Customary marine tenure in Australia

Edited by Nicolas Peterson and Bruce Rigsby

SYDNEY UNIVERSITY PRESS

Originally published in 1998 by Oceania Publications

This reprint edition published in 2014 by SYDNEY UNIVERSITY PRESS

© Sydney University Press 2014

Reproduction and Communication for other purposes

Sydney University Press
Fisher Library F03
University of Sydney NSW 2006
AUSTRALIA
Email: sup.info@sydney.edu.au

National Library of Australia Cataloguing-in-Publication entry

Title: Customary marine tenure in Australia / edited by Nicolas Peterson and Bruce Rigsby.

Edition: Reprint edition.

ISBN: 9781743323892 (paperback)

Subjects: Aboriginal Australians--Land tenure.

            Marine resources--Australia.

            Marine resources conservation--Australia.

Other Authors/Contributors:

            Peterson, Nicolas, 1941–, editor.

            Rigsby, B. (Bruce), editor.

Dewey Number:

            333.20994

Cover image

This painting on masonite was collected at Yirrkala by R. and C. Berndt in 1946–47. The artist is not recorded. Entitled *Bremer Island turtle hunt*, it shows a canoe, turtles, sailfish and waves breaking on the reef, a description supported by the famous artist Wanjuk Marika. Image P2070, from the Macleay Museum, University of Sydney.

Contents

List of Figures

Note to the 2014 edition

Peter White

Most Australians are used to the concept of land ownership. The idea of ownership of areas of sea and its resources is foreign to them, but not to coastal Aboriginal communities. The papers in this volume demonstrate how this concept is developed in various communities, and some of the general implications of this. Originating in a session of papers at a conference in 1996, the papers in this volume were originally published as Oceania Monograph 48 in 1998. It was later reprinted, but this 2014 reprint will allow its important concepts to have wider circulation. Two more recent publications which expand those here are J. Bradley, *Singing Saltwater Country* (Allen & Unwin, 2010) and M. Somerville and T. Perkins, *Singing the Coast* (Aboriginal Studies Press, 2010).

Preface

Nicolas Peterson and Bruce Rigsby

This volume has its origins in a conference session held at the 1996 Australian Anthropological Society Meetings. The purpose of the session was to make a beginning towards enlarging our collective knowledge and understanding of the range and variety of contemporary indigenous systems of marine tenure. As has been widely commented on, such systems, both here and abroad, have received little attention until the last twenty years, yet there is not only a significant identification and involvement with the sea among indigenous peoples in Australia but it also plays an important subsistence role in the life of many Aboriginal and Torres Strait Islander communities around the continent. This importance is now coming to public notice following the passing of the *Native Title Act* 1993 (Cth) with more than 120 applications for determination being lodged over the coastal waters by the end of 1997.

In April 1997 proceedings began in the Federal Court in the first application for recognition of native title in the sea in the case of *Mary Yarmirr and others v the Northern Territory of Australia and others* before Mr Justice Olney.

Unlike the Mabo case and the recognition of native title in the land, the Yarmirr case comes against a background of a paucity of published research into indigenous marine tenure. In the light of the land claims experience it seems important to build up knowledge and understanding of the complexities of the marine tenure systems among the public, government, lawyers and the judiciary if Aboriginal and Torres Strait Islanders claims and rights are to be understood and assessed properly. We see this volume as a first step in the process.

We would like to thank Anthea Bundock for assistance in preparing the manuscript and Kevin Cowan for drawing the figures. We would also like to thank Oceania's editorial and office staff, and the two anonomous readers for their helpful suggestions for improving the volume.

1

Introduction

Nicolas Peterson and Bruce Rigsby

Until the 1970s, indigenous systems of marine tenure received little attention not just within Australian waters but worldwide (see Ruddle and Akimichi 1984, 1–5). The reasons for this are complex but without doubt one of the more important is the widespread European understanding that the seas are open to all. This has resulted in the indigenous relationship to the sea being seen only in terms of resource usage and in the many and complex indigenous systems of near-shore marine tenure worldwide becoming invisible.

Over the last three decades, however, research on indigenous marine tenure has received considerable attention partly in response to the failure of fisheries development schemes and partly in response to decolonisation. In the Pacific, in particular, much research has been driven by the belief that traditional systems of marine tenure can be harnessed and/or revived in order to manage near-shore marine resources in a sustainable way (e.g. see Ruddle 1994).

In Australia the interest in marine tenure is even more recent and it was not until the 1980s that the first studies started to appear in response to the *Aboriginal Land Rights (Northern Territory) Act 1976 (Cth)*. Section 73(1)(d) of this Act provides for reciprocal legislation to be passed by the Northern Territory under which Aboriginal communities can apply to close sections of the sea adjoining Aboriginal land for two kilometres off-shore. This resulted in Section 12(1) of the *Aboriginal Land Act 1978 (NT)*, which became the first statutory granting of some limited rights over the sea. Before the sea is closed the Administrator of the Northern Territory may refer the matter of closure to the Aboriginal Land Commissioner for investigation and recommendation.

The statutory test for closure is based on the proof of the right to exclude strangers. Only two applications for closure of the seas have been made to date, in the area around Milingimbi and Howard Island on the Arnhem Land coast,[1] although research for two others was carried out in the 1980s: Croker Island (see Palmer and Brady 1984) and Groote Eylandt (Palmer 1983).

With the Mabo No. 2 judgement in 1992 and the subsequent passing of the *Native Title Act 1993 (Cth)* which contemplates that rights and interests in the sea may be recognised (see s6 and s223), interest has escalated enormously so that marine tenure is set to become a key native title issue. However, it should be emphasised that the statutory right to negotiate does not apply to 'off-shore' areas (s234(8a)) and proposed amendments to the Act will ensure the priority of fishing industry interests over native title, limiting indigenous people only to a right to apply for compensation.

Although native title is now driving the interest in marine tenure, it is important to maintain some conceptual separation between research for an ethnographic documentation of such tenure and research for an application for the recognition of native title rights in the sea, although the two are, of course, closely related. Court rulings and legal discourse are now defining and structuring the kinds of evidence required for a native title application, placing limitations on a purely ethnographic account concerned with local categories, perceptions and

---

1 The two cases are the Castlereagh Bay/Howard Island decided in 1988 and the Milingimbi, Crocodile Islands and Glyde River Area decided in 1981 by the Aboriginal Land Commissioner. The other cases have not been pursued for two reasons: first, sea claims were proving expensive to research and it was decided it was more cost effective to give priority to land claims. Second, and clearly related, the rights conferred on people achieving a sea closure are minimal since any person with an existing fishing licence is not affected by the closure. Since it was mainly the fishermen that were causing the problems the closures were not nearly as effective as they might appear to be.

understandings, some of which may have only a marginal place in the evidence required by the court.

In this introduction we will begin with a discussion of the issues raised by the ethnographic blind spot regarding marine tenure and its relationship to property theory. We will then overview the literature on Aboriginal people's relationships with the sea, and the relationship between marine tenure and native title before turning to a discussion of the papers in this volume. We conclude with a brief section on the legal terminology associated with the sea.

A blind spot: property rights in the sea

The extent of the blind spot regarding customary marine tenure (CMT) is extraordinary in retrospect. Norman Tindale (1925–26), Lloyd Warner (1937), Fred Rose (1960), Steve Hart and Arnold Pilling (1960), Ronald Berndt (1964; 1970; 1976), Les Hiatt (1965), David Turner (1974), Betty Meehan (1982) and Nancy Williams (1986) all worked with coastal peoples in Arnhem Land and addressed issues of land tenure, or the use of sea, yet they make no mention of the kind of estates or interests in the sea that they describe on the land.[2] This blind spot is not confined to Arnhem Land as Sandra Pannell's contribution shows, but appears to apply to the whole continent. There is, however, an early and highly significant reference to ownership of the seas in the Torres Strait, although it was consigned to a footnote. Anthony Wilkins noted:

> I think there is what may be termed a spatial projection of
> the idea of proprietorship. As foreshore rights of landed
> property extend not only over the adjacent reef *but to the*
> *water over it* [emphasis added]—as in the case of fish caught

2   Ronald Berndt (1976:map 5) provides a map of estates on Elcho Island which includes the sea within some of them but he makes no comment in the text about the sea as part of the estate. Nancy Williams (1986:92) mentions 'management of land and marine resources' but only makes a passing comment about the sea.

within the area—so the inhabitants of certain areas appear to have a pre-emptial right to certain distant fishing stations which lie off their part of the coast (1908:167 fn l).

This appears to be widely true of Aboriginal marine tenure systems.

The first passing reference to sea estates appears to be by Mr Justice Woodward in his First Report in 1973 (1973:33), while the first brief published anthropological writing specifically on marine tenure was in reaction to the inquiry by the *Joint Select Committee on Aboriginal Land Rights in the Northern Territory* in 1977. Howard Morphy and Paul Memmott made submissions to this inquiry explicitly dealing with estates in the sea.[3] Athol Chase's writing on east coast Cape York appear to be the first substantive anthropological analysis carried out before the stimulus of landrights although published later (see Chase 1980 and Chase and Sutton 1981). Other early reports are by Ian Keen (1980), Stephen Davis (1982; 1984), Kingsley Palmer (1983) and Kingsley Palmer and Maggie Brady (1984), all arising out of the Northern Territory legislation and the papers by Ian Keen, Ian Crawford, Moya Smith and Kingsley Palmer in the special issue of *Anthropological Forum* 1984–5. The more recent literature reflects the concern with management (e.g. see Gray and Zann 1988; Cordell 1991; Smyth 1993; Sutherland 1996).

This raises the possibility that the late discovery of marine tenure in Australia is because it is only a recent development. It might be argued, for instance, that under the impact of landrights legislation and the possibility of closing the seas in the Northern Territory, there has been an extension of the land based arrangements out into the sea so that open access has given way to a common property system (see Rigsby). It is evident, looking beyond Australia, that not all coastal peoples have systems or probably ever had systems of marine tenure. Property theory would explain this in terms of the economic costs and benefits related

---

3 Ian Keen also made a submission to this Committee about the sea emphasising the spiritual importance of the coastal waters and sites in the sea. At the end of his submission he does say, 'Waters are of the clan and moiety of the adjoining coast...' (1977:1098).

to maintaining such property rights while anthropologists have documented a range of cultural reasons.[4]

Alternatively, it might be, as Palmer (1988) has suggested that customary marine tenure systems are fragile so that they disappear quickly under the impact of colonialism. Palmer does not suggest why they might be fragile but one factor could relate to the policing of rights and the difficulties created when outsiders introduce new and radically changed maritime techologies which are only differentially available. New technology can also, however, strengthen and extend relations with the maritime environment as the relatively recent introduction of the dugout canoe in the Top End of Australia makes clear (see below).

Yet another possibility is that longstanding practices and arrangements of a more informal nature have firmed up under the impact of the growing prevalence of legal and rights discourses in Aboriginal affairs. This seems possible from a consideration of property theory. If we focus on property as first and foremost a relationship between people in respect of something rather than a relationship simply with a thing *per se* (see Rigsby this volume), attention is focussed on control. A property relationship entails one person controlling or regulating the behaviour of the other in respect of that thing in one of a number of ways. With changes in technology and better understandings among Aboriginal people of the way in which the Australian legal system works, the uncodified and relatively informal indigenous modes of expression of these rights of control have been translated into the language of the encapsulating society.

Control in relation to the right to exclude (i.e. exclusive possession) and the right to alienate have always had a central place in European notions of property. Where there is a recognised right to exclude, the question of its enforcement arises. Normally, of course, such rights do

---

4   Polunin (1984:269–272) documents a number of cases. For example, the Tanga Islanders of Papua New Guinea had a supernatural dread of the sea in a context where the land was much more productive, and the Balinese have strong land/sea opposition seeing the mountains as pure and the sea as polluted.

not need to be enforced since property rights are respected and there are culturally recognised ways of negotiating access. Nevertheless, there does have to be a mechanism and an expectation that people will enforce their rights if they are breached. The difficulties associated with exercising rights of control over an extensive land estate in a hunter-gatherer context are great enough but people can be tracked and signs of one sort or another put up to warn people off. At sea, neither of these options is available. The basic control of the sea thus rests on sight, which is the same sense that is the initial basis of a social relationship with somebody or the reactivating of it: that is, one perceives their presence. Aboriginal people say, and it is consistent with other practices, that they constantly monitor the sea and those on the shore expect those coming into their field of vision to travel directly towards them to declare their intentions to those living on the shore.[5] If they fail to do this, and have not previously arranged permission for access, they have breached accepted social practice and the assumption is that because they are behaving furtively they are there with illegal or malicious intent. Arnhem Landers speak of Europeans who come into their sea estates without seeking permission as 'sneaking' in (e.g. Croker Island Transcript 1997:704).

This construction of Aboriginal sea country practice is reinforced by their practice on land of setting fire to the bush when travelling cross-country to announce an impending arrival (e.g. see Heath 1980:536). That is to say, people make themselves visible at a distance to establish their existence and then they proceed straight to the camp where they expect to find the local residents (Heath 1980:536).

The importance of sight is further underlined by its role in defining the dimensions of Aboriginal sea estates. It is common for people to say,

5 Dharlwangu people in northeast Arnhem Land told Peter Toner, a graduate student in the Department of Archaeology and Anthropology at ANU, that the light reflecting off wet canoe paddles can be seen at a great distance. This is something they sing about (see also Berndt 1948:96). See Rose (1994:Chapter 9—Seeing property—especially pages 269,292–293) for a fascinating account of the place of vision in property relations.

when asked how far out to sea their sea estates go, that they go 'to the horizon' (e.g. this has been documented for the Tiwi (Davis and Prescott 1992:49); and the people of the Croker Island area (Peterson and Devitt 1997)). This field of vision is extended both by the distances people can see from elevated points and by the area they can see when at their farthest point of travel from land. Victor Prescott (quoted in Davis and Prescott 1992:49) records that in the mid-eighteenth century, Naples and the Ottoman empire signed an agreement to protect shipping in the area of sea that could be seen from the shore. Of course, as Paul Memmott and David Trigger's paper makes clear, people had an interest in areas way out of sight both in terms of their deep involvement with clouds and more mundanely through their travels into distant waters particularly in the past with Macassans, pearlers, fishers and missionaries. And the Sandbeach people of eastern Cape York Peninsula (see Rigsby and Chase this volume) say their estates extend to the outer reefs of the Great Barrier Reef, which are generally well out of sight beyond the horizon.

One of the difficulties for Aboriginal people in sustaining this definition of the extent of their sea estates is that rarely do they use these more distant areas. Thus the rule of thumb is that standing on the shore a person can see about 20 kilometres out to sea. While there are areas where people did cross such distances of open water, it seems improbable that Aboriginal people went out 20 kilometres beyond the most northern parts of their land estates along much of the Top End coast unless there were islands to be seen. However, just because parts of the sea country were not used, visited or policed does not make them any less part of their sea country as Australia's difficulties with parts of its sea territory in the southern ocean, which are rarely visited and/or unpoliced and almost unpoliceable, makes clear.[6]

---

6 For instance, see the article in the *Bulletin*, 1 July 1997, page 13. 'Anarchy in the Antarctic. Toothless law: foreign vessels are plundering fish stocks in Australian territory'. The article emphasises the great difficult of policing waters that are 4500km from Perth.

As Memmott and Trigger also suggest, when people moved into centralised communities the ability of the estate owners to control their sea estates declined substantially and, at the same time, the sea within easy reach of such communities tended to become an area in which all people in the settlement have similar *de facto* access rights. Rigsby and Chase in their chapter report the same thing for the Lockhart River community but note that the 'public', that has free access to the sea near the community, is the local Aboriginal one and there are complaints when outsiders enter the area. Thus around settled village communities, permission to use the sea country is rarely sought, although in the smaller communities the senior estate owner will usually receive a portion of any turtle or dugong caught there.

Thus centralisation and the fact that most anthropologists have worked in such centralised communities would seem to be important in understanding the invisibility of marine tenure. The parallel with the ownership of the land on which these communities stand is illuminating. Until the advent of village councils in the late 1960s the fact that the land on which an Aboriginal village stood was owned by a small fraction of the resident population certainly went unremarked by Europeans who treated the village areas as open-access areas. However, elections for the village councils started to make the formerly invisible owners visible and they have since become even more evident with the emergence of the idea of rental payments for certain facilities established in the villages. Along with this has gone the decline in the significance of some other rights in some areas, in particular, rights to country through conception in some fringe desert areas, since now far too many people are conceived in the same place threatening the rights of those people with descent interests.

If there is exclusive possession there has to be permission seeking. Yet while Aboriginal people will readily agree that people from other tenure groups should seek permission to fish or hunt in their sea-land estate, when asked if they have ever refused anybody permission to do so, they nearly always say they have not. This, then, appears to undermine the claim that there is real permission-seeking behaviour and might be taken to suggest that our ethnographic practice is creating rights and interests that do not really exist, rather than recognising that our codification of ethnographic practice for articulation with the state entails such objectification and transformation.

The issue of permission giving is complex. Both in the past and today the people from whom others are normally seeking permission are relatives. Thus unless relationships have become tense or have broken down, in which case people would not ask, people know that their relatives will say yes unless there are exceptional circumstances. One such circumstance is the common practice of closing parts of the sea closely associated with a deceased person because of intensive use or because they were a senior owner of the area. It is significant that in the Croker region, for example, when people are asked why they seek permission they say it is out of 'respect'. This parallels directly the practice of spouses in our own society where each has a car and one wishes to borrow the other's car: normally they would never expect to be refused but they ask out of respect and to acknowledge the other's ownership or possession. If there were tensions leading to a divorce, neither spouse would probably ask to borrow the other's car and their property rights would become explicit in a legal setting.

The fact that people have a firm expectation that any close relative with whom they are in good standing will not refuse them access to their estate can lead to the conversion of this expectation, in the context of a legalistic discourse, to an assertion of this as a right because, normatively speaking, they know they will not be refused. Yet this is clearly not a right but only a strong expectation because there is no ability to enforce this expectation nor are there any obligations associated with such relationships that relate directly to the estate.

It is interesting too that when talking about excluding people or not granting them permission, the refusal of permission to Europeans is normally completely overlooked even though today this is the most common form of exclusion or attempted exclusion of people from sea estates.

Thus the maintenance of these relatively subtle forms of control of the behaviour of others is easily lost in the contexts of access to radically different technologies that allow people to appear and disappear with speed, and who are not accountable to people on the shore because they are in no long standing social relationship with them. Customary marine tenure in places like Australia does indeed seem to be fragile.

Another feature of European property notions as they relate to the sea is that it is only the seabed that is capable of being owned.[7] This in turn gives control of the column of water above it and all that is in or on it. Aboriginal people's notions of sea tenure clearly encompass the seabed in many areas. Sharp (this volume) quotes a Groote Eylandter saying 'we don't follow the water, we follow the land under the sea...' (see also Bradley) and Charlie Wardaga from Croker Island commented:

> That boat go on top and really—on the bottom—[is] that Dreaming. Every boat and every big ship, he go top, but that bottom one, that Dreaming, [it's] inside there ...Aboriginal culture goes right to the bottom—and to the shore (see Peterson and Devitt 1997:6–7)

Wardaga is referring to one of the best known of the ancestral figures, the Rainbow Serpent, which is found throughout Australia wherever there are bodies of water, particularly large bodies of water. Around the coast these spirit beings, of fearsome power, lie beneath the water on the sea bed and can be easily disturbed by things thrown carelessly overboard or in other ways (e.g. Heath 1980:546; Peterson and Devitt 1997). Thus around Croker Island meat and fatty substances should not be thrown overboard in many places because it is feared that this will arouse the local Rainbow Serpent.

---

7   But note that Christy (1996) speaks of the increasingly common replacement of open access conditions by property rights regimes in the world's fisheries.

Access to the maritime environment in historical perspective

It is evident that Aboriginal access to the sea has undergone a number of changes. The most recent of these, prior to European arrival, was the adoption of the dugout canoe in one of several forms. Its adoption clearly facilitated sea travel, made it possible to reach distant islands more easily and regularly and influenced hunting and fishing patterns. Outside of eastern Cape York the dugout canoe seems to have been taken up only in the last three hundred years or so.

The first people to arrive on the greater Australia land mass some 60,000 or more years ago had to cross at least 80km of open sea probably landing them somewhere in what is now western Irian Jaya (see Butlin 1993:14–34). This was an extraordinary early feat of seamanship and one that must have been repeated a number of times. Yet despite this uniquely early engagement with the sea, it cannot be said that most coastal Aboriginal peoples are truely maritime in the sense of being seafarers, but rather that they are intensive users of near-shore waters in mixed economies.[8] Further, the distribution of the various forms of watercraft at the time of Europeans arrival was complex and discontinuous with a zone of more than two thousand kilometres westwards along the Great Australian Bight being devoid of any watercraft at all (see Davidson 1935:3). This regional diversity has been documented by Davidson, who argued that the distribution of the four principal types of craft—dugouts with one or two outriggers or none; bark canoes of single or several sheets of bark; complex rafts of two or more logs or rolls of reed or bark; and simple rafts consisting of only one log or

---

8 Rhys Jones concluded from his comparison of three Arnhem Land groups, the Anbara Gidjingali who combine access to land and sea roughly equally, the Matai Gidjingali who are basically inland people but with seasonal access to coastal resources at important times and the truely inland Ritharmgu that, 'There are no structural differences between any of these economic systems' (1980:129).

roll—reflects the chronology of their invention and/or introduction (see Davidson 1935:8; Akerman 1975; Jones 1976; Rowland 1987).

Only in Cape York did people have substantial sea going canoes. These measured from 24–30 feet long and had double outriggers as far south as Princess Charlotte Bay and single outriggers to the south. They could hold three, four or more people but the life of such canoes could be less than a year because of borers or cracking (see Thomson 1934:243–244; Baker 1988:185). There is no doubt that the bigger canoes in the far north of Cape York Peninsula came from New Guinea via the Torres Strait, mainly by trade, but people did learn to make them locally.[9] When they were first acquired is unknown but there is good evidence for the diffusion of fish hook technology down the east coast in the last thousand years and it is possible that dugouts may have diffused at the same time (Rowland 1981).

Elsewhere around the continent people used bark canoes or canoe-rafts whose normal range seems to have been limited to between 6.5–13 kilometres (see Jones 1976:260). The construction of these bark canoes varied considerably. Some were made from a single piece of bark and were only suitable for use in calm water (see Davidson 1935; Baker 1988:180) but others were made from several pieces of bark sewn together and were better suited for the rougher conditions of open sea travel (Baker 1988:180). Stories of the stitching coming apart at sea with resultant loss of life are not uncommon and are reported from Maningrida and the Borroloola area (see Cooke and Armstrong this volume; Baker 1988:181; Bradley 1997). Some bark canoes were large enough to hold six men in the Borroloola area (see Spencer and Gillen 1912:484).

Despite their fragility, there is no doubt that people hunted turtle and dugong from such boats using harpoons made from various woods or stingray spines (e.g. see Heath 1980:534; Bradley 1991:96). However, this must have been a more difficult enterprise than from a dugout canoe and it would not have been possible to get the animals into the

---

9 See footnote 15, Chapter 12 which records empty dugouts drifting down on to eastern Cape York beaches.

bark canoes in most cases. Rather, they would have been tied up along-side and towed back (see Baker 1988:183; Heath 1980:533).

At some relatively late stage, probably in the late seventeenth or early eighteenth century, Macassan trepangers started regularly visiting the north coast of Australia between Broome and the Borroloola area introducing not only dugout canoes, through trade, but metal harpoon heads and axes.[10] It seems safe to assume that the unsinkable dugouts expanded the range of travel and brought islands that were uninhab-ited or difficult of access within easier range and greatly increased the effectiveness of dugong and turtle hunting. The best evidence for this is provided by Scott Mitchell (1994: Chapter 14) who shows on the basis of archaeological work in the Cobourg Peninsula—Mountnorris Bay area of the Northern Territory that no dugong bones and few turtle remains are to be found in pre-Macassan middens in this area. He makes a strong case for what he calls a 'sea change' in Aboriginal economies in this area following access to the new technology which saw a 'dramatic' increase in the intensity with which large animals were exploited and a shift in settlement pattern with larger groups of cores-idents and decreased mobility, as indicated by the size and structure of midden deposits.

Fred Rose has made a similar argument for Groote Eylandt. He claims that before acquiring the dugout canoe Groote Eylandters were unable to hunt dugong and turtle and he estimates that the population would have been only one-third of the 300–350 recorded by Tindale in the 1920s because of the lack of access to the resources of the sea (see Rose 1961:526–529).[11] This would seem to be overstating the impact because the bark canoes did enable the people to get out to the islands,

---

10 The most likely date based on documentary evidence is around 1720AD (see Macknight 1986) although radio carbon dates could be taken to suggest that regular contact started up to 800 years ago. Macknight, however, rejects these dates (see 1976:98).

11 Tindale (1925–6:110) makes the interesting estimate that 'There are probably more than twenty-five big sailing canoes in the possession of the islanders in 1921–1922.

as the archaeological evidence makes clear (Clarke 1994). But it does seem likely that turtle and dugong featured less often in the diet prior to these innovations and it may have been that turtles were most commonly captured when they came onto the beach to lay their eggs.[12] It is significant that while Bryce Barker (see paper, this volume) has evidence of turtle bones in deposits on the Whitsunday Islands going back 6000 years, he did not find any dugong bones at all.[13]

The date of the adoption of the dugout canoe could have some bearing on native title especially where there are offshore islands some distance from the coast. Two issues are involved here: the period at which the area came under British sovereignty and the evidence for when people took up the dugout canoe.

Sovereignty over Australia was declared in three stages.[14] The east coast of Australia westwards to 135 degrees east longitude (i.e. just east of Milingimbi) was taken up by the British in 1788; the area westwards to 129 degrees of east longitude in 1825 although the north coast around Fort Dundas-Cobourg Peninsula was taken over in 1824; and the rest of the continent between 1826 and 1831. Exactly how these declarations of sovereignty affect the sea is a complex legal issue. What is of interest here is how the documentation for the adoption of the dugout canoe correlates with these dates.

---

12 Douglas and Rebecca Bird describe this practice among Torres Strait Islanders (1997).

13 This could be because of how the animal is butchered and the bones treated. Certainly in some areas the remains of turtles and dugong should, in theory, be disposed of in the sea, in keeping with a need to keep key elements of land and sea associated things apart. The mutual antipathy between things of the land and things of the sea is best documented from Mornington Island (see Cawte 1974). However, if turtle bones could find their way into deposits there seems no good reason why dugong bones would not also.

14 There are complex legal issues involved here, especially in relationship to the sea which, apparently, may not have been resolved as yet. The purpose here is only to flag what might possibly emerge as an issue: the timing of the introduction of the dugout canoe.

Along the north coast of Australia the earliest recorded sightings of Aboriginal people actually in a dugout canoe seems to come from March 1818 when a dugout canoe was taken from a group of Aboriginal people near Goulburn Island (King 1827:67). King, (1827:138) however, also reports that the 'principal rajah' of one of the Macassan fleets whom he interviewed in Timor in 1818 told him that 'Their small canoes are frequently stolen from them' indicating that Aboriginal people had access to such canoes before this date, although for how long and in what numbers is unclear.

In this respect it is interesting that it seems from what Aboriginal people have said that they rarely made dugouts themselves until the Macassans stopped coming at the turn of the century (see Warner 1937:459; Thomson 1937 quoted in Baker 1988:181; Worsley 1954:61–62; Heath 1980:532–533; Baker 1988:181).[15] According to Mitchell (1994:124) the first reference to Aboriginal manufacture of dugouts on the Cobourg Peninsula is to be found in Earl, who was writing in 1846. However, he goes on to say that such indigenous dugout manufacture 'may not have been common at this time'.

Each Macassan prau brought between three and seven dugouts (*lepa-lepa*) with them (see Mitchell 1994:28) for getting around. They also brought large dugout canoes with one or two outriggers (*balolang*) for dredging trepang. At the end of the season it was the *lepa-lepa* canoes that were given to or traded with the Aboriginal people. Although Aboriginal people had access to iron axes long before the Macassans stopped coming it seems quite compatible with Aboriginal ideas about knowledge and rights to make things, that making dugout was largely left to the Macassans.[16] Given that dugouts seem to have lasted up to

---

15 Mitchell (1994:124) discusses this matter in respect of the Cobourg Peninsula and says that the first reference to an Aboriginal manufacture of a dugout there is to be found in Earl writing in 1846. However, he goes on to say that such indigenous dugout manufacture 'may not have been common at this time'.

16 Warner (1937:536) records a myth in which the figure identified with Arnhem Landers, a dog, refuses many items of material culture offered

three years on average (Baker's 1988:185–186) there was no need for Aboriginal people to make them themselves in view of the annual visits. However, it seems that as soon as the Macassans stopped coming, the Aboriginal people started making them along the northern coast.

Another interesting aspect of adoption of dugouts is that outside Cape York and the east coast of Australia (see Davidson 1935 for distribution), they were never fitted with outriggers. This is despite the fact that Warner reported that Macassans used outriggers on the Arnhem Land coast and some of the Aboriginal people he worked with knew about them. He put their failure to adopt them down to their conservatism (1937:459).

Aspects of the economic and cultural relationships with the sea

Suprisingly, given that much of the coast was among the most densely populated areas of the continent, systematic documentation of the economic usage of the sea is almost absent. There is only a single substative quantitative study of use of the sea. This is Betty Meehan's superb ethnography (1982) based on work around the mouth of the Blyth River in Arnhem Land and focused on shellfish collecting but including a comprehensive range of subsistence data (1977). Prior to Meehan, Margaret McArthur (1960:95) had published some limited quantitative material on three populations in eastern Arnhem Land based on a total of 60 days of observation, as against Meehan's (1982:45) 334 days. Interestingly, neither of these studies makes even passing mention of marine tenure despite the fact that in Meehan's case she briefly covers

---

to him by the Macassans, including canoes, because, he says, 'I want you to be a Macassar man. I am a black man. If I get all these things I will become a white man and you will become a black man'. According to Mitchell (1994:124), the first reference to Aboriginal people manufacturing dug outs in the Cobourg Peninsula area of the Northern Territory is from Earl.

land tenure. Some, often quite fragmentary, quantitative material is available on turtle and dugong hunting mainly from the east coast and Torres Strait (see Bird and Bird 1997 for particularly rich data; Bradley 1997; Johannes and MacFarlane 1991; Neitschmann 1985; Smith 1988). Beyond this there appears to be no other substantial quantitative information.

There is, however, an enormously rich archaeological literature dealing with coastal economies that is too large to consider here (but see Bowdler 1982) that supplies irrefutable evidence of the longterm economic significance of the sea. Suffice it to say that it goes to the earliest periods where evidence has not been inundated by sea rises. Of most interest here is the widespread documentation of fish traps in the sea around the continent (although absent from some areas such as in the Sand-Beach Region) and the all pervasive shell middens and less common shell mounds. The latter two manifestations of sea use are important because they represent congealed female labour and stand as enduring monuments to women's intensive involvement with the sea which can be easily overlooked because it is largely in the intertidal zone (see Meehan 1982).

Another important aspect of the use of the sea especially along the north coast of Australia was for producing commodities for exchange. In this respect it is clear that Aboriginal people collected materials such as pearl and turtle shell *on their own initiative* for exchange with Europeans and/or Macassans. Brierly (quoted in Mitchell 1994:98) makes this quite clear with his comment that Aboriginal people kept pearl shell hidden from Europeans because they preferred to trade it with Macassans. Another reference to the independent collection of sea produce for trade is from Alfred Searcy, the Sub-Collector of Customs at Darwin from 1882–1896, (1909:32–3) who reports that:

> The natives [of the Arnhem Land coast] collected the pearls during the absence of the Malays for whom they saved them and received in exchange grog and tobacco. On all the outlying reefs at low-water pearl-shell could always be procured.....

> The Malays took away immense quantites of tortoise shell
> which was also collected by the natives.

Earl commented in 1846 on the contrast between the Aboriginal people
of the Cobourg area and other Aboriginal people in terms of their 'progress' towards commerce:

> ... it is upon the northern coasts, where aborgines have long
> held intercourse with a people not greatly superior to them-
> selves ....[that] They have here made the first step towards
> an improved condition. They have acquired the rudiments
> of commerce, and although the cultivation on the soil has
> not yet been attempted, they have learned to collect the nat-
> ural productions of the country, with the view to exchanging
> them for food of a superior quality to that which their own
> land affords. A considerable number have paid one or more
> visits to Macassar, residing there for months together, which
> has familiarized them with the language and manners of the
> people of that country, and may probably lead to a closer in-
> tercourse, should the Macassars establish themselves upon
> the coast (Earl 1846:118)

Aboriginal people also sold their labour to the Macassans and were
sometimes paid in canoes (e.g. Macgillivray 1852:147). It is much less
clear whether, at any time, Macassans felt the need to pay Aboriginal
people for the right to work the trepang or pearlshell beds in recognition of their ownership rights in the sea.

Indigenous interest in the sea encompasses a great deal more than
subsistence, as the anthropological literature makes clear. While this literature is silent about marine tenure until the 1980s, it records rocks,
reefs and sandbanks out to sea as named places, some as sacred sites
(e.g. Berndt 1964; Tindale 1962) and the existence of ancestral dreaming tracks crossing over water to Arnhem Land. Thus Paul Foelsche,
a Darwin policeman, in 1881 records a female ancestral figure,
Warramurragundji, coming from over the seas and much more recently
Catherine and Ronald Berndt (1952) documented the Djangkawu cycle
which follows the travel of two sisters across the seas of the Gulf of
Carpentaria making a landfall in eastern Arnhem Land.

The social construction of the sea and seascapes is, as these papers show, complex and varied but in all areas there is not suprisingly a strong identification with the sea. This has been best documented by John Bradley in his paper here and more extensively in his thesis (1997; see also Peterson and Devitt 1997) In much of Arnhem Land life force comes from the sea in the form of fish and the souls of the dead migrate to island homes, off to the northeast, or in the case of the Tiwi to the smudge of land on the horizon to the south. On a grander scale every-where there are foundation stories of human and non-human forces and beings fashioning the seascapes, creating islands, reefs, currents, deeps and imbuing these places and others beneath the sea or along the shore with great power. These powers, places, ancestral heroes and relationships are celebrated in myth, song, ceremonies, paintings and the practices of everyday life.

The real dangers and fears faced by sea users and coastal dwellers have cultural objectification in places that allow for the controlling or unleashing of storms, cyclones, waterspouts, winds, rains and, more rarely, even more powerful catastrophic forces (e.g. see Peterson and Tonkinson 1979; Peterson and Devitt 1997). Commonly, ancestors are thought to control access to sea resources (e.g. see Cooke and Armstrong, and Rigsby and Chase, this volume) such that people fishing or hunting for the first time in an area need to be introduced to them by an owner of the sea estate or run the risk of no success. Elsewhere the hunter and the hunted are understood to be in a complex symbiosis where they need each other (see Bradley this volume).

Marine tenure and native title

Ethnographically speaking, the fact that much recent work on tenure has been carried out for sea closures and native title applications means there has been a pervasiveness of legal discourse in the ethnography of marine tenureship just as there has recently been for land tenure. This tends to alienate Aboriginal people from their own experience and practice at the same time as it makes those experiences and practices recognisable by the state. Thus the above account of the behaviour expected of people travelling at sea, which is the specific cultural form that the expression of ownership rights takes, is translated into rules and concepts of boundedness. Legal requirements have another, more positive, consequence which is to concentrate attention on ethnographically complex issues that might otherwise go unexamined.

Although no applications for the recognition of native title have yet been finalised some of the legal parameters are now becoming clearer as a result of legal prosecutions. So far the two most relevant deal with men prosecuted for breach of fisheries regulations.

The only extended discussion of the legal issues involved in demonstrating native title in the sea has been provided by Mr Justice Kirby in his judgement in the appeal of the Mason v Tritton case heard in March 1994 in the NSW Supreme Court (delivered in August 1994), the background to which is provided by Scott Cane. This case dealt with a man arrested on the South Coast of NSW for having more than the prescribed number of abalone in his possession. Mason's defence was that he was exercising his native title right to fish and therefore outside the scope of the fisheries regulations. Mason lost his case. The reasons for this are discussed by Cane but they were technical so that the nature of his claimed right was never tested.

Kirby's judgement, however, provides a useful discussion of issues involved with rights in the sea, particularly the issue of the 'right to fish' and the nature of the evidence required to prove native title. Formally, these requirements are the same for land and sea. Mr Justice Kirby outlines four requirements. The evidence must be sufficient to demonstrate:

1. That traditional laws and customs extending to the right to fish were exercised by an indigenous community immediately before the Crown claimed sovereignty over the Territory (this date varies across the continent—see above)

2. That the person seeking recognition of their native title is an indigenous person and is a biological descendant of that original indigenous community or group

3. That the person and their immediate descendants have, subject to the general propositions outlined above, continued, uninterrupted, to observe the relevant traditional laws and customs and

4. That the person's activities or conduct in fishing is an exercise of those traditional laws and customs (Kirby 1994:21–22).

Kirby (1994:31) comments that a person seeking recognition of their native title rights 'faces a difficult evidentiary task'. Just how difficult has yet to become apparent and clearly will vary in different parts of the continent as the papers here show. The most difficult ethnographic task is, in situations like those discussed by Bryce Barker and Scott Cane, to find the language to describe the system of traditional laws and customs regulating fishing, where they still exist, and to define the group that holds these laws and customs.

Another relevant fishing case relates to three Western Australian Aboriginal men in the Derschaw case, who also relied on a 'native title rights' defence when prosecuted in 1993 for netting 66 mullet in Six Mile creek near Port Headland against regulations. Although they too lost their case it does not necessarily mean that proof of native title is extremely difficult (see Kennedy 1996:31–2 and Derschaw et al 1996 for a discussion of this case).

A central issue raised by implication in the Mason case is one that is clearly going to recur. Is there a native title right which is commercial in nature: can people sell the products of the sea (or land for that matter) obtained under a native title right? Does the existence of bartering between families in the past, trading with the Macassans or across the Torres Strait, provided the basis, given an already accepted legal notion of tradition as dynamic and evolving, for commercial exchange in the present (see Kilduff and Lofgren 1996:16. They seem quite confident that it does).

The central issue raised by the Derschaw case, where the fish were to be consumed by some of the 300 people attending a funeral, is whether fishing regulations can limit a native title right to fish. Lachlan Kennedy (1996:32) is of the opinion that they do not, relying on s211 of the Native Title Act 1993, which had not been enacted at the time

Derschaw was charged. Section 211 provides that where the enjoyment of native title rights involves hunting, fishing, gathering, or a cultural or spiritual activity, and there is a law which prohibits persons from fishing other than in accordance with a licence or permit, the need for a licence or permit does not apply to native title holders when fishing to satisfy their personal, domestic or non-commercial community needs and they are exercising their native title rights (Kennedy 1996:32). In this Kennedy has been proved correct, as the decision of October 1996 in the case of Eaton v Yanner in the Mt Isa Magistrate's Court indicates. Prosecuted under the *Queensland Fauna Conservation Act* for taking crocodiles for food, Murandoo Yanner was acquitted on the grounds that he was exercising his native title rights.

The papers

The first paper is by Bruce Rigsby and provides a survey of property theory considering two general theories for the emergence of property rights: the social contractarian argument that they arise as an alternative to constant conflict over the use of land and resources; and the conventional economists' position that property rights emerge in land and resources when the gains from assigning property rights outweigh the costs of foregoing them. He then considers the character of property rights and provides a useful checklist of rights that will help fieldworkers. He concludes with a consideration of tenure types, drawing attention to the term 'common property', which has been used somewhat confusingly to signify both joint communal property and open-access situations.

Nonie Sharp documents the existence of customary marine tenures in Europe, some of which survived beyond the seventeenth century, when the consolidation of state power led to the concept of territorial seas and absorbtion of these tenures as if they never existed. Like other authors Sharp asks why it has taken anthropologists and others so long to recognise and acknowledge these customary systems of marine tenure. Obviously a complex of factors was involved, including the need to keep other nations at a distance and, in the European context, the effects of the enclosure of the commons movement which meant that ordinary people became more committed to open access to the coast and the seas.

Scott Cane discusses the situation of Aboriginal people on the south coast of NSW where people have been interacting with Europeans since first settlement. His paper relates to the research he carried out for the Mason v Tritton case in which an Aboriginal man was prosecuted for having too many abalone in his possession and sought to advance as his defence that he was exercising his native title right to fish. The paper raises two key issues: the first relates to the harvesting of sea resources for sale rather than use; the second to what way, if any, the fishing practices of Aboriginal people in the settled parts of Australia differ from those of many non-indigenous Australians who have fished all their lives.

Both Bryce Barker and Patrick Sullivan, in different ways, also deal with people like those on the south coast of NSW whose systems of customary marine tenure have undergone radical transformation under the impact of European arrival.

Bryce Barker, an archaeologist, is able to show that the people with traditional interests in the Whitsunday Islands have a long history of sea use going back 6000 years. This usage has continued down to the present day but it is not now, if it ever was, associated with any elaborate system of sea tenure. It involves simply the collective use of the region by a group of interrelated families who see themselves as holding the area communally. What chance does such a long history of use have of recognition, he asks, when it is not characterised by any developed system of customs and traditions.

Patrick Sullivan describes the system of tenure among the Yawuru in the Broome area of Western Australia. He argues that the tenure-holding unit is best characterised as the 'society'. He describes a complex system of relationships to sea and land under which people have attachment to localised areas on the basis of conception, birth, link through either parent or long knowledge and association and, at the same time, enjoy rights in the combined land and water of the wider 'society' which, following Berndt, he defines as the widest functional grouping characterised by interactions for ceremonies. This is not a grouping that excludes others from entry onto land and sea but one that does exclude others from the right of possession. Thus in the system that Sullivan describes the sea is held as communal property among all members of the society, rather than some much smaller group, and this he believes to have been a long-standing arrangement which is partly accounted for by the ecology of both the land and sea elements of their country.

Memmott and Trigger's account of tenure in the central part of the Gulf of Carpentaria presents a radical contrast to the kind of system reported by Sullivan. Formally the patrilineal clan-based land system is extended into the sea and there is well-defined boundary location close to the coast in the intertidal zone but fuzzier boundaries further out to sea. However, on land as in the sea, people have the expectation of ready access to the estates of their grandparents in many cases. Rather unusually for Australia, there is a term for the senior male of a clan, *dulmada*, in whom some authority lies in respect of regulating the use of the resource of all parts of the estate. Along the coast and on reefs out at sea there are important places which can be used either to create storms or to make them abate. This seems to be a common feature in many areas: a range of sites that can create heavy rain, strong wind, waterspouts or cyclones or to cause these events to disappear.

Kingsley Palmer discusses the system of tenure in the Groote Eylandt area of the Gulf of Carpentaria which is broadly similar to that described by Memmott and Trigger. While land-based interests extend out into the sea, movement across the sea seems less regulated, although permission is required. The seascape is structured around the travels of mythological beings responsible for the creation of many places, some of which are dangerous.

John Bradley writes about the area immediately to the west of that discussed by Memmott and Trigger. He considers the significance of the sea in the constitution of Yanyuwa identity, looking at the attachment as expressed in the language and in song. He shows how the same terminology used for land-based features is applied to the seabed confirming a widespread interest in it. A complex symbiotic relationship, expressed as kinship, exists between animals and their environment, as well as between sea animals and their hunters, who are seen as mutually benefical to each other, such that if hunters do not hunt dugong, their numbers will decrease. Likewise, if sea birds do not hunt fish, then both fish and birds will suffer.

Geoffrey Bagshaw provides a case study from the Crocodile Island region of the north coast of Arnhem Land. The unique feature of this study is that unlike elsewhere the system of tenure in the sea in this area is not an extension of the system found on the adjacent land. Here, where there is a patrilineal moiety system, the muddy waters (*gapu dhulway*) adjacent to the coast are said to be affiliated with one moiety, regardless of the moiety affilation of the adjacent land and the clear deep blue water (*gapu marumba*) further out to sea is affiliated with the other moiety. It is interesting, however, that the seabed appears to have the moiety affiliation of the land to which it is adjacent.

This contrast between the two kinds of salt water is similar to the one that the Tsimshianic-speaking peoples (the Southern Tsimshian, Coast Tsimshian, Nishga and Gitksan) of the northern coast and hinterland of British Columbia draw between *laxmo ʾon* 'the inshore, sheltered salt channels and estuaries' and *laxsiilda* 'the open, blue sea'. However, there is no evidence that the two kinds of salt water articulate with the interregional phratry /moiety system found in the region.

Peter Cooke and Gowan Armstrong describe the situation about the Liverpool River region of the Arnhem Land Coast. Here there is a primary emphasis on patrifilial rights but a complex of other rights and interests allow people access to a range of sea country. They also describe an interesting ritualised fishing expedition, *Lurra*, held by the Kunabidji to persuade the ancestors to be generous in allowing people to make good catches. Having participated in the *Lurra* men could harvest seabird eggs on Haul Round Island in the portion of the Island allocated to their clan, the football oval-sized island being divided up between the clans on the opposite mainland.

Bruce Rigsby and Athol Chase deal with the life of the Sandbeach People of the east coast of Cape York, a region where some of the most maritime-oriented Aboriginal people are found. Their maritime orientation was first described by Donald Thomson in the 1930s and it has, of course, since undergone the kind of change common around Australia. The pre-European technology of dugout canoes with outriggers has been replaced by aluminium dinghies and fibreglass boats powered by outboards. But the sea, and land, as property still plays a central part in economic and social life and in social relations.

Michael Southon discusses the Kauareg people's traditional knowledge of the seas around the Prince of Wales and neighbouring islands in the southern part of the Torres Strait. Central to their marine tenure is the mythological figure Waubin, who created many features on and around the islands.

Finally, Sandra Pannell provides a provocative postmodern challenge to the idea of CMT and indeed the kinds of ethnographically based studies that make up this volume. She argues that the term customary marine tenure has come to be so all-embracing that it is in danger of becoming meaningless and of producing the very categories and beliefs it is said to be a study of. Rather than an empirical reality, it is coming to stand for an endangered reality, for a system of tenure that is community-based, traditional, caring, conservative, sustainable, sensitive, primitive and associated with the past as against the self-interested open-access systems of European ideas about the sea.

Terminology

The legal definition of the seaward boundaries of the states and territories and of the various categories of sea distinguished in legislation is complex. Any legal or other action for which these definitions are relevant requires professional legal advice but it seems useful to provide a basic guide to the key terms used to refer to the sea.

It is significant and suprising that the issues surrounding sovereignty in the sea around Australia were not confirmed by legislation until the 1970s with the passing of the *Seas and Submerged Lands Act 1973*, (Cth. See Meyers et al 1996:39). In February 1983, the inner limits of the Australian territorial sea were defined as required by Section 7 of this Act. The greater part of this baseline is the low water line along the coast, which is defined as the 'Lowest Astronomical Tide, which is the lowest level which can be predicted to occur under average meterological conditions' (Australia 1988:3). The rest of the baseline consists of straight lines as follows:

1. Lines across the mouths of rivers which flow directly into the sea.
2. Bay-closing lines to enclose certain bays not more than 24 nautical miles wide at their mouths; and
3. Straight baselines to enclose waters where the coastline is deeply indented and cut into, or where there is a fringe of islands along the coast in its immediate vicinity (Australia 1988:3).
4. Four bays of historical significance in South Australia (Anxious, Encounter, Lacepede and Rivoli).

From this territorial sea baseline the following categories of waters are distinguished:

Internal waters: waters between the baseline and the shore. These waters are not to be confused with 'inland' waters which are those whose connection is with the land although they may be open to the sea. These waters are controlled by the states and territories.

Coastal waters: waters between the baseline and three nautical miles out to sea. These have been vested in the states and territories since 1979.

Territorial sea: waters between the baseline and twelve nautical miles out to sea. The first three nautical miles are the Coastal Waters controlled by the states and territories and the other nine nautical miles are controlled by the Commonwealth.

Exclusive Economic Zone: this runs from the 12 nautical miles line to 200 nautical miles out to sea from the territorial sea baseline.

The territorial sea baseline is a baseline under international law and does not represent state boundaries which, are generally further landward of the baselines (Australia 1988:4).

The distribution of control of the various fisheries between state and Commonwealth is also complicated. For example, while most fisheries are controlled by the states and territories within their waters some may be controlled by the Commonwealth.

References

Akerman, K. 1975. The double raft or *kalwa* of the West Kimberley. *Mankind* 10:20–23.

Australia, Attorney-General's Department. 1988. *Australia's territorial sea baseline*. Canberra: AGPS.

Baker, R. 1988. Yanyuwa canoe making. *Records of the South Australian Museum* 22(2):173–188.

Berndt, R. 1976. Territoriality and the problem of demarcating sociocultural space. In *Tribes and boundaries in Australia* (ed) N. Peterson. Canberra: Australian Institute of Aboriginal Studies. Pp. 133–161.

1970. *The sacred site: the western Arnhem Land example*. Canberra: Australian Institute of Aborignal Studies.

1964. The Gove dispute: the question of Australian Aboriginal land and the preservation of sacred sites. *Anthropological Forum* 1(2):258–295.

1952. *Djanggawul: an Aboriginal religious cult of north-eastern Arnhem Land*. London: Routledge and Kegan Paul.

1948. Badu: islands of the spirits. *Oceania* 19 (2):93–103.

Bird, D and R. 1997. Delayed reciprocity and tolerated theft. *Current Anthropology* 38(1):49–78.

Bowdler, S. (ed). 1982. *Coastal archaeology in eastern Australia.* Canberra: Department of Prehistory, Australian National University.

Bradley, J. 1997. *Li-Anthawirriyarra, people of the sea: Yanyuwa relations with their maritime environment.* Unpublished PhD thesis. Darwin: University of the Northern Territory.

1991. Li-Maramanja: Yanyuwa hunters of marine animals in the Sir Edward Pellew group, Northern Territory. *Records of the South Australian Museum* 25(1):91–110.

Butlin, N. 1993. *Economics of the dreamtime: a hypothetical history.* Cambridge: Cambridge University Press.

Cawte, J. 1974. *Medicine is the law: studies in psychiatric anthropology of Australian tribal societies.* Adelaide: Rigby.

Chase, A. 1980. *Which way now? Tradition, continuity and change in a north Queensland Aboriginal community.* Unpublished PhD thesis. Brisbane: University of Queensland.

Chase, A. and Sutton P. 1981. Hunter-gatherers in a rich environment: Aboriginal coastal exploitation in Cape York Peninsula. In *Ecological biogeography of Australia* (ed) A. Keast. The Hague: Junk. Pp. 1818–1852.

Christy, F. 1996. Thalassorama: the death rattle of open access and the advent of property rights regimes in fisheries. *Marine Resource Economics* 11:287–304.

Clarke, A. 1994. *Winds of change: an archaeology of contact in the Groote Eylandt archipelago, northern Australia.* Unpublished PhD thesis. Canberra: Australian National University.

Cordell, J. 1991. Managing sea country: tenure and sustainability of Aboriginal and Torres Strait Islander marine resources. Canberra: ESD Secretariat.

Croker Island Transcript, 1997. Mary Yarmirr, Mandilarri-Ildugij Peoples and Others and Northern Territory of Australia and Others. In *Transcript*

of Proceeding of the Federal Court of Australia before Mr Justice Olney.
Darwin: Auscript.

Davidson, D. 1935. The chronology of Australian watercraft. *Journal of the Polynesian Society* 44(1):1–16; (2):69–84; (3):137–152; (4):193–207.

Davis, S. 1984. *Aboriginal tenure and use of the coast and sea in northern Arnhem Land.* Unpublished MA thesis. Melbourne: University of Melbourne.

1982. Report on the Castlereagh Bay and Howard Island sea closure application 2 vols. Darwin: Aboriginal Sacred Sites Protection Authority.

Davis, S. and Prescott, V. 1992. *Aboriginal frontiers and boundaries in Australia.* Melbourne: Melbourne University Press.

Derschaw *et al.* 1996. Derschaw, Clifton and Murphy v Sutton. *Australian Indigneous Law Reporter* 2(1):53–63.

Earl, G. 1846. *Enterprise in tropical Australia.* London: Madden and Malcolm.

Gray, F. and Zann, L. (eds). 1988. *Traditional knowledge of the marine environment in northern Australia.* Townsville: Great Barrier Reef Marine Park Authority.

Hart, C. and Pilling, A. 1960. *The Tiwi of north Australia.* New York: Hart, Reinholt and Winston.

Heath, J. 1980. *Nunggubuyu myths and ethnographic texts.* Canberra: Australian Institute of Aboriginal Studies.

Hiatt, L. 1965. *Kinship and conflict in Arnhem Land.* Canberra: Australian National University Press.

Johannes, R. and MacFarlane, J. 1991. *Traditional fishing in the Torres Strait islands.* Hobart: CSIRO Division of Fisheries.

Jones, R. 1980. Hunters in the Australian coastal savanna. In *Human ecology in savanna environments* (ed) D. Harris. London: Academic Press. Pp. 107–146.

1976. Tasmania: aquatic machines and off-shore islands. In *Problems in economic and social archaeology* (ed) G. Sieveking, I. Longworth and K. Wilson. London: Duckworth. Pp. 235–263.

Keen, I. 1980. *Report on the Milingimbi closure of the seas hearing.* A submission to the Aboriginal Land Commissioner.

Kennedy, L. 1996. Exercising native title hunting rights: Derschaw v Sutton. *Aboriginal Law Bulletin* 85:31–32.

Kilduff, P. and Lofgren, N. 1996. Native fishing rights in coastal waters and territorial seas. *Aboriginal Law Bulletin* 81:16–17.

King, P. 1827 *Narrative of a survey of the intertropical and western coasts of Australia performed between the years 1818 and 1822.* (2 vols). London: John Murray.

Kirby, J. 1994. Judgement in Mason v Tritton and another on appeal in the Supreme Court of New South Wales. Pp. 1–55.

Macgillivray, J. 1982. *Narrative of the Voyages of the H.M.S. Rattlesnake.* (2 Vols). London: T. and W. Boone.

Macknight, C. 1986. Macassans and the Aboriginal past. *Archaeology in Oceania* 21:69–75.

1976. *The voyage to Marege: Macassan trepangers in northern Australia.* Melbourne: Melbourne University Press.

McArthur, M. 1960. Food consumption and dietary levels of groups of Aborigines living on naturally occurring foods. In *Records of the American-Australian Scientific Expedition to Arnhem Land*, Volume 2. Melbourne: Melbourne University Press. Pp. 90–135.

Meehan, B. 1982. *Shell bed to shell midden.* Canberra: Australian Institute of Aboriginal Studies.

1977. Man does not live by calories alone: the role of shellfish in a coastal cuisine. In *Sunda and Sahul: prehistoric studies in southeast Asia, Melanesia and Australia* (eds) J. Allen, J. Golson and R. Jones. London: Academic press. Pp. 493–531.

Meyers, G., O'Dell, M., Wright, G. and Muller, S. 1996. *A sea change in land rights law: the extension of native title to Australia's offshore areas.* Perth: National Native Title Tribunal.

Mitchell, S. 1994. *Culture contact and indigenous economies on the Cobourg Peninsula, northwestern Arnhem Land.* Unpublished PhD. Thesis. Darwin: Northern Territory University.

Morphy, H. 1977. The ownership of the sea in north-east Arnhem Land. *Hansard of the Joint Select Committee of Aboriginal Land Rights in the Northern Territory*, 3rd May. Pp. 1100–1103.

Nietschmann, B. 1985. Hunting and ecology of dugongs and green turtles, Torres Strait, Australia. *National Geographic Society Research Report* 17:625–652.

Palmer, K. 1988. Status of documentary information on Aboriginal and Islander fishing and marine hunting in northern Australia. In *Traditional knowledge of the marine environment in northern Australia* (eds) F. Gray and L. Zann. Townsville: Great Barrier Reef Marine Park Authority. Pp. 4–19.

1983. *A report prepared in support of an application to control entry onto seas adjoining Aboriginal land.* Darwin: Northern Land Council.

Palmer, K. and Brady, M. 1984. *A report prepared in support of an application to control entry onto seas adjoining Aboriginal land: Croker Island and other islands, N.T.* Darwin: NLC.

Peterson, N. and Devitt, J. 1997. *A report in supoort of an application for recognition of native title to areas of sea by the Mangalara, Mandilarri-Ildugij, Murran, Gadura, Mayarram, Minaga and Nganyjaharr of the Croker Island region.* Darwin: Northern Land Council.

Peterson, N. And Tonkinson, M. 1979. *Cobourg Peninsula and adjacent islands land claim.* Darwin: Northern Land Council.

Polunin, N. 1984. Do traditional marine 'reserves' conserve? A view of Indonesian and New Guinean evidence. In *Maritime institutions in the western Pacific* (eds) K. Ruddle and T. Akimichi. Osaka: National Museum of Ethnology, Senri Ethnological Studies No. 17. Pp. 267–283.

Rose, C. 1994. *Property and persuasion: essays on the history, theory and rhetoric of ownership.* Boulder: Westview Press.

Rose, F. 1961. The Indonesians and the genesis of the Groote Eylandt society, northern Australia. *Beitrage Zur Volkerforschung* 11:524–531.

1960. *Classification of kin, age structure and marriage arrangements amongst the Groote Eylandt Aborigines.* Berlin: Akadamie-Verlag.

Rowland, M. 1987. The distribution of Aboriginal watercraft on the east coast of Queensland: implications for cutlure contact. *Australian Aboriginal Studies* 2:38–45.

1981. Radiocarbon dates for a shell fishhook and disc from Mazie Bay, North Keppel Island. *Australian Archaeology* 11:1–17.

Ruddle, K. 1994. Traditional marine tenure in the 90s. In *Traditional marine tenure and sustainable management of marine resources in Asia and the Pacific* (eds) G. Smith, D. Goulet, S. Tuqiri and M. Church. Suva: University of the South Pacific. Pp. 6–45.

Ruddle, K. and Akimichi, T. 1984. Introduction. In *Maritime institutions in the western Pacific* (eds) K. Ruddle and T. Akimichi. Osaka: National Museum of Ethnology, Senri Ethnological Studies No 17:1–9.

Sharp, N. 1997. Why indigenous sea rights are not recognised in Australia: the 'facts' of Mabo and their cultural roots. *Australian Aboriginal Studies* 1:28–37.

Smith, A. 1988. *An ethnobiological study of the usage of marine resources by two Aboriginal communities on the east coast of Cape York Peninsula.* Unpublished PhD thesis, James Cook University of Northern Queensland.

Smyth, D. 1993. *A voice in all places: Aboriginal and Torres Strait Islander interests in Australia's coastal zone.* Canberra: Resources Assessment Commission.

Spencer, W. And Gillen, F. 1912. *Across Australia* (2 Vols). London: Macmillan.

Storey, M. 1996. The black sea. *Aboriginal Law Bulletin* 79:4–8.

Sutherland, J. 1996. *Fisheries, aquaculture and Aboriginal and Torres Strait Islander peoples: studies, polices and legislation.* Canberra: Department of the Environment, Sports and Territories.

Thomson, D. 1934. The dugong hunters of Cape York *Journal of the Royal Anthropological Institute* 64:237–262.

Tindale, N. 1962. Geographical knowledge of the Kaiadilt people of Bentinck Island, Queensland. *Records of the South Australian Museum* 14(2):297–336.

1925–26. Natives of Groote Eylandt and of the west coast of the Gulf of Carpentaria. *Records of the South Australian Museum* 3:61–102, 103–134.

Turner, D. 1974. *Tradition and transformation: a study of Aborigines in the Groote Eylandt area, northern Australia.* Canberra: Australian Institute of Aboriginal Studies.

Warner, L. 1937. *A black civilization: a social study of an Australian tribe.* New York: Harper and Brothers.

Wilkins, A. 1908. Property and inheritance. In *Reports of the Cambridge expedition to the Torres Strait: sociology, magic and religion of the eastern islanders,* Vol 6 (ed) A. Haddon. Cambridge: Cambridge University Press. Pp. 163–167.

Williams, N. 1986. *The Yolngu and their land: a system of land tenure and the fight for its recognition.* Stanford: Stanford University Press.

Woodward, A. E. 1973. *Aboriginal Land Rights Commission: First Report July 1973.* Canberra: Australian Govelrnment Publishing Service.

Worsley, P. 1954. *The changing social structure of the Wanindiljaugwa.* Unpublished PhD thesis. Canberra: Australian National University.

2

A survey of property theory and tenure types

Bruce Rigsby

> [I]f kinship be regarded as the social instrument that structuralizes the fundamental roles which individuals play toward each other as persons, property as a social institution is the instrument that structuralizes the roles which individuals play in the complex system of human relations that prevail in regard to the ownership of valuable objects, whether material or not (Hallowell 1955[1943]:246).

> [P]roperty is always a contested concept ... [and it] changes over time (Radin 1993:119).

In the evolutionary anthropology of the past century and its successors up into the 1950s, property was a notable concept, but with the rise of new interests in and concerns with ecology and evolution, property and tenure (or ownership) were by and large replaced by terms such as territoriality, range and use[1] in anthropological studies of people/

---

1   Barnard and Spencer (1996:625) wrote:
territoriality A slightly ambiguous term which may refer either to cultural mechanisms to define or defend territory or to observed behaviour indicating a preference for remaining within a given teritory. The term is is common use in archaeology and social anthropology (especially in reference to hunter-gatherers), but often has ethological connotations (emphasis in original). Some early notable references to works that exemplify the shift to cological and evolutionary approaches are Damas (1969a, 1969b) and Lee and De Vore (1968). Amongst Australianists, Peterson (1975, 1976, 1986 plus other items) and Hunn and Williams (1982) are significant. Williams (1997) includes a section on 'Territory/ Territoriality' that surveys the broader literature, including contributions

land relations. In our country, following the 1992 Mabo No. 2 decision and the federal Native Title Act 1993, Aboriginal and Torres Strait Islander people's rights and interests in land under their traditional law and custom are recognisable by the common law where they have not been extinguished by acts of the Crown or other adverse acts. This sea change in the law respecting indigenous land rights has implications for anthropological work in native title and other land-related actions. We need to refamiliarise ourselves with the theory and concepts of property and ownership, but at the same time, we should continue to study territoriality, range and use.

Keesing (1981:67–75, 212, 213) distinguished cultural structure from social structure in the same way that Goodenough (1969:329–330) earlier differentiated cultural anthropology from social anthropology. The first is a system of organised knowledge and rules or principles held by social actors which we infer from our observations of their behaviour (including their speech and discourse), while the second is a system of patterned regularities we can infer from the same kinds of observations. In other words, we observe what people do and say, and we can model this either as a cultural system of organised knowledge and rules for action or behaviour or as a social system of patterned regularities of action or behaviour. Both perspectives are important for us as we seek to analyse and describe how people own and use land. If we take seriously the requirements that Mabo No. 2 and the *Native Title Act 1993* established, then we anthropologists and our clients must present to native title tribunals and federal courts evidence of fact and expert opinion that there is an ongoing system of traditional laws and customs

---

by anthropologists. We suggest that it would be useful to explore the relationships amongst terms arranged by proportional analogy such that:

| property | : | estate | : | possession | : | occupancy | etc. |
| territoriality | : | range | : | defence | : | use | etc. |

One might speculate that the linkage of the institution of property with bourgeois liberal economic and political theory was also related to anthropologists' shift to evolutionary and ecological approaches.

that connects people to their land and waters. This includes a system of tenure, as well as a system of use. Customary marine tenure[2] adds to the challenge that the study of property and the traditional Aboriginal ownership of land pose for us. Cordell (1993:163) observed that 'land and marine tenure may be divisible for the sake of analysis, but from indigenous coastal peoples' perspectives[,] they are indivisible'. The point is important not only as a representation of indigenous beliefs and values, but also as a statement that terrestrial and marine tenure should be analysed and described in a single account, using the same kinds of terms and relations amongst them.

Tenure, property rights and objects of property

There is a wider body of theory that we can draw upon to better understand Aboriginal tenure systems.[3] The concepts of tenure (or ownership)

2   Any serious consideration of customary marine tenure in Australia must refer to the work of John Cordell. It was Cordell's (1989) excellent collection of papers on sea tenure that helped to frame a general field for study, and it is his (Cordell 1992, 1993) less inclusive term 'customary marine tenure' that has captured a wider audience. Hviding (1996:388–389) noted that he introduced the term 'customary marine tenure' in 1987, published as Hviding (1989), and he provided a brief discussion of his choice of wording. Hviding (1996) is a superlative monograph, comprehensive in its coverage and elegantly written. We sometimes abbreviate customary marine tenure to CMT here.

3   There is an extensive literature on property which includes earlier writers such as Locke, Hume, Proudhon and Bentham and extends to the present day (e.g. Munzer 1990; Radin 1993; Rose 1994). In another context, I (Rigsby 1997:31–34) sought to gain a perspective on the anthropological literature that American anthropologists might have drawn on to analyse and describe Indian systems of land tenure during the period the Indian Claims Commission operated, and this led me to read more widely in the property literature. Up until about 1955, anthropology texts often included chapters or sections on property (e.g. Boas 1938; Herskovits 1948, 1952[1940]; Lowie 1920, 1940, 1948) and the

and property are at its centre. Tenure and property always involve three terms; in symbolic logic, we say that the predicate 'own' takes three arguments. We can formalise them in the proposition 'A owns B as against C', as did Brewer and Staves (1995:3); Hallowell (1955[1943]:239) and Paul (1987:193). This contrasts with the simpler 'A owns B', as in popular discourse and in Snare (1972:200), who spoke of 'the special relationship which may hold between a person and a physical object called "owning"'.[4]

Tenure or ownership is the relationship of A to B as against C, while property, strictly speaking, is the rights that A has in B, the thing that A owns as against C. Hallowell (1955[1943]:239) noted that the term 'property' has two common senses: it signifies both the object that is owned, as well the rights that are exercised over it.[5] He argued, citing economists and lawyers, that the term should be restricted to the first sense. We accept his view and will use 'object of property' for the second sense (see also Rose 1994:253, 263; Waldron 1988:30). It also bears noting that B need not in fact be a physical object, but can be incorporeal knowledge, for example, see Lowie (1929).

---

wider social science literature included contributions from anthropologists (e.g. Lowie 1933). By and large, these anthropological writings were more descriptive, historical and encyclopaedic than analytical, but Radcliffe-Brown (1952[1935]) and Hallowell (1955[1943]) are exceptions. Anthropologists have been conspicuously absent from the more recent literature, and economists, historians, lawyers, philosophers and political scientists have been prominent contributors. In all its years, the Annual Review of Anthropology has not run a general overview article on land tenure, although Shipton (1994) surveyed the literature on African land tenure.

4   However, all Snare's rules make reference to persons (C) other than A. Hann (1996:454) observed that 'most anthropologists would now agree that rights over things are better understood as rights between people'. Munzer (1994:15ff) contrasts the 'sophisticated' relational view of property with the 'popular' view of property as things.

5   See also the discussion in Williams (1986:202), which cites Hohfeld (1964), but does not privilege one sense over the other.

The inclusion of two personal (or group) arguments (namely, A and C) makes the owning relationship a social one. There is no property in nature apart from humans. As Demsetz (1967:346) expressed it:

> In the world of Robinson Crusoe property rights play no role. Property rights are an instrument of society and derive their significance from the fact that they help a man form those expectations which he can reasonably hold in his dealings with others. These expectations find expression in the laws, customs, and mores of a society. An owner of property rights possesses the consent of fellowmen to allow him to act in particular ways. An owner expects the community to prevent others from interfering with his actions, provided that these actions are not prohibited in the specification of his rights.

The property relationship is also a cultural phenomenon, i.e. it is based on symbolism, the arbitrary assignment of meaning. Marshall Sahlins (1996:1) recently reminded us that Leslie White used to say that an ape could not recognise the difference between holy water and distilled water for there is no chemical difference, only a symbolic one. Snare (1972:200) speculated that a Martian would understand little of our daily social life if he did not comprehend that much action makes sense only in the context of the property institution:

> For example, he would completely miss what we are doing when we sell an automobile or give a gift or steal an apple. After all, a stolen apple doesn't *look* any different from any other apple.

The triadic formulation of tenure and property relationships also recognises the insight encapsulated in the conventional definition of rights *in rem* as rights which A holds in B 'as against the world' (Radcliffe-Brown 1952[1935]:33; Munzer 1990:31; Rose 1994:271). The phrase 'as against the world' not only quantifies the C argument, but in so doing, it introduces the condition that ownership implies the right to exclude others from possession, occupation and use and enjoyment of the object of property, for example, land (see Munzer 1990:89).

41

Common law courts and tribunals in land rights cases here and overseas have generally insisted on evidence that a claimant group has exercised its right to exclude others from its land, i.e. the right of exclusion is a *sine qua non* of ownership. In its absence, there is no ownership—there is no property.[6]

However, the triadic formulation of tenure and property relationships remains incomplete as formulated because it fails to note that they exist only in the context of wider cultural and social systems which have internal and external dominion[7] dimensions. It fails to note that the A and C parties constitute a polity, that is, a rule or norm-generating and—maintaining community, and it fails to note that the set of parties in C can generally be partitioned into those who are members of the polity and those who are not, for example citizens and residents vs foreigners, kin vs strangers, us vs them, etc. The quantification of C as 'as against the world' has the same defect.

In the first respect, property relationships exist as a subset of the social relationships in a polity, and its members customarily and conventionally acknowledge and observe one another's property rights. Phrased another way, members of a polity hold beneficial or proximate titles (Sutton 1996a) in land and other objects of property. The polity itself, however, exercises dominion internally, that is, it sets the parameters of tenure and title.[8] For example, in state-based polities, the

6 Several writers (Williams 1982; McCay 1987) have commented on the difficulty of getting evidence for one indigenous group excluding others because public ideology stresses sharing and generosity. See below for further discussion of the right to exclude.

7 Dominion is the aspect of sovereignty that polities exercise with respect to the ownership of land and waters in their territories. In earlier discourse, dominion was contrasted with sovereignty. The two terms respectively translate the Latin *dominium* and *imperium*, from Roman law and jurisprudence. Contemporary political thought sees dominion related to sovereignty as part to whole, not as a coordinate function of a polity.

8 Walker (1980:1221) defined 'title' as '[t]he legal connection between a person and a right constituted by some act or event having legal significance. Every right which a person has attaches to him by virtue of

state typically exercises rights of escheat, eminent domain, taxation and regulation. The latter may include zoning, building restrictions and requirements, etc. All these relate to its holding of the radical or under-lying title to its territory. In classical and contemporary Aboriginal Australia, a non-state-organised polity, the leading men and elders of a region exercise the underlying title by mutually confirming one anoth-er's group proximate titles and by dealing with problematic cases, for example where a group dies out and/or where succession, boundaries, divided rights and the like are contested and disputed (Sutton 1996a).

In the second respect, polities have external relations with other polities, for example, state-based polities regulate whether and how non-citizens may hold property rights in their territories. In the common law countries, the courts have consistently held over the past few centuries that only the state (e.g. the Crown in Commonwealth countries) can acquire rights in land recognisable by its law in other territories. Only a state can acquire radical title to the territory (or a part of it) of another polity. Private individuals cannot do so. But to return to the triadic formulation of tenure and property relationships, the point is that the members of a polity cannot expect to have their property rights automatically recognised and respected by members of another. Tenure systems, i.e. systems of property rights, always exist in an 'international' inter-polity context. During the colonisation of the New World and our own country, it was often the case that the members of the indigenous

---

some title, and rights of the same character, e.g. ownership of goods, may be vested in different persons by virtue of different kinds of titles, by making, by gifts, by purchase, by inheritance, and so on'. He also noted that '[i]n land law 'titles' or 'title deeds' denote those deeds which evi-dence a person's title to particular land, which require to be examined by a prospective buyer and which are transfered to him on completion of the purchase'. This definition seems incomplete for we generally speak of title with respect to some object of property to which rights and interests attach. Thus broadened, title as a legal connection can be used cross-cul-turally, but in its sense as a sign of that connection, we note that in societies that lack writing, title deeds may be manifested in speech, song, dance, artistic designs, etc.

43

non-state-based polities did not have their property rights recognised by settler members of the colonising state-based polities, or even by the colonising polity itself. Such was the case with the property rights of Aboriginal people in land and waters under their own traditional law and custom until the Mabo No. 2 decision in June, 1992.

The origins and functions of property

Property is universal, an institution found in all human societies (Smith 1985:404, 407–408), and property in land similarly is universal—see Hallowell (1955[1943]:242–244), who noted that the denial that hunter-gatherers and pastoralists own land was 'linked with the pseudo-history of the social evolutionary theories of the nineteeenth century' and referred readers to Herskovits (1940) for evidence they own land. Hallowell (1955[1943]:249) concluded that one of the 'primary contributions [of the institution of property] ... to a human social order and the security of the individual' is that 'individuals are secured against the necessity of being constantly on the alert to defend [valuable] objects [of property] from others by physical force alone' (see also Rose 1994:296). This is because in human societies, we internalise norms and values with respect to property. Over and above the anticipation and fear that other owners will exercise force and commit violence against us, we are motivated not to trespass by the wider 'moral, religious, or legal penalties' that may operate if we do not do our duty. The institution of property probably has an evolutionary history like those of kinship[9]

9 See the opening quotation above from Hallowell (1955[1943]:246). He credited Bunzel (1938:340) for the insight of their parallelism. Smith (1985:404–406) argued that in the Old World, humans shifted from hunting and gathering to agriculture as climatic change, 'overkill' or whatever resulted in the 'loss of the favoured easy prey [which] substantially increased the opportunity cost of hunting and gathering compared with agriculture'. He also suggested (p. 406) that '[a] good working hypothesis is that property rights and exchange predate the Agricultural Revolution' and he argued this on the basis of the ethnographic evidence got from

and language that takes them back at least to the emergence of *Homo sapiens sapiens*. Phrased another way, we have always been territorial, like other contemporary hominoids, but when we became landowners, acquired kinfolk and began to speak modern-type language, we also became human.[10]

But if property is very old in our species, its specific objects nonetheless have shallower histories. It is a truism of our discipline that not all the plant and animal species and natural phenomena found in the environment of a particular society are recognised as resources and assigned value in its culture. No doubt many Aboriginal groups knew of the presence of gold in their countries before non-Aboriginal prospectors and miners invaded their lands, but there is no reason to believe that gold was the object of specific property rights and interests in the indigenous tenure systems as it later became. Similarly, Aboriginal people have probably owned and used the beach and littoral areas of their estates for millenia, but whether they owned and used the offshore areas (especially the reefs and seagrass beds) where most dugongs and sea turtles are found in another question. This leads us to the question of what are the conditions under which particular things become objects of property.

In the history of thought on the origins of property (see Umbeck 1981:50–64), several kinds of theories were proposed. Much early Western thought (from the Greeks onward) regarded property as originating from God, so that property rights were considered to be 'natural' and people were obliged to respect them. The philosopher Locke argued in the 18th century that land and things became property only when humans invested their labour in their production, but a century earlier, Hobbes developed a social contract theory which survives in current theories. Hobbes' *Leviathan* (1951 [1651]) situated the original contract

---

hunter-gatherers studied during the past hundred years.

10 Smith (1985:404) proposed that to be human means to use language, tools, organization, property rights and exchange, but that only exchange is unique to humans. We disagree and restrict language and property rights similarly.

squarely in human society and the acquisitive, maximising propensities of people. For Hobbes, the right each individual had to the use of his own physical power or labour was the only natural right. In the absence of any agreements, people must live in a continual state of 'warre' with their neighbors. 'It is consequent also to the same condition, that there be no propriety, no dominion, no mine and thine distinct; but only that to be every man's that he can get: and for so long as he can keep it' (Hobbes 1951[1651]:83–84, cited by Umbeck 1981:1, 51).

In *The Social Contract*, Rousseau (1938[1762]) took issue with Hobbes' view that 'Might makes right', but he contributed to helping to understand the costs associated with the original contract. He concluded that where resources have little or no economic value, a contract regulating their use would probably not be made. Rousseau (1938[1762]68–69, cited by Umbeck 1981:53) wrote:

> Unfriendly and barren lands, where the product does not repay the labour, should remain desert and uncultivated, or peopled only by savages; lands where men's labour brings in no more than the exact minimum to subsistence should be inhabited by barbarous peoples: in all such places all polity is impossible.

Umbeck (1981:53) thought it possible to assemble 'a fairly full theory of the creation of private property rights from the work of Hobbes and Rousseau'. Where there are no agreements, rights are determined by personal violence and force. In such situations, much potential income is lost that could be got by contracting with others to grant and recognise exclusive rights to property. However, the contract will be costly to form and enforce. Given the costs, the gains from contracting increase with the value of the resources to be made private property.

Umbeck (1981:53) also noted that the social contract theory fell into disfavour after Rousseau and for nearly two centuries the relationship among property rights, contract and the state was forgotten or ignored. He said that it was reintroduced into modern price theory by way of the literature on 'externalities'. Umbeck (1981:53–64) reviews the development of the externality concept from Pigou (1938) and Knight

(1924) through Coase (1960), Gordon (1954) and Cheung (1970, 1974) to Demsetz (1967).[11]

Demsetz (1967:350) proposed that property rights emerge, i.e. they are assigned, 'with the emergence of new or different beneficial and harmful effects'. Communities assign property rights 'when the gains of internalization become larger than the cost of internalization'. By 'internalization', Demsetz means that the beneficial and harmful effects of actions, such as hunting, fishing, mining, cutting timber, etc. then are brought squarely to bear on owners as they so act and exercise their property rights.[12]

The primary empirical case that Demsetz examined in support of his theory was that of the development of private property rights in land amongst Northeastern Algonkian peoples.[13] Originally, men

---

11   Common (1988:79) wrote: 'An external effect, or *externality*, exists when the activity of a firm or a household gives rise to consequences for other firms or households, which consequences are not intentional and do not figure in the costs or benefits associated with the activity as perceived by the originating firm or household. A good example of an externality is the release by a firm of polluting waste products in some environmental media.' See also Neher (1990:225) and Tisdell (1993:4–5).

12   See also Neher (1990:159) and Tisdell (1991:55). Anderson and Hill (1975) is in the same vein as Demsetz (1967).

13   See Leacock (1954) and Hickerson (1967), who argued that precontact Northeast Algonkians owned land communally and that the ownership of hunting territories by famiies and individuals developed as a result of their involvement in the fur trade. Rose (1994:26, 200, 287), Schmidtz (1994:51–52) and Waldron (1988:7–9) recapitulated Demsetz' account. Gordon (1954:134–135) referred to Speck (1926) and Malinowski (1935) when he wrote that 'stable primitive cultures appear to have discovered the dangers of common-property tenure and to have developed measures [i.e. private property in land] to protect their resources'. Speck was an early advocate of the view that Northeast Algonkian family hunting territories were precontact. Berkes' (1989b) chapter, 'Cooperation from the Perspective of Human Ecology' in Berkes (1989a) surveyed and analysed new empirical material on James Bay Cree hunting territories and he corrected and criticised Demsetz' (1967) analysis thoroughly.

hunted game primarily for food and the furs they required for their own use. There was no need to assess the impact of one's own actions on the stocks of game nor to assess the effects of others' hunting the same game on one's own chances. But with the advent of the fur trade, the exchange-value of furs increased greatly as also did the scale of hunting. It then became advantageous for hunters to husband and conserve fur-bearing animals by hunting over only a portion of their land each year in rotation and by excluding trespassers and punishing poachers. The assignment of property rights in specific territories was a response to the new conditions. They allowed a community to adjust to new cost-benefit possibilities where the costs of not assigning property rights had become greater than the costs of assigning them.[14]

Umbeck (1981) proposed a contractarian theory for the emergence and assignment of property rights in land. His primary empirical case was California for perhaps two decades from the discovery of gold in 1848. The United States acquired California from the Mexican Republic by treaty the same year, and the new military governor abolished Mexican law, which had regulated mining previously. The 200,000 or so miners who rushed into the territory encountered a situation where they were technically trespassers and there was no American law regulating access to minerals on public lands. The new state government did not commence activities until 1850 and did not fund a law enforcement operation for a few more years. But as Umbeck (1981:5) noted, '[y]et by 1850..., miners had organized into groups and had agreed upon explicit contracts in which exclusive and transferrable rights to land were assigned to individuals within a given mining area or district. By 1866 over 500 separate and distinct districts were formed, each with their own system of property rights'. He also observed that while the contracts varied in some respects, each 'explicitly enumerates the rights that each miner shall be allowed in choosing between alternative land uses and the amounts of land each miner can claim as his own property'.

Umbeck's social contract theory is grounded in the human capacity for violence and it attempts to identify situations where the cost

---

14   Smith (1975) is in the same vein.

of violence leads people to forego it and to enter into property rights arrangements with one another. He (1981:28) wrote:

> For property rights to exist, some individuals must be able to exclude others from using or deriving income from a good. Ultimately, this ability to exclude depends on violence. Any contract in which individuals explicitly agree to assign and maintain exclusive rights will succeed or fail depending on the group's ability to use or threaten to use violence. The contract, if it is formed, must assign to each individual the exclusive rights to property equal in value to what the individual could get through personal violence. This distribution is predictable, given the relative abilities of individuals in violence and, [for example,] mining and the relative productivity of land. In order for the contract to be formed, ... [two] conditions are necessary: there must be economies of scale in violence, and there must be some advantage to being 'first.' These two conditions are not sufficient. The third condition, which is necessary and sufficient, is that there are positive costs of contracting, these costs must be less than the gains [of violence and not contracting].

Umbeck (1981:60–64) criticised Demsetz' account of the instituting of private property rights amongst Northeastern Algonkians in response to the fur trade, and he argued that his own contractarian theory was mutually exclusive with Demsetz' externality-based theory. Umbeck (1981:64) contrasted the two theories, and he concluded:

> property rights do not emerge from nowhere. They are subject to individual choice. Because individuals in the real world have chosen not to assign property rights to regulate all possible margins of resource use, the decisions about resource use are not necessarily made outside the market. Rather, it is an indication that the market for property rights is not without costs. It is more economical not to assign rights to some resources and, in so doing, allow them to be used in ways different from private property. To observe a resource, the rights to which have never been assigned, and to label its use externality, is to label our ignorance of the rel-

evant constraints. To suggest ways to remedy this externality without studying the relevant constraints is to demonstrate our ignorance.

...Before any type of economic activity—Crusoe islands aside—can take place, there must be some type of contract specifying who has what rights to what resources. All individual production decisions... are constrained at many margins by contracts... Every time a good is exchanged, some type of contract is implied. The contract is the basic building block of economic activity. Only by understanding the contractual constraints under which each individual operates and the costs associated with new contractual arrangements will economics ever be able to explain the wide range of human behavior we observe every day.

No matter which of the theories—Demsetz' or Umbeck's—we opt for, both are relevant to customary marine tenure in Australia, for they lead us to believe that property rights in offshore sea country and its resources only developed when Aboriginal people got watercraft that made them accessible and when they acquired technology and techniques that made the hunting of dugongs and sea turtles on reefs and seagrass beds possible.[15] Similarly, property rights in bailershell, cone

---

15   It is generally accepted that the first colonisers (in the biogeographical sense) must have had seaworthy watercraft (perhaps rafts) to make the journey to Greater Australia successfully, but it is not clear that that tradition of making and using such watercraft continued without interruption to the present. With respect to dugout canoes, which make offshore waters, islands, etc. accessible, it is generally accepted that the Macassans brought dugouts to the Top End several centuries ago, and that the single- and double-outrigger technology found in Torres Strait and along the northeastern coast of our continent at the time of European contact derives ultimately from Melanesian sources. Some scholars believe that simple dugout technology (without outriggers) on the east coast, whatever its ultimate origins, dates back several millenia, while others consider the dugout-*cum*-outrigger complex to have arrived from Melanesia only in the past few centuries. Dugout canoes not infrequently drift in to the

shell, giant clams, mother-of-pearl shell and other reef resources would have arisen with new demand and with new technology and techniques to harvest them. Groups assigned property rights in the new resources when it became too costly not to do so, whether by way of reduced production or of increased intergroup violence.

The character of property rights

Property rights are a subset of the rights[16] that members of a society (or polity or community) have and exercise, and one way to identify them is simply to list them. For example, A.M. Honore (1961; summarised by Becker 1977:18–19; see also Munzer (1990:22) and Waldron (1988:49)) proposed that the 'full' or 'liberal' concept of ownership included eleven kinds of rights, which are:

The right to possess—that is, to exclusive physical control of the thing owned. Where the thing cannot be possessed physically, due, for example, to its 'non-corporeal' naure, 'possession' may be understood metaphorically or simply as the right to exclude others from the use and other benefits of the thing.

---

east coast of Cape York Peninsula. In November, 1975, Athol Chase and I saw a small (less than two metres) single-outrigger canoe that had drifted onto the beach near our camp on the mainland near Cape Sidmouth. It was seaworthy and the children played about with it. In May, 1997, we saw another small single-outrigger canoe beached not far north of Cape Sidmouth, but it was holed or split. Chase saw larger (six metres or more) double outrigger canoes washed onto Night Island and the beach near the Pascoe River in the 1970s. Aboriginal people say that such canoes come from the Solomon Islands. It is unclear whether their ancestors first acquired dugouts with outriggers by constructing them from such models or whether Torres Strait Islanders introduced the complex and instructed people in their construction.

16 See Williams (1986:123–124, endnote 7.) for a good discussion of the notion of 'right'.

The right to use—that is, to personal enjoyment and use of the thing as distinct from 3 and 4 below.

The right to manage—that is, to decide how and by whom a thing shall be used.

The right to the income—that is, to the benefits derived from the foregoing personal use of a thing and allowing others to use it.

The right to the capital—that is, the power to alienate the thing and to consume, waste, modify, or destroy it.

The right to security—that is, immunity from expropriation.

The power of transmissibility—that is, the power to devise or bequeath the thing.

The absence of term—that is, the indeterminate length of one's ownership rights.

The prohibition of harmful use—that is, one's duty to forbear from using the thing in certain ways harmful to others.

Liability to execution—that is, liability to have the thing taken away for repayment of a debt.

Residuary character—that is, the existence of rules governing the reversion of lapsed ownership rights.

Although Honore considered the total complement comprised full ownership in 'mature legal systems', he said that none was essential to ownership—even the right to possession could be restricted.

Scholars have generally considered that the right to exclude others from entry and use is criterial or diagnostic of property rights in land, but Hallowell (1955[1943]:239–240) observed some time ago that our Western view that exclusive possession and use are essential to the property relationship is 'only one specific constellation of property rights, a limiting case, as it were', and that absolute property rights are not found in any society. Sutton (1996a:9–14) recently examined the right of exclusion in indigenous Australian systems of land tenure. He noted (1996a:11) that acts of physical exclusion are rare, and he considered that the right of exclusion has been overemphasised. He concluded (p. 14):

That such a right is in many cases qualified.

That such a right is only one aspect of the relevant exclusionary powers.

That exclusive possession is at core an exclusive right much more than it is right to exclude.

That even when it is a right to exclude, the most important things from which the possessors may exclude others are rights of identification with land, fundamental decision-making over land, and uses or alterations of land that cause permanent and significant depletion or destruction, rather than mere physical presence on the land.

Other have considered that the right to alienate (see Honore's right 5) is necessary, else there is no property. For example, Justice Blackburn wrote in the Milirrpum Decision, 'I think that property, in its many forms, generally implies the right to use or enjoy, the right to exclude others, and the right to alienate' (cited by Williams 1986:199) However, this restriction overlooks and ignores the classical work of Maine[17] that communal landed property in some societies is inalienable and people acquire rights in it, not through purchase or inheritance, but through their gaining membership of the perduring corporation that owns it. As Williams (1986:91) noted, succession to land amongst the Yolngu was not well understood by anthropologists in 1970 nor was the topic developed clearly in evidence during the hearings. The insistence that the right to alienate is criterial to property is perhaps based upon the mistaken assumption that land is always a commodity (something that can be bought and sold) in a system of market exchange based upon contracts between buyers and sellers. But as we have just noted, real property existed before the emergence of markets for land in complex societies, and certainly it existed long before the emergence of capitalism.

In analysing and describing Aboriginal systems of tenure, the Honore listing is helpful to insure one has comprehensively listed the

---

17   See footnote 33 below.

several kinds or property rights. Certainly, one must modify, reformulate and expand some of them, say, to note that owners have certain ceremonial rights in specific sites, that owners have the right to be asked for permission to enter and use country, etc. What is missing in Honore's listing are 'the right to state 'proper' (customary-lawful) possessive claims over land, [and] the right to speak for, on behalf of, or even authoritatively *about* the country and its content as cultural property (i.e. to represent it, in both senses)' (Sutton 1996a:12). These are universally found in Aboriginal tenure systems.

Types of property right systems

Berkes[18] and Farvar (1989:9–10) and Tisdell and Roy (1996:4), resource and development economists, identified four ideal types of tenure systems ('property regimes')[19]. These are (we have slightly rephrased their definitions):

---

18   I came across the Berkes (1989a) volume only toward the end of my research and writing of this chapter and I have not had the opportunity to make as much use of it here as it merits. It includes papers by anthropologists, e.g. Acheson (1989) and Freeman (1989), and papers treating CMT, e.g. Acheson (1989), Baines (1989) and Ruddle (1989). I recommend the book as a significant work to readers on property. The journal *Marine Resource Economics* has also published articles bearing on CMT and common property issues, e.g. Ruddle (1988); Ruddle, Hviding and Johannes (1992); Yamamoto (1995) and Christy (1996).

19   Munzer (1990:25, 89, 92–93) contrasted private property with public property: 'The identification of the owners or right-holders facilitates additional terminology. If the owners are identifiable entities distinguishable from some larger group, there is *private property*. The most common example is individual private property, where an individual person is the owner—in severalty, as lawyers say. Other sorts of private property exist when the owners or right-holders are persons considered together, such as partnerships and co-tenanies, or are artificial entities that represent the financial interests of persons, such as corporations. Contrasted with private property are various sorts of *public property*. Here the owners are the state, city, community, or tribe. Some forms of ownership involve a

1. Private property, where rights are held by individuals and their corporate counterparts.
2. State property, where rights are held by the state.
3. Communal property (Latin *res communis* 'common property'), where rights are held by a community of users.
4. Open-access property (Latin *res nullius* 'no one's property'), where access is free and open to all.

The term communal property has a long history. In the nineteenth century, anthropologists such as Morgan, as well as Marx and Engels, regarded the evolution of human society—and specifically, the emergence of capitalism—to have involved the replacement of communal property by private property. More recently, Teh and Dwyer (1992:1–2), an introductory property law text, also distinguished communal property from private property and noted that '[t]he general non-recognition of communal property in Anglo-Australian law is traceable to the growth of capitalism in western civilisations'. Demsetz (1967:354) defined 'communal ownership' as rights 'which can be exercised by all members of a community', and gave the example of the right to walk on a city footpath. The Mabo No. 2 decision did not use the term

---

mixture of private and public property rights.' Waldron (1988:38–46) distinguished private, collective and common property, and he considered corporate property in contemporary market-based economies to be a 'mutation of private property' (pp. 57–59), but noted that it could also be a form of collective property too. Radin (1993:2, 11, 16–17, 104, 233) distinguished personal property from fungible property. The former is constitutive of personhood, and the latter is not. Radin (1993:233 n44) wrote: 'If an object is fungible it is perfectly replaceable with money or other objects of its kind. If it is personal it has become bound up with the personhood of the holder and is no longer commensurate with money.' Her distinction corresponds closely to the one that Carrier (1995:10) drew between possessions and commodities, respectively, and I believe, better characterises their differences. Carrier's conceptualisation of terms and their interrelations misses the point that what we humans exchange are objects of property. One cannot properly exchange what one does not own or have property rights in.

communal property, but used a series of phrases that leave no doubt that the High Court believed that traditional Aboriginal rights and interests in land were such that it was communal property. The phrases used are 'communal rights and interests in land', 'communal native title', 'communal title', 'communal proprietary interest', 'communal usufructory occupation', 'communal occupation', 'communal lands', 'common law communal native title' and 'traditional communal title'.[20]

The relationship of communal property to the term common property bears some examination because the latter term is sometimes used to signify both common property and open-access property as defined above by Tisdell and Roy (1996). For this reason, Cordell (1989:6) was careful to distinguish sea tenure from 'common property, the catch-all notion invoked to categorize fishing, fishermen and particular management problems associated with fisheries'. He wrote (Cordell 1989:4) 'that the world's inshore seas, at least from the standpoint of many traditional fishing societies, may not or should not be thought of as common property—that is, in the sense of open access, a precondition for many Western legal and theoretical usages of the term'. Here Cordell alluded to the common property resource model that Hardin (1968) popularised in his well-known paper, 'The Tragedy of the Commons'.[21] Cordell (1992:35–36) later said that Hardin's and his sympathisers' model does not 'accurately portray fishermen's and indigenous people's attitudes and actions in using marine resources, scarce resources, and sea space, or to guide management of traditional economies'. Cordell (1993:162) further noted that 'CMT institutions are distinct from ... open-access commons or 'common pool' resources'.

In an endnote, Cordell (1989:22–23) expanded on the point:

> There is still no consensus regarding the fisheries definitions, theories and models of common property advanced by econ-

---

20   We cite no specific passages here, but we searched the electronic text of the decision with our wordprocessor to assemble them.

21   Demsetz (1967), Gordon (1954) and Scott (1955) are in the same vein as Hardin (1968).

omists... Disagreement over terminology in part reflects a tendency to interchange and indiscriminately use 'common property,' the 'commons,' 'common pool,' 'communal,' 'public domain' and 'public good.' For example, Ciriacy-Wantrup and Bishop (1975) argue that common property rights refer to a condition in which a number of owners are coequal in their use rights, Others disagree, pointing out that [the existence of] use rights violate[s] the basic assumptions of the common property model: free and open access...

Thus, Cordell identified two distinct views of common property in resource and environmental economics. CMT fits within one of them 'as a special system of property rights within the framework of common property resource management problems' (Cordell 1992:13). CMT also exemplifies 'community-based or joint property' (Cordell 1992:19).[22]

Ciriachy-Wantrup and Bishop (1975), Quiggin (1986) and McCay (1989; 1987) wrote at greater length about the conflict between these two models of common property, and all expressed the view that the 'tragedy of the commons' or open-access regime misapplies the term property to situations where there is in fact no property.[23] McCay (1989:205) put it as 'what is everybody's is nobody's', while Ciriachy-Wantrup and Bishop (1975:713) phrased it as 'everybody's property is nobody's property'.[24] The open-access regime certainly does not fit the

---

22 See also Cordell (1992:2), where he notes that 'it is the quality of shared or joint tenure that sets CMT systems in question here apart from forms of state ownership or private property'.

23 The equation of open access situations with common property is conventional in the resource and development economic literature, e.g. see Common (1988:224), Neher (1990:5, 29, 51, 88–89, 225), Clark, Munro and Charles (1985:100), Tisdell (1991:36, 63–64, 107–121, 147) and Tisdell (1993:7, 12). See Christy (1996) for a critical overview of the current period in which property rights regimes are replacing open access conditions in fisheries around the world.

24 Neher (1990:88) also wrote, 'If all property were common property, all property would be everybody's property, and everybody's property would be nobody's property'.

situations of property rights that villagers had in the commons as we know them from English history. It may be empirically more applicable to situations where 'resource raiders' ignore indigenous property rights, as discussed by Ganter (1994) with respect to beche-de-mer, pearlshell, trochus and sandalwood in northeastern Australia. Tisdell and Roy (1996) disambiguated the two senses of common property, as did Berkes and Farvar (1989) before them, by separately designating them as 'communal property' and 'open-access property' (but as we have seen, some scholars regard the latter term as an oxymoron).

Common property and joint property

The term common property also occurs in the common law tradition, where it contrasts particularly with joint property, but that tradition also uses modifying terms which describe how property rights are distributed over and amongst individuals and groups. It speaks of rights which are held jointly, in severalty, in common or in division.[25] This leads us

25 Rights in severalty are rights that an individual person holds to the exclusion of others. Where two (or more) persons hold rights, Radcliffe-Brown (1952[1935]:44–45) distinguished among rights in common ('A and B have similar and equal rights over Z and these are such that the rights of A will not conflict with those of B'), joint rights ('A and B (or any number of persons) exercise jointly certain rights over Z') and rights in division ('A has certain rights over Z and B has certain other definite rights'). We discuss rights in common and joint rights below. Radcliffe-Brown (1952[1935]:44) observes that rights in division 'may be defined either by custom or by a specific contract, or agreement. An example is the relation of owner and tenant of a leased land or building'. Brewer and Staves (1995:17) refer to rights in division in seventeenth and eighteenth century England thus: '...It cannot be the case... that in this period[,] older, multiple-use rights to property were simply supplanted by a rise of absolute property rights [held by individuals]... In the seventeenth and eighteenth centuries, even interests in land were divided among owners and renters, mortgagors and mortgagees, owners with life estates and remaindermen, or owners with legal interests and owners with equitable

to review Stanner's (1969) unpublished paper, 'The Yirrkala Case: Some General Principles of Aboriginal Land-Holding'.[26] Stanner prepared the paper for the plaintiffs' lawyers as an attempt to reduce the traditional land tenure system to principles constructed with terms deriving from the Roman and common law traditions, but it was not submitted to the court. Amongst other things, Stanner discussed the distribution of property rights over and amongst individuals and groups. He (1969:2) wrote:

> It is unquestionable that all the [A]boriginal peoples who have been studied adequately had a conception of land as property. The three ideas necessary to the conception demonstrably coexisted. That is, (a) an idea of ownership under right of title, (b) an idea of corollary right of possession, and (c) an idea of correlative or connected rights of occupation and use. There were also customary rules determining with whom rights properly lay and by whom they could be properly exercised.
>
> In [A]boriginal understanding land was much more than property in our sense; ownership was more intrinsic; title, right and possession were embedded in different doctrines; and use and occupation were articulated into a highly distinctive body of social habits; but there was a sufficient coincidence between their underlying ideas and ours in relation to all these matters to justify the use of European terms, provided there are accompanying explanations.
>
> The three ideas mentioned were at the foundation of [A]boriginal society insofar as it involved land. Taken together, they support an inference that there was a real if unverbalized conception of 'estate' in land, and that there was a true

interests.'

26 I thank Nancy Williams for providing me with a copy of Stanner (1969) and for telling me a bit about its history. Williams (1986:35, 101–104, 141, 163–164, 202) used and cited Stanner (1969) extensively; Sharp (1996) did the same.

'system' of land-holding, occupation and usage in rational connection with the circumstances of aboriginal society.

Stanner (1969:3) noted that some anthropologists have tried explain the Aboriginal relationship of ownership between people and land by saying the people belonged to the land, rather than the land belonged to the people. He thought it to be a true statement, but 'vague and mystical'. We believe the statement to be half-true as phrased.[27] Both clauses are indeed true, but they do not contrast as the *rather than*-complementiser signifies. Thus, it is true both that Aboriginal people belong to the land and that the land belongs to Aboriginal people. The predicate in the first clause signifies inalienable possession, the whole-to-part relationship. Inalienable possession is the relationship of a person's body (the physical site of the self) to their head. Aboriginal people are part of their land because they incarnate spirit that comes from it. The predicate in the second clause signifies alienable possession, the socially and culturally constituted phenomenon of ownership. Alienable possession is the relationship of a headhunter to his severed trophy. Rephrased, we can say that Aboriginal people belong to the land and they own the

---

27 In an earlier piece, I (Rigsby 1993:147) attacked 'the silly notion that 'traditional Aboriginal wisdom is that the land owns the people who live on it' (Kaufman 1992:38)' for being 'a romantic construction of Aboriginal people that is both untrue and politically harmful to their interests'. I quoted the late Jack Bruno's Yir-Yoront text which translates closely as:
I am the owner of [this] country.
It's my property.
They will never take away this our land.
They will not take it from us.
For we want to keep walking about in plenty of room.
I have also heard many Lamalama people assert that they own specific land and sea country. Having read and pondered Stanner's statement, I have changed his analysis and understanding of the complex proposition it encodes and developed them further. See also pp. 200–201 on Sandbeach People's religion below. Williams (1986:102, 199) provided other references to the view that the land owns Aboriginal people, that Aboriginal people belong to the land. Note also Davis (1989:39–40).

land, but not that the land owns them (except in a secondary metaphorical sense).

Stanner further elucidated the relationship between people and land by describing it as dual. That is, the relationship was at once *in animam* 'in spirit'[28] and *in rem* 'in a thing'. In other words, the relationship had both spiritual and material dimensions. The root[29] of Aboriginal title derived from the 'historic-genetic' relation of the owning group to particular land *in animam* (i.e. part-to-whole), and the group's *in rem* relationship (i.e. its ownership of the land) resulted from it and depended upon it. Stanner (1969:3) described this dual relation of ownership as a first fundamental axiom.

Stanner's second fundamental axiom was that 'the clearest, most unequivocal, most enduring and most perfect ownership-relation between persons and land' was that 'between a patrilineal descent group (clan) or similar group and a more or less definite tract or region or set

---

28   Stanner used the phrase *in animum*, but this was an error. He incorrectly selected the masculine noun *animus* 'intellect, judgement, courage, commitment', where he plainly intended the feminine noun *anima* 'soul, vital principle, life'. The preposition *in* governs the accusative case in such phrases, so that we purists must use 'rights *in animam*' with the feminine accusative singular form of the noun, not *in animum* with the masculine accusative singular form of another noun. Don Barrett, my Latinist colleague at The University of Queensland, enlightened me on these linguistic matters.

29   The 'root' of a title is the historical event which gave rise to it. There were no written title deeds to record, for example, that so-and-so acquired such-and-such land by purchase or grant of the Crown. Instead, Aboriginal people in the north know and tell how the Dreamings or Story-Beings fashioned specific landscapes and perhaps 'sat down' in a place to remain for all time. The root of their title derives from the specific creative acts of the ancestral beings during the Dreamtime or Story-Time and from the unbroken links of spirit that connect them, their deceased ancestors (called the 'Old People' on eastern Cape York Peninsula) and specific land. It is their spiritual relationship to land which gives rise to their *in rem* relationship to it.

of localities or places' (1969:3). We need not dwell on the point, but we note there has been extensive debate the past three decades or so over the character of owner groups in classical and contemporary Aboriginal social organisation. Whatever position one takes, one surely must recognise that significant property rights are vested in groups, but at the same time, people are linked to land and to one another through multiple, cross-cutting ties (Rumsey 1996).

Stanner's axioms rested upon fundamental postulates that Aboriginal people did not conceive to be open to question. Three postulates were:

Human life was indivisibly corporeal and spiritual because each person as corporeal being incarnated one or more spiritual elements 'which had entered or affected or become one with the embryo at or about the time of conception' (1969:4). These pre-existed conception and they persisted after death at least for a time. Importantly, these numinous beings came from a specific place or made themselves known at a specific place. This indissoluble connection of a person to their place of origin by 'a spiritual link externally manifest in land as an outward and visible sign' was the relation *in animam*.

The corporeal and spiritual elements were so indissoluble that each person 'was 'with' or 'of' a locality, or a locality was 'with' or 'of' him or her' (1969:4). Thus specific country or land was intrinsic to the identity of persons and owning groups.[30]

---

30 One can find much evidence for this around the country in the indigenous language patterns for clan names and for personal names which are constructed with place names. For example, Lamalama speakers call the Olkola-speaking clan who have Dog Story as their main totem, *Mbatorrarrbinh* 'People who have Dog [Story]', while they call certain of their close neighbours *Mbarimanggudinhma* 'People from Ngudinh [country]'. In the southern part of the Sandbeach Region—see chapter 12 below—significant members of a clan were sometimes named for important places in their estates. For example, Old Man Monkey Port Stewart was called *Aakurr Yintyingga* 'Yintjingga Country' after the indigenous name for the Port Stewart area, and Old Lady Emma Claremont was

Some empirical data are in order here. Sunlight Bassani explained to Rigsby (1995) that the land or ground around Port Stewart is part of his group, just the same as the trees, the animals, 'anything you name', shade, etc. 'That's our family', he concluded. This is a clear statement that Lamalama people share spirit with their land. It also asserts that Lamalama people and their land are parts of a whole universe of social actors.

> Each member of an owning group was related to their land *jointly* 'with every other member of the group, without distinction of sex. age, status or any other criterion. The relation was truly joint, as distinct from common or several, in a sense closely analogous to the European conception of the 'four unities' of joint tenancy' (Stanner 1969:4).[31]

In the common law tradition, the four unities criterial to joint ownership or tenancy are (a) title—each co-owner must acquire by virtue of the same instrument or act, (b) possession—each co-owner must be entitled to possession of the whole property, (c) interest—each co-owner must acquire the same interest, and (d) time—each co-owner must acquire the rights at the same time (Hardy Ivamy 1993:145; Martin 1990:220; Rutherford and Bone 1993:185–186; Walker 1980:667). Stanner (1969:4) noted that all these conditions were met, except that

---

called *Ngaachi Yalmarraka* 'Yalmarraka Country' after a major place at the mouth of Breakfast Creek. The former name is Uuk-Umpithamu and the latter is Umpila.

31 Note that Cordell (1992:2, 19) correctly identified CMT ownership as joint—see endnote 22—but in common law terms, the object of joint ownership is joint property, not common property. Driver (1961:244, 245, 252) also identified joint property as a major type amongst Native American peoples. Lowie (1929:557, 559) said that amongst the Hidatsa 'children inherit the right of jointly buying proprietary rights from their own father' and amongst the Nootka, 'the lineage of eldest-born descendants virtually consititutes a joint-company as regards the relevant rights'. Also Hiatt (1962), Williams (1986) and Sharp (1996) speak of joint ownership of their land by Gidjingarli, Yolngu and Meriam people, respectively.

the unity of time in Aboriginal ownership 'extended to the unborn and the dead as well as the living'.

The common law tradition distinguishes joint ownership or tenancy from co-ownership or tenancy in common 'in that joint tenants have one interest in the whole, and no interest in any particular part', whereas '[t]enants in common have several and distinct interests in their respective parts which may be in unequal shares and for interests of unequal duration' (Burke 1977:2:1748). Tenants in common hold property by unity of possession because none of them knows their own individual part, but this is the only unity in the ownership because they may hold different kinds of interest, they may hold from different sources of title and their interests may vest in each at different times.[32]

Stanner (1969:8) later expanded his argument for joint ownership by noting that '[t]he estate could not be diminished by the deaths of any of the joint owners; it remained the undivided property of the survivors; it did not, in a strict sense, pass by 'inheritance' between generations but remained 'in' the dual spiritual-corporeal stream of life—certainly, no one could be 'disinherited'.[33] He also wrote 'that the rights were vested, not severally in individual persons, or in common between persons, but jointly in a particular kind of kinship group'(1969:9).

---

32 Rumsey (1996:4, 8, 9) speaks of 'rights-in-common', but his phrase seems to signify in an ordinary English way that people share the same interests, not that they have different interests.

33 This formulation built on the understanding of Maine (1931[1861]) that: 'Ancient law ... knew next to nothing of individuals. Property was held and transmitted not by private citizens but by corporations of blood relatives linked by descent in the male line and putatively descended from a common male ancestor. Corporate identity was perpetual; corporate property was undivided, unmalleable, and sometimes absolutely inalienable... Neither ethnology nor classical scholarship supported the view that human social life began on the basis of contracts between individuals. What they suggested, rather, was that society had evolved *towards* contract and private property from an earlier condition in which the rights of individuals were defined and protected on the basis of their status as members of corporate descent groups (Hiatt 1996:14).

A lawyer, we believe, would be unlikely to accept Stanner's qualification of the unity of time and would not accept his argument that traditional Aboriginal land tenure meets all the criteria for common law joint tenure. But of the forms of common law tenure, it most closely resembles joint tenure.

Stanner (1969:10) also noted that there might be a few areas of land in the Yirrkala region that were 'areas of commonalty' or 'box up' places. He thought these lay outside the clan estates and 'on the hunting ranges of merging or overlapping bands', but they 'in no way threaten or qualify the clan estates'.

Here we believe that Stanner's analysis went offtrack when he spoke of 'areas of commonalty'. We know what he intended in ordinary English, but in legal terminology, we think it more accurate to regard 'Murri roads' and 'company land' (to use the Cape York Creole and Aboriginal English terms) again as the joint property of two or more owner groups and their members,[34] not as their common property.

To summarise this far, we have considered Stanner's arguments that Aboriginal property rights in land are held jointly, not in common, not in severalty (individually), and not in division. Becker (1977:25) also noted that:

> When a thing is jointly owned in the full liberal sense, for example, any disposition of the thing by one person without the consent of the others is a violation of their rights of ownership—even if one has taken no more than one's share [but one's individual share is not known in joint ownership! BR]. Joint ownership means joint management, and more fundamentally, joint right to the capital.

In the Cliff Islands and Lakefield National Parks land claim transcripts, there is much evidence for joint Lamalama ownership of their estate, and we give just one bit of it here. When Rigsby examined Sunlight Bassani on the topic of whether he could sell or give away part of the

---

34 See also Hiatt (1962:279–280) on 'company' or joint ownership of land amongst the Gidjingarli.

Lamalama estate, he included in his reply:

> If I'm going to sell him, if I say I'm going to sell it, I might
> be get killed from somebody else, my family, 'What do you
> want to sell that country for? That's our country'. (dftT1808/
> fnlT1875)

This makes reference to the need to consult with other joint owners on matters of import, and thus it is evidence for joint ownership.[35]

Finally, Stanner (1969:8–9) spoke of 'several classes of less precise rights which lay with people who were not of the true joint owners' and he called such people 'secondary right-holders'. He distinguished amongst:

1. Wives who 'had virtually an unconditional right of residence on and occupation and use of their husbands' lands *in rem*'
2. Husbands who 'had a clear but probably less express right to visit, occupy and use his wife's clan lands'.
3. 'A woman's children [who] had an express right to visit, live on, occupy and use the lands of her patrilineal clan and in many cases they had as well some degree of right to use the lands *in anim[a]m*'.
4. Men and women who 'had acknowledged ritual duties ... involving persons or categories of persons in other clans', amongst other rights, had 'a right of entry into that clan's domains and, while there, to support from the resources of that clan'.
5. 'A somewhat undifferentiated general public right to limited visitation, occupation and use by the owners' consent'.

These certainly must be part of any adequate analysis and description of Aboriginal tenure systems. It is also clear that individuals and groups may sometimes transform secondary rights into primary property rights[36] over time in a variety of circumstances relating to succession, regencies and even land claim actions.

---

35 See also Williams (1886:80) on the need to consult within a Yolngu clan.

36 Williams (1986:175) preferred 'presumptive' and 'subsidiary' to primary and secondary, while Sutton (1997) spoke of 'transferrable' and 'transferred' rights.

Conclusion

In this chapter, we surveyed property and tenure generally. We identified communal property as an ideal type of tenure system. We noted that the phrase 'common property' signifies two different situations amongst resource and environmental economists, while it signifies something else again in the common law tradition. One sense is that of communal property, which is the indigenous property regime attributed to Aboriginal people, and the second is that of open-access property. For its part, the common law distinguishes common property from joint property. We also reviewed Stanner's argument that most Aboriginal property rights in land are held jointly, not in common, not in severalty (individually), and not in division.[37] We accept Stanner's argument and the observations of other anthropologists regarding joint tenure in Aboriginal Australia, and we suggest that the communal property regime as an ideal type should be interpreted also as joint tenure.

References

Acheson, James M. 1989. Where have all the exploiters gone? Co-management of the Maine lobster industry. In *Common property resources: ecology and community-based sustainable development* (ed) Fikret Berkes. London: Belhaven Press. Pp. 199–217.

Anderson, Terry and Hill, P. 1975. The evolution of property rights: a study of the American west. *Journal of Law and Economics* 18:163–179.

---

37 The point also has some importance for our understanding of corporateness because Radcliffe-Brown (1952[1935]:34, 44, 45) and Williams (1986:95–96) both proposed that it is the joint ownership of property in land that makes groups corporate. While we now recognise that Aboriginal people have multiple cross-cutting links and ties to one another and to land and that they are members of a variety of social categories and groups, we must surely also recognise that they also are members of corporate groups that perdure by virtue of their ownership of land.

Barnard, Alan and Spencer, Jonathan (eds). 1996. *Encyclopedia of social and cultural anthropology*. London and New York: Routledge.

Baines, Graham B.K. 1989. Traditional resource management in the Melanesian South Pacific: a development dilemma. In *Common property resources: ecology and community-based sustainable development* (ed) Fikret Berkes. London: Belhaven Press. Pp. 273–295.

Becker, Lawrence C. 1977. *Property rights: philosophic foundations*. London, Henley and Boston: Routledge and Kegan Paul.

Berkes, Fikret (ed). 1989a. *Common property resources: ecology and community-based sustainable development*. London: Belhaven Press.

Berkes, Fikret. 1989b. Cooperation from the perspective of human ecology. In *Common property resources: ecology and community-based sustainable development* (ed) Fikret Berkes. London: Belhaven Press. Pp. 470–88.

Berkes, Fikret and M. Taghi Farvar. 1989. Introduction and overview. In *Common property resources. ecology and community-based sustainable development* (ed) Fikret Berkes. London: Belhaven Press. Pp. 1–17.

Boas, F. (ed). 1938. *General Anthropology*. Boston: D.C. Heath and Company. [see index entries on property, many by Ruth Bunzel].

Brewer, John and Staves, Susan. 1995. Introduction. In *Early modern conceptions of property* (eds) John Brewer and Susan Staves. London and New York: Routledge. Pp. 1–8.

Bunzel, Ruth. 1938. The economic organization of primitive peoples. In *General anthropology* (ed) Franz Boas. Boston: D.C. Heath and Company. Pp. 327–408.

Burke, John (ed). 1977. *Jowitt's dictionary of English law*. Second edition. Volume 2. London: Sweet and Maxwell.

Carrier, James. 1995. *Gifts and commodities: exchange and western capitalism since 1700*. London: Routledge.

Cheung, Steven N.S. 1974. A theory of price control. *Journal of Law and Economics* 17:53–71.

1970. The structure of a contract and the theory of a non-exclusive resource. *Journal of Law and Economics* 13:49–70.

Christy, Francis. 1996. Thalassorama: the death rattle of open access and the advent of property rights regimes in fisheries. *Marine Resource Economics* 11:287–304.

Ciriacy-Wantrup, S.V. and Bishop, Richard C. 1975. 'Common Property' as a concept in natural resources policy. *Natural Resources Journal* 15:713–727.

Clark, Colin, Munro, Gordon and Charles, Anthony. 1985. Fisheries, dynamics, and uncertainty. In *Progress in natural resource economics: essays in resource analysis by members of the Programme in Natural Resource Economics (PRE) at the University of British Columbia* (ed) Anthony Scott. Oxford: Clarendon Press. Pp. 98–120.

Coase, Ronald H. 1960. The problem of social cost. *Journal of Law and Economics* 3:303–344.

Common, Michael. 1988. *Environmental and resource economics: an introduction*. London and New York: Longman.

Cordell, John. 1993. Indigenous peoples' coastal-marine domains: some matters of cultural documentation. In *Turning the tide: papers presented at the conference on indigenous peoples and sea rights*. Darwin: Faculty of Law, Northern Territory University. Pp. 159–173.

1992. Managing sea country: tenure and sustainability of Aboriginal and Torres Straits Islander marine resources. Report on indigenous fishing and ecologically sustainable development (ESD) Fisheries Working Group. St Lucia: Department of Anthropology and Sociology, University of Queensland.

Cordell, John (ed). 1989. *A sea of small boats*. Cultural Survival Report 26. Cambridge, Massachusetts: Cultural Survival, Inc.

Damas, David (ed). 1969a. *Contributions to anthropology: band societies. Proceedings of the conference on band organization. Ottawa, August 30 to September 2, 1965*. Ottawa: National Museums of Canada. Bulletin No. 228. Anthropological Series No. 84.

1969b. *Contributions to anthropology: ecological essays. Proceedings of the conference on cultural ecology*. Ottawa, August 3—6, 1966. Ottawa: National Museums of Canada. Bulletin No. 230. Anthropological Series No. 86.

Davis, Stephen. 1989. Aboriginal tenure of the sea in Arnhem Land, northern Australia. In *A sea of small boats* (ed) John Cordell. Cultural Survival Report 26. Cambridge, Massachusetts: Cultural Survival, Inc. Pp. 37–59.

Demsetz, Harold. 1967. Toward a theory of property rights. *American Economic Review* 57:347–359.

Driver, Harold E. 1961. Chapter 14: Property and inheritance. In *Indians of North America* (ed) Harold E. Driver. Chicago: University of Chicago Press. Pp. 244–264.

Freeman, Milton M.R. 1989. Graphs and gaffs: a cautionary tale in the common-property resources debate. In *Common property resources: ecology and community-based sustainable development* (ed) Fikret Berkes. London: Belhaven Press. Pp. 92–109.

Ganter, Regina. 1994. *The pearl-shellers of Torres Strait: resource use, development and decline, 1860s-1960s*. Carlton, Victoria: Melbourne University Press.

Goodenough, Ward H. 1969. Frontiers of cultural anthropology: social organization. *Proceedings of the American Philosophical Society* 113(5):329–335.

Gordon, H. Scott. 1954. The economic theory of a common property resource: the fishery. *Journal of Political Economy* 62:124–142.

Hallowell, A. Irving. 1955. The nature and function of property as a social institution. In *Culture and experience*. Philadelphia: University of

Pennsylvania Press. Pp. 236–249. [Reprinted from Journal of Legal and Political Sociology 1:115–138(1943)].

Hann, CM. 1996. Property. In *Encyclopedia of social and cultural anthropology* (eds) Alan Barnard and Jonathan Spencer. London and New York: Routledge. Pp. 453–454.

Hardin, Garrett. 1968. The tragedy of the commons. *Science* 163:1243–1248.

Hiatt, L.R. 1996. *Arguments about Aborigines: Australia and the evolution of social anthropology*. Cambridge: Cambridge University Press.

1962. Local organization among the Australian Aborigines. *Oceania* 32:267–286.

Hardy Ivamy, E.R. (ed). *Mozley and Whiteley's law dictionary*. Eleventh edition. London: Butterworths.

Hobbes, Thomas. 1951[1651]. *Leviathan: or the matter, forme and power of a commonwealth ecclesiastical and civil*. Oxford: Mowbray.

Herskovits, Melville J. 1952. *Economic anthropology: a study in comparative economics*. Second edition. New York: Alfred A. Knopf. [Published originally as *The Economic Life of Primitive Man* in 1940].

1948. *Man and his works. the science of cultural anthropology*. New York: Alfred A. Knopf.

Hickerson, Harold. 1967. Some implications of the theory of the particularity, or 'atomism', of northern Algonkians. *Current Anthropology* 8(4):313–343.

Hohfeld, W.N. 1964. *Fundamental legal conceptions* (ed) W.W. Cook. New Haven: Yale University Press.

Honore, A.M. 1961. Ownership. In *Oxford essays in jurisprudence* (ed) A.G. Guest. Oxford: Oxford University Press. Pp. 107–147.

Hviding, Edvard. 1996. *Guardians of Marovo lagoon, practice, place, and politics in maritime Melanesia*. Pacific Islands Monograph Series 14.

Center for Pacific Islands Studies, School of Hawaiian, Asian, and Pacific Studies. Honolulu: University of Hawaii Press.

1989. *All things in our sea: the dynamics of customary marine tenure, Marovo Lagoon, Solomon Islands.* NRI Special Publication 13. Boroko, Papua New Guinea: National Research Institute.

Kaufman, Tina. 1992. SBS Television program guide, 10 August–4 September. *Modern Times.* Pp. 38–39.

Keesing, Roger. 1981. *Cultural anthropology: a contemporary perspective.* Second edition. New York: Holt, Rinehart and Winston.

Knight, Frank H. 1924. Some fallacies in the interpretation of social cost. *Quarterly Journal of Economics* 38:582–606.

Leacock, Eleanor B. 1954. The Montagnais 'hunting territory' and the fur trade. *American Anthropologist* 56:3, Part 2.

Lee, Richard B. and Irven De Vore (eds). 1968. *Man the hunter.* Chicago: Aldine-Atherton.

Lowie, Robert H. 1948. *Social organization.* New York: Rinehart and Company.

1940. *An introduction to cultural anthropology.* New York: Rinehart and Company.

1933. Land tenure: primitive societies. In *Encyclopaedia of the social sciences* (ed) Edwin R.A. Seligman. Volume 9. London: Macmillan. Pp. 76–77.

1929. Incorporeal property in primitive society. *Yale Law Journal* 37:5:551–563.

1920. *Primitive society.* New York: Horace Liveright.

McCay, Bonnie J. 1989. Sea tenure and the culture of the commoners. In *A sea of small boats* (ed) J. Cordell. Cultural Survival Report 26. Cambridge, Massachusetts: Cultural Survival, Inc. Pp. 203–227.

1987. The culture of the commoners: historical observations on old and new world fisheries. In *The question of the commons: the culture and ecology of communal resources* (eds) B. J. McCay and J. M. Acheson. Tucson: University of Arizona Press. Pp. 195–216.

Maine, Sir Henry Sumner. 1931[1861]. *Ancient law: its connection with the early history of society and its relation to modern ideas.* London: Humphrey Milford, Oxford University Press.

Malinowski, Bronislaw. 1935. *Coral gardens and their magic.* In two volumes, London: Allen and Unwin.

Martin, Elizabeth M. (ed). 1990. *A concise dictionary of law.* Second edition. Oxford: Oxford University Press.

Munzer, S. R. 1990. *A theory of property.* Cambridge: Cambridge University Press.

Neher, Philip A. 1990. *Natural resource economics: conservation and exploitation.* Cambridge: Cambridge University Press.

Paul, Ellen Frankel. 1987. *Property rights and eminent domain.* New Brunswick, New Jersey and Oxford: Transaction Books.

Peterson, Nicolas. 1986. *Australian territorial organization.* Oceania Monograph 30. Sydney: University of Sydney. (in collaboration with Jeremy Long).

Peterson, Nicolas (ed). 1976. *Tribes and boundaries in Australia.* Social Anthropology Series No. 10. Canberra: Australian Institute of Aboriginal Studies.

Quiggin, John. 1986. Common property, private property and regulation. The case of dryland salinity. *Australian Journal of Agricultural Economics* 30(2,3):103–117.

Pigou, A.C. 1938. *The economics of welfare.* Fourth edition. New York: Macmillan.

Radcliffe-Brown, A.R. 1952. Patrilineal and matrilineal succession. In

Structure and function in primitive society. Glencoe, Illinois: The Free Press. Pp. 32–48. [Reprinted from *The Iowa Law Review* 20:2(1935)].

Radin, Margaret. 1993. *Reinterpreting property.* Chicago: University of Chicago Press.

Rigsby, Bruce. 1997. Anthropologists, Indian title and the Indian Claims Commission. In *Fighting over country: anthropological perspectives* (eds) D.E. Smith and J. Finlayson. Centre for Aboriginal Economic Policy Research Monograph 12. Canberra: Centre for Aboriginal Economic Policy Research, Australian National University. Pp. 15–45.

1993. Review of Barry Alpher, Yir-Yoront lexicon: sketch and dictionary of an Australian language. *Canberra Anthropology* 16 (2): 146–148.

Rose, C. M. 1994. *Property and persuasion: essays on the history, theory and rhetoric of property.* Boulder, Colorado: Westview Press.

Rousseau, Jean Jacques. 1938[1762]. *The social contract.* New York: Dutton.

Ruddle, Kenneth. 1989. Solving the common-property dilemma: village fisheries rights in Japanese coastal waters. In *Common property resources: ecology and community-based sustainable development* (ed) Fikret Berkes. London: Belhaven Press. Pp. 168–184.

1988. Social principles underlying traditional inshore fishery management systems in the Pacific basin. *Marine Resource Economics* 5:351–363.

Ruddle, K., E. Hviding and R.E. Johannes. 1992. Marine resources management in the context of customary tenure. *Marine Resource Economics* 7:249–273.

Rutherford, Leslie and Sheila Bone (eds). 1993. *Osborne's concise law dictionary.* Eighth edition. London: Sweet and Maxwell.

Rumsey, Alan. 1996. Aspects of native title and social identity in the Kimberleys and beyond. *Australian Aboriginal Studies* 1:2–10.

Sahlins, Marshall. 1996. 'Sentimental pessimism' and ethnographic experience: or, why culture is not a disappearing object. Unpublished paper. 119 pp.

Schmidtz, David. 1994. The institution of property. In *Property rights* (eds) Ellen Frankel Paul, Fred D. Miller, Jr. and Jeffrey Paul. New York: Cambridge University Press. Pp. 42–62.

Scott, Anthony. 1955. The fisheries: the objectives of sole ownership. *Journal of Political Economy* 63:116–124.

Sharp, Nonie. 1996. *No ordinary judgement: Mabo, the Murray Islanders' land case*. Canberra: Aboriginal Studies Press.

Shipton, Parker. 1994. Land and culture in tropical Africa: soils, symbols, and the metaphysics of the mundane. *Annual Review of Anthropology* 23:347–377.

Smith, Vernon L. 1985. Comment. In *Progress in natural resource economics: essays in resource analysis by members of the programme in Natural Resource Economics (PRE) at the University of British Columbia* (ed) Anthony Scott. Oxford: Clarendon Press. Pp. 403–421.

1975. The primitive hunter culture, Pleistocene extinction, and the rise of agriculture. *Journal of Political Economy* 83:727–755.

Snare, Frank. 1972. The concept of property. *American Philosophical Quarterly* 9 (2):200–206.

Speck, Frank G. 1926. Land ownership among hunting peoples in primitive America and the world's marginal areas. *Proceedings of the 22nd International Congress of Americanists*. Rome, II. Pp. 323–332.

Stanner, W. E. H. 1969. The Yirrkala case: some general principles of Aboriginal land-holding. Unpublished manuscript. Pp. 1–12.

Sutton, P. 1997. *Possession, occupation and Aboriginal native title*. Draft discussion paper prepared for the National Native Title Tribunal. Pp. 1–15.

1996a. The robustness of customary Aboriginal title under Australian pastoral leases. Manuscript. 36 pp. [A shorter version of this paper was published as The robustness of Aboriginal land tenure systems: underlying and proximate customary titles. *Oceania* 67:7–29].

1996b. *Families of polity: post-classical Aboriginal society and native title.* Discussion paper published by the National Native Title Tribunal. 77 pp.

Teh, Gim and Dwyer, Byron (eds). *Introduction to property law.* Second edition. Sydney: Butterworths.

Tisdell, Clem. 1993. *Environmental economics: policies for environmental management and sustainable development.* Brookfield, Vermont: Edward Elgar Publishing Company.

Tisdell, Clement A. 1991. *Economics of environmental conservation: economics for environmental and ecological management.* Amsterdam, London, New York, Tokyo: Elsevier.

Tisdell, Clem and Kartik Roy. 1996. Governance, property rights and sustainable resource use: analysis with Indian Ocean rim examples. *Working Papers on economics, ecology and the environment.* Working Paper No. 1. St Lucia: Department of Economics, University of Queensland.

Umbeck, John R. 1981. *A theory of property rights. With application to the California gold rush.* Ames: Iowa State University Press.

Waldron, J. 1988. *The right to private property.* Oxford: Clarendon Press.

Walker, David M. 1980. *The Oxford companion to law.* Oxford: Clarendon Press.

Williams, Nancy M. 1997. Territory, land, and property: milestones and signposts. Unpublished review paper prepared for the Academy of the Social Sciences in Australia. 37 pp.

1986. The Yolngu and their land: a system of land tenure and the fight for its recognition. Canberra: Australian Institute of Aboriginal Studies.

1982. A boundary is to cross: observations on Yolngu boundaries and permission. In *Resource managers: North American and Australian hunter-gatherers* (eds) Nancy M. Williams and Eugene S. Hunn. Washington, D.C.: American Association for the Advancement of Science. Pp. 131–153.

Williams, Nancy M. and Eugene S. Hunn (eds). 1982. *Resource managers: north American and Australian hunter-gatherers*. Washington, D.C.: American Association for the Advancement of Science.

Yamamoto, Tadashi. 1995. Development of a community-based fishery management system in Japan. *Marine Resource Economics* 10:21–34.

3

Reimagining sea space: from Grotius to Mabo

Nonie Sharp

In a 'restrained critique' of the proceedings of the World Fisheries Congress in July 1996,[1] Sir Tipene O'Regan, Chairman of the Waitangi Tribunal Fisheries Commission, took issue with the failure of fishermen and fisheries managers across the world to examine two assumptions of their marine strategies: first, the right of open access to coastal seas; and second, what he termed 'the bone fish-hook syndrome', the belief that customary marine tenures are antithetical to modern marine management strategies.

Examination of these two assumptions from a historical perspective may help to clarify emerging marine issues in post-Mabo Australia. In the light of the High Court decision on native title in June 1992, such an inquiry may offer a way of coming to terms with an under-examined question: to what extent has the privileging of the dominant European construction of sea space precluded serious or meaningful recognition of the inherited rights to sea domains characteristically adjoining the lands of coastal indigenous people.

Sir Tipene graphically challenged the dominant belief that territorial seas are simply adjuncts of centralised states, that marine resources are simply the property of all citizens of that state: 'When someone wants to take what is someone else's, they say it belongs to everyone' (O'Regan 1996). This, he said, is the way open access to coastal seas came to rule historically.

---

1 Developing and Sustaining World Fisheries Resources: The State of Science and Management, Second World Fisheries Congress, Brisbane, 28 July 1996, Closing Session, Issues and Outcomes.

This right to take was justified by the ideology of backwardness: 'the bone fish-hook' label is another way of saying that the more industrious peoples have the right to expropriate the less advanced (as defined by them) in the name of progress and civilisation. Whether on land or sea, this was the doctrine as self-righteous as it was brutal that underlay the inexorable course of colonial expropriation of lands and local marine territories. Sir Tipene was thinking of settler colonies like New Zealand and how islands surrounded by bounded clan and family owned plots of sea were declared to belong to all citizens to use and enjoy, so erasing any other construction of seascape from the historical memory of the coloniser though not from the minds of the colonised.

He could just as easily have been referring to the historical process whereby the locally-based heritable rights to foreshore and adjacent seas bordering the coasts of Europe came to be eclipsed and incorporated into state coastal seas. State territorial seas are only as old as the centralised states which began to become dominant political entities in Europe in the seventeenth century. When English jurist, John Selden (1663:282), wrote in *Mare Clausum: The Right and Dominion of the Sea 1663* how the mainland and associated islands, together with their adjoining seas, 'made one Bodie' of Italy, how the creation of the state sea was the means of 'keeping other nations at a distance' he was writing under the shadow being cast by the demise and disappearance of the sea holdings of many coastal groupings. Clans and other groupings were treated dismissively, their laws and customs were classified as primitive, and they themselves were often written off as racially inferior. Events in Ireland and on the Celtic fringe of the British monarchical state as a whole provide a stark and melancholy instance of the way the colonial model with its underpinning ideology of racial inferiority, was developed and perfected, foreshadowing what Hechter (1975:80) calls 'its more notorious overseas cousin'.

In the period immediately prior to the consolidation of the British state under the Tudors and the declaration of the four surrounding seas as the one 'British sea', the seafaring coastal septs of western Ireland were continuing to follow Brehon law, a body of written Irish law. Ancient coastal holdings may have extended out a distance of nine waves, a 'measurement' recorded in the legend of an ancient battle that brought the Milesians to Ireland.[2] Brehon law, practised on land and sea by Irish septs and families, was reviled by English statesmen being seen by them as primitive. Making an explicit comparison of the Irish with 'the natives of the New World', Edmund Spenser saw 'the refusal of the Irish to give up their barbarian customs and clannish pride' and 'conform willingly to ... self-evidently superior English practices', as evidence 'that they are a barbaric race who must be broken by famine and the sword' (Cairns and Richards 1988:5, 4).

In the English conquest of Ireland between the twelfth and sixteenth centuries, certain clans defended themselves successfully in battle and 'in defiance of English law' against expropriation of their land-sea property, so that by the sixteenth century one half of Connaught was back in the hands of the clans (Butler 1925:197, 202). In that period, the O'Donnell family was called 'King of the Fish' in northwest Connaught; the coastal waters adjoining land of the O'Malley sept centred at Clew Bay, County Mayo, west Connaught, were known as 'O'Malley waters' and the head of that family 'issued licences to Spanish, French and English fishermen to fish his sea domains' (Chambers 1986:38); and foreign fishermen paid fishing dues to the Sullivan-Beare (Bere) of Bantry (Butler 1925:29). In 1601, the thirty-oared galley commanded by Grainne (Grace) O'Malley 'proved troublesome' when first attacked by the twenty-one-gun Royal Navy warship *Tramontana* off the coast of Donegal, a sea-battle that has lapsed largely from historical memory (Glasgow 1965–66:302).

However, while the Brehon laws, together with a construction of sea space based upon local land-sea domains, survived long after their

---

2 See M. Heaney, Over Nine Waves: the Milesians come to Ireland, in Heaney, 1994:50–55; cf Kelly forthcoming 1996:290 who points to fishing entitlements at this distance from the shore. Of the *Muirbretha* 'sea-judgments', a lost text of Irish law, three quotations have been preserved (Kelly 1991, Appendix I, S53:276–77). I thank Martin Hoare for his expert advice on written sources on Irish coastal rights in history.

official replacement by English law (Chambers 1986:46, cf. Butler 1925), lack of scholarly inquiry into the clans' interrelationship with the sea, is integral with a culture of ignorance that characterises the colonial imagination. In the name of the right to open access to state territorial waters, local customary rights of land-sea holders in the colonial world were denied in a historical process that also rendered them invisible in Europe. In calling into question the universality and the 'naturalness' of open access, customary marine rights may be seen not simply as *exceptions* peculiar to settler colonies and independent coastal states, but as characteristic of coastal clans, villages and communities in a variety of historical times and situations. These 'times and situations' include our own, both with respect to marine territories in former external colonies and to marine tenures in peripheral parts of Europe. For identifiable historical reasons, these have managed to survive well into this century, even until the 1990s.

An exemplary case is the Norwegian cod fishermen's self-regulatory fishery which they have operated in the Lofoten Island area for the century since 1897 when long-standing fishing rules and practices were enshrined in the 'Lofoten Law'. The immediate social context of this codification was the desire of the cod fishermen to shake off the power of the landowner-merchant class whose actions had led to 'the exclusion of the poorest fishermen' (Jentoft and Kristoffersen 1989:357). A spectacular clash at the entrance to a site known as Trollfjord in 1890, between small fishermen acting in concert and the big shipowners, led directly to the small-holders' legislation of 1897. So began an era of almost 100 years of a self-regulated fishery. Small-scale fishermen continued to follow customary rules respecting local inheritance of plots of sea and fishing grounds whose origins stretch back over a millennium (Örebech 1993:4).

Few writers have addressed the subject of indigenous rights to the sea within the larger framework of cultural contrasts in representations of sea space. Even fewer have addressed what Sue Jackson (1995:87) calls 'the imperial history of landscape construction'. With the broad aim of demonstrating 'how the pervasive and dominant European perceptions of environments and social space have impeded indigenous aspirations to own and manage the sea', she points to a social construction in which 'the land, quite unlike the sea, has emerged as a commodity or property which has an economic value'.

Some cultures, Aboriginal and Torres Strait Islander among them, do not observe this 'cultural distinction between land and sea', constructing land and sea property into a seamless web of cultural landscape. Nor do they ascribe an economic value to that construction in dissociation from culture; the economic and the religious, the material and the spiritual, are embedded within the one whole (Sharp 1996). In the Murray Island (Mabo) Land Case, plaintiff Reverend Dave Passi explained with passion how he could not sell his land because it was part of himself and his family line; selling it would mean trespassing against Malo's Law, the traditional law of the Meriam. The right to own land is accompanied by a responsibility: my father gave me 'every right and all the responsibility', witness Gobedar Noah told the court (Supreme Court of Queensland, Transcript: 2108; hereafter TQ; Sharp 1996:77–81). That responsibility entails the obligation to care for it and, in return, to receive its 'gifts' to share it with those on whose behalf one acts as landholder today and for future times and people. This, an inalienable system, contrasts with the dominant European perspective in which the individual alone owns this object: possession here is utilitarian-economic and self-evidently a *real* property right.

The Meriam, a sea people whose totems come almost exclusively from the sea, have an expression, *gedira gur* 'the sea that belongs to the land', where land (*ged*) also means homeland or place. So when plaintiff James Rice explained in court how his father, Loko, showed him his land and sea boundaries at Dauar as a child: 'This is our boundaries, this is our land. This is our reef', he was speaking of *ged*, his land; and in the same breath he was talking about *gedira gur*, the sea that belongs to that land. In forming a web of association through sites named and tracks made by ancestors, mythical and human, they become and are experienced as an undetachable part of Meriam identity. Such proprietal indivisibility of land and sea territories and estates is characteristic of coastal Aboriginal and Torres Strait Islander peoples (Keen 1984; cf Smyth 1993:17). Their law creates a moral obligation impelling them to act in certain ways, a part of their socially made human make-up that led one Yolngu elder to say how their feelings for their sea territory were part of their body and blood forcing them to defend it. 'It is something deep within us', a Meriam elder told me in 1996. Recognising the vast gap in ways of seeing, Allen (1992:2), a former Northern Land Council lawyer, concludes that to achieve legal recognition of the sea water component of indigenous territories, the first task 'is to make them understandable, comprehensible, to non-indigenous people'.

In seeking to identify the cultural roots of the dominant perspective on the sea within the history of European expansionism, this chapter is framed by, and takes its bearing from, these key positions within a wider picture. In the following three sections, this chapter considers the social and cultural origins of the belief in freedom of the seas/open access and its undisputed role as an ideology of European maritime powers; it gives an account of its limited contestation in Australia; and it argues that, under contemporary global conditions, indigenous maritime peoples' move to take primary responsibility for inherited seas may be seen as an important opportunity to create management regimes which develop economically viable fisheries in a culturally and environmentally sustainable way.

Ruling local sea rights out of the imagination: the cultural roots

So complete was the enshrinement in statute and in mainstream public consciousness of the belief that sea space cannot be conceived as the property of a local group, that only in the last thirty years has the idea of customary right of local coastal groups to sea territories become the subject of scholarly inquiry or public debate. The few ethnographic field studies of local ownership of sea territories carried out in the 1970s, mainly among indigenous peoples on the periphery of settler colonies, were often seen as discoveries of 'unique, rare or isolated systems' (Cordell 1989:15).

Local sea territories are a form of territorial sea in the sense of being culturally inseparable from adjacent land masses. The difference between *local* sea tenures and *state* sea territories may be located broadly within a contrast between community and society. In each case there is sea belonging to land, but the principles of that 'belonging' differ in quality. With 'local' sea tenures the right to land-sea domains is embedded in persons whose central being is created in face-to-face interrelations. Land-sea property is held and bequeathed by a person on behalf of a family, clan or other group of associated persons. With 'state' sea tenure the right to the sea is not a right on behalf of a tangible group of persons associated with a geographical locale. It has been removed from the level of the face-to-face and reconstructed as an impersonal, abstract right vested in a monarch or state acting for all the citizens of a polity. It is given legal expression as public rights where every citizen has the right to use and enjoy the coasts.[3] Local property rights along the coasts make a geographical but not a (major) cultural distinction between wet and dry land. State sea territories also belong to land, but they have been severed from dry land property held characteristically in alienable title.

In neither case can a rightholder to sea refuse to accept that right. When a father at the island of Mer is bequeathing his land and reefs and lagoons and outer fishing stations, his son can not conceivably say 'I'll just have the dry land. Forget about the reefs and waters.' Nor can a coastal state refuse its territorial sea. As Lord McNair stated in the *Anglo-Norwegian Fisheries Case* (1951): 'International law does not say to a State: "You are entitled to claim territorial waters if you want them." *No maritime State can refuse them*' (International Commission of Jurists, Report 116:160 as cited in Symmons 1993:45; Symmons'

---

3 For a classificatory scheme and discussion of various forms of rights pertaining to land and sea, see Sharp 1998.

emphasis). Here again, land and sea are also associated culturally, but according to radically different principles to those in local face-to-face coastal communities.

Why has it taken so long to recognise the existence of *local* sea tenures in coastal waters? Cordell (1989:9) suggests that the association of property rights with land and the tendency for knowledge of contemporary sea tenures to be located within oral tradition has meant that customary rules relating to sea property have been followed largely unbeknownst to officials and officialdom. His observation spoke strongly to me as I began the project from which this chapter is drawn, in 1995.

On the island of Skye, a Gaelic poet, and keeper of cultural tradition, told me how stone fish-traps, very numerous until the second half of the nineteenth century, when they were declared illegal and largely destroyed by the landlords, were owned by certain families and clans. One of the surviving four I saw at Sconser was reminiscent of the fish-traps at Mer. Evans (1979, Fig 75:228) details the way similar stone fish-traps were used by local fisherfolk in the last half-century in County Down, Ireland. Taylor's (1981:782) study of fishermen of the hamlet of Teelin, south Donegal, illustrates how Teelin villagers, miraculously by-passed by the enclosures, continued to uphold and follow locally evolved social rules and mores in salmon fishing in contemporary times, including the right to exclude outsiders from their community ('far-siders'), based on their assumption of ownership of and use rights to their estuary: the 'by-laws' and code of rules they followed were their own, not those laid down by the national government.

These oral accounts of surviving marine rights, which included seaweed rights and the use of standing stones as foreshore property boundaries on the geographical and social margins of Britain and Ireland, matched written accounts of surviving rights.[4] Yet I found no

4 Jentoft and Kristoffersen (1989:355) refer to the ninth International Seminar on Marginal Regions, Skye and Lewis, 5–11 July 1987. 'Seaweed rights' refer to the rights to harvest seaweed (also known as wrack), which was used traditionally as an agricultural fertiliser.

comparative account of local sea territories in the Old and New Worlds. Customary marine tenures of indigenous people of the non-European colonial world tended to be seen as exceptions and were treated as 'curios'.

The origins of the invisibility of ancient and contemporary local sea territories lie in the revolutionary transformation of feudal and pre-feudal, clan-based land-sea tenures, largely completed in England by the end of the eighteenth century (Thompson 1975). From the seventeenth century onwards, this transformation found legal expression in the concept of state territorial seas, which had been established before 1600 in international law through the work of Gentilis.[5] Rights to territorial seas and their resources then moved from the customary marine rights of local coastal inhabitants to the Crown. Coastal waters continued to be integral with coastal lands, but sovereignty over these waters shifted from local inhabitants with fields more or less adjoining the sea, to monarchical states. Inherited coastal territories or domains were absorbed into greater state territorial seas *as though they had never existed*.

In practice, the Crown frequently granted lease rights to large landowners as private property rights, effectively excluding the traditional owners from the coasts and fisheries. The right to fish in tidal waters in Britain had been enshrined as a public right under the Magna Carta in 1215 (Netboy 1968:165). However, as McCay (1987:198–99) notes, 'this freedom was abridged and supplemented by claims of the Crown and landowners and the development of complex common-law rights', so that '[o]pen access to the fisheries of England and Wales was gradually whittled away'. Not only did the idea of free access to coastal waters by the citizens of developing monarchical states often find brutal expression in the uprooting of coastal families and clans in the process of the obliteration of ancient heritable sea tenures, but also, to the extent that

5 P.T. Fenn concludes that after the work of Gentilis (1550–1608) 'it is literally correct to speak of territorial waters in international law', Origins of the Theory of Territorial Waters, *American Journal of International Law* 20, 1926:478.

local tenures survived in isolated and sometimes residual form, they were rendered invisible in the name of the Crown. As Selden (1663: Preface) wrote in 1663: 'the King of Great Britain is Lord of, the Sea flowing about'.

The period of the rise of imperial maritime powers saw the doctrine of freedom of the high seas expounded by Dutch jurist, Hugo Grotius, become joined to market goals, so creating a belief of immense persuasive power. The origins of this belief lie in what is taken to be natural law, where things in a state of nature cannot be alienated as private property, and where water and air are seen as by their nature a gift for all to share in. The lasting appeal of Grotius' *Mare Liberum*, a book of only seventy-six pages published secretly in 1603–04 and appearing under his name in 1633, may be sought among the philosophical and cultural roots of the belief that the surrounding ocean was a gift of God to all peoples 'speaking through the voice of Nature'.

Grotius drew upon the works of ancient scholars, especially the pre-Christian jurists Virgil, Ovid, Cicero and Seneca: 'the air, the sea and the shore', according to Virgil, 'are open to all men'; sun, air, waves 'are public gifts' Ovid wrote; nature herself 'enjoins its [the sea's] common use' (Donellus IV, 2 as cited in Grotius 1972:30). But unlike Seneca, who inveighs against those who cross the ocean '*for gain*' (Knight 1920:9), Grotius' *Mare Liberum* was part of a treatise which he had been asked to prepare in support of the Dutch East India Company, on whose behalf he was legal adviser and advocate (and apparently kin to one of its more influential directors).

The counter-right to dominion and power over the seas, the subject of John Selden's treatise *Mare Clausum*, was written in the context of Britain's search for the legal means to exclude Dutch fishing vessels from her territorial waters. This right was remembered almost exclusively as in opposition to Grotius' thesis.[6] Selden's work lacked the power to stir

---

6 Yet both Grotius and Selden accepted the principle of state sovereignty over territorial waters (Grotius 1925:209–10; 1972:30–31). As Prescott has noted, before Grotius wrote, 'the concept of territorial waters was firmly established' (1975:35–36, cf Grotius 1925:214). For a further discussion of

the emotions in the same way as the belief in freedom of the seas. As a member of the London-based Grotius Society (Cole 1919:17) wrote of *Mare Liberum*, in appealing to laws 'written in the minds and on the hearts of every individual' Grotius 'appealed to the common sense of mankind for what was fair and right'. Like a biblical text, its thesis was not up for discussion, still less for critique (cf. Knight 1920:4).

Above all, the lasting quality of Grotius' ideas is found in the profound cultural political role they were destined to play. The imperial wave rose in a crescendo among the modern Ulysses of the nineteenth century. The freedom to sail beyond the sunset, an idea whose magnetic pull was entwined with the hope for the freedom of the human spirit, the God-given chance to venture out into the dread and glorious oceans stirred ancient dreams. The right to navigate freely the widest expanses of oceans was also the indispensable condition for the reconstruction of the heartlands of the rising imperiums of Europe. This very freedom guaranteed the inexorable and rapid development of property in land as an economic commodity value. In turn, it ensured that rising industrial capitalism would tear apart the old structures of agriculture, crofting and fishing, leaving vast numbers of land-less and sea-less people with the freedom only to sell their labour power. Herein lies the tragic paradox of the 'freedom of the seas'. The belief in private property as the centre of human values sat back to back with the belief in freedom of the seas as a natural right, for 'water is a moveable, wandering thing and must of necessity continue common by the law of nature', wrote Sir William Blackstone (II, 1979:18), famed eighteenth century English jurist.

In the turbulent wake of the evictions from land-sea territories after 1845 in the British Isles and Ireland following the Enclosure Acts, the practical possibility of open access to the coasts in the New World had special appeal to the settlers and their descendants, people whose sensibilities had been heightened by a sense of outrage at the wrongs suffered by their forebears. In the popular imagination, freedom of the seas took on a generalised meaning: the unfettered right to fish anywhere, the

the ideas and assumptions of Selden and Grotius, see Sharp 1995.

right of any citizen to the sandbeaches and the coastal seas of coastal states, and the world seas as an international commons.

The social processes that placed ancient sea tenures of Europe into remission or at least cast them into shadow are the same ones which hide sea tenures in colonial settings from the perceptions of people in dominant cultures. These social processes also contribute to the fragmentary character of information on customary rights to the sea.

Behind the effective blotting out of local sea rights in dominant cultural representations of sea space lay three facts of social history and cultural assumption: two relate to the triumphal march of propertied classes on a course heralding the social annihilation of social formations which upheld local smallholder rights, whether as clan right or property in common. The first relates to the formation of states within the context of the rivalries of sea powers to capture the oceans for their exclusive navigational use (Grotius) and the need to keep 'other Nations at a distance' (Selden II, 1663:282). Free access to navigate the high seas for imperial endeavour and the need to exclude others from coastal waters, form the two sides of the coin of rising state imperiums. The second concerns the accumulation of capital and the transformation of the countryside in the interests of an ascendant capitalist-merchant class and their alliance with a landlord class. This process rose to prominence in eighteenth and nineteenth-century England and Scotland. In eighteenth-century England the inexorable thrust of capital accumulation was registered in the *Black Act* of 1723, which restricted 'non-monetary use rights' by outlawing the forest commons (Thompson 1975:244). In the nineteenth century the enclosures uprooted vast numbers of families from inland and coastal areas all over the British Isles and Ireland, resulting in starvation, a landless class and forced emigration. 'Freedom of the seas' became an ideological justification for destroying the 'natural' rights to *ferae naturae*, experienced as the right to a fish for the pot or a faggot for the fire (McCay 1989:205).

A third fact rests within a contrast between cultural assumptions. The uprooted and hidden social forms embodied in local inherited sea tenures followed a different set of principles to those of the tenures that usurped them: a significant manifestation of this difference is that like land the sea was not represented as simply water-bearing resources to be exploited: the aim was to conciliate the land or the sea, not to conquer it. The Irish conceived of the sea as part of 'Otherworld' (Heaney 1994:56–62), to be respected, even placated, a withholding space as well as a giving place. In the late nineteenth century, the Shetland Islanders continued to use an ancient secret deep-sea language at the *haaf* or fishing ground, a custom shared with fishermen of Norway, the Faroe Islands and probably throughout the areas of the Viking influence (Drever 1935–46:235). This *haaf* language substituted certain names secret to fishermen for their usual names, these being mainly Old Norse words, many of them of ancient Sami origin, some of them being the words of a devotional language or words drawn from Eddic poetry (Drever 1935–46:236). They included 'old worship words' for sun, moon, sea, land and fire; secret words belonging to the ritual of fishing, including the boat and its launching, the destination, hauling the fish; and 'protective' words substituted for those tabooed at the *haaf* (240). Pálsson and Durrenberger (1983:521) consider folk beliefs among Icelandic fishermen early this century: the ability of an individual to catch fish or 'fishiness' was seen as 'part of a grand design' and fish caught were spoken of as 'gifts of God'.[7]

One may readily agree that secret languages and belief in luck or magical notions sit awkwardly beside modern Enlightenment-inspired ideas of progress. Small-scale, low-technology fisheries, the social structures that hold them in place and the cultural meanings that underlie their social practices, the law and custom that regulated their practice

---

7 John Spence (1935–46) recalls fishing at a deep-sea fishing area off the Shetland Islands in the summer of 1875 in an eighteen-foot sixern or *haf*-boat, divided into six compartments or 'rooms'. The skipper, 'a man of great moral worth' (Spense 35–46:36) and elder of the Established Church was, like other fishermen of his time, most meticulous in his 'observance of time-honoured customs' of fishing. Care was taken to avoid ballast stones with white veins through them for it was believed they brought the white waves that might cover the boat.

(e.g. Brehon law), are readily forgotten and pushed aside, the practitioners are taken to be backward, in many ways akin to the indigenous clan societies of those parts of the globe which were brought into the European orbit through the colonial process. Once the dominant perspective is de-naturalised, however, one may seek to understand the principles of difference, a task of some practical urgency today. Perhaps the relativising of the conception of a *mare nullius* of the coasts, a particular social construction with a very short time span in the history of humanity, leaves a way open to discern the mental patterning and the aesthetic unity of other 'cultural ways'.

Contesting the dominant perspective: some beginnings in Australia

Against the background of hitherto taken-for-granted assumptions, one may examine some of the processes by which the total hegemony of the open-access/state-territorial seas position has begun to be contested in practice over the last decade and particularly since 1993. Significant events in the marine sphere have led to some reassessment of old policy positions in post-Mabo Australia, but not to the relinquishment of underlying premises.

Although hundreds of pages of testimony of maritime Yolngu people along the Arnhem Land coast were devoted to people's explanation of their perspectives on sea space at the beginning of the 1980s, there is little evidence of a recognition by fisheries managers of the depth or meaning of the difference in Aboriginal perspective to the European-Australian one. Certainly seas around Milingimbi and Castlereagh Bay were closed as a result of the hearings.[8] And although efforts were made by some commercial fisheries leaders to show proper respect for Aboriginal concerns and priorities, more than a decade went

---

8 Aboriginal Land Commission (1980, 1982), Transcripts of Proceedings, *Closure of Seas, Castlereagh Bay and Howard Island Area Public Hearing,* Darwin.

by without significant change. It took an event believed by fisheries officers and commercial fishermen to place in jeopardy the commercial fishing industry in the Gulf of Carpentaria,[9] to move from a 'cult of forgetfulness' about Aboriginal claims to a modest programme of recognition. This was the announcement by the Anindilyakwa clan leaders and elders of their intention to lodge a sea-closure application seaward of the mean low-tide mark around Groote, Bickerton and other surrounding islands. The perspective behind this announcement, made at the 'Turning of the Tide' conference held at the Northern Territory University in July 1993, was the Anindilyakwa people's aspiration to manage the local marine environment of which they are the recognised owners and custodians under Aboriginal law (Josif 1993:21–22).

From the perspective of the Aboriginal community, the motivating reason for their decision was that increased use and greater exploitation of the marine environment by outsiders 'is having a cumulatively detrimental effect on some marine species' habitats', and that some activities are a threat to cultural sites: 'we don't follow the water, we follow the land under the sea...', one elder stated (Josif 1993:22). It was the same position taken by custodians in neighbouring areas along the Arnhem Land coast (Aboriginal Land Commission, Sea Closure 1980–82: *passim*).

The Anindilyakwa people's move acted 'as a trigger galvanising the industry into action'.[10] The action led to a series of moves finding public expression in the establishment of eight regional consultative bodies known as Fisheries Committees taking in the 87 percent of Northern Territory coastline inhabited by Aboriginal people.[11] These committees comprise commercial, recreational and Aboriginal fishing

9 The Northern Prawn Fishery is regulated by the Australian Fisheries Management Authority, and other fisheries are controlled by the Northern Territory government.

10 Department of Primary Industries and Fisheries official, notes of conversation with author, Darwin, 4 July 1996.

11 The 'coastline' includes 'the area under Northern Land Council responsibility', Fisheries Committee, Charter, nd. This takes in coastline and off-shore islands from the western side of the Gulf of Carpentaria

representatives who are referred to by officials as being in 'partnership', even in 'co-management' with them. While useful, these committees only provide channels for hearing and tackling grievances. They enlighten Aboriginal people on resource management activities already in place, on licensing rules and their relation to sustainability and begin and end with consultation (Fisheries Committee, Charter nd:1–2).

Despite this change, the basic assumptions of non-indigenous Australia remain as they were: no-one owns the water or the sea-bed and the fish are conceived as a resource that belongs to everyone. Property rights or primary caretaking rights to a marine locality are foreign to this way of thinking. At the same conference at which the Anindilyakwa claimed primary rights, public servants responsible for fisheries put the perspective of official government circles on public rights to coastal seas:

> Fish and aquatic life are common property resources and the NT and Commonwealth Governments have the responsibility to manage the fishery resources in its adjacent waters on behalf of the whole community. This is undertaken under the provisions of the Fisheries Act 1988, and subordinate legislation (Grey and Lea 1993:1).

Closer to the ground, officials argue that Aboriginal coastal people would gain nothing from rights to the sea: given the habits of fish, small plots of sea could not enclose them and modern fisheries management requires large areas of sea to be viable commercially.

The foray into the area of consultation with Aboriginal people by representatives of the dominant culture makes some concessions to their wishes in regard to conservation of fish and respect for cultural sites; it recognises, puts to use and often sets out to extend their body of knowledge and expertise on dugong and turtle. But it does not address the question of Aboriginal perspectives in any basic way. The Anindilyakwa are interested in learning and exchanging as they and their Yolgnu

---

through Arnhem Land to the far reaches of the Territory adjoining Western Australia.

neighbours did with the Macassans, who recognised their ownership of the land, paying tribute to each land-sea owner for access rights to the foreshore (Thomson 1949:51). They accepted elements of techno-logical change, incorporating them into their economy; they extended their cultural symbols in a way that did not diminish or destroy them. Today they seek 'to implement a comprehensive marine management program' which involves other groups in the area. In a co-management scheme to which commercial and recreational fishermen, government agencies and fisheries contributed, the Anindilyakwa would be happy to accept new ideas and technologies but 'as primary caretakers' they see 'the last word' as lying with themselves (Josif 1993:24).

The reasons for that stance have been explained on countless occa-sions: by Yolngu in the sea closure hearings or for that matter by the Meriam of the Murray Islands in the hearing of 'the facts' in the Supreme Court of Queensland in 1986 and 1989 in the Mabo case. Again and again in the former hearings, Yolngu coastal people expressed two closely related concerns which they backed up with examples from their experience: that outsiders' activities will deplete the area of fish, mess up the estuaries and rivers with old nets and gear and generally fail to observe rules Aboriginal people hold dear to themselves and their chil-dren; and they will fail to respect the centres of creation beings, burial sites and other cultural sites. They explained the cultural arbitrariness for them of two kilometres, the distance beyond the low-water mark recommended by the Aboriginal Land Rights Commission that tradi-tional coastal estates may extend: 'When Aboriginals sing our sacred songs we don't start it from two kilometres ... our ceremony songs start off from right out in the ocean' (Aboriginal Land Commission, Sea Closure, Transcript of Proceedings, Darwin and Milingimbi 1980–81:143–44; hereafter Transcript).

Witnesses contrasted *balanda* (white people's) relationships with the sea as 'just a sea' for enjoyment and the dollar with their own: the seas are 'something that means something to our people, something that we belong to' (Charles Manydjarri, Transcript: 145). Significant places are 'linked to you with feelings'. Sea places are not just nature out there; nor are other parts of the environment: 'The thunder and clouds and birds ... is the feeling of the people'. That interrelationship is part of the round of life where the budding of flowers on land is a sign of the right time for certain sea life (Mr Mawunydjii, Transcript: 22 June 1981:184; cf 167, 172–73).[12] In disclosing some of their beliefs in the hearings, they often drew back as they approached matters of central belief, giving voice to a lifetime of experience that *balanda* are incapable of understanding: 'It is just beyond your understanding', said Mr Gaykamanu, as he sought to explain the idea that 'Every bit of land means something to Aboriginal people' (Transcript: 185). Flowers, birds, fish *tell*; you have to be able to listen. The witnesses were revealing a different sensibility, a different psychological make-up. The sea gives back to those who respect it: 'It [our tie with the sea] is something which is part of our blood and body that is forcing us and telling us what to do...' (Mr Weluk, Transcript: 143).

Thus they may approach the matter of fishing differently to many *balanda*: the sea gives back to those who know and respect it. So, for example, live-release sports fishing is offensive to Aboriginal people. Returning a hooked fish violates their sense of what is morally acceptable. Cree fishermen of Chisasiki, Canada express a similar repulsion and they see tagging too as a mark of disrespect to the animal. They say 'you eat what you catch, you do not kill more than you need, and you approach the task of fishing with basic humility and modesty' (Berkes 1989:195). Nevertheless, even in rejecting the idea that *balanda* could ever understand how feelings, visions and dreams about a place may be a way of linking you with it, Charles Manydjarri appealed to the judge face to face, reflecting wistfully on the melancholy of dwindling Aboriginal cultures 'on the edge of Australia': 'because you are interested you are very welcome', he said. Perhaps this may help you to 'get a feeling from the Aboriginal people here so you can help us' to 'win the victory' (Transcript: 146). To be taken seriously in practice as primary caretakers.

12 See also Meriam custodian Sam Passi (Au Bala): 'I use nature for my book' (Sharp 1993:51–52).

The most imaginative, flexible and intelligent *balanda* persons concerned with fisheries organizations and management do respect the Aboriginal way of doing things and the time is ripe for them to educate the *balanda* fishermen about how Aboriginal people feel about the sea. Nigel Scullion, Chairman, Australian Seafood Industry Council, sees the outlook for co-operation as a rosy one because 'there is so much goodwill from the Aboriginal people and to a large degree from the [non-Aboriginal] fishermen' (notes of conversation with the author, Darwin, 8 July 1996). In his view, the key to the rosy future is consultation, and this must be culturally appropriate. The issue remains that even such an enlightened business person does not relinquish the cultural assumption about open public rights to state territorial seas.[13]

Overcoming the bone fish-hook label: sharing the coasts?

A major sea transformation is underway globally, signalled firstly by the expansion of competitive economic resource pursuits at sea including deep sea bed mining and secondly by a redivision of the seas whereby state territorial seas are expanded to 200 nautical mile Exclusive Economic Zones (EEZ). These changes may hasten 'the imminent demise of individual fishermen and small business operators in coastal waters (O'Connor and O'Connor 1994:4). On the other hand, the United Nations Convention on the Law of the Sea requirement for each coastal state to determine its own total allowable catch (TAC) carries the rider that where domestic industry is unable to meet all of a TAC, the state has an obligation to offer licences to outsiders for the remainder of the catch quota. In this context, the initiatives being taken by Aboriginal and Torres Strait Islander maritime cultures towards re-assuming the

---

13 He identified the 'cultural value', which he believes is shared by 97 per cent of Australians, that the beaches and coastal seas are the preserve of all citizens, not of any one group (Nigel Scullion, 'Late Night Live', 21 May 1996; cf 'Lateline', 28 August 1996).

role of primary guardianship of marine resources and coastal management, might reasonably be welcomed as an opportunity, not feared as a threat.

The thrust of globalisation is to hasten destruction of local cultures through the processes intrinsic to systems geared to economically rationalist goals. This was the process that produced anger and frustration among cod fishermen in arctic Norway when in 1990, in the interests of 'efficiency' as conceived by Government officials, small boats skippered and worked by their owners lost their full participation rights in the fishery (Maurstad 1992, 1995; Örebech 1993, 1995). Side by side with this 'tragedy of the commoners' as McCay (1989:206–10) has called it, is a trend towards the creation and encouragement of regimes that require participation of so-called 'user groups'. A review by Sen and Raakjaer Nielsen (1996:21, cf 23) of twenty-two case studies concluded that in almost all the fisheries studied co-management regimes had been established to relieve the consequences of overexploitation. In such cases co-management is clearly 'a form of crisis management'.

There is a shocking irony in destroying the old sea tenures and then imposing stewardship on user groups. Sen and Raakjaer Nielsen (1996:11–12) cite a Zambian case where the right to participate in a crisis management fishery was conditional on the fishermen and their families leaving their fishing camps or their own villages and 'emigrating' to artificially created lakeside fishing villages on Lake Kariba. By contrast, along Australia's northern coastline, and in other places, the sea territories of indigenous peoples remain relatively healthy and most of their owners have the will to act as their primary caretakers. The Yolngu people of Galiwin'ku (Elcho Island) and the Meriam of the Murray Islands, for example, are putting their perspectives on their inherited sea territories into the public realm and demanding the right to responsibility for the management of their seas (Ginytjirrang Mala 1994, 'Salt Water People', SBS 18 September 1996; Day 1993; Media Release, Mer Island, 6 December 1993; *Maber Newsletter*, nos 1–3, 1996).

In addressing the basic issue of cultural contrast in representing sea space, the world-historical picture tells us that the problem in finding a future is more deep-seated than the differences between indigenous and non-indigenous perspectives as they manifest themselves in countries like Australia and New Zealand, or in Canada, the United States or South Africa. A wider problem is the long-term failure to take small-scale locally managed marine activities seriously. As Rettig, Berkes and Pinkerton (1989:286) observe, until about the mid 1980s most fisheries managers treated self-managed fisheries, coasts and waterways 'as anthropological curiosities'. They point to a veritable 'treasure chest' of 'success stories' reported in the late eighties of 'informal co-management' from a range of community situations. A body of work built up by a succession of Norwegian scholars, mainly from arctic Norway, has been able to demonstrate that the success of the Lofoten cod fisheries was contingent on the fishermen taking *informed responsibility* for the marine environment and in relation to one another (Eythorsson 1992, 1995; Maurstad 1992, 1995).

Similarly, the example of Kowanyama community, some 1,200 people with fifty kilometres of coastline and centred on one of Australia's largest delta systems on the south east of the Gulf of Carpentaria, challenges the view, often unstated, that Aboriginal communities cannot handle the demands of modern resource and environmental management. At a conference hosted by the Kowanyama community in 1990, a locally-based program to 'keep the rivers and lands healthy for future generations' was initiated. Its basis is community ownership, its starting point the special attachment of the people to land and waterways, its brief the maximisation of indigenous management 'in a way meaningful to the community' (Sinnamon 1996:4). Its masthead is self-governance, its project is local, not regional or national. Their success comes from having made their plans work themselves. In the words of John Clarke, Kowanyama community ranger and Australia's first Aboriginal fisheries inspector: 'We at Kowanyama don't want a joint management agreement. We are the landowners. We want to control the land the way we want it. Not how they [the land and fisheries managers] run it' ('Salt Water People', SBS Television, 18 September 1996). The community has developed first-hand ties with the coastal Lummi Indian people of Washington State, where contact and new knowledge are placed in the service of a *local* project. Unlike the slogan of Western-based environmental groups in the 1990s who said 'think globally, act locally', the agenda of the Kowanyama people is 'think locally, act locally, but exchange knowledge with others even far away and as equals in order that we and they may each act in our own domains more effectively'. As Dwyer (1994:95) has noted, the 'concern of indigenous systems is with the resident group and not with outsiders, their ambit is species and habitats that contribute to human well-being (both secular and sacred) and not with all species and habitats ...'

Rettig, Berkes and Pinkerton (1989:281–82) have drawn attention to the self-regulatory impulse of base communities and its relevance to the success of co-management systems. They argue that where long-existing local cultures, indigenous and non-indigenous, with customary norms and values independent of national cultures, continue, they may develop an ongoing practical commitment to conservation practices. Thus they are 'naturals' for largely self-regulatory co-management regimes. They suggest that indigenous groupings 'have a head start' on local-level conservation because group boundaries and obligations to members of the group are defined by kinship and territorial systems (Rettig *et al.* 1989:282).

The work of Norwegian scholars with small coastal communities gives substance to this contention, both in regard to the application of traditional ecological knowledge in fisheries management and to the delicate decisions of maintaining the integrity of the group and its shared ethic within the general province of social boundary maintenance in the admittance of new members to the group. Eythorsson (1992:1–11) considers the importance of traditional local knowledge among Sami and Norwegian coastal communities who share an ethic of concern for the species. Rettig and others (1989:282) suggest that non-indigenous local communities may never develop the indigenous 'spiritual kinship to the fish nor the actual kinship to other community members'. However, the work of Drever and Spence (1935–46) on the persistence of the deep-sea language among Shetland Islanders in the late nineteenth century with its strong components of a secret religious language suggests perhaps that the distinction between aboriginal and non-aboriginal is less salient than the distinction between the differing social forms of 'community' and 'society'.

Conclusion

Spokespeople for many indigenous maritime cultures have stated publicly their wish to be primary caretakers of their marine environments. In following the customs and beliefs about the sea of their ancestors, they also see themselves as modern people wishing to earn a living from the sea. Above all, it is their own unique perspective on the sea that assures them that they know what is best for saltwater country. Peter Yu (1995:2), Executive Director of the Kimberley Land Council, confirms what people have said all along the coast: 'We are not just another "user group" of a limited resource'. In Jull's (1993:111) words, each follows 'the imperative of a unique social culture'.

Perhaps the biggest impediment to recognition of this right is the belief that exercise of the right to particular marine areas means the 'imprisonment' of marketable resources in locked-up areas of coast. This view is fuelled by self-fulfilling policies that deny indigenous people the chance to earn a living from their ancestral sea domains. A report of an investigation into indigenous aspirations and their bearing on ecologically sustainable development possibilities gives a resounding 'no' to the notion of keeping their sea domains as backwaters:

> What people desire above all is to bear the brunt of responsibility in controlling access of outsiders to land and associated sea territory. Also uppermost is a desire to earn a living from ancestral resources, and not have them locked up unilaterally by government agencies as empty 'wilderness' areas. (Commonwealth, *Ecologically Sustainable Development Working Groups, Final Report—Fisheries* [1991:65] as cited in Sutherland 1996:17)

This resounds with the strategies proposed by the Anindilyakwa who seek 'a co-operative marine management regime' (Josif 1993:22), or those of the Steering Committee of Manbuynga ga Rulyapa, which called for 'An Indigenous Marine Protection Strategy' on 8 November 1994.

However, there is reason now to believe the (sea) horse may have bolted. Aboriginal people are seeking legal empowerment. Claims to seas around Croker Island, western Arnhem Land were heard in court during 1997, other claims from sea owners along the coast of Arnhem Land are in preparation, and in October 1997, more than one hundred and twenty land-sea claims were before the National Native Title Tribunal. For a number of reasons, some of them a result of the imposition of rules derived from the European perspective on open coastal access (Sharp 1997), consideration of native title was restricted to land above the high-water mark in the Mabo case. The Meriam are now moving towards completing the process of recognition of land-sea rights. They have established a Sea Rights Committee, whose newsletter is *Maber*, the Meriam name for the giant triton or *bu* shell, blown in pre-colonial times as an alarm signal calling the warriors together to respond to an enemy or emergency (*Maber Newsletter*, April, May, June editions, 1996).

A lesson from the experience of Meriam people in their land case is that without practical moves for culturally and environmentally sustainable development, a court success may have a hollow ring. Many Meriam people wish to accept the challenge of making their own future. For nearly five years many of them have struggled to create a viable community fishing economy in a way which respects and conserves land-sea country for future generations. They look forward to a self-determining situation like that now developed at Kowanyama. Events there led Aboriginal fisheries official and community leader, John Clarke to say: 'It's superb. I like what we're doing' ('Salt Water People', SBS Television, 18 September 1996).

Notes

This chapter is a revised and expanded version of Sharp, N. 1996. Fron Grotius to Mabo. *Arena Journal* 7:111–129. It draws on Sharp, N. 1996. *Reimagining sea space in history and contemporary Life: pulling up some old anchors.* Darwin: North Australia Research Unit, Australian National University, Discussion Paper no. 5:1–31.

References

Aboriginal Land Commission 1980. Sea closure, *Bathurst Island, Melville Island and Millingimbi land claim*, transcript of proceedings before His Honour Mr Justice Toohey, Aboriginal Land Commissioner, Darwin.

Aboriginal Land Commission 1982. *Closure of seas, Castlereagh Bay and Howard Island area public hearing*, transcript of proceedings before Justice Sir William Kearney, Aboriginal Land Commissioner, Darwin.

Allen, D. 1994. Salt-water dreaming. In *Surviving Columbus: indigenous peoples, political reform and environmental management in north Australia conference* (ed.) Peter Jull. Darwin: North Australian Research Unit, ANU.

Berkes, F. 1989. Co-management and the James Bay agreement. In *Co-operative management of local fisheries* (ed.) E. Pinkerton. Vancouver: University of British Columbia Press. Pp. 189–208.

Blackstone, Sir W. 1979. *Commentaries on the laws of England*, 4 vols. Oxford: Clarendon Press. (Facsimile of the first edition, University of Chicago Press, 1765–69.)

Butler, W.F.T. 1925. *Gleanings from Irish history*. London: Longmans.

Cairns, D. and S. Richards 1988. *Writing Ireland: colonialism, nationalism and culture*. Manchester: Manchester University Press.

Chambers, A. 1986. *Granuaile: the life and times of Grace O'Malley*. Dublin: Wolfhound Press.

Cole, S.D. 1919. The highways of the sea. In *Transactions of the Grotius Society*, vol.IV, *Problems of war* (Papers read before the Society in the year 1918). London: Sweet and Maxwell. Pp. 15–25.

Cordell, J. 1989. Introduction: sea tenure. In *A sea of small boats* (ed.) J. Cordell. Cambridge, MA: Cultural Survival. Pp. 1–32.

Day, R. 1993. Sea rights, traditional boundaries and modern fishing in Mer Island waters. In *Turning the tide: conference on indigenous peoples and sea rights, 14 July–16 July 1993: selected papers*. Darwin: Northern Territory University.

Drever, J. 1935–46. 'Taboo' words among Shetland fishermen. In *Old-Lore miscellany of Orkney, Shetland, Caithness and Sutherland*. Vol. X. London: Viking Society for Northern Research, University College.

Dwyer, P.D. 1994. Modern conservation and indigenous peoples: in search of wisdom. *Pacific Conservation Biology* 1:91–97.

Evans, E.E. 1979. *Irish folk ways*. London: Routledge and Kegan Paul.

Eythorsson, E. 1992. *Sami fjord fishermen and the state: traditional knowledge and resource management in northern Norway*. University of Manitoba occasional paper: Pp. 1–13.

1995. Who should have a voice in management of local marine resources? Paper given to the Fifth Common Property Conferences, Reinventing the Commons, Bodø, Norway, 24–28 May.

Fenn, P.T. 1926. Origins of the theory of territorial waters. *American Journal of International Law* 20: 465–82.

Ginytjirrang Mala 1994. Manbuynga ga Rulyapa, Arafura Sea, marine strategy, Darwin. Pp. 1–9.

Glasgow, T. Jr, 1965–66. The Elizabethan navy in Ireland (1558–1603). *The Irish Sword 7*, 291–307.

Grey, D.L. and R.J. Lea 1993. Fisheries in the Northern Territory: their management and Aboriginal involvement. In *Turning the tide: conference* on indigenous peoples and sea rights, 14 July–16 July 1993: selected papers. Darwin: Northern Territory University.

Grotius, H. 1925. *The law of war and peace, De Jure Belli ac Pacis Libri.* Indianapolis: Bobbs-Merrill.

1972. *The freedom of the seas or the right which belongs to the Dutch to take part in the East Indian Trade.* New York: Orno Press (Latin and English texts on opposite pages). Facsimile of Oxford University Press, New York, 1916. Ruan Deman Magoffin transl. *Mare Liberum.* 1st Latin edition 1633.

Heaney, M. 1994. *Over nine waves: a book of Irish legends.* London: Faber and Faber.

Hechter, M. 1975. *Internal colonialism: the Celtic fringe in British national development 1536–1966.* London: Routledge and Kegan Paul.

Jackson, S.E. 1995. The water is not empty: cross-cultural issues in conceptualising sea space. *Australian Geographer* 26(1) May: 87–96.

Jentoft, S. and T. Kristoffersen 1989. Fishermen's co-management: the case of the Lofoten fishery. *Human Organization* 48(4): 355–65.

Josif, P. 1993. An overview of Anindilyakwa aspirations to manage the marine environment adjacent to their lands under two laws. In *Turning the tide: conference on indigenous peoples and sea rights, 14 July–16 July 1993: selected papers.* Darwin: Northern Territory University. Pp. 21–24.

Jull, P. 1993. *A sea change: overseas indigenous-government relations in the coastal zone.* Consultancy report, Resource Assessment Commission, Coastal Zone Inquiry, Canberra.

Keen, I. 1984. Aboriginal tenure and use of the foreshore and seas: an anthropological evaluation of the Northern Territory legislation providing for the closure of the seas adjacent to Aboriginal land. *Anthropological Forum* 5, 421–39.

Kelly, F. (ed.) 1991. *A guide to early Irish law.* Dublin: Institute for Advanced Studies.

1996. *Early Irish farming*. Page proofs from the author, 27 March 1996.

Knight, W.S.M. 1920. Grotius in England. In *Transactions of the Grotius Society, vol. V, Problems of peace and war*. (Papers read before the Society in the year 1919). London: Sweet and Maxwell. Pp. 1–38.

McCay, B. 1987. The culture of the commoners. In *The question of the commons: the culture and ecology of communal resources*, B.J. McCay, and J.M. Acheson. Tucson: University of Arizona Press. Pp. 195–216.

1989. Sea tenure and the culture of the commoners. In *A sea of small boats* (ed.) J. Cordell. Cambridge, MA: Cultural Survival. Pp. 203–27.

Maber Newsletter 1996. Sea rights committee, Mer Island, April, May, June editions.

Mabo and Others v the State of Queensland and the Commonwealth of Australia, in the High Court of Australia, No. 12 of 1982. Transcripts of proceedings before High Court of Australia, Supreme Court of Queensland 1984–89. Determination pursuant to reference of 27 February 1986 by High Court to Supreme Court of Queensland to hear and determine all issues of fact raised by the pleadings, particulars and further particulars in High Court action B12 of 1982, 16 November 1990 (Determination). *Eddie Mabo v State of Queensland* (1992) 66 *Australia Law Journal Reports* 408 (High Court, Full Bench, 3 June 1992).

Maurstad, A. 1992. Closing the commons—opening the 'tragedy': regulating north-Norwegian small-scale fishing. Paper given to Third Common Property Conference of the International Association for the Study of Common Property, Washington DC, 17–20 September.

1995 Customs in commons—commons in court: fishermen's customary practice and statutory law concerning the cod-fishery in north Norwegian waters. Paper given to the Fifth Common Property Conference of the International Association for the Study of Common Property, Bodø, Norway, 24–28 May.

Netboy, A. 1968. *The Atlantic salmon: a vanishing species?* Boston: Houghton Mifflin.

O'Connor, 'C. and M. O'Connor 1994. Mabo and the law of the sea convention: state and national implications in the changing position of Australia as an international maritime state. *Maritime Studies* 74:1–15.

O'Regan, T. 1996. Maori fisheries rights and the New Zealand fisheries management regime. Paper presented to Second World Fisheries Congress, Brisbane, 29 July.

Örebech, P. 1993. The legal right to Norwegian fisheries participation with a special emphasis on the Lofoten cod fisheries. Paper given to the Man and Biosphere Conference, 21 February.

1995 Public and common private property rights: how to protect and preserve inalienable rights? Paper given at Researcher Training Course, Legal change in north/south perspective, Copenhagen, 22–25 November: 1–41.

Pálsson, G. and E.P. Durrenberger 1983. Icelandic foremen and skippers: the structure and evolution of a folk model. *American Ethnologist* 10(3):511–28.

Prescott, J.R.V. 1975. *The political geography of the oceans*. Devon: David and Charles.

Rettig, R.B., F. Berkes and E. Pinkerton 1989. The future of fisheries co-management: a multi-disciplinary assessment. In *Co-operative management of local fisheries: new directions for improved management and community development* (ed.) E. Pinkerton. Vancouver: University of British Columbia Press. Pp. 273–86.

Selden, J. 1663. *Mare Clausum. The right and dominion of the sea*, 2 vols, London: Andrew Kembe and Edward Thomas.

Sen, S. and J. Raakjaer Nielsen 1996. Fisheries co-management: a comparative analysis. Paper presented to Second World Fisheries Congress, Brisbane (*Marine Policy* 20(5)).

Sharp, N. 1993. *Stars of Tagai: the Torres Strait Islanders*. Canberra: Aboriginal Studies Press.

1995. The freedom of the seas: ruling inherited sea tenures out of the imagination. Unpublished paper, 1–54.

1996. *No ordinary judgment: Mabo, the Murray Islanders' land case.* Canberra: Aboriginal Studies Press.

1997. Why indigenous sea rights are not recognised in Australia: 'the facts' of Mabo and their cultural roots. *Australian Aboriginal Studies* 1:28–37.

1998. Terrestial and marine space in human imagination and social life. Unpublished paper. Pp. 1–26.

Sinnamon, V. 1996. Co-management and self-governance: contemporary indigenous natural resource management. Paper prepared for conference on Conservation outside nature reserves, University of Queensland, Brisbane, 5–8 February.

Smyth, D. 1993. *A voice in all places: Aboriginal and Torres Strait Islander interests in Australia's coastal zone*, Consultancy Report, Resource Assessment Commission, Coastal Zone Inquiry, Canberra.

Spence, J. 1935–46. The days of the old Shetland sixern, *Old-lore miscellany of Orkney Shetland Caithness and Sutherland* (Old-Lore Series) 3:36–41.

Sutherland, J. 1996. *Fisheries, aquaculture and Aboriginal and Torres Strait Islander peoples: studies, policies and legislation.* Canberra: Department of the Environment, Sport and Territories, Commonwealth of Australia.

Symmons, C.R. 1993. *Ireland and the law of the sea.* Dublin: The Round Hall Press.

Taylor, L. 1981. 'Man the fisher': salmon fishing and the expression of community in a rural Irish settlement. *American Ethnologist* 8(4):774–88.

Thompson, E.P. 1975. *Whigs and hunters.* London: Allen Lane.

Thomson, D.F. 1949. *Economic structure and the ceremonial exchange cycle in Arnhem Land.* Melbourne: Macmillan.

Yu, P. 1995. Native title and its potential impacts on fisheries management. Paper presented to the Third Australasian Fisheries Managers Conference, 1–4 August.

4

Aboriginal fishing rights on the New South Wales South Coast: a Court Case

Scott Cane

This paper arises from the prosecution of seven Aboriginal men from the South Coast of New South Wales. The men were arrested in possession of mussels, rock lobsters and between 12 and 1,450 abalone in 1991 and 1992. The Department of Fisheries claimed these to be illegally obtained. They saw the men as poachers—a serious offence with significant penalties, fines, confiscation of diving equipment and possible jail terms. The men claimed their arrest was an infringement of their customary rights. These rights, the men contested, existed and continued to exist regardless of government quota systems and fishing licenses imposed over the last 30 years. There was nothing, they observed, in the *Fisheries and Oyster Farms Act (1935)[1]* that specifically extinguished their rights. The men were, however, prosecuted as criminals and the NSW Land Council sought to defend them and their traditional rights.[2]

---

1 This Act was the earliest regulatory Act referred to in the prosecution and in subsequent hearings. There appear to have been no other regulatory Acts between 1901 and 1980. The Coastal Water (State Powers) and the Coastal Waters (State Titles) Acts (Commonwealth) were enacted in 1980 to empower the States to make laws in relation to the seabed (also the Application of Laws (Coastal Sea) Act 1981). The Fisheries and Oyster Farms Act of 1935 was amended in 1989 (Fisheries Regulation 1989) (Robert and Katz 1994, Court of Appeal record sheet 1994).

2 Their case was argued by Blake Dawson and Waldron and later Horowitz Bilinsky.

The case first went to the Magistrates Court, then the Supreme Court and finally the Court of Appeal. The outcome recognised the existence of a traditional right to fish but questioned whether the defendant[3] was actually practising that right at the time of his arrest. The case entailed archaeological and ethnographic documentation and complex litigation which at times seemed removed from the traditions in question.

Many of the legal and contextual aspects of the case are, in a sense, beyond the arena of this ethnographic case study but are recounted as they provide a flavour and a sense of the reality of the process of determining traditional rights in court. The legal issues are complex and people have differing views on them.

The paper provides a background to the case by outlining the sequence of events leading up to and surrounding the hearings and offers some observations about the legal outcomes. It also summarises the archaeological and ethnographic material presented to the court and comments on the nature of data collection. The original investigation entailed the documentation of genealogical, anecdotal and historical information for over 300 people, in 25 families spread between Sydney and eastern Victoria over the last 140 years (Figure 4:1, Cane 1992 a and b). This was a substantial task which resulted in the production of a linear, and rather frank, historical account of the association amongst the men charged, their ancestors, the sea and the South Coast. The original account of fishing on the South Coast of New South Wales has been condensed and organised so as to outline the family connections amongst the defendants as simply as possible and place them in the broader historical and geographic setting.

---

3   Only one of the seven men was actually tried—Mason.

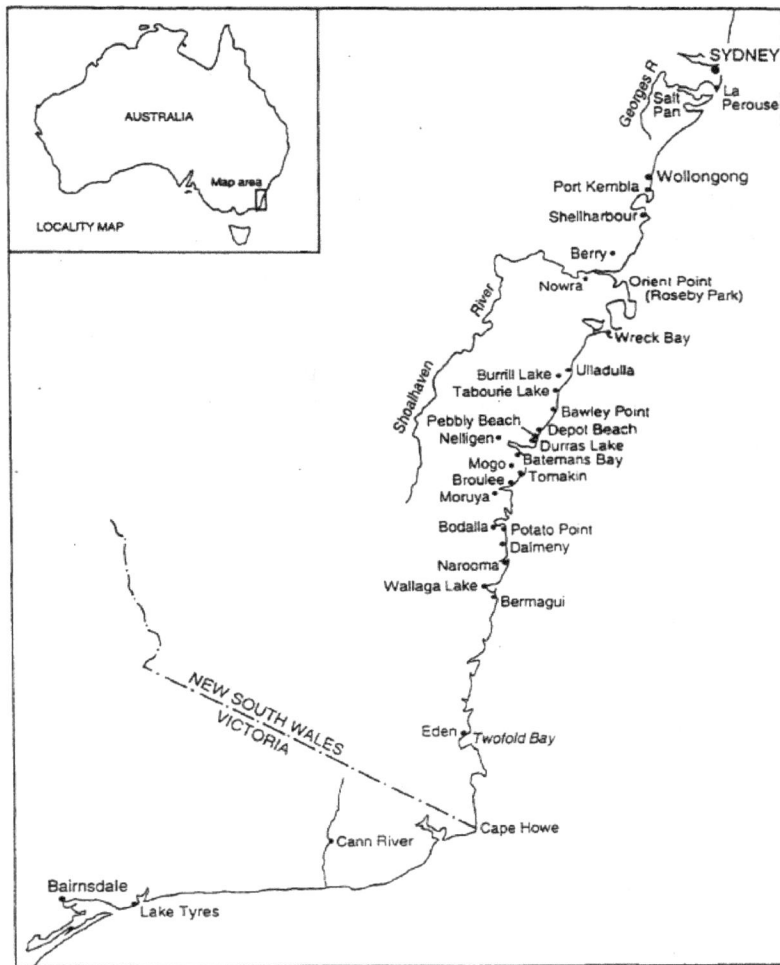

Figure 4:1 The south coast of New South Wales

Some background to the investigation

The court cases took place between 1992 and 1994. The seven[4] men involved were arrested for poaching on the South Coast of New South Wales, between October 1991 and March 1992 (see Figure 4:2). Those charged were summoned to appear before the Batemans Bay Local Court in April 1992. An adjournment was sought in order to have the hearing transferred to Sydney where the case was resumed in July 1992. The ethnographic and archaeological material was presented at this hearing, but the case was then adjourned until March 1993 to allow time to review the material and to consider the significance of the issues at hand.[5] This hearing was lost by the defendant and an appeal was made to the Supreme Court in October 1993. This appeal was also lost and the case was again appealed before the Court of Appeal in August 1994

An investigation was commissioned by the New South Wales Aboriginal Land Council in mid-June 1992 to determine the legitimacy of the traditional rights claimed by the defendants. This study was conducted over the course of three weeks between the time of notification and the hearing in the Local Court in Sydney.

It may surprise some readers that such an important case was prepared in such a short time. There may have been a number of reasons for this. The timing of the case was obviously a significant factor, as the men were charged between October 1991 and March 1992, and appeared in the Local Court in July that year. Thus there were only a

---

4   An eighth man, Clarke Chatfield was also involved. His family came to the South Coast from Dubbo in the 1960s and does not have an established history of fishing on the South Coast of NSW.

5   The issue of native title was virtually unheard of in July 1992. The High Court decision had just been made and copies of the determination could only be obtained from the High Court. There was no Native Title Act yet and there was little political debate about the consequences of native title. Nevertheless, the magistrate appeared troubled following the presentation of the archaeological and ethnographic evidence, suggesting his realisation of the significance of the issue at stake.

few months separating the charges and the hearing. Cost may also have been a factor, and presumably many of those involved had other commitments which prevented the planning and organisation of the case until quite late in the proceedings.

Figure 4:2: Summary of charges against defendants, October 1991–March 1992

Defendant	Charge	Defence
Brierly	8 rock lobsters, 1 cm under size	Not intending to keep undersized fish
Carriage	97kg (1,450) abalone	For annual community football barbecue
R. Masson	92 abalone	Only 40 abalone, non-commercial, for family
Nye	12 abalone	Always dived for abalone, can't get licence
Stewart	17 abalone	To be shared between two divers
	39 abalone—33 under size	Unemployed, for wife and 7 family members
Carter	(with Stewart, above)	Accompanying Stewart and Carriage on dive
K. Mason	160 abalone	Charge 'a lie', only a small quantity of abalone
	Threatening an inspector	Inspector threw diving gear off cliff
	77 abalone	'A lie'—had one lobster and six abalone
	18 litres of mussels	For family, unaware of legal limit on mussels

Preparing the defence for the case commenced with a meeting held at the Regional Land Council in Narooma, NSW at which there was a strong desire to assert and defend what the men perceived as their traditional rights. Several concerns were raised at this meeting.

The first was that the case would be the first traditional fishing rights case in Australia. As such it would be an important case and all involved should be mindful of the responsibility they carried in mounting and participating in it. If the case were a success, the men and others involved would be applauded. If the case failed, then those involved would be criticised and a bad precedent could be set for others with stronger comparable rights. As it turned out, these concerns were unjustified as the legal outcome was ambivalent and the case provided some useful insights, rather than negative precedents.

The second concern related to the fact that only one witness was to be called. The legal advice was that it was safer to call an 'expert witness', who might be able to withstand the critical and skilful attack of an opposing Queen's Council, than to expose a defendant who could unwittingly convict himself. This was a significant strategic decision that was ultimately to backfire. The original intention was to protect the defendants from the adversarial rigour of the court. The defence appeared not to know who might be called so they chose the safest course of defence: use one 'expert witness', myself.

There seemed to be no intention on behalf of those representing the defendants to prevent the exposure of some weakness in the defence or to bypass the relationship between each defendant and their espoused traditional right. As no-one knew which of the defendants would be called before the court first there was not (and could not have been) an intentional strategy of protecting one witness as against another or any witness because of any weakness in their claim. Each had varying historical associations with the sea, and each had varying degrees of experience and confidence in court.

Thirdly, it was made clear that I had only stood before a Queen's Council once, had rarely spoken in Court and was nervous about doing so. It was also noted that I had precious little time to gather whatever information was available and consult whoever might be able to speak with authority on the depth and duration of the traditional fishing practices within the indigenous community. There were only three weeks before the case went to court. There were seven key defendants, allowing just three days' research time per person, ignoring time for travel, organisation, historical research and report writing. It was likely that little could be documented in the available time and it was possible that much would be anecdotal and inadmissible in court.

The legal view seemed to be that something was better than nothing and, given the critical urgency of the cases and the fact that some of the men might go to jail, something had to be done. The defence also believed there was a lack of awareness of the significance of the High Court's Mabo decision and native title more generally at the time. There seemed to be a view that any evidence presented to the court might be accepted, without opposition, before the implications of the evidence were grasped. It would be something of a surprise attack in which the acceptance of unopposed ethnographic evidence would implicitly verify the existence of a traditional right to fish. It was also assumed that additional information could be submitted later or introduced through cross examination if necessary.

In view of the severe shortage of time a strategy had to be adopted that would maximise the documentation of essential information. There was no time to observe, participate in, document or analyse the 'ethnographic experience'—or even observe much of the fishing customs of the South Coast people in action. Although fishing activities were occurring throughout the investigation (see below), there was no time to wait on the beach for the tide, the wind and the swell to go fishing. There was no opportunity to participate significantly in fishing activities, document the distribution of collected foods, calculate the nutritional returns, estimate the proportions and determine the commercial and subsistence values of the seafood harvested. We did not have the time for, and questioned the value of, defining the meaning of tradition in this fishing community, nor did we have the opportunity to specify the laws and customs that may comprise those traditions. The best evidence one could hope to achieve was a comprehensive historical account of who fished and who did not, an account from which the tradition of fishing and its associated rights would be evident, if it existed. It must be remembered that at this stage of the prosecutions, it was not even clear whether the defendants were from the South Coast, let alone whether they had a history of fishing.

Thus the history of each defendant's family and their association with the South Coast had to be documented before the alleged traditional fishing right could be ascertained. The presence or absence of a traditional fishing right would become apparent through an historical narrative and the presentation of accurate, unembellished individual historical accounts. If there was a strong and continuous association between a defendant, the South Coast and fishing, then we assumed the tradition of fishing would be shown; the tradition would plainly be seen to have continued through history and into the present. Equally, if there were no historic and geographic links between a defendant, the South Coast and fishing, then it would be clear that there was no tradition of fishing and no traditional right. There would also be situations in which the historic experiences of the defendants would fall between these two extremes. It was difficult to predict how history would present itself until the investigation was complete, but it seemed plain that the courts would have to adjudicate on some cases that were less clear-cut than others. Thus it was obligatory to provide clear and detailed evidence so the courts could make a reasonable assessment of the nature of the traditional right.

With these issues in mind an intense effort was made to research accessible material: reports, journals, church records, old newspapers, regional historic sources and community notes, tape recordings and histories. Interviews were also arranged and undertaken with each of the defendants, their families and elderly community members living in Wallaga Lake, Narooma, Mogo, Batemans Bay, Ulladulla, Jervis Bay and Berri. The names of individuals supplying this information were not associated with material in the original reports so as to minimise any repercussions after the hearings.[6]

Time pressures were such that material was collected during the day, drafted and dictated in the evenings, couriered to Sydney in the morning, returned by fax that night, read and re-faxed that night as other text was dictated and couriered to Sydney. In this way the text was researched and drafted simultaneously—and completed within the time available. Final additions were written into the text at midnight on the day before the first hearing in Sydney.

By the time the hearing was convened historical material had been gathered for five of the seven defendants: Nye, K. Mason, Carriage, Stewart and Carter. No information had been collected for Brierly and R. Mason, the defendant later called before the court. A supplementary investigation was then completed for Brierly and R. Mason and submitted in September 1992. Two other studies were completed at the same time as the ethnographic investigation. One (Colley 1992) examined the archaeological evidence for abalone fishing on the South Coast of NSW and the other, (Egloff 1992a) reported on the significance of coastal maritime resources to Aboriginal communities on the South Coast. Copies of the ethnographic study were circulated to each of the Aboriginal families involved in the case and sent out for review.

The process of review was used as an effective means of verifying and checking the information contained within the original report and insuring against any surprises in court, should the counsel representing the Department of Fisheries also have been getting expert advice. The report was sent to Egloff (1993) and Sutton (1993), both of whom provided excellent, although different, reviews. They pointed to both positive and negative aspects of the study and identified relevant information which had been missed. Foremost amongst these were

---

6 The Aboriginal people included Jean Carter, Nick Carter, Joanna Lonesborough, Laurel Carriage, Joey Carriage, Phyllis Carriage, Symalene Carriage, Stan Carriage, Jack Carriage, Keith Nye, David Nye, Gladys Nye, Danny Chapman, Kevin Mason, Ron Mason Snr and Jnr, Vivian Mason, Leo Ritchie, Betty Gill, Alan Brierly, Thomas Brierly and John Brierly.

the genealogies and ethnographic notes made by Norman Tindale at Wallaga Lake in the late 1930s. These were held by the South Australian Museum, which kindly copied and sent the relevant family trees a few days before the court hearing in March 1993.

A summary of the material presented to the court

The material presented to the court focused on the prehistoric evidence for abalone collection and the historic evidence for fishing amongst the defendants living on the South Coast of New South Wales. The archaeological evidence demonstrated that abalone consumption was moderately important in precontact coastal societies on the South Coast and that abalone had been harvested for the last 3,000—4,000 years at Currarong and into the historic era at Durras North (Colley 1992:10).

More recent investigations (not presented to the court) of coastal archaeological sites around the nation indicate that abalone collection is a stronger, more dominant feature of the archaeological record in southern New South Wales than anywhere else in the country with the exception of coastal Tasmania and some sites in western Victoria. The earliest evidence for abalone collection comes from the Nullarbor Plain, some 12,000–16,000 years ago (Cane 1995, 1996).

The archaeological evidence from the South Coast also points to a mixed and intensified exploitation of the sea. This contrasts with the situation in northern New South Wales, where marine exploitation was more selective, and in neighbouring Victoria, where marine exploita-tion appears to have been secondary to the exploitation of the coastal plain (Bailey 1975; McBryde 1982; Gaughwin 1981; Frankel *et al.* 1989; Cane 1995).

On the South Coast of New South Wales the settlement pattern was semi-nomadic with some movement inland (Poiner 1976:199). Exploitation of the coast intensified over the last 2,000 years with evi-dence of overexploitation of local shellfish resources in some areas

(Burrill Lake and Currarong; Lampert 1971:61) and a shift from open shore to estuarine shellfish between 1,200 and 700 years ago (Sullivan 1987:97). This change was accompanied by an increase in the range and quantity of littoral resources exploited (Sullivan 1984).

Primary marine resources included shellfish, fish, seabirds and mammals. The technology used to obtain these food items included shell blades (for prizing shell fish from rocks), canoes, shell fishhooks, spears with bone points, hoop nets, traps and weirs (made of branches), baskets for storage, torch light for night fishing and poisons from various plants (Lawrence 1968; Nicholson and Cane 1994).

A significant aspect of the prehistoric and protohistoric economic record is that fishing generally, as distinct from abalone collection specifically, was the key economic activity in South Coast communities. As mentioned in the original report:

> ...fishing was an important economic activity in which abalone collection was an integral part ... it is illustrative to note that during the two weeks spent collecting information for this paper I observed one family collecting small numbers of abalone for food, yet also observed members of the same family collect two loads of salmon, one three and a half tonnes and the other just over three tonnes. Clearly the difference in magnitude is very great...In this sense the traditional relevance of various components of the fishing economy have not seen drastic change in Aboriginal society. What has changed is European perceptions of a small and now scarce component of that larger economic base (Cane 1992a:2,3).

The earliest historic observations of traditional fishing on the South Coast come from mariners between 1798 and 1826. They speak of the great desire of indigenous people for fish, observed the remain of fish and seals at Aboriginal camps and saw them actively involved in European-like fishing practices, notably netting, a tradition they already practised with their own nets, and which is still active today (Plate 1: Collins 1798; Grant 1801 and D'Urville 1826, quoted in Cane 1987:32, 33; Roseman 1987:61; also Lawrence 1968; White 1987).

Land-based settlement after this period—through to the 1840s—brought territorial conflict, warfare, massacre and poisoning of the people on the South Coast. There is reliable evidence that people were successful in maintaining and adapting traditions to the new economic circumstances (Cameron 1987; Rose 1990). Tribal people were recorded assisting the settlement process with traditional skills and resources. A resident in Moruya noted, in 1837, that 'shortage (of food) was at times acute. Aboriginal people saved the settlement several times from starvation by supplying fish and oysters' (in Cameron 1987:78). Whether or not these products were bartered or sold is unclear, but it is clear that traditional foods were being sold later in the century: 'about 50 blacks were camped at Blackfellows Lake, on the Bega River between Bega and Tathra, some of who worked for wages and some sold honey and fish' (in Cameron 1987:78). The application of Aboriginal fishing traditions to support the European economy seems to have begun shortly after colonisation and survives today, through bartering and direct sale. Many of the defendants have no independent income and regularly trade fish, abalone and crayfish for meat and other goods.

Aboriginal men and women were involved in the European whaling industry from the outset, although it is unknown whether they received money or goods for their labour. Two boats were ' manned entirely by Aborigines' at Twofold Bay in 1839 (Letter to Colonial Secretary, quoted in Organ 1990:246) and three Aboriginal crews were working in Eden in 1844. One elderly Aboriginal man in the region adopted the name of the famous artist and whaler Sir Walter Oswald Brierly, and was actively involved in whaling in the 1840s (Mead 1985; Davidson 1986). One of his descendants, Allan Brierly, was a defendant in this case.

Between 1829 and 1846 indigenous people between Wollongong and Broulee were described as selling fish and subsisting 'from their ordinary pursuits of hunting and fishing' (Organ 1990:282) and, as access to land diminished in the 1840s through settlement, forestry and pastoral developments, 'people in the district (Broulee) depend more on the sea than the bush for food' (Census information for 1846, in Organ 1990:284, 285).

A formal request to the New South Wales Government by Aboriginal people for fishing boats occurred in 1876 and, by 1878, people in Roseby Park, Bega, Eden and Moruya were fishing with government boats and equipment. Census information reveals that indigenous people in Moruya were described as 'remarkably well off and can earn the same wages as Europeans' with income earned from four fishing boats (Bayley 1975:122; Organ 1990:336, 340, 342).

Between 1885 and 1905, a number of reserves were set up between Milton, Tomakin, Tuross and Wallaga Lake on the South Coast.[7] These were 'intended as a residential base from which to fish' (Goodall 1982:34, 43). People also began to get seasonal work with farmers, such as small fruit and pea farmers. Others worked in timber mills. Most continued to subsist through fishing and the government provided another 18 boats to South Coast people (Goodall 1982:43, 58).

Life at the end of last century was captured through the eyes of an Aboriginal artist, Mickey the Cripple, at Ulladulla. His painting reflects camp life, ceremonial activity and the getting of traditional foods. The most relevant paintings in the context of this paper feature sailing ships, fish, fishing boats and fishing. The paintings conveys the broad focus of Aboriginal interests and activities at this time, and imply that at least half of their customary interests centred on the sea (see Sayers 1994: colour plates 15,16,17,19,20).

A number of the families of the defendants appear in the historical record during the early years of settlement. The Carter family, for example, were living in the Cobargo district, 'when white man first came around'[8], probably the 1820s. They were also among the first people at Wreck Bay (under the name Hadigadi, see Egloff 1981).

7   Reserves notified on the South Coast included: Dalmeny (1861), Moruya (1875), four at Tuross Lake (1878–1880), Birroul Lake (1877), Tomakin (1884), Wallaga Lake (1891), Tathra (1893), Ulladulla (1892), two at Roseby Park (1900), Batemans Bay (1902), Narooma (1913), Jervis Bay (1917), Wreck Bay (1930s), four at Wallaga Lake (1906,1909,1931,1949) (Thomson 1979).

8   Recorded by N. Tindale at Wallaga Lake, 3/1/1939.

The Stewart family are first recorded on the South Coast in the mid-1800s. Their children were born at Wallaga Lake in the 1870s[9] and lived at Corunna Lake near Narooma in 1892[10], exactly 100 years before their descendant, Andrew Stewart, was arrested for poaching.

The Carriage family were at Batemans Bay before the 1850s, and family members are recorded in marriage and birth in 1859, 1863, 1869 and 1899[11]. The family did not move from Batemans Bay and Joey Carriage was arrested in the area in 1992.

The early members of the Mason family were living at Bega in 1867 and and eastern Victoria in 1887. At this time the family were recorded 'getting native food like swans eggs, black fish ... and luderick'[12] (Pepper 1980:75–77).

During and after the First World War, South Coast families had very little employment opportunities and depended heavily on fishing. Fish were used for subsistence and sold to market. The commercial success of indigenous fisherman was such that between 1914 and 1918, non-Aboriginal fishermen began to protest through the Fisheries Department to the Aboriginal Protectorate Board. Aboriginal people were seen as a threat to non-Aboriginal fishing livelihoods (Goodall 1982:32, 115, 174).

---

9   K. Stewart was born to 'Governor' Stewart and Bessie Kaine in 1872. He married Emily Walker (born 1974) on 15/7/1892 at Wallaga Lake.

10   V. Mason, oral history transcript 1992.

11   The earliest family members were James Pittman and Jane Nicholson, whose child John Pittman was born at Clyde River in 1859 (d. Batemans Bay 1915). Robert McCauley and Margaret Nicken had a daughter Margaret, born in the Shoalhaven in 1863 (d. Batemans Bay 1924). She married John Pittman and their daughter married Christopher Carriage, son of Eliza Spriggs and Christopher Carriage. Christopher and Eliza's first child was born at Araluen in 1869.

12   Luderick (Paragus auratus) are a school fish that inhabit mangrove lined creeks and estuaries. They are now a commercial fish with an average national annual catch of around 500 tonnes (Kailola et al. 1993).

Pressure was also applied to give land to returned soldiers during this period and 75% of reserve land allocated the previous century was revoked. Eight reserves were revoked on the South Coast. Some near Narooma were still being used as fishing bases (Goodall 1982:227, Plate 3).

The family of the defendant Keith Nye was fishing near Ulladulla and Durras at the turn of the century and at Wreck Bay after the First World War, where they built humpies before the present community was established. The family packed up their boats and nets, and rowed back to Broulee (over 100 km.) as more Aboriginal people came to Wreck Bay.[13] The family then settled near Batemans Bay where they lived in a tin humpy at Tomakin. They were known as beach fisherman (fishing for mullet, salmon, flathead and bream). Members of the Carter family were also living in Wreck Bay, and moved between there and Wallaga Lake. Members of the family fished and collected oysters. They married into the Mason family before the Second World War.

Early members of the Mason line were settled at La Perouse (Kevin Mason) and Batemans Bay (Ronald Mason) at the turn of the century and lived around the South Coast in subsequent decades. All were fishermen in those early years. The family of Kevin Mason subsequently became sleeper-cutters and boxers after the First World War. The family of Ron Mason continued to live at Batemans Bay (Nelligan) after the First World War. They made their own boats and nets and were known by the name 'Katu' or 'Katungil' meaning 'sea people' (also Eades 1976:87). The family adopted the name Cooley around this time in recognition of their association with some Chinese people living nearby.

Members of the Cooley family married into the Stewart family. The Stewarts were also living on the South Coast, but farming and working in the wood mills. The family stayed with the land, subsequently becoming more involved in timber milling than fishing. Two members of the Stewart family also married Carriages. The Carriages are recorded at Pebbly Beach in 1899 and 190, where they are remembered fishing with the Nye family. The Carriage family were still living at Pebbly Beach in

---

13   Oral history, A. MacLeod (1992); also Rose (1976).

1922 and 1925, when members of the family married Stewarts.[14] Four family members were fishing and others had begun working in the mills with the Stewarts.

Throughout this period the Brierly family lived in Eden (and were involved in the moribund whaling industry). In 1922 they moved from Eden to the mouth of the Moruya River, where they remain today. Much of their original land has been resumed to build the Moruya airport, but the local boat ramp is still called Brierly's Landing. The family house overlooks the river mouth. Family members married into the Mason line and become distant relations to the Masons. All the men of the Brierly family were fishermen and one was drowned at sea.

Thus by the Second World War a number of South Coast family connections had been made. Brierlys had married Masons, Masons had married Stewarts, Stewarts had married Carriages, and Carters had married Masons. Some families were heavily involved in fishing: some were not. As a group, however, fishing remained the dominant community means of subsistence. This communal tradition continued throughout the next four decades and ultimately led to the sequential arrest, prosecution and defence of various family members in 1992.

The social and economic situation of the Depression continued for these families after the Second World War. There was a short period of employment near the close of the war (Long 1970), but then people returned to seasonal work—fruit and pea picking, timber cutting and fishing—as regular employment evaporated. The fishing skills of people living on impoverished South Coast settlements were capitalised on by the government, whose policies encouraged 'self supporting fishing stations' like Roseby Park, Wallaga Lake and Wreck Bay.[15] Fishing was the most important source of income for people at Wreck Bay. Three people

14 Compilation of births, deaths and marriages by N. Cregan 1981–2, from the Clyde River and Batemans Bay Historical Society.

15 A photograph in DAWN, a magazine for Aboriginal people of NSW shows Reg MacLeod, Archie Moore and Sam Ardler fishing at Wreck Bay in 1954 (vol. 3, series no. 11).

owned their own boats. Others were involved in the transportation and selling of fish (Long 1970:59).

By and large, however, fishing activity on the South Coast was informal, geared towards subsistence rather than significant economic returns. Aboriginal people were described as having little part in the South Coast fishing industry and as having difficulty managing, financing and maintaining commercial fishing operations. The fishing industry provided limited employment opportunities with most families involved in the same forms of subsistence activities they had practised since settlement: fishing, vegetable picking and forestry work (Scott 1969).

The Carters were living at Wreck Bay through this era. Fishing continued, but the tradition was changing. Boats were bigger and fishing activities went further afield. Eight of the Brierly children fished, for example, but now moved between Eden and Broulee in pursuit of fish for harvest. One family member worked on a trawler, travelling as far as Newcastle and Bass Strait. The family had their own 45–foot boat, but lost it in a flood on the Moruya River. Another of their children died at sea.

The father of the defendant Kevin Mason married into a family from southern Victoria. He fished, but the Victorian family were mostly pea-pickers. Members of the family of Ron Mason married into the next generation of Stewarts, reinforcing existing family connections amongst the Mason, Stewart, Carter and Carriage families. Four members of the Mason family were fishing.

The Carriage family was still living at Batemans Bay. The aunt of Joey Carriage married into the Nye family in 1948. She was the mother of Keith Nye, another defendant in the fishing case. His parents moved to Jervis Bay, camping and fishing for mullet, before travelling to Ulladulla. All the men of the Nye family fished. The seasonal catch was mullet through February and March, blackfish in April, salmon through winter, 'travelling fish' i.e. mullet and salmon, through the spring, and bream at Christmas.

The fishermen were apparently paid a penny per pound for salmon and a shilling for big bream. They caught lobster 'by the bag full', but only took abalone 'for a feed'. This generation 'didn't touch them, got nothing for them'. The father of the defendant Keith Nye apparently liked to eat abalone. Men who fished in that era described working hard and long hours, often rowing their 16–foot boats from Wreck Bay to Ulladulla and East Lynne (over 140 km). The women minded the children, spotted fish, pulled nets, sewed nets and packed boxes of fish.

The Nye family were, by this time, a well established fishing family and lived almost entirely at Barlings Beach, where there was an Aboriginal camp of about eight huts. They spotted fish from a pole and had their own gear and a double ended boat.[16] This tradition continues today with the Nyes being one of the few remaining licensed beach fishermen in NSW.[17]

The father of the defendant Andrew Stewart married one of the Nye family, completing the family connections between all subsequent defendants. All the Stewarts were timber workers at this stage.

The last thirty years have seen increased documentary evidence of Aboriginal life on the South Coast. Local people have collected much of this themselves sporadically between 1965 and 1992.[18] This information reveals an attenuated core of language and mythology, but highlights the significance of the sea in that remnant body of original

16   A detailed account of the fishing interest and enterprises of the Nye family is given in Rose (1976).

17   Licences to fish became available in the 1940s. At the time, the licenses were valued at the equivalent of $5. Many people fished without a license and many of those with licences lost them as fees increased to $300–$500 through the 1960s. The Nyes maintained licences for four rowing boats and three nets: garfish, prawn and 'beachfish' (salmon and mullet).

18   1965: Frank Cooper—Browns Flat; Ernie Andy—Bega, Percy Davis—Batemans Bay; Dave Carpenter—Roseby Park; Walter Davis, Walter Brierly and Des Picalla—Bega. 1966: Arthur Thomas—Wallaga Lake; Percy Mumbulla—Tomerong; Sid Duncan—Nowra.

knowledge. Twenty-two words survive which are associated with the sea and its exploitable content. Remnant myths are also documented, the most significant of them relate to the sea and the coast (Eades 1976; Rose 1990). Twelve personal histories[19] have also been recorded over the last 35 years which portray coastal life, fishing exploits, seasonal movement, school fishing, night fishing, prawning, crabbing (for bait), lobster collection, shellfish collection (pipis, mussels, oysters and abalone), spearfishing, spear construction and identify a variety of fishing spots between Wallaga Lake and Wreck Bay.

These local accounts are supported by more detailed investigations of language, community histories, economic activity, expressions of Aboriginality and cultural heritage. Themes of the sea pervade these accounts (Bell 1965; Scott 1969; Eades 1976; Rose 1976; Attenbrow 1976; Poiner 1976; Carter 1984; Cane 1987). They indicate that fishing remained an important means of subsisting and earning money. Salmon fishing was still a dominant activity with over 100 tonnes being landed in one month during spring in the late 1980s.[20] These sold for around $700 a tonne i.e. $70,000 for the monthly haul.

The need to fish and the assumed right to fish continued throughout the period. Members of the South Coast community requested that their customary fishing rights be recognised and in 1980 a Select Committee of the Legislative Assembly recommended legislation be

---

19   1965: Percy Davis, Batemans Bay; Charlie Parsons, Wallaga Lake; Herbert Chapman, Wreck Bay; Dave Carpenter, Roseby Park.
1990: Col Walker—Nowra.
1991: Amy Williams—Wreck Bay.
1992: Mary Duroux—Moruya; Barbara Roach—Moruya; Muriel Chapman—Batemans Bay; Leo Mason—Narooma; Shirley Foster; Brenda Ardler—Wreck Bay (no date).

20   An undated newspaper clipping reads 'Salmon are running on the coast... 24 tonnes was netted off North Congo by the Nye and Jessop brothers. They dragged in over 100 tonnes for the last October, 56 tonnes in one haul and the cannery pays $700 a tonne' (value of 56 tonnes—$39,200).

enacted to do so (1980:87). Individuals continued to openly breach Crown Law in spite of the cumulative risks. Breaches escalated consistently over the last 20 years. One defendant has been arrested 12 times and has spent 45 days in jail. The regularity with which the offences have occurred says something about individual economic need, resistance to fishing regulations, and the conviction and belief in the community's historic traditional right to fish. A brief summary of the present situation follows.

The Nyes are recognised by both long-term Aboriginal and non-Aboriginal residents of the South Coast as an established fishing family. All the male members of the family fish. The defendant, Keith Nye, grew up at Barlings Beach, dropped out of school and went fishing. He fished with his father's gear until his father died. Keith lost interest for a while and his gear was taken over by his first cousin (his 'brother' in Aboriginal custom). Keith remained unemployed and returned to free diving[21] and line fishing, selling fish for money and trading it for food. He has been diving for 17 of his 35 years. He was arrested with 12 abalone (see Figure 4:2).

Joey Carriage has fished and harvested abalone most of his life. He sold abalone for six pence a pound in his youth. His nickname is Snapper, after his grandfather,[22] with whom he fished as a child. His mother is Keith Nye's aunt and Joey has often fished and cleaned abalone with the Nyes. He was arrested with 97 kg of abalone (possibly worth $10,000 if sold) in the company of Nick Carter and Andrew Stewart.

---

21 I dived with Keith one afternoon near Rosedale during this study. We both dived while his wife sat on the shore minding three children, observing our progress and being on hand to take any catch. Keith Nye found eight crayfish amongst the weed in a gathering landscape that appeared over fished and barren. He demonstrated excellent water skills, marine knowledge and gathering ability, comparable to the knowledge and skills I have seen in 18 years of working with indigenous people in the Western Desert.

22 Who caught a snapper on a piece of string as a child.

Nick Carter was born in Berry and went to school in Jervis Bay. Nick is also a fisherman, having travelled to Darwin to work on the prawn trawlers. He has been unemployed since his return and now fishes between Wreck Bay and Batemans Bay. His wife is the daughter of a fisherman from Roseby Park.

The mother of Andrew Stewart is also a Nye. Andrew works primarily as a timber miller and was arrested with 39 abalone.

Allan Brierly grew up at Moruya and spent most of his life at sea. He could row a boat at the age of three and was taken out of school by his father 'to work with fishing boats'. He is a licensed fisherman and still lives with and works for his father, under the direction of his eldest brother. The family have their own gear: freezers, boats, vehicles and nets. He was arrested with undersized lobster.

Kevin Mason was also born at Berry. His father described him as 'mad on mutton fish' (abalone) as a child. The family were poor and Kevin gathered 'goanna. porcupine and abalone' in his childhood. He travelled with his father, fishing between Bermagui and Cape Conran. He then worked in Sydney before returning to the South Coast. He is well known and liked in the region. His nickname is the Phantom because of his elusive and independent personality. He is a well known fisherman, and has a number of legendary fishing exploits attributed to him (shark attacks and the like). Two of his three brothers are fishermen. He was facing seven charges accrued between 1991 and 1992 for over 200 abalone, 18 litres of edible mussels and failing to comply with and threatening a fisheries' officer.

His nephew is Ron Mason, the defendant whose case was tried in court. Ron was 26 years old at the time. He first dived at the age of five, has worked primarily as a deckhand on fishing boats and now has a Class Five skipper's ticket. Ron was arrested with 92 abalone. All his gear was taken by the Fisheries Inspector and he was publicly stripped down to his underwear in the main street of town.[23]

---

23   See the statement of Ron Mason in relation to Summons (2) before

The hearings and their outcomes

The hearing for Ronald Mason took place in the Magistrate's Court in Sydney on 1 March 1993. I found the cross-examination a trying and confusing process, bearing out the fears of the defendants and their legal representatives that the court is a tense, hostile and disempowering environment, draped in ethnocentric bias, shrouded in mystifying technicalities and fortified by adversarial processes.[24]

The issues addressed in the process of cross-examination related to the area in which the charges took place, whether or not the defendant was a member of the South Coast Aboriginal community of that area, the role of fishing in traditional society, the history of disputation amongst tribal groups in respect of the right to fish, the nature of post-colonial evidence for the assertion of fishing rights to a particular area, the nature of fishing customs and the exclusive nature of those customs.[25]

Two months later the Magistrate handed down his decision on the evidence and arguments put before him. His key determination was that:

> I am satisfied that the following facts have been established. Firstly that the defendant is an aboriginal (sic) and a descendant of the Mason family whose members have inhabited the South Coast area of New South Wales since the eighteen eighties and second that the Mason family, together with a number of other aboriginal families have traditionally fished those coastal waters for abalone as a major source of food, however there is in my view a factual question which arises in this case, namely whether the defendant was in fact ex-

the Downing Street Local Court Thursday 23rd April 1992. page 2. The inspector took his flippers, bootees, wetsuit top and bottom, goggles, snorkel, knife, netbag and weight belt.

24 See McCallum (1993) for a comprehensive account of the power imbalance between Aboriginal claimants and Governments.

25 Transcript: Triton vs R. G. Mason, Downing Centre 1 March 1993.

ercising a customary or traditional right on 9 October 1991 when he shucked and then possessed 92 abalone. As I have already said the defendant did not give evidence in this case and therefore there is no evidence before me as to the defendant's intentions in relation to the subject abalone. In other words there is no evidence that the defendant either intended to consume the abalone himself or to make mem available for consumption by the immediate members of his family or to exchange them for other food. Accordingly I am not satisfied that the defendant has established as a matter of fact that he was exercising a customary right to fish for abalone on 9 October 1991 (Clugston 1993:3).

The Magistrate thus accepted the traditional right of the defendant to fish, but was not convinced Mason was practising that right at the time of his arrest. The obvious question that arises from this observation is that if the defendant was not exercising a traditional right, then what right was he exercising? The implicit answer is that the defendant was exercising a commercial right, although there was no evidence before the Magistrate that this was the case either. So the question hangs in the balance. A traditional right appears to exist, but the defendant appears not to have been practising it. Is this a legitimate verdict? Should Mason have taken the stand? What would have been the result if Mason had stated the abalone were for himself and his immediate family? What would have been the Magistrate's determination if Mason was intending to sell them—as had been the historic practice of his people for the last 150 years?

The Magistrate then went on to consider whether or not the right asserted by the defendant was a land right or usufructuary right recognised by Australian common law. He concluded that 'a customary right to harvest abalone is not linked to any claim for native title to the submerged lands adjacent to the South Coast of New South Wales' and that the:

decision of the High Court in Mabo Number 2 does not support the proposition that the common law now recognises customary aboriginal (sic) fishing rights such that a claimed

> right must first be extinguished by legislation before an ab-
> original exercising such a right is obliged to comply with leg-
> islation effecting that right (Clugston 1993:4).

Mr Justice Young of the New South Wales Supreme Court[26] was less sympathetic to Mason's case than the Magistrate. He compared 'native peoples' with a 'type of primitive company', contrasted the traditional rights claimed on the South Coast with those of the Cook Islands,[27] denied the existence of both proprietary and usufructuary rights, considered the latter to have as much real property value as a 'title of honour or an advowson' and indicated that he believed the current legislation did not discriminate against Aboriginal people because it was established to regulate the activities and competing rights of 'all people'.

His judgment concluded that the evidence presented to the Magistrate's Court failed to disclose a 'group of people living in community who had settled rights and privileges under a system of laws and customs which they all respected' (Chalk 1993:1). Further Mason was not, apparently, a biological descendant or connected with the relevant Aboriginal people who once exercised traditional and customary rights on the South Coast of New South Wales.[28]

This judgment is also interesting as it raises the issue of the existence of a commercial right to fish as against a traditional right to fish. Justice Young's assessment was that the expansion of a traditional right to fish for subsistence to a right to fish for commercial gain 'would be such an expansion of the right as to be a different right'. He admitted the 'line may be difficult to draw' but observed 'it is often easy to recognise when that line has been crossed' (Young 1993:21,22). He did not say

---

26 Supreme Court of New South Wales Common Law Division: Mason v Triton: Coram J. Young: Hearing Sept. 1993, judgment Oct. 1993: pages 1–35.

27 The source referred to by Justice Young is quoted as Crocombe's *Land Tenure in the Cook Islands* (Oxford University Press 1964).

28 Account of Supreme Court ruling as summarised in Kirby P. Supreme Court of New South Wales, Court of Appeal, Mason v Triton, August 1994:4.

when that line might have been crossed, but he obviously believed it had been. A logical inference is that the decisive crossing took place when indigenous people first began selling fish early in the last century, as the South Coast was just being colonised. If so, it is hard to accept that Aboriginal fishing traditions on the South Coast ended before European settlement, let alone European customs, had taken hold in southern New South Wales.

Following the failure of the appeal before the Supreme Court, another appeal was lodged to the Court of Appeal. This appeal centred on the interpretation of usufructuary practices, the existence and nature of native title, the exclusivity of that traditional right, the nature of evidence for traditional fishing, the content of the traditional right and whether or not the appellant was exercising a traditional right (Roberts and Katz 1994).

The Court of Appeal dismissed the appeal due to a lack of evidence.[29] The primary deficiency in the evidence appears to have been that the defendant did not give personal testimony as to whether or not he was practising his traditional right at the time of arrest. Justice Kirby (1994:26) develops the point as follows:

> Why, I therefore ask myself...did Mr. Mason not give evidence that he was collecting the abalone in question within the ambit of the traditional and long practiced native entitlement which he set out to prove? He went to so much trouble to establish his genealogical legitimacy and the relevant practice of Aboriginal fishing for abalone back to the 1880s. Why would he fail to complete the chain of relevant evidence by the next logical step of bringing himself and his actions within that practice...he left unproved a vital link in respect of which the evidentiary or forensic onus was certainly on him. I cannot believe, in a case otherwise so well prepared and presented, that this was an accident or oversight. The only other inference available is that Mr. Mason's evidence, if it had been called, could not have supported his claim that

---

29   Court of Appeal Record Sheet: File no/s: Ca 40620/93; CT 12048/93: Gleeson C. J., Kirby P., and Priestley J. A. August 1994.

what he was doing at the time of his apprehension was in exercise of his native title rights as an Aboriginal Australian. For example, that it was for sale of the abalone to the general commercial fish market... That was fatal to the appellant's attempt to prove his exemption from the operation of the regulation.

This position is the same as that reached by the Magistrate. It is a position that was disputed by the counsel for the appellant who countered that:

If there was a right to take abalone for any purpose...then the appellant's intentions were irrelevant. If, on the other hand, the traditional right was limited in the way suggested by the Magistrate, then oral evidence by the defendant was not the only way in which his intention could be established. The prosecution evidence itself established that the abalone had been taken for non-commercial purposes: the abalone were shucked on the shore immediately after taking and then transported by the appellant to his residence, the appellant being a member of the group which traditionally took abalone for food (Roberts and Katz 1994:9).

It is clear with hindsight that even if the abalone were collected with commercial intent,[30] an argument may have been mounted that this fell within the ambit of contemporary traditional practice. There was, it is now clear, no particular advantage (as the ruling from the Court of Appeal suggests) in hiding the possibility. A commercial right may have been successfully argued and its presentation would certainly have placed the issue on the table for future resolution.

One of the judgments from the Court of Appeal queried the strength of the evidence supporting the broader claim for traditional rights. One judge observed that 'more needed to be proved to comply with the requirements' of native title (Priestley 1994:12). As the historical records are scanty and rarely provide enough detailed information to connect a specific family with their traditional and customary activity

---

30 The abalone were probably worth between $1,000 and $2,000.

consistently through history in a particular geographic location there may be difficulties in this regard. The evidence for the association of the Mason family with the South Coast and traditional fishing activities was not, in my opinion, the strongest amongst the men charged, but it was reasonably comprehensive nonetheless. This difficulty was identified in Cane (1992b) and recognised in Kirby (1994:19).

Yet not all the judges were of the same opinion as to the strength of the written evidence. Justice Kirby (1994:34) for example, observed:

> The appellant, in my view, sufficiently established, by evidence of others, his genealogy as descended from Aboriginal Australia. He sufficiently established that his forebears traditionally fished, including for abalone... (but) held back from giving evidence that the abalone which he himself had been fishing... were within his asserted native title right.

The concern, however, from an ethnographic (if not legal) perspective is that the Magistrate in the Local Court and some of the judges in the Court of Appeal appear to have missed some of the evidence that was put before them. They may thus not have given Mason's traditional rights the recognition and consideration they were due. Determinations from both courts refer to the Mason line extending back to the 1880s, whereas in fact it extends back to (and beyond) the 1860s. Both refer to R. Mason as follows:

> He is a descendant of the Mason family, tracing to Paddy Sims (sic) who originally came from the La Perouse area and who I quote, 'apparently did a bit of fishing and lived off rations and either lived on or fished at Bear Island' (sic). The Mason line is coastal with part of the family emerging from the coastal districts of Victoria between the Cann River and Bairnsdale and the rest from the Illawarra Region, Nowra to La Perouse (in Clugston 1993:2; Kirby 1994:17).

This reference is slightly misquoted but, more importantly, refers to the family of *K*. Mason—another of the defendants—not R. Mason, the defendant before the court. K. Mason is R. Mason's uncle. K. Mason's brother and R. (Ron) Mason's father is also called R. (Ron) Mason, so one can understand the confusion. But this hardly excuses a failure to correctly address the evidence.

The family of K. Mason are related to Paddy Simms and spreads from south Sydney to Eastern Victoria (as referred to in the judgments) while the family of R. Mason relates to the Stewart family and concentrates more closely on the South Coast (and not referenced in the judgments). There is an indirect connection between R. Mason (defendant) and Paddy Simms on his father's side, but this is only part of the story.[31] The name Mason is taken from Ron's grandmother's first husband. Little is known about him except that he was a sailor, died, and had no relationship to Paddy Simms. Ron's grandfather then married a Ritchie but all the children kept the name Mason. So some children are actually Ritchie (such as K. Mason) and are descendants of Paddy Simms (about 1880) and others (R. Mason) are not.

More significantly Ron Mason is related, through his mother (Ella), to the Sutton, Cooley, Walker, Kaine and Stewart families, all of which were more involved with the sea and fishing activities than the Ritchie-Simms family line. Thus the failure of the judges and the magistrate to recognise a fishing tradition among the Mason (Simms) line is in error. The judges in the Court of Appeal either missed, misread or failed to refer to the evidence in relation to the key, maternal, side of the family of R. Mason. The presentation of and references to the ethnographic material strongly suggest that the judges (and magistrate) made a determination on evidence for the wrong person.

---

31 See section 5. of Cane 1992a for K. Mason and Section 1. of Cane 1992b for the defendant, R. Mason. The relationship was also discussed in cross examination and purposefully summarised for the Local Court (Table 2).

Figure 4:3: Family chronologies as summarised for the Magistrate in 1993

Period	K. Mason	R. Mason
pre 1880		South Coast, through Stewart (Kaine, Walker, Austin; Narooma area).
1900	Simms:[1] fisherman, La Perouse.	Ella (English), marries Simms[2] (La Peruse). Stewart marries Walker (Wallaga Lake/Narooma).
1920	Ritchie marries Simms (who marries Ryan, fisherman, La Perouse). Son Ritchie with Mclennan (with Simms; fisherman, La Perouse, then Stewart: part fisherman, Wallaga Lake).	Ella marries Sutton (Roseby Park, Jervis Bay), related to Carter (Ardler (?),Timbery); fishing families from South Coast.
1940	Ritchie (fisherman) marries Thomas (then Mason, sailor) from Lake Tyres; subsistence and field work Carter; South Coast fishing families; 3	Ella (Wreck Bay) marries Stewart (Nowra), related to Timbery Cooley (Carriage, Brierly) and Ella's fishing.
Present	Mason; fishing, South Coast, related to Ella (Stewart, Cooley); 3 fishermen Carter, Stewart, Cooley, Brierly,	Mason (Nowra), marries Ella (Wollongong); 6 family members fish, 2 children fish. Related to fishing families; Timbery, Williams.

Conclusion

Reflecting upon the experiences of this South Coast fishing case, one cannot help but ask how things might have been done differently. What

---

32 Paddy Simms.

33 Tinnie Simms (woman).

can be learnt from the experience? By asking these questions, however, one is implicitly asking how, in other circumstance, might the fishing rights case on the South Coast of New South Wales have been won.

The determinations by the courts indicate that sufficient evidence was provided to have 'established the ingredients necessary *in law* to succeed in a claim for native title in respect of a right to fish' (Kirby 1994:33, his emphasis) although I believe a stronger case could have been made if more time had been available and we had had a better understanding of the requirements for proving native title.

Should I have undertaken the investigation, given the time constraints? One is inclined to say no, but it is one thing to stand on the professional high ground and contemplate what should be done and how others might do it, and it is another to be confronted by seven defiant and tense men who are about to face court and, in at least one case, a possible jail term. Nevertheless, there is a lesson to be learnt for the future. There is a greater advantage in having one's ethnographic material in order before a case goes to court than in having to prepare it with the date of the court case fixed and imminent.

As it was, of course, none of these considerations may have influenced the outcome of the case greatly. The primary problem for the task of determining the presence or absence of a traditional right to fish was that the defendant 'failed to provide sufficient *evidence* to *prove* that he actually had been exercising such a native title' at the time of his arrest (Kirby 1994:33 his emphasis). It is absolutely clear that in future the defendants or the applicants must be in the witness box. The second issue is that more attention should have been given to the formal descriptions of the traditions and rights claimed and to the nature of the group that held them, as Kirby's judgement makes clear.

As a final comment I should say, my original impression of the case was one of suspicion and misgiving with respect to the alleged traditional right to harvest abalone. But after tracing the historical experiences, family connections and geographic association of the families involved in the case, my view changed. One cannot but help being struck by the tenacity with which the tradition of fishing has been maintained throughout the historical experiences of the last 150 years on the South Coast. The evidence indicates that, in one of the most settled parts of Australia, with one of the longest histories of European settlement, there is a continutity of Aboriginal fishing practices and traditions traceable back to the earliest historic period.

The traditions and practice today are clearly different to those in existence before contact but moulded by and adapted to, rather than being washed away by, the great changes in social and environmental circumstances.

While many would perceive the process of historic change as considerably weakening, if not destroying the original traditions, I would argue that these historic experiences have in fact given fishing an added significance. They are the very core of present day tradtion and community association with that tradition is as strong today as ever. Further while any exclusive rights associated with the original tradition may have expired, commercial rights associated with the historic tradition have emerged in their place.

In conclusion, the resultant history and associations of people and fishing on the South Coast appears to have broad concurrence with the general propositions of native title (Brennan in *Mabo v Queensland (No. 2)*: 50). The research reported on indicates that the defendants are indigenous people, the biological descendants of an indigenous group who exercised traditional and customary fishing rights on the South Coast of New South Wales. Although the customs of the group have changed over time, the tradition of fishing has not been abandoned.

The local Aboriginal community may find it difficult to understand how a member of a group whose native title rights can be proven in law and who has a demonstrable biological, historical, geographic and cultural association with that group can be acting outside the traditions of that group. The knowledge of their right to fish seems ingrained in the fishing families on the South Coast and contemporary pressures on this right seems to have created a stronger than ever determination to protect it. There appears to be a strong sense of injustice within the Aboriginal community in reaction to European perceptions and regulation of that right. The defendants see themselves as victims of a hostile social and commercial environment. They would argue that what was once a prehistoric economic activity (*viz.* the taking of abalone) and then a necessary historic component of their subsistence economy is now an illegal activity. History will judge: all one can do in the meantime is collect the relevant information as faithfully as possible and let the judicial system make its determination. In the meantime one can almost guarantee that resistance to and infringements of the common law will continue until the traditional right is recognised and steps are taken to accommodate it.

References

Attenbrow, V. 1976. Aboriginal subsistence economy on the far south coast of NSW, Australia. BA (Hons) thesis. Sydney: University of Sydney.

Bailey, G.N. 1975. The role of molluscs in coastal economies and the results of midden analysis in Australia. *Journal of Archaeological Science* 2: 45–62.

Bayley, W.A. 1965. *History of the Shoalhaven*. Nowra: Shoalhaven Shire Council.

Bell, J.H. 1956. The economic life of mixed blood Aborigines on the south coast of New South Wales. *Oceania* 26: 181–189.

Bowdler, S. 1995. Offshore islands and maritime explorations in Australian prehistory. *Antiquity* 69(266): 945–958.

Brennan, J. 1992. Mabo v the State of Queensland (No.2) June 1992 High Court of Australia, copy of the court's reasons for judgment prior to formal revision and publication. Canberra: High Court.

Cane, S.B. 1987. *An archaeological and anthropological investigation of the armament depot complex in Jervis Bay, NSW*. Report to the Department of Housing and Construction, ACT. Canberra: Anutech.

1992a. *Aboriginal fishing on the south coast of NSW*. A report to Blake Dawson and Waldron, and the NSW Land Council.

1992b. *Aboriginal fishing on the south coast of NSW: a supplementary report to Blake Dawson and Waldron, and the NSW Land Council.*

1995. *Nullarbor antiquity: archaeological, luminescent and seismic investigation on the Nullarbor Plain.* A report to the National Estate Grants Program, Australian Heritage Commission, ACT.

1996. *A coastal heritage, site gazetteer.* Draft manuscript to the National Estate Grants Program, Australian Heritage Commission, ACT.

Cameron, S.B. 1987. *An investigation of the history of the Aborigines of the far south coast of NSW in the nineteenth century.* BLetts thesis, Australian National University.

Carter, J. 1984. *Aboriginality: the affirmation of cultural identity in settled Australia.* MA thesis, Australian National University.

Chalk, A. 1993. Mason v Triton—south coast fishing rights. Horowitz and Bilinsky, solicitors, Sydney; fax—23 October 1993.

Clugston, R. 1993. *New South Wales v R.G. Mason, transcript no 181a/93.* Sydney: Local Court Sutherland.

Colley, S. 1992. *Archaeological evidence for abalone fishing by Aboriginal people on the NSW south coast.* Report to Blake Dawson and Waldron.

Court of Appeal 1994. Mason v Triton, record sheet and determinations by C.J. Gleeson, P. Kirby and J.A. Priestly. File nos. Ca 40620/93: C112048/93.

Davidson, R. 1988. *Whalemen of Twofold Bay.* Canberra: Pirie Printers.

Dawn Magazine. 1954:3(11).

Eades, D. 1976. *The Dharawal and Dhurga languages of the NSW south coast.* Canberra: Australian Institute of Aboriginal Studies.

Egloff, B.J. 1981. *Wreck Bay: an Aboriginal Fishing Village*. Canberra: Australian Institute of Aboriginal Studies.

1992. A draft report on the significance of coastal maritime resources for Aboriginal communities on the south coast of New South Wales to the South Coast Regional Aboriginal Land Council, and Blake Dawson and Waldron.

1993. *Aboriginal fishing on the south coast of New South Wales*. University of Canberra.

Frankel, D., D. Gaughwin, C. Bird and R. Hall 1989. Coastal archaeology in south Gippsland. *Australian Archaeology* 28:14–25.

Gaughwin, D. 1981. *Sites of archaeological significance in the Westernport catchment*. Ministry for Conservation, Victoria.

Goodall, H. 1982. The history of Aboriginal communities in NSW, 1909–1939. PhD thesis. Canberra: Department of History, Australian National Univeristy.

Kailola, P.J., M.J. Williams, P.C. Stewart, R.E. Reichelt, A. McNee, and C. Grieve 1993. *Australian fisheries resources*. Canberra: Bureau of Resource Science and the Fisheries Research Development Corporation.

Kirby, P. Court of Appeal: Mason v Triton. File nos. Ca 40620/93: C112048/93.

Lampert, R. 1971. Burrill Lake and Currarong: coastal sites in southern New South Wales. *Terra Australis*, 1. Canberra: Australian National University, ACT.

Lawrence, R. 1968. *Aboriginal habitat and economy*. Canberra: Department of Geography, Australian National University.

Legislative Assembly 1980. *The first report from the select committee of the Legislative Assembly upon Aborigines, Part 1*. Government Printer NSW.

Long, J. 1970. *Aborigines and settlements: a survey of institutional communities in eastern Australia*. Canberra: Australian National University Press.

McCallum, A.G. 1993. Dispute resolution mechanisms in the resolution of comprehensive Aboriginal claims: power imbalance between Aboriginal claimants and governments. Master of Laws, York University, Ontario.

McBryde, I. 1982. *Coast and estuary: archaeological investigations on the north coast of New South Wales*. Canberra: Australian Institute of Aboriginal Studies.

Mead, T. 1985. *The killers of Eden*. Sydney: Angus and Robertson.

Nicholson, A. and S.B. Cane 1994. Pre-European settlement and use of the sea. *Australian Archaeology* 39:108–118.

Organ, M. 1990. *A documentary history of the Illawarra and south coast Aborigines, 1770–1850*. Aboriginal Education Unit, Wollongong University.

Pepper, P. 1980. *You are what you make yourself to be. The story of a Victorian Aboriginal family 1842–1980*. Melbourne: Hyland House.

Poiner, G. 1976. The process of the year among Aborigines of the central and south coasts of NSW. *APAO* 11(3):186–206.

Priestley, J.A. 1994. Court of Appeal: Mason v Triton, File nos. Ca 40620/93: C112048/93.

Read, P. 1988. *The Hundred Years War*. Canberra: ANU Press.

Roberts, P. and L. Katz 1994. Mason v Triton written submission of appellant for the Court of Appeal.

Rose, L. (ed.) 1976. A quiet revolution in Mogo—an account of an Aboriginal community. Unpublished manuscript.

Rose, D. 1990. *Gulaga: a report on the cultural significance of the dreaming to Aboriginal people*. Sydney: Forestry Commission, NSW.

Roseman, H. 1957. *The voyage to the south seas by Jules S.C. Dumont D'Urville*. Translated by Roseman. Melbourne: Melbourne University Press.

Sayers, A. 1994. *Aboriginal artists of the nineteenth century*. Melbourne : Oxford University Press.

Scott, W.D. and Co. 1969. Report on a reconnaissance of means of Aboriginal advancement on the south coast of New South Wales. Sydney: Scott and Company.

Sullivan, M.E. 1984. A shell midden excavation at Pambula Lake on the far south coast of New South Wales. *Archaeology in Oceania* 19(1):1–15.

1987. The recent prehistoric exploitation of edible mussel in Aboriginal shell middens in southern New South Wales. *Archaeology in Oceania* 22:97–105.

Sutton, P. 1993. Aboriginal fishing rights on the New South Wales south coast. A review for Horowitz and Bilinsky, solicitors, Sydney, NSW.

Tindale, N. 1939. Field genealogies, held with the South Australian Museum Adelaide.

Thomson, S. 1979. Land alienation and land rights: a preliminary social history of south coast Aboriginal communities. BA (Hons) thesis. Armidale: University of New England.

White, D. 1987. Aboriginal subsistence and environmental history in the Burrill Lakes region, NSW. Unpublished BA (Hons) thesis. Canberra: Australian National University.

Wright, D. 1987. Aboriginal subsistence and environment in the Burrill Lake region, NSW. BA (Hons) thesis. Canberra: Australian National University.

Young, J. 1993. Judgment on Mason v Triton, Supreme Court of New South Wales, Common Law Division. Proceedings number 12048 of 1993.

5

Use and continuity in the customary marine tenure of the Whitsunday Islands

Bryce Barker

This paper looks at some of the problems in identifying customary marine tenure (CMT) in the Whitsunday Islands of the central Queensland coast which is an area where, although continuous use can be demonstrated, detailed knowledge of the former clans and their estates are now largely unknown.

The contemporary community in the Whitsunday region is represented by the Giru Dala Council of Elders, an incorporated body which represents traditional and historical Aboriginal and Islander peoples in the region north of Bowen (Juru and Bindal), Collinsville (Biria), Proserpine, extending south to just north of Mackay (Gia) and the Whitsunday Islands [northern Cumberlands] (Ngaro) (Figure 5:1). Issues relating to native title in the Whitsundays were first raised when members of the Giru Dala Council of Elders expressed concern about aspects of the Great Barrier Reef Marine Park Authority's (GBRMPA) management of dugong and turtle populations within the park, especially as it relates to traditional hunting (I. Butterworth pers comm.). Under increasing pressure from GBRMPA, the Department of Environment, conservation groups and individual scientists to curtail and ultimately cease hunting these species, Giru Dala expressed concern that their traditional hunting of turtle and dugong was being blamed for the general decline in species numbers. It was in this context that I began to consider the possibilities of establishing native title under Mabo in the Whitsunday Islands and the possible native title ramifications if traditional hunting were banned. It should be made clear that the Giru Dala Council of Elders are not currently pursuing this direction, but have a general philosophy of self-sufficiency revolving around notions of wider community involvement and participation. In this context, and on their own initiative, the Giru Dala Council of Elders plays a significant role in the management and use of the Great Barrier Reef Marine Park, encompassing the central region of the Queensland Department of Environments National Park. At present they have considerable input into the strategic plan for the central region, have representatives on decision-making bodies relating to traditional hunting and fishing (specifically, dugong and turtle) and are consulted in regard to permit applications for tourist projects and developments.

Since the *Native Title Act (1993)* surprisingly little has been discussed about the status of sea-rights in regard to native title. Apart from sections 223 (1) and 223 (2) of the *Native Title Act (1993)*, which defines native title as including 'communal, group or individual rights and interests of Aboriginal peoples or Torres Strait Islanders in relation to land or waters including fishing rights and interests', very little of a specific nature relates to native title in sea country (Mabo vs The State of Queensland [No. 2] 1992). This is ironic given the pivital role of Murray Islanders in bringing about the Act, a group who have been described as:

> belonging to one of the most marine-oriented and sea-life dependent indigenous societies on the planet,[who] got native title to land above the high water mark but dropped sea claims due to insufficient evidence of traditional marine ownership (Cordell 1993:159).

Although the important role of the marine environment to Torres Strait cultures is generally recognised, this is not so much the case in relation to mainland Aboriginal peoples whose coastal use is often portrayed as a more shore-based system, revolving around estuarine mangrove communities and involving a large, often seasonal hinterland component. The perception of Australian Aboriginal groups as essentially land-based may be one of the contributing factors to the relative lack of recognition and discussion of CMT as it relates to mainland coastal Australia.

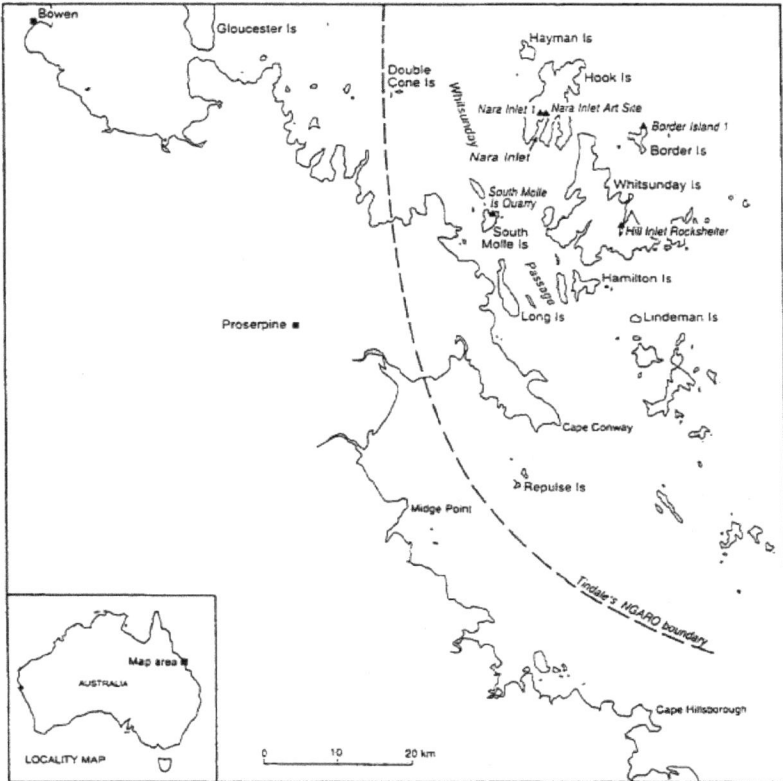

Figure 5:1 The Whitsunday Islands

A recent regional archaeological study in the Whitsunday Islands on the central Queensland coast (Barker 1995) has shown that, as with other Queensland coastal peoples on Cape York and the Gulf of Carpentaria, a socio-economic system based on the sea was and is in place. From the historical and archaeological evidence it is clear that the Whitsunday peoples were a marine people who lived on the very fringe of the large steep inaccessible islands and derived their subsistence principally from the sea. These people had sophisticated three-piece bark and outrigger canoes in which historically and archaeologically

149

documented open sea voyages of over 30km were a commonplace occurrence. Hunting of open sea biota including turtle, dugong and even whale was a major subsistence activity in which they utilised a complex marine hunting technology including detachable harpoons, bone, shell and turtle shell fishhooks and spears. This system is not just a case of 'boundaries of ancestral estates not ending at the shoreline' (Bergin and Lawrence 1993:32) hinting strongly at land as being more, or of equal importance to the sea. In the Whitsunday Islands, the evidence indicates that the sea, reefs and tidal flats were far more important than the land, and there is little evidence archaeologically that the terrestial flora and fauna of the islands were economically utilised in any major way. The archaeology in the Whitsundays has demonstrated the continuous use of marine resources from 9000 years ago with major changes to a highly specialised maritime system from after 3000 years ago (Barker 1991). Marine resources predominate in all the sites excavated in the Whitsunday Islands. Although this should not be surprising, given that they are all coastal sites, it is clear that the coastal occupation and settlement pattern is an accurate reflection of a broader, essentially maritime system (Barker 1991, 1995, 1996).

In this context, there seems to be nothing to justify separating land and sea in regard to native title, something which I would argue has more to do with European notions of land as ownable and the sea as common property, than with indigenous notions of ownership and use. The lack of clear recognition/definition, both generally and under Mabo for native title claims based on notions of CMT, places indigenous claims to sea in an inferior position to that of land-based title claims, and sets up a false dichotomy between rights over land and sea.

The historical background to the Whitsunday Island peoples is an essential component in understanding their contemporary position in regard to native title. The Whitsunday people were first recorded by Cook in 1770, and from that time, they maintained continuous and largely mutually beneficial contact with shipping passing through Whitsunday Passage. Historical accounts of trade involving among other things, turtle and fish for bottles and nails, are also supported by the archaeology (Barker 1995). From 1860 when permanent mainland settlement in the region by Europeans began with the establishment of Port Denison (Bowen), relations deteriorated. From 1860 until 1879 there are five accounts of attacks on shipping, including the attack and burning of a schooner, the Louisa Maria, and numerous other shore-based skirmishes. In about 1879, in response to the attack and burning of the Louisa Maria, the Queensland Native Mounted Police were active in the area. This led to an account in 1881 of a frightened group of fifty island people consisting of some old people and some children, clustered around the Dent Island Lighthouse for protection (Coppinger 1883). It appears that most of these people were eventually taken to Port Denison (Bowen), which had a large fringe camp. It is clear, however, that the island people's physical presence persisted with occupation still in place in the late 19th century. For example, one of the contemporary elder's grandmother was born on Whitsunday Island, probably in the mid 1880s.

Walter Roth recorded Whitsunday Island people there in the late 1890s and Joseph W. Hawkes, a resident of South Molle Island, recorded a detailed 'dreaming' story told to him by 'Goolgatta' in 1901. Accounts of the island Aboriginal people being employed for logging, pastoral and early tourism ventures on the islands in the 1920/30s, as well as the recording of word lists from two individuals in the 1930s, all attest to the continuous physical presence of Whitsunday peoples from the late 19th century right through to contemporary times (Hawkes 1901; Roth 1910; Whitley 1936; Thora Nicholson pers comm.). All of the contemporary descendants, however, were born and live on the mainland, or Palm Island, Bowen, Proserpine and Mackay. 'Traditional' knowledge relating to the sea and islands still exists, consisting of stories relating to marine species, and knowledge of specific locations, including reef and mangrove systems as well as relating to the outer Barrier Reef itself.

Figure 5:2 Presence of turtle bone in Border Island 1 archaeological site

Date (years)	Excavation Unit	Depth (cm)	Weight (gms)
150	1	3.5	9.85
	2	9.8	8.97
	3	12.9	2.38
	4	15.6	
	5	17.4	5.52
	6	20.7	0.26
	7	23.0	2.42
3,089	8	26.8	54.50
	9	30.1	0.62
	10	32.1	2.77
	11	35.1	4.77
	12	37.8	12.20
6,940	13	40.9	3.80

It is clear from the archaeological and historical record that turtle and dugong hunting was one of the major subsistence activities of the Aboriginal people of the Whitsunday region, a practice which has been carried out from at least 6,940 years ago and became increasingly important after 3000 years ago. It is evident that turtle (and probably dugong) were a sustainable resource over thousands of years, providing the staple meat food for an estimated minimum of 100 people (Barker 1995). The Whitsunday peoples are now being pressured to cease a traditional subsistence activity in which there is clear evidence of sustainable use over thousands of years, including up until the period of massive tourism and recreation activity beginning from the late 1970s. It is clear that the Great Barrier Reef Marine Park Authority are reacting to the steady decline in numbers of turtle and dugong in the region, something Giru Dala have also been very much aware of. Obivously, Giru Dala along with the GBRMPA and other interest groups recognises the importance of conserving these species, which is why it voluntarily reduced its quota of dugong from 40 in 1994 to 30 in 1995 and just three in 1996, as well as introducing a voluntary ban on all turtle hunting in 1996. And yet as far as Giru Dala are concerned, the real issue of why turtle and dugong numbers continue to decrease has not been addressed by government agencies. The ecological impacts of the activities of developers, canefarmers, professional fisherman and tourist operators, all important economically in the local, regional, national and international settings, have not been targeted in the same way as those relating to traditional hunting.

Figure 5:3 The relative importance of dietary resources in archaeological sites in the Whitsunday region

	NIL		NIAS		BI1		HIRS1	
	kg	%	kg	%	kg	%	kg	%
Shellfish	978.2	7.7	685.8	14.5	102.3	2.9	1185.7	15.1
Fish	7999.2	63.6	364.0	7.7	1280.0	36.7	4368.0	55.8
Turtle	3520.0	28.0	3360.0	71.2	2100.0	60.3	1800.0	23.0
Terrestrial	65.1	0.5	303.8	6.4	—	-	465.0	5.9
TOTAL	12562.2		4713.6		3482.3		7818.7	

Consequently, the Giru Dala Council of Elders has drawn on the archaeological data relating to the traditional hunting and management of turtle and dugong to argue against the banning of hunting of these species and to demonstrate continuous 'traditional use'. For example, in the Border Island 1 site, turtle was hunted as a resource from initial occupation at just after 7000 years ago and is present continuously right up until the historical period (Figure 5:2). Furthermore, although the bulk of the cultural material in all the sites excavated is shellfish, it only comprised a small proportion of the overall dietary component.

Fish and turtle were the two most important animal foods throughout. Together they contributed 91.6% of meat weights at Nara Inlet 1, 78.9% at Nara Inlet Art Site, 78.8% at Hill Inlet Rockshelter 1 and 97.0% at Border Island 1. In contrast, terrestrial fauna never contributed more than 7% of total meat weights and shellfish contributed a maximum of only 15.1%. Overall, fish comprised 49% of the total meat in all the sites, turtle comprised 37.7%, shellfish comprised 10.3% and terrestrial fauna comprised 2.9% (Figure 5:3). Although no dugong bone has been excavated, the prehistoric technology was fully geared to the hunting of large marine mammals including, possibly, whale, and there is no reason to doubt that dugong was taken in prehistory. Indeed dugong hunting was a major subsistence activity described historically and there are well documented taphonomic and cultural reasons as to why dugong bone is not found archaeologically (Minnegal 1984, Barker 1995).

Despite the external pressures and voluntary restrictions, the contemporary Aboriginal communities' strongest links to the islands and sea today relate to their enduring use of the marine subsistence base, especially of turtle and dugong. For all the descendants young and old, turtle and dugong were and are important food sources for the community. These particular foods are especially important during occasions such as family gatherings and other community occasions.

From my informal discussions with Giru Dala members, it emerged that their notions of CMT are almost wholly linked to *use* in regard to hunting dugong and turtle. It could be said fron the archaeological, historical and anthropological evidence that Giru Dala can demonstrate continuous hunting and fishing in the Whitsunday Islands and that this fulfils the condition under the *Native Title Act (1993)* that the indigenous inhabitants must have maintained a continuous connection with the land according to the group's traditional laws and customs in order for native title to still exist. Furthermore, it could be argued that Giru Dala's exemptions from state laws banning the killing of turtle and dugong constitute tacit acknowledgment of prior use and proprietary rights.

Ultimately it is the role of the National Native Title Tribunal, the Queensland Native Title Tribunal or the Federal Court to rule whether or not a continuous connection has been maintained by the indigenous inhabitants in the Whitsundays. I believe that this connection is clearly demonstrable. However, even taking into account the proviso in the Act that the Tribunal acknowledge the changing nature of cultures, it may be problematic as to whether continuous resource procurement and use on its own will be enough to prove native title has not been extinguished. For example, Justice Brennan emphasised the need for the occupancy or connection to be *in accord with a system of laws and customs* of a community or society (Bartlett 1993:10). Indeed findings by Justices Brennan, Deane and Gaudron further elaborate on this point by stating that native title rests in a traditional connection with or occupation of the land under the *laws and customs of the group and that the substantial maintenance of the connection must be established* (Bartlett 1993:10). Just what type and to what degree claimants are expected to have maintained traditional connection according to laws and customs is unclear. I agree with Cordell (1993:163). who states:

> CMT traditions are dynamic, living customs; nowhere are they 'pure' traditions. There is no question that colonial impacts on indigenous groups, beginning with the frontier experience, [consequent enculturation], interaction with European legal institutions, commodity market exploitation of marine products have all modified local custom. The point is, however, while CMT may not be what they once were, and cannot live up to some idealised past (a fictive state usually constructed by Europeans), they should not be regarded as broken-down traditions, but living customs linked to basic livelihood and resource management tasks, which Islanders and Aborigines constantly relate to new conditions, incorporating new knowledge.

Native title has ostensibly been extinguished already over large areas of the coastal shoreline in the Whitsundays by past grants of certain leasehold interests, specifically relating to tourism, as well as in land lying under tidal navigable rivers or streams, existing canal estates, under designated Queensland harbours and, significantly, in all coastal land between high and low water mark. Although this relates to land under sea, the extinguishment of native title in coastal land between high and low water mark effectively deprives coastal peoples of control over a major component of their resource base. This is especially so in the Whitsundays where there is a tidal range of over 4 metres. This encompasses vast areas of mangrove, fringing reef and mud flat, as well as a range of significant cultural sites such as fishtraps and a stone arrangement. Furthermore, this is the zone of development in the region with the greatest impact in regard to the sea and its resources, encompassing as it does marina developments, canal estates and various tourism ventures.

If the Native Title Tribunal does find that the demonstrated continuous resource use of the Whitsunday region constitutes a traditional connection with or occupation of the land and sea under the laws and customs of the group, and therefore determine that native title exists, then the issue of turtle and dugong hunting becomes crucial. If in this context, GBRMPA bans traditional hunting then it may be effectively extinguishing native title. If native title hinges on traditional hunting it is imperative that it continues to ensure native title is not extinguished.

To conclude, it would appear that the recognition of customary marine tenure in the Whitsunday Islands, and in many other coastal domains in Australia, would generally centre on interpretations of continuity of use and how the notion of use according to custom and laws is established or interpreted. I suspect that it will ultimately be found that a considerable gap will emerge between contemporary indigenous concepts of CMT and legal definitions of the same.

References

Barker, B. 1991. Nara Inlet 1: coastal resource use and the holocene marine transgression in the Whitsunday Islands, central Queensland. *Archaeology in Oceania* 26: 53–79.

1995. *'The sea people:' maritime hunter gatherers on the tropical coast. A late holocene maritime specialisation in the Whitsunday Islands, central Queensland coast.* Unpublished PhD thesis. Brisbane: University of Queensland.

1996. Maritime hunter gatherers on the tropical coast: a social model for change. In *Australian archaeology '95: proceedings of the 1995 Australian Archaeological Association annual conference* (eds) S. Ulm, I. Lilley, A. Ross. St Lucia: University of Queensland. *Tempus* Vol 6.

Bartlett, R. 1993. Aboriginal sea rights at common law: Mabo and the sea. In *Turning the tide: conference on indigenous peoples and sea rights, 14 July 1993: selected papers.* Darwin: Northern Territory University. Pp. 9–21.

Bergin, D. and A. Lawrence 1983. Aboriginal and Torres Strait Islander interests in the Great Barrier Reef Marine Park. In *Turning the tide: conference on indigenous peoples and sea rights, July 1993: selected papers.* Darwin: Northern Territory University. Pp. 25–53.

Coppinger, Dr. R.W. 1883. *Cruise of the Alert in Patagonian and Polynesian waters.* Paternoster Row: W. Swan Sonnenschein and Co..

Cordell, J. 1993. Indigenous peoples' coastal-marine domains: some matters of cultural documentation. In *Turning the tide: conference on indigenous peoples and sea rights, July 1993: selected papers.* Darwin: Northern Territory University. Pp. 159–157.

Hawkes, J.W. 1901. The Weeneenee bird. Unpublished manuscript. Brisbane: John Oxley Library.

Minnegal, M. 1984. Dugong bones from Princess Charlotte Bay. *Australian Archaeology* 18: 3–72.

Roth, W..E. 1901–1906. North Queensland ethnography, Bulletins 1 to 8. In *The Queensland Aborigines* Vol 2 (ed.) K.F. MacIntyre. Facsimile Edition 1984. Victoria Park: Hesperian Press.

Whitley, G.P. 1936. Aboriginal names mostly of marine animals from north Queensland. *Mankind* 2: 42–44.

6

Salt water, fresh water and Yawuru social organisation

Patrick Sullivan

This is a case study of the customary rights in 'sea country' of the Aboriginal people of the Broome region, who nowadays live mostly in the town itself. Broome does not immediately present itself as a town where Aboriginal culture, in all its richness of myth, ritual, language and group relationships, has an unbroken link with pre-colonial practice. It is more usual to view the town as having a modern creole culture.[1] However, both these views of contemporary Broome culture are true. A large proportion of the present Aboriginal population of the town belong to families that began to move into camps on the town's outskirts after the Second World War and who brought with them, and retain, knowledge of myth, ritual, local language and subsistence lore. Recently all these aspects of local culture have undergone revival. The people that are the subject of this paper call themselves Yawuru and Djugan, and most agree that these are simple locational dialectical differences of the same language and culture grouping (see Hosakawa 1991:1–2).[2]

---

1 This is particularly celebrated in the works of me musician and writer Jimmy Chi with his musicals Bran Nue Dae and Corrugation Road, but see Hosokawa (1994).

2 In this paper, following popular usage, the term Yawuru is often used for both Yawuru and Djugan. There is another group, which calls itself Goolarabooloo, simply meaning 'coastal people', which has a more complicated attachment to the land. This paper does not concern their social organisation or attachment to the sea since these have not been the subject of such intense study. The three named groups, and others, come together under the name Rubibi, which refers to Broome town (see Sullivan 1996).

The setting

The town itself lies on the shores of Roebuck Bay at the base of the Dampierland Peninsula in the Kimberley region of north-west Western Australia. In practice, when Broome people speak of 'Kimberley' they mean further inland at Halls Creek and Fitzroy Crossing, and express in this way quite unself-consciously their sense of their own uniqueness. The town is undergoing a sustained development boom based on tourism (Jackson 1996a: 14). Between 1976 and 1986 the population of the shire doubled with most of this increase in the town (Shire of Broome 1993:6). This was probably due largely to the sealing of the road from Port Hedland in the west. The population of the town itself is predicted to increase by about a third in the next ten years from its present estimate of 10,476 to about 15,337 (Hames Sharley 1996). The current Aboriginal population of the town is 3166 (Jackson 1996b:2) and one estimate of the proportion of Aboriginal people to non-Aboriginal people in the town itself puts it at 21.2% (Jackson 1996b:1). Despite the overall increase in Aboriginal population its proportion to non-Aboriginal people has dropped almost 10% since 1976 (Sullivan 1989:7). Aboriginal people in Broome have also undergone steadily worsening impoverishment over this period (Jackson 1996b). Of particular relevance to the subject of this chapter, Yawuru uses of the sea, is the importance of caught food. An Australian Bureau of Statistics survey in 1994 reported that 45% of Broome Aboriginal people surveyed 'worried' or 'sometimes worried' about going without food, while the national Aboriginal and Islander average for these concerns was 29%.

Aboriginal culture in this area is under threat, not from loss of knowledge and breakdown of tradition—these have seen a strong revival in recent years—but from being swamped by the sheer numbers of non-Aboriginal people. Cultural conflict is finely balanced at present, and large areas of town land are under claim for recognition of the existence of native title. This has placed a pause on the release of new residential land to accommodate the population increase, as well as on new tourist related developments, and it has empowered the Aboriginal community to begin to negotiate their future security. This paper is based on information collected in support of these claims.

In this chapter a number of propositions are developed, some of which are well founded while others are simply suggestions for discussion and analysis. These are that a system of customary land and sea ownership law exists in the shared knowledge of the Yawuru community. Use of the land is not distinct from use of the sea: in other words Yawuru people hunt and forage in the sea and the assertion of rights in the sea is essentially the same as the assertion of rights in the land. The system of ownership is felt to extend to all who claim descent from Yawuru or Djugun ancestors. Within this group there is attachment to smaller areas on a number of grounds, including descent, residence, knowledge and birth spirit (called *rai* in this region). By the manipulation of these factors the people achieve a higher degree of flexibility in their belonging to areas within the the larger group's territory than may be common elsewhere in Aboriginal experience. This is so pronounced that it is impossible to talk of patrilineal descent being the primary principle of land ownership, or of a clan-based society, as many unrelated individuals may have primary attachment to the same small named areas and most individuals will have attachment to several. Consequently, there is a strong ideology of common ownership of all the land. There is also a sense of belonging to 'land right-holding communities' that are not coincident either with linguistic boundaries or small family territories.

Yawuru country is where the arid grasslands of the Great Sandy Desert meet the sea. There are no freshwater creeks and few semi-permanent freshwater lakes. Fresh water is found in springs and soaks for much of the year. The land is low lying. The region is known for its extreme tidal variations (about 7 metres) and is subject to both monsoonal rains and frequent inundation from tropical cyclones. In other words, from time to time much of the country floods with spring tide salt water, and for long periods monsoonal rain floods also lie over much of the land making it impassable. This is a time of abundant fresh water but limited food resources. Off the coast there are areas of shallows stretching for several kilometres out to sea which are mud flats at extreme low tides and permit wading to reefs and sandbars. It is an area, then, where water, salt and fresh, is a constant, and constantly changing, feature of the people's lives. At times the sea itself is dry as the tide recedes almost to the horizon. At other times the land is awash. In some seasons it bakes in more than 40 C of heat and fresh water is scarce. Throughout the year the Yawuru make and made use of land, sea, mangrove creek, mud flats and reefs, but in all of these they needed, on the one hand, to be highly mobile to adapt to the rapid diurnal as well as seasonal changes in topography and landscape, and on the other hand they were constrained in their exploitation of changing food stocks by the distance they could move from a small source of fresh water either *in situ* or carried in a baler shell. No doubt there are a number of adaptations that could have been made to these circumstances. Elsewhere in Australia different forms of social organisation may well be described in precisely the same circumstances. Nevertheless, the adaptation favoured by the Yawuru is flexibility in the distribution of land and sea rights supported by an ideology of relatedness and common property among those of the same and related languages.

The system of belief, group relationship and land and sea use which derives from particular local conditions is still held among the Aboriginal people of Broome. This chapter is a demonstration of this, as the information in this case study has been taken from contemporary interviews, and these were by no means limited to the old. Some of the information here relates to past practices, but a very recent past, within the experience of many older people. It constitutes a body of contemporary knowledge. Inasmuch as it is currently known, it also underpins contemporary practice. As long as it is preserved it will not have 'died out' and will remain the cultural inheritance of all Aboriginal people who belong by right to the Broome region. Many of the traditional owners have covered the area on horseback while droving or mustering, and several of the elder inhabitants have walked extensively over it. Despite only limited access to one of the three local pastoral stations, many younger Aboriginal people of the town still regularly visit and use their traditional lands.

Uses of land and sea food sources

As a coastal people the Yawuru depend for most of their protein on the sea, but the pindan (semi arid scrub country) as well as providing some traditional meat sources, is also rich in vegetable foods and medicines. One recent inspection of a typical town block close to a main road identified within about twenty minutes fourteen plant species currently used, and this without moving more than fifty metres in any direction. This knowledge of the use of the land continues to be handed down among Yawuru families. Throughout their lives their members have eaten the foods of the land and learned to recognise its scarce waters. Hosakawa says:

> The country is rich in marsupials (of small to medium size), birds, reptiles, marine fish and shells. Traditionally Yawuru people lived by gathering wattle (*Acacia*) seeds, various edible tubers and bush fruits (during my 1986 fieldwork, over 90 species of edible and/or useful native plants were identified (Hosakawa 1988a; Lands 1987)), as well as by fishing, gathering shells (mainly in the mangrove swamps) and catching wallabies, sand monitors, flying foxes, and birds (particularly Native Hens, Crested Pigeons and Australian Bustards) (Hosakawa 1991:1–2).

These sources of meat were an important part of the diet of the older people as they grew up, which otherwise was largely limited to occasional salt beef, flour, tea and sugar. They remain an important basic food source as Aboriginal incomes are almost universally very low and Broome food and housing costs high. But these are not only food sources, they are important social identifiers that bind local Aboriginal people to each other as members of a particular society, and which link them to an ancient tradition. Hunting and fishing practices are consciously carried out to reaffirm their distinction from the increasingly embracing white population.

Women in general are the most knowledgeable about edible fruit and vegetable species, their locations, seasons, and preparation. Even quite young women who mainly live in town can provide copious information on the subject.[3] While the pindan was used in the past, and can sustain life today with the knowledge of the traditional owners, the sea and the coastal fringe is their principal milieu. The tidal creeks and some parts of the coastline are fringed with mangrove thickets that both harbour important food sources and are themselves used as part of the diet. Mangrove fruit is collected and allowed to ferment for one or two weeks in the steep muddy bank of a tidal creek. Following this, it is washed and boiled. Previously this was done in a baler shell over coals, nowadays it is in a billy with a stew. The mangrove also harbours crab, which are speared with a sharpened stick, dug and hooked from their holes, or yanked out of the shallows on a baited line. In the hot season, fruit bats roost low in the mangrove for shade and the cool breeze. They are easily knocked down with a stick. Ten or more can be taken at a time. Since they eat only fruit, the entire bat is edible.

The sea itself offers the richest and most varied diet. Naturally, the coastal people of the region have developed their most refined food gathering techniques and knowledge for harvesting its resources. Fishing techniques are determined by the topography and tidal patterns. The extremely high tides of the region and the existence of reefs and sandbars not far from shore, require a variety of methods of harvesting. At high tides fish can be speared by wading from the shore or from rock formations, as can turtle and dugong. Their location can be assessed from the frequent low cliffs, but local people are also adept at spotting shoals or the shadow shape of a turtle from the shore. Tindale's field notes from 1953 also record the use of a sort of net:

---

3 The book Mayi (Lands 1987) is evidence both of the extensiveness of this knowledge and of its currency, and the unpublished Yawuru Seasons (Lands and Mann 1990) provides a wealth of contemporary envirnmental information.

> The Jawuru used to fish using masses of grass which they pushed about like a net to corner and entangle fish. Such a 'net' was called 'marukutju:n'. With it they got plenty of fish. Any kind of grass could be used, as also the tendrils of Cassytha (Tindale 1953:773).

At low tide, fish traps, called *jimbinundira* or *kurljan*, come into play. They may nowadays be made of chicken wire and star pickets driven into sand at the outlet of a small subsidiary of a tidal creek. Knowledge is retained, however, of the traditional method which is to drive mangrove stakes into a prepared foundation of specially placed rocks which form a large pool. Spinifex or boughs are woven into the base of these stakes and this prevents the fish swimming out when the tide recedes. They are taken by hand, with spears or with specially designed fishing boomerangs which have concave faces.

At low tide it is possible to wade for long distances to outlying reefs and sandbars. The mudflats traversed are rich sources of shellfish, whose many varieties make up the numerous middens sometimes found several kilometres inland. For instance, at Cockle Well (Baldargi) on Roebuck Plains station some 20 kms from Broome, centuries of use of this water source has raised the ground into a significant mound. Kunin, or Fisherman's Bend, on Broome's outskirts is also such a raised midden, there is another at Crab Creek, and a prominent one in the town between Malingbar community and the Mangrove Hotel.

Stingray can be taken in the shallow waters as the tide recedes. When the flowers, *nyal nyala*, of the *guardo* tree are in bloom it tells the people that stingray are fat. When alarmed they flatten themselves in the sand of the shallows. The hunter must be skilful in assessing their location and orientation so as to avoid the thrashing of the poison tail when the spear strikes. Dugong sighted in the shallows also dive. The technique here is for several men to surround the animal and stir up the sand with their feet to make it rise when it can be speared or dived upon.

On gaining the reef, plant poison, *bunjuda*, may be used to stun the fish trapped in rockholes, or they may be speared. Shellfish such as *jagoli* can be got on the reef. Large amounts of the remains of these can be found on top of Warwan hill at Wadagungu rock-hole, testimony to the distances they would be carried to a camping ground. Sometimes turtle are trapped by the retreating tide and then easily overturned and killed. Otherwise, they can be dived upon when found swimming off reef ledges. Dugong also are caught by diving onto them. When alarmed, this airbreathing mammal tends to close its nose flaps and submerge. The method in this case requires stuffing the nostrils with spinifex gathered for this purpose, or a loin cloth, and allowing the animal to drown. It can then be floated to shore on the incoming tide, providing a rich source of meat and fat.

Local people observe six seasons. *Bargarna* is the cold dry season. It is time to leave the reefs and go for salmon in the creeks. They can be speared offshore in numbers if their 'track' can be found, as can barramundi, but they must first come into the creek, so it is only a matter of waiting and they can be easily caught. There is a particular wind, the water is choppy and dirty, and the salmon are in the creek whether ebbing or flowing.

This is followed by *Wirlburu*, a transitional season. Then it is *Larjar* season, in late September, October and November, the lead up to the monsoon. This is called 'married turtle time' when turtle eggs in the beach sand are plentiful. The reef fish are fat and it is a good season for barramundi, oysters and crabs (though when the crabs have eggs, they are left alone).

The full wet season, *Mankala*, is not good for fishing. Attention turns to goanna and turkey. Fishing may continue but with care taken for sudden storms. After the rain, the fish are hungry and feed well. Barramundi are taken in the late rains, and stingray. After the rain, in *Marol* season, it is still quite warm and humid, there is dew on the ground in the morning and a cool wind from the east. It is possible to return to fishing on the reef, but the fish are not so fat as during *Larjar*. Year-round fish can be taken then such as mullet, queenfish, whiting and trevally. Then it is *Bargarna*, the cold season, once more and time to leave the reef fish to mate, spawn and fatten and turn attention to the tidal creeks.[4]

All people who live by the sea have knowledge of the tides and seasons. They know the hazards and the beneficial techniques. That this is distinctly local Broome region Aboriginal knowledge is true, however, in two senses. The brief summary of a detailed local knowledge revealed here has been handed on from one generation to another during the actual practice of hunting, fishing, gathering and camping over thousands of years. Some of it, such as when the salmon are running for instance, may be known by non-Aboriginal people, but it is not shared knowledge. Hardly any sharing takes place. That some superficial and obvious aspects of a society's knowledge may be known by members of another society does not make it common knowledge or lessen the fact that this knowledge belongs to the former society and is one of its markers.

One distinction is that Aboriginal food gathering is carried out with low impact techniques and with attention to spreading the impact across a variety of habitats and species according to their reproductive needs. Non-Aboriginal approaches in Australia generally use high technology, are geared to maximal immediate returns, and frequently are confined to single species and locations. Local Aboriginal people frequently show dismay at the waste in non-Aboriginal fishing methods, both recreational and commercial. Another important distinguishing feature is that the Aboriginal people of Broome fish to feed their families. The concept of family includes numerous individuals. Unlike non-Aboriginal people, they can never have caught 'too much' fish. While non-Aboriginal people are frequently observed to throw away fish they believe to be non-valuable, Broome Aboriginal people say that the only things they themselves leave behind are the guts, scales and bones.

---

4   While most of this information comes from fieldnotes I have benefited from access to the unpublished Yawuru Seasons (Lands and Mann 1990) to clarify some points.

This practice of intense use, rather than widespread catching, is bound up with the serious view they take of animal species as both food and medicine. The water in which shellfish have been boiled is said to cure depression and saltwater fish to relieve stress. Theirs is not a simple recreational use of natural resources or optional food supplements. There is deep-seated conviction, even in contemporary Broome Aboriginal thought and activity, of a relationship, even a form of identity, between individuals, their group, the features and creatures of the land, the myths of its creators and their appropriate rituals, and their own rights to own and use the land. The following sections will describe conception totemism, which is a primary regulator of land attachment, then the means by which attachment to land is expressed at the local level, followed by wider scale groupings which celebrate the myths of the land and sea in ritual.

Aboriginal knowledge of gaining food from the natural world is produced in a system of meaning and belief quite distinct from any other. Most obviously, there is the ritual that surrounds hunting and fishing activity. In at least one instance this is related to secret male initiation ritual. One old women remembers that her grandfather would walk alone into the mangrove to find a *burgo* tree. Here he would perform a secret ritual involving blood that otherwise is confined to initiation practice. He would sing the appropriate verses and draw to him large fish called *dinga*.

Reef fish trapped in rock pool fish traps are similarly imbued with the power and secrecy of male ritual. The men sing sacred verses on the outgoing tide that women and children are not allowed to hear, and the fish are pulled back and trapped on the reef. Only initiated men are allowed to gather them from the trap. These songs, and other songs to charm species, placate spirits or celebrate places associated with hunting, fishing and gathering are taught to young men when they go through the various stages of their initiation. In particular, this is a feature of the *Walawalang* stage of the initiation cycle. Worms (1957:216–219) recorded two songs, one of which equates the seasonal appearance of turtles to aspects of men's secret initiation ritual.

The existence of 'increase sites' where particular rituals are carried out to ensure the continuity of species has been well-documented (e.g. Elkin 1933:284). The term 'increase' is widely accepted to be a misnomer as the intention is rather to maintain an existing balance and ensure success in hunting. It is widely believed that this practice has largely died out. This may be because early observers imbued it with a kind of formality (it was required to be carried out by nominated categories of individuals using prescribed ritual formulae at distinct places) that it has either lost or never in fact had. In the Broome region, places where songs may be sung to attract food species are still well-known. One, for instance, is near the old jetty and several others along the coast from Willie Creek to Broome. The practice varies from the singing of particular songs at particular locations, to the singing of particular verses in any location to ensure success the next day, to simply calling out to the spirits of the place at a creek or reef when arriving for fishing after a long absence.

Spirit beliefs, food resources and group relationships to land

Among the spirits which Broome fishers and hunters call out to after a long absence are those that are said to enter a woman as the essence of the child she is to give birth to (cf. Tonkinson 1978; Merlan 1986). These are called *rai*. The means of entry is usually a food species she has eaten. The child is frequently born with the mark of the spear, digging stick, bullet or other implement upon it. Thus each individual is linked to naturally occurring species, precise locations, father and mother (it is usually the father who has done the hunting or at least has 'dreamed' the child spirit the woman has ingested) and the world of spirits and mythic ancestors. In many areas of Australia, the spirit children are said to have been left at natural features of the landscape by the mythical heroes who created or discovered the world and passed on its law to humans. This is not always the case in the Broome region. *Rai* here can be associated with a mythological site, in which case they are said to belong to the mythological being associated with the site, but in many instances they appear to be simply spirits of place. They are always linked to a natural species because it is that which acts as the means of transmission of the spirit to the woman who will give it birth. More fundamentally, the *rai* belongs to a site which its human manifestation will also have rights over and responsibilities for. Many of these sites are in the sea, usually in coastal reefs and rocks.

The belief in the unity of spirit, land/sea myth, and person is not compartmentalised in people's thought under a particular label such as 'folklore' or 'fairy-story'. It is firmly held even by the young. A person's *rai* place is as real to them as their birthday, even where not previously known. One young man was recently shown a rock in the sea called Miniriny near Cape Villaret as his origin place. He was impressed, imbued with a new sense of responsibility for the area, and showed a sense of fulfilment at piecing together these aspects of his social identity. Children may be claimed as the *rai* of deceased individuals, or as the special wards of an older person able to see *rai* in people. In an example of the latter, an old man once complained that one of his *rai* was missing from a particular location, he described her to others, particularly her long hair. Not long after this, a baby girl was born with the long black hair that led the man to identify her as his missing *rai*. Even the *rai* places of people long dead are discussed as matters of record, helping to determine where they belonged.

The complexities of *rai* belief in the Broome region bear much examination. They are one among the many markers of Aboriginal culture that distinguishes it from that of non-Aboriginal people. Their particular significance for present purposes, however, is to situate the economic activity of hunting, fishing and gathering in a wider framework of religious belief, and as an important means, perhaps the most important currently, by which people regulate and negotiate their particular and unique rights over areas of land and sea within the common land heritage of the whole society. This 'anchoring' of the individual to sites, myths and groups makes spirit-child belief the central and pivotal element in social organisation. So far this chapter has discussed some of the more empirically verifiable aspects of Yawuru material culture and religious practice, the nexus of these and Yawuru social organisation now requires attention.

Some interpretations of Aboriginal statements may lead to an assumption that primary attachment to land is by descent from the father, sometimes from the mother, but *rai* belief integrates with this and cuts across it, making the system infinitely more flexible. Broome region Aboriginal people will often say that they 'come from' a place or 'belong to' a place because their father came from such a place. They can also say that their mother came from a place and nowadays among the younger generation they may refer to a grandmother or great grand-mother who 'came from' somewhere. On the face of it this could be a system of patrilineal descent groups, with one or two alternate systems, such as through maternal filiation, producing the odd anomaly. This is, in fact, the way that Elkin (1933a) viewed it, but it does not stand up to examination. All knowledgeable informants so far interviewed say that persons who come from the same place may marry each other. Their offspring then have both parents from the same place. This is bi-lateral descent, neither patrilineal nor matrilineal. Moreover, family groups who are not directly related may all come from the same place. One instance concerns three prominent Yawuru men, now dead, who all 'came from' a place called Marar. The families do not believe themselves to be closely related nor does the ideology of descent insist that these three men ought to have been. The pattern that emerges is not one of small clan-like groups with delimited named areas of land tracing their origin to a common male ancestor. It is one of several family groups establishing primary rights to a 'home' area by a number of means, including having their *rai* from the place, while still enjoying rights over the combined land and sea of the wider group.

Belonging to a country

Some of the means of establishing attachment to a place within the territory should be examined. A person can establish attachment to a place if a parent or other significant forebear 'came from' or 'belonged to the place'. One very old Yawuru ritual leader, when asked to explain this, used the example of a man who will be called here Billy. It is know that his father 'came from' or 'belonged to' Marar on Thangoo station, despite the fact that he was of mixed Asian descent, removed to Beagle Bay at an early age, and spent most of his life in Broome town. Billy, according to the elder of the group, 'comes from' Broome because he was born there, raised a family there, lives there (despite considerable periods of absence in Katherine and Port Hedland). Billy, however, can 'claim' Marar, or 'get' Marar according to the old man. Asked what this means he says he can build a paddock there or a house, go hunting there, in other words live and use it by right. This does not mean that he cannot go anywhere else in the people's common land nor that they cannot enter Marar. According to the same informant one can go, quietly; one might mention that one is going to the person who 'comes from there' but not in the sense of asking permission. Nearly all of these named sites where people belong or come from are coastal and provide use of the sea and and mangrove creeks.

The question is, from the point of view of Billy's future grandchildren, where would their grandfather have 'come from', Broome, Marar or somewhere else entirely?

The answer to this is that, in local Aboriginal terms, a person comes from the area socially determined to be theirs by a consensus absorbed into the body of knowledge of the oldest surviving authoritative individuals. Whether indeed the remembered old man who was Billy's father came from Marar by birth, conception totem, adoption, mother, father, or some other means is neither known nor considered consequential. Nor, if it were not for the existence of written records, would it be to Billy's grandchildren. His 'home' area would be a matter of record in the thought and knowledge of the community, enjoying a truth not subject to any other form of reference.

Nevertheless, the level of consensus about where a recently deceased person belonged, whatever the mechanism of their belonging, does place some constraints on their descendants. It is one among the many parameters of the system. One means of escaping it and coming from an area more congenial, practical, politic or emotionally and spiritually satisfying is, as mentioned, to 'follow' a mother or other relative. Another is to return to the area of one's birth-spirit. A third may be to acquire deep knowledge of the features of a region including its mythology and associated ritual, though usually this is consolidated by reference to one of the other mechanisms.

These can be summarised as:

Descent or inheritance through one line or another

Birth

Conception spirit or *rai*

Knowledge and association. (cf Peterson 1986:59–60)

Of these the two that cannot be gainsaid are descent and *rai*, even though, as discussed, descent only operates to the extent of the oldest community member's memory and there is no necessity among community members to insist that it is the principle that stretches back to the beginning of time in any particular case, and a *rai* association cannot be falsified.

The main way a person may end up with attachment to an alternative home area than their father is by the finding of their birth spirit in another area. In an another paper Elkin (1932:330–1) pays considerable attention to this:

> More research remains to be done in the Kimberlies with regard to the local organization, totemism and mythology, before the roles of the father and the locality in totemic descent can be finally determined. But on the south-east of the Kimberlies and right through Central Australia...it is the local principle which predominates. A person's country is that

> in which he is conceived...or born....This is usually the father's country. The point is that in aboriginal thought in the Kimberlies and other areas where I have worked, the father is closely associated with the local horde and its totems, and therefore patrilineal and local descent amount to much the same thing, though, as I have already stated, the local principle with its spiritual, sacred and mythological associations seems to be primary and the more fundamental of the two.

It is clear that by 'local principle' and 'local descent', which Elkin here contrasts with 'patrilineal descent' he means the peoples' statements that they 'come from' or 'belong to' an area rather than, primarily, a clan group with rights over that area. Although, as he says, this may amount to the same thing, it is very important to note the effect of the cases in which it does not. In particular, conception spirits allow individuals to have attachment to areas through a means other than patrilineal descent. Elkin makes an unusual statement when he identifies the principle of attachment to an area, rather than membership of a clan group, as the 'primary and the more fundamental of the two' means of land association. This does more than simply add one alternative means of recruitment to a local group, it has two highly significant consequences for the clan model.

Firstly, there is the uncertainty it introduces about the continuity of descent. At any generation level the principle of attachment may have been 'alternate' making the descent line shallow indeed. Secondly, and more importantly, there exist in the group with primary rights over a small named area individuals, and over time families, that are not related to each other, since some of them form attachment by descent alone, some by another means (principally birth-spirit) and some by descent from these last. Clans, then, to the extent that they exist as any more than an anthropological abstraction, are neither the main land-owning nor land-using group.

It is interesting that Elkin's own fieldwork case studies support this view. One person noted by Elkin (1933a:267–8) in his discussion of the *ngura* relevant to this claim belonged to a different *ngura* and totem than his father and brothers by means of his birth spirit. Two others, one a headman, belonged to the *ngura* of their mother, or mother's brother's (which amounts to the same thing). One was found as a spirit in one *ngura*, had their totem revealed in a dream as coming from another, and was born in a third.[5]

The situation, then, is extremely flexible. If indeed this flexibility is seen to have always been the case, and, despite his comments to the contrary Elkin's (1933a:268–70), information indicates that it was, we can no longer think of these means of gaining rights in land and sea as variants on a norm, but instead as themselves constituting the system. The picture then emerges of a people whose members each have particular attachment to relatively small area of homeland, an attachment they may have achieved by a number of means and share with close kin as well as those who may not be directly related. They hunt, fish and perform ceremonies over a wider area of land where they feel themselves to have rights in common with a larger group. They travel over wider areas still, where they feel themselves to be at the invitation or on the sufferance of other large groups. The boundaries of communal ownership do not lie between small family or clan groups, but between the latter two larger social groupings. In this region at least, a right-holding community may overlap the stated boundaries of linguistic domains, and conversely, need not assert its rights to the entire territory of either linguistic domain.

In 1959 Berndt published a seminal paper on 'The Concept of The Tribe in the Western Desert of Australia' which made the distinction between land-owning groups (the clan, which he called simply 'the local group') and land-using groups (the band, which he called 'the horde') (1959:98, 103). More importantly for the subject under discussion, he rejected the concept of the tribe as not applicable in this area and not the widest functional grouping. This latter he called a 'society' and its prime characteristic was interaction for ceremonies. His description

---

5 Ngura is glossed by Elkin as 'country' but can mean something as simple as camp or hearth. Similarly, the Dampierland 'buru' is often translated by anthropologists as 'clan estate' but has the literal meaning 'ground'.

is useful for the Broome situation. He (1959:104) finds, as well as the local forms of association already discussed, two others: the cult lodge (clans sharing a totemic association with a complex of mythic sites in a 'track') and a wider unit formed by hordes coming together seasonally for ceremonies

This last unit he calls 'a society' and he identifies it as 'the widest functionally significant group'. He (Berndt 1959:105) wrote of it that:

> The significance of this wider unit rests primarily on the degree of interaction taking place among its members. Traditionally, those who occupy (not necessarily own) contiguous stretches of country would more probably be found coming together for seasonal meetings, and contacts between them would be stronger than with those further away. But this nucleus, by no means fixed since wandering was the norm, would consist of members of different local groups, different hordes and different dialect units. We cannot speak of it as a kin group, although relationships between members included in it would be articulated in kin terms. Further, representatives of more distant local groups and hordes might be present: the occasional coming together of those who are for the greater part of the year living apart, visits from areas relatively far away, are a notable feature of such gatherings. It is those who meet regularly and consistently, even if intermittently—and are closely involved in reciprocal duties and obligations—who make up the widest functionally significant group.

The land/sea-owning group described here as a society is exclusive, not inasmuch as it would exclude others from entry into and use of the land and sea, but that it would exclude them from the right of possession. The principles of membership of the land/sea-owning group cannot be found in the narrowly defined clan or cognatic descent group, nor even in the broader tribe or language group. They are found in the interrelation between these two forms of land/sea group identification and the wider group that performs the ritual of, and holds other esoteric knowledge of, the land and sea. While these principles of membership of the land/sea-owning group can be described, it is not possible from this to definitively list all members who possess, or potentially possess, the necessary characteristics. The concept of 'the land/sea-holding society' is an abstraction from the actual practices of assertion of affiliation to named tracts, demonstration of knowledge. socially accepted lines of descent, and assertion of competence in and rights over linguistic domains. These are socially determined, sometimes by consensus and sometimes in dispute. Resolution of the question of who, in every instance, holds title is not by reference to a membership list or suitable adherence to a check-list of criteria. It is by a continuing process of community debate, assertion, reference to authorities, precedents and even signs and portents beyond the experience of current European-based systems of tenure. None of this calls into question the existence of communal native title in the sea, only the difficulty of giving it corporate expression in terms that are required for its recognition as a form of Australian land/sea-tenure.

Notes

The research and much of the text of the paper was contracted by the Kimberley Land Council. I am grateful for permission to reproduce it. I also wish to thank those who provided their cultural information, especially: Doris Edgar, Cissy Djiagween, her brother who is deceased, Mary Tarran, Francis Djiagween and Frank Sebastian. I am grateful to Sue Jackson of Macquarie University School of Earth Scineces and the North Australia Research Unit for generous provision of some of her work-in-progress research material.

References

Berndt, R.M. 1959 The concept of the 'tribe' in the western desert of Australia. *Oceania* 30:81–107.

Elkin, A.P. 1932. Social organisation in the Kimberley division, north-western Australia. *Oceania* 2(3):296–333.

1933. Totemism in north-western Australia: the Kimberley division. *Oceania* 3(3):257–296.

Hames, Sharley 1996. *Land use indentification study*. Broome: Local Government Development Project.

Hosakawa, K. 1991. *The Yawuru language of west Kimberley: a meaning-based description*. Unpublished PhD thesis. Canberra: Australian National University.

1994. Retribalisation and language mixing: aspects of identity strategies among the Broome Aborigines, Western Australia. *Bulletin of the National Museum of Ethnology (Osaka)* 19(3).

Jackson, S. 1996a. *When history meets the new native title era at the negotiating table: a case study in reconciling land use in Broome, Western Australia*, a discussion paper. Darwin: North Australia Research Unit, Australian National University.

1996b. Land use planning and cultural difference. Paper presented to the Tracking knowledge: northern landscapes, past, present and future workshop. Darwin: North Australia Research Unit, Australian National University.

Lands, M. 1987. *Mayi: some bush fruits of Dampierland*. Broome: Magabala Books.

Lands, M. and M. Mann 1990. *Yawuru seasons*. Unpublished resource kit.

Merlan, F. 1986. Australian Aboriginal conception beliefs revisited. *Man* 21:474–91.

Peterson, N. 1986. (in collaboration with Jeremy Long). *Australian territorial organisation*. Oceania Monograph No:30. Sydney: University of Sydney.

Shire of Broome 1993. *Broome planning study*.

Sullivan, P. 1996. Authority, conflict and appropriate land holding bodies. Paper delivered to Australian Anthropological Society and Australian Institute of Aboriginal and Torres Strait Islander Studies Native Title workshop, Canberra, September 1996.

1989. *Wattle Grove, traditional affiliation, history ans social circumstances of Yawuru people*. Report to the Aboriginal Development Commission, Broome.

Tindale, N.B. 1953. Anthropological field notes on the University of California, Los Angeles University of Adelaide anthropological expedition, north-west Australia, 2 vols. Adelaide: South Australian Museum.

Tonkinson, R. 1978. Semen versus spirit child in a western desert culture. In *Australian Aboriginal Concepts* (ed.) L.R. Hiatt. Canberra: AIAS. Pp. 81–92.

Worms, E.A. 1957. The poetry of the Yaoro and Bad, north-western

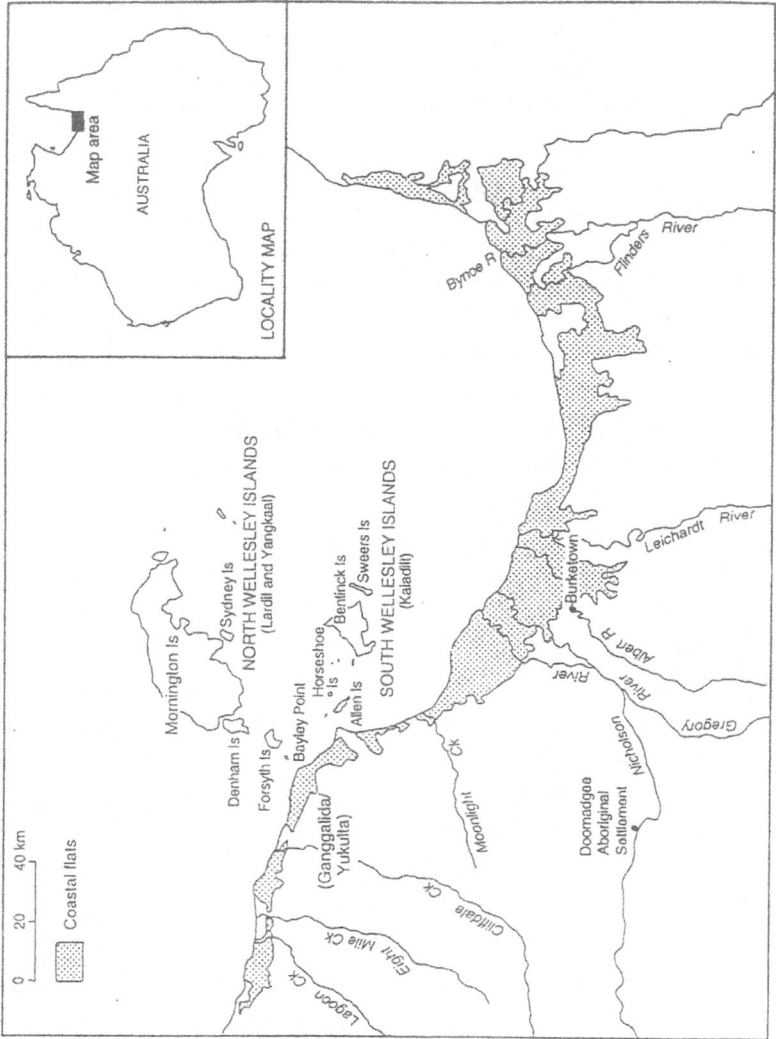

Figure 7:1 The southeastern Gulf of Carpentaria

7

Marine tenure in the Wellesley Islands region, Gulf of Carpentaria

Paul Memmott and David Trigger

This paper presents ethnographic material concerning four Aboriginal groups in a region of the southern Gulf of Carpentaria, namely the Lardil, Yangkaal, Ganggalida and Kaiadilt. At least for some decades now people have used these language names as 'tribal' or group identifying labels. [1] The languages are closely related, and on the basis of linguistic analysis constitute a 'Tangkic' sub-group, the latter term deriving from the common word, *tangka*, meaning 'person' (Evans 1995: 9). The homelands and seas of these language groups are in the vicinity of the Wellesley Islands and adjacent mainland coast (Figure 7:1).

Indigenous classification of coastal environments

All these groups designate the marine environment as distinctive in its difference from inland areas. The Lardil people of Mornington Island (the largest of the North Wellesley group) classify their land and seas into two categories, 'inside country' and 'outside country' (Memmott 1983:34). The 'inside country' consists of what we might term the interior land systems, constituted by tussock grasslands, open low eucalypt woodlands and scrub lands. This landscape is distinct from the geologically much more recent coastal land systems which are known among

---

1 The name 'Ganggalida' is also known in published literature as 'Yukulta'. However, during the past two decades, at least, it is the former term which has been used for both the language and the people or 'tribe' identifying with it. Keen (1983: 192) points out that *'ganggalida'* literally means 'word' or 'language'.

Lardil people as 'outside country'. The coastal areas are made up of tidal flats, sand-based cheniers and ridges, and interspersed cliffs, boulder beaches, off-shore wave-cut platforms and reefs. Figure 7:2 presents key properties of 'inside' and 'outside' country on Mornington Island, indicating among other things that most 'story place locales' are situated in the coastal 'outside country' and that this is also the landscape most modified by Lardil occupants.

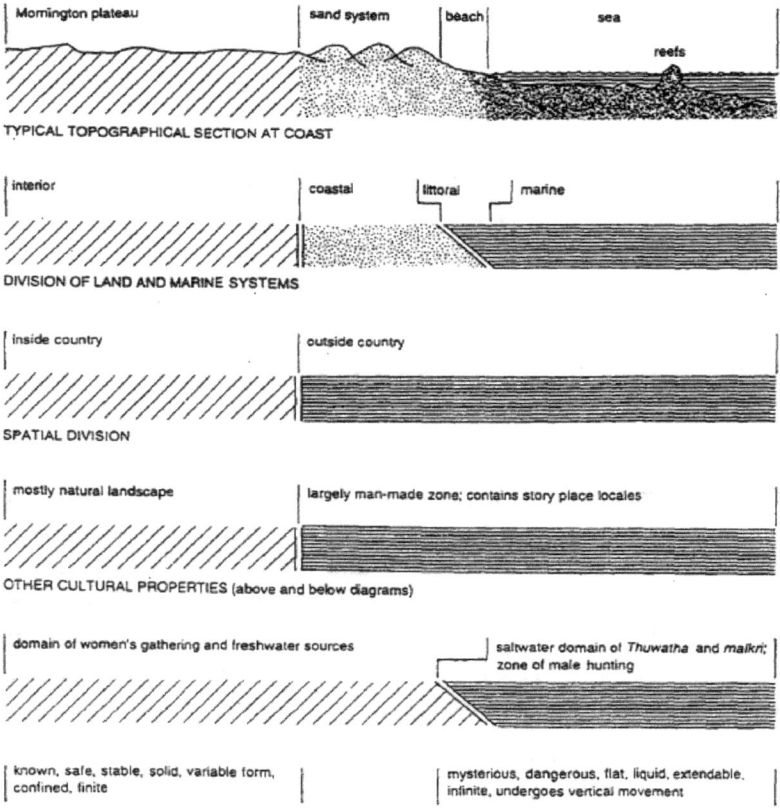

Figure 7:2 The Properties of inside and outside country on Mornington Island

Similarly, according to Tindale's research in the early 1960s (1977: 247–9), the culture of the Kaiadilt people of Bentinck Island (in the South Wellesleys) was focused very much upon the coastal parts of their island. Tindale suggests that most subsistence activities occurred in shore areas. He presents a map drawn by a young Kaiadilt man which places the sea (*mala*) in the centre of this man's conceptual representation of his country, such that the perimeter of Kaiadilt territory is the coastline enclosing the sea (Figure 7:3). This is a powerful representation of the centrality of the sea in Kaiadilt perceptions of their territory.

In the case of the coastal Ganggalida people on the mainland, Trigger (1987: 72–4) has described how the traditional indigenous view is that the 'land' or 'mainland' begins at the inland limit of the saltpan, which also marks the dimensions of what is generally known as 'saltwater country'. Figure 7:4 shows this limit, designating a coastal strip of 'saltwater country' extending southwards for distances varying between three and ten kilometres from the beach. Sand ridges are labelled 'islands' (*murndamurra*), the same term used for offshore islands (see also Figure 7:5). Thus, the coastal strip is regarded as environmentally and culturally distinctive from further inland, and as the domain of 'saltwater people'. Throughout the islands and the coastal mainland there is a strong prohibition against mixing the material and spiritual properties of 'land' or 'inside' country with those of the saltwater domain; all language groups share the belief that illness and death can follow from mixing saltwater and land-based foods and the 'fat' or internal essence of land animals must be washed from the body before having contact with the sea (Evans 1995: 17–18; Memmott 1982).

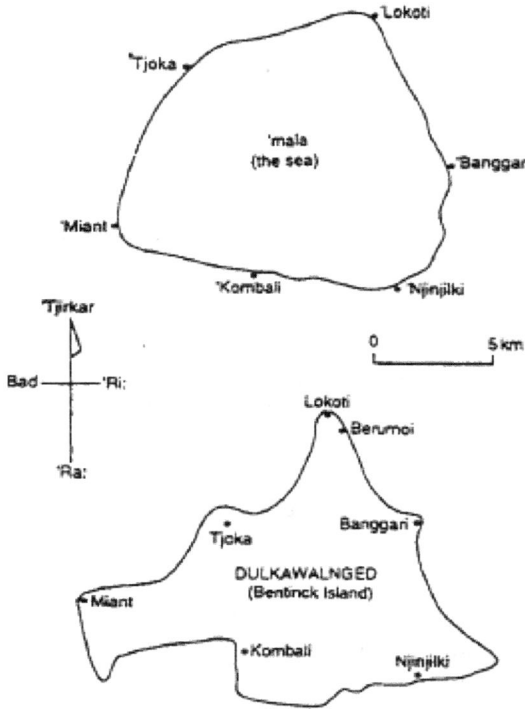

Figure 7:3 Drawing by Kaiadilt man showing his concept of his country. Below is a comparative sketch map of Bentinck Island (after Tindale 1977:248)

Customary use of coast and seas

Throughout the Wellesley Islands, coastal places are used for hunting and collecting sea foods, which continue during the 1990s to contribute substantially to the local diet; resources obtained include turtle, dugong, fish, oysters, shellfish and crabs. Many rock wall fish traps (Lardil: *derndernyn*; Kaiadilt: *ngurruwarra*) have been constructed in parts of the littoral zone on the islands, whilst other rock or reef traps lie totally within the sea. It is generally believed that these traps were built by mythic ancestors. The North Wellesley

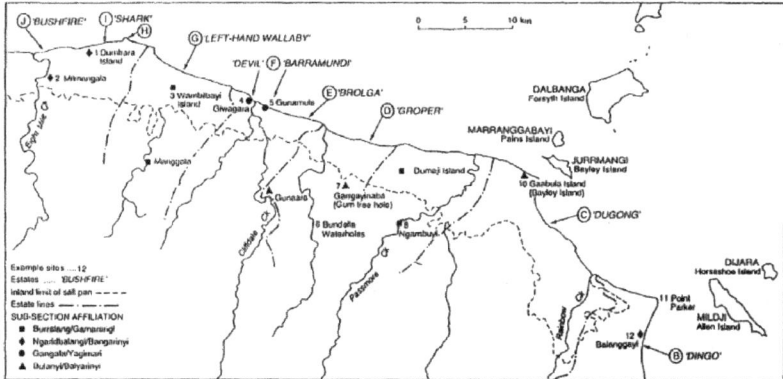

Figure 7:4 Coastal mainland Ganggalida country

Islanders believe their traps were shaped by the first Lardil people Maarnbil, Jirnjirn and Diwaldiwal who brought culture and language to Mornington Island (Memmott 1979: 205–9). Evans (1995: 16) reports the Kaiadilt view that the original construction of the many traps in the South Wellesleys is attributed to *Bujuku* (Black Crane) and *Kaarrku* (Seagull), but that older people also recall the contribution of human labour to building and maintaining fish traps. In the vicinity of Bayley Point and Point Parker on the mainland coast, the rocks comprising fish traps are similarly believed to be the flesh of the *Bijarrba* (Dugong) Dreaming ancestor. Senior Ganggalida people in the early 1980s, when asked, acknowledged human agency in their accounts about the historical construction of the traps; however, the mythic association with the rocks from which the traps were built, conflates this ancestral human agency with Dugong Dreaming itself.

Figure 7:5: Schematic Representation of Ganggalida Classification of Environmental Zones in the Mainland Coastal Area

malara	mirlaja/ mala/lilu	ngar-nda	dumuwa	gabara	gin.gara
'sea'	go back/ sea/north	'beach'	[multiple ridges]	'saltpan'	'flat country'
	[intertidal zone]		'sand ridge'		[on other side of saltpan]
		area containing murndamurra, 'islands'			
'saltwater country'					'mainland' 'land' wambalda

Across the region, we have estimated a total of some 334 individual traps (located at 108 sites) on the islands and along the mainland coast.[2] In general, most of the smaller islands have a relatively dense distribution of traps and sites. Bentinck Island in Kaiadilt country is enormously rich in this respect. Whereas on the Lardil people's Mornington Island, our calculation is one site containing traps for roughly every 20 km of coastline, on Bentinck Island we have an average of one site every 0.9 km and a figure of one trap per 0.4 km. While participating in the recording of fish traps on Sweers Island in 1983, a senior Kaiadilt man casually listed six fish species, four kinds of shark and two types of stingray that were easily available for capture when routinely caught behind the trap walls with the receding tide. Clearly, there were many further species which could have been elicited; Evans (1995:17) notes for the Kaiadilt that 'most food came from the sea and estuaries'.

---

2   Since the early 1980s, we have carried out collaborative research on the fish traps with Richard Robins of the Queensland Museum, comprising of visits to trap locations, counts from a low-flying aircraft and examination of aerial photographs. Extensive analysis of these data is proceeding at the Queensland Museum.

On the Wellesley Islands, people have continued to manufacture and in many cases use customary repertoires of artefacts for sea hunting and fishing (e.g. pronged fishing spears and spear throwers). Traditional technology has been supplemented with commodities from the wider Australian society including dinghies, outboard motors, steel spear prongs and nylon (for fishing lines and nets).

Since the establishment of a mission in 1914 in the southwest corner of Mornington Island the Lardil population has become gradually settled into residence at a single location. Nevertheless, from the 1970s a number of outstations have been developed and some families now live intermittently in decentralized camps and settlements in their homelands. In any case, hunting, fishing and gathering practices have continued throughout this century as activities especially focused upon the coast and adjacent waters. An important customary use of the seas was (and remains) that of travelling around and between the islands, to and from the mainland, and along the mainland coast. In the early contact period, rafts (Ganggalida: *walbuwa*; Lardil: *walba*; Kaiadilt: *walbu*) were used as an apparently longstanding traditional form of watercraft. Canoes (both sewn bark and dugouts) were also used throughout this century and probably earlier (see Trigger 1987: 80–1).[3] Powered boats have now replaced rafts and canoes.

The continuity in marine travel practices should not be characterised as only focused on obtaining food but as also encompassing social and ritual interaction among different groups and between people and their country. This form of ongoing interaction would appear continuous from pre-contact times, especially within the domains of the different language groups, but also between the coastal mainland and

---

3 In earlier times, some missionaries on Mornington Island wilfully destroyed canoes. This practice was aimed at discouraging the butchering of dugong and turtle in the vicinity of the Mission in order to minimize shark attacks on the dormitory children who were required to bathe regularly in the sea. Despite such setbacks, Lardil people can be said to have adapted and maintained their traditional hunting and fishing activities throughout the mission era (1914—1976).

the North Wellesley Islands; the latter travel was facilitated by a chain of islands, shallow waters and sandbanks exposed at low tides.

The Kaiadilt people were traditionally much more isolated by an expanse of difficult to traverse waters of some 13 km at its narrowest point. Tindale's (1962a; 1962b; 1977) general suggestions about the extreme isolation of the Kaiadilt should be qualified by the facts of similarities between aspects of their traditional society and various mainland cultural forms (Trigger 1987). In the context of our research, there have been occasions during the past two decades when Kaiadilt persons have suggested that in the past there was intermittent interaction with mainlanders. Nevertheless, the results of intensive linguistic analysis lead Evans to suggest (1995:26) that (having migrated to the South Wellesleys from the mainland between 500 and 1000 years ago) 'whatever contacts there were, that did not end in death or exile, must have been separated by decades of isolation' (1995:17); he also mentions (1995:18) that nothing was obtained by the Bentinck Islanders via trade in times prior to European colonisation.

Throughout the past 50 years, Kaiadilt people have lived in close contact with the Lardil at the main residential township on Mornington Island, just as Ganggalida people have lived mainly at Doomadgee some considerable distance away from the coast. However, during the last couple of decades, there has been an increasing presence of people on both Bentinck Island and in mainland coastal Ganggalida country. Both these outstation movements (from Mornington Island in the case of the Kaiadilt, and from Doomadgee on the part of the Ganggalida) have been driven by a keen interest in maintaining broad cultural links with ancestral lands and seas. Kaiadilt people have had to re-establish their presence in the South Wellesleys after they were moved to Mornington Island Mission in 1947–8 (Tindale 1962a: 260); and Ganggalida people similarly began returning to their coastal domain from the late 1970s after being congregated some 100 km inland at Doomadgee Mission from the 1930s (Trigger 1992).

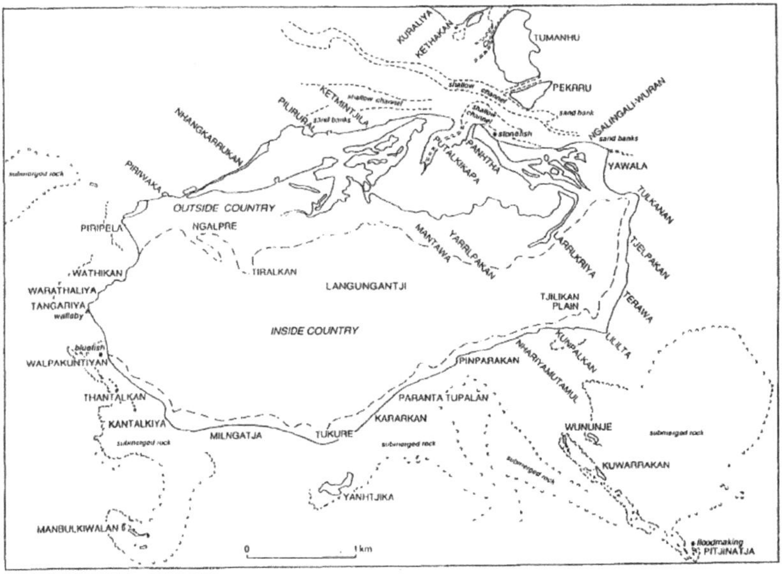

Figure 7:6 Lardil geography of Langungatji, Sunday Island

Widespread mapping throughout the Wellesley Islands and on the mainland has demonstrated that there is an intensity of indigenous geographic knowledge focused on the coastal land systems. There is typically a concentration of place names in these areas; indeed, it would seem that few parts of the coastal land systems were unnamed. In comparison, the interior areas of the islands contain few place names (see Memmott 1983: 51; Tindale 1962a: 276).

As well as designating various features along the shore, certain coastal place names are also used to identify adjacent offshore sea areas. In some cases, prominent features in the sea such as reefs, rocks, oyster banks, sandbars, or sand spits may have a specific name, especially if such a place is of sacred significance; e.g. Bijinaji, the floodmaking place in an underwater reef off Langunganji (Sydney Island, in the North Wellesleys) or Bangarnayirrb (Locust) Reef to the southeast of

Ringurrng (Sweers Island, in the South Wellesleys). To give an idea of the intensity of coastal place naming, there are over 35 names recorded around the perimeter of Sweers Island in Kaiadilt country (an island of approximately 8.6 km x 2 km); similarly, in the case of Sydney Island in Lardil territory (5 km x 2.6km), there are over 30 place names around its perimeter (Figure 7:6). This gives an average of about one named place for every 350–500 metres of coastline. Tindale's map of Bentinck Island (1962a) similarly presents a densely named coastal strip of country (and see Figure 7:4 for coastal Ganggalida country on the mainland, though this Figure shows only a small proportion of the named sites).

The intensity of coastal naming reflects the tendency for people to have traditionally spent much of their time living on the coast. Among the Lardil, most camps were located on the sand-based coastal systems and people maintained an orientation to the sea. A primary advantage of living in this location is ease of access to food resources. Such residential areas are within daily range of most of the land and marine systems, ensuring a great variety of habitats for many animals and plants, and an abundance of resources for artefacts and shelter manufacture. Furthermore, there were specialised locations on the coast such as turtle and dugong hunting camps (Memmott 1983:52).

Among Lardil and Kaiadilt people, there is a large body of customary knowledge concerning the marine environment, its plants and animals, the weather, tides and the behaviour of the seas. There is a detailed classification of the seasonal cycle, and extensive knowledge of the nature of offshore winds, the movements of fish schools, the times of the fattening offish and the reproduction of sea animals. As well as various techniques used to catch sea resources there are traditional practices associated with the consumption of certain species. While these practices have been maintained much more among those residing on the islands (including some people who would identify as mainlanders) coastal Ganggalida traditions mirrored the Lardil and Kaiadilt cultures in respect of this knowledge. For example, butchering of dugong was a rule-governed exercise right throughout the region, with different parts of the animal ideally being distributed to people of different status.[4]

Social and territorial organisation

Coastal clan estates appear to be a fundamental territorial unit of the four language groups discussed in this paper. In both the Lardil and Ganggalida cases, the dimensions of estates are defined by boundaries at roughly right angles to the shore line. While quite fixed by geographic markers on the coast, these estates may extend somewhat indefinitely out to sea or into the interior land systems. The boundaries of the coastal estates would appear to be subject to fission and fusion over time due to demographic changes, disputes, political activity and so on.

The culture of the Lardil exhibits a strong patrilineal ideology whereby coastal lands and seas are held by patricians and ownership rights are transmitted from male ancestors. People can also assert rights over country through connections to grandparents other than one's father's father; however, this would seem to have been practised more commonly among the Kaiadilt and Ganggalida peoples. Lardil individuals, as with the other language groups, also claim rights and interests in their birth-place, and flexible processes of succession most likely operated widely, according to demographic changes and political processes.

Lardil estate groups would commonly designate a senior person (usually a man) as a type of leader, somebody who was particularly responsible for decisions about use and management of bush resources, including important offshore foods such as dugongs and turtles. Such a person was referred to as *dulmada* in the Lardil language. Tindale

---

4 Bradley (1991) provides a detailed depiction of such knowledge among the Yanyuwa people whose territory is in the vicinity of the Sir Edward Pellew Islands, some 250 km to the west. Mainland Ganggalida people have had considerable historical contact with groups and individuals from Yanyuwa country, this interaction seemingly having intensified since European colonisation.

(1962:273) has reported for the Kaiadilt that 'the eldest living male' of each patriclan estate-owning group is known as *dolnorodangka* (*dolnoro* being the term for the estate itself and *dangka* simply the word for man). Evans (1995:19) corroborates these data with the comment that each clan estate belonged to 'a patrilineal clan headed by a *dulmarra dangkaa* ('land-having man'), whose permission was required before hunting or fishing on his land'. Similarly, our understanding of the traditional Ganggalida terminology is that the sequence of patrician estates along the mainland coast were known as *dulmarra* (now more commonly termed 'countries' in English) and that a senior influential male member of the owning patriclan could be termed *dulmarra dangka*.

One aspect of the ideal role of the Lardil *dulmada* or estate boss, in the area of environmental management, is a rule concerning the hunting of dugong and turtle in marine estates. A hunter venturing into another clan's marine estate should provide the local *dulmada* with certain cuts of meats from any dugong or turtle which is caught in that estate. While this rule is still given regular verbal expression today at Mornington Island, the practice of actually distributing meat in this fashion was disrupted from the 1920s and 1930s, when the entire regional population of Mornington Island gradually moved to live in the mission village. For since that time most people have in fact hunted close to the mission township and have not followed the prescriptive rule about meat distribution. Yet with the advent of the outstation movement over the last ten years, together with land rights and other forms of cultural resurgence, there has been some repopulation of the coastline around the island by small residential groups; and with this phenomenon has come both a degree of increased coastal surveillance by those occupying estate shores and a revitalization of the rule systems governing the management and sharing of local resources.

Such proprietorship over estate resources is also evident in the Kaiadilt case. During an inspection of fish traps on Sweers Island in 1983, a senior man explained how the *dulmarra dangka* would traditionally camp close to certain fish traps, to be on guard against *wungiji dangka*, 'stealing man', that is to say other Kaiadilt persons who might try to sneak into an estate to steal fish and other foods from the traps. Evans (1995: 19) mentions that this role of influential clan leader would be 'passed to a brother or son by a sort of verbal deathbed will' upon the death of the Kaiadilt *dulmarra dangka*.

Religious properties of coast and seas

Throughout the study area there are 'story' or 'Dreaming' places (known for example among Kaiadilt people as *jungarrba dulka*, 'big [i.e. important] place', see Evans 1995: 22), many of which constitute classical increase centres. Ritual actions performed by Aboriginal people at such a place are believed to activate the reproduction or fertility process of the totemic entity there. Some of these places are said to maintain particular plant or animal species, whilst others give rise to meteorological phenomena; for example there are story places for dugong, shark and fish species and for making tidal floods, cyclones and strong winds.

On the islands, almost all story places are located in the coastal land systems, either on the coast itself or offshore in the sea. For example, a site known as Ngawilan comprises three rocks rising from the sea near the eastern end of Mornington Island, which the Lardil believe to be the bodies of their ancestors, the first humans who came into their country. It is believed to be dangerous for outsiders to interfere with story places, which is why there is a perceived need to protect and manage these areas and exclude unhosted outsiders.

Totemic 'energies' are transmitted from story places to humans who are born (or in some cases, spiritually conceived) near a story place, or who preside over and regularly occupy the locale (e.g. the *dulmada* in the case of the Lardil). These people then possess a close identity with their story place and its occupants. Evans (1995: 20) points out for the Kaiadilt that:

> Children are believed to show physical or temperamental resemblances to their conception totems—for example, a 'dugong' child may have a squashed ear like that of a dugong, or

193

> a 'rainbow' child may have a powerful temper like that of the
> rainbow serpent *thuwathu*.

Thus, the totemic entities provide personal subjective links into an invisible but co-existing spiritual world, a realm of non-human spiritual forces which thereby influences profoundly everyday life experience. The right of social identity with elements of this spiritual realm is linked inextricably to rights in coastal lands and seas. Many individuals have totems or Dreamings that are from the saltwater domain. For example, the leader of the Kaiadilt homeland movement in the 1960s and 70s was Darwin Moodoonathi, known as *Ngarrawurna* or 'Bluefish'. This is one of the eight main totems among Kaiadilt people, the others all similarly belonging within saltwater country and seas: *bijarrba* (dugong), *thuwathu* (rainbow), *dibidibi* (rock cod), *kulkiji* (shark), *thandamanda* (water spout), *rukuthi* (casuarina tree) and *walbu* (raft) (Evans 1995: 20). On Mornington Island it has been common to hear individuals referred to as 'Rock Cod' or 'Shark' or 'Barramundi', i.e. using names referring to the Dreaming with which they are associated closely.

For the Lardil there is a close relationship between story places and sacred knowledge. By frequenting a story place locale, individuals may receive gifts of knowledge via dreams. Such knowledge appears to be qualitatively different for each particular story place and we might thus describe a 'territorialisation' of Lardil cosmology. The knowledge obtained from the realm of Dreamings is often in the form of songs with accompanying dances, each of which encompasses one or more associated designs used in performance. For example, there is a chest design for the splash of saltwater on the beach.

Much religious knowledge recounts the creation of aspects of the environment by mythic ancestral beings. An example from coastal Ganggalida country on the mainland is *Bijarrba* (Dugong) Dreaming, which emerged from a fresh water hole some 17 km inland, to then proceed down a watercourse to the sea; on the way, Dugong was speared, its flesh turning into rocks as a consequence of being treated haphazardly by people. After proceeding through the saltwater to the off-shore islands this Dreaming went westwards through the sea towards Yanyuwa country. From the Lardil perspective, at the time of these mythic ances- tors, it is believed that much of the sea was in fact land, and Gununa (Mornington Island) was part of a large peninsula. Most of the coastline is believed to have been created or fashioned by ancestral Dreamings and in some areas they submerged parts of the land beneath the sea. Thus, many of the travel paths and places created on land by these mythic forces are today part of the sea and sea bed.

Examples include certain sacred histories which recount how var- ious ancestral Dreamings cut through the land to make channels for the sea in the North Wellesleys—between Forsyth and Francis islands, Forsyth and Andrew islands and Denham and Mornington islands. Other histories tell how islands were 'cut out'—for example, the South Wellesley Islands of Mirrimanki (Albinia), Durathi (Margaret), Kandingarrbayi (Bessie), Nathayiwinda (Douglas) and Baltayi (Fowler) islands. It is worth noting that such 'creation' of the islands is consis- tent with the process of eustatic sea level changes of the post-glacial Pleistocene and the Holocene, some 6500 years ago, when the Wellesley Islands came into existence according to scientific accounts of the geo- logical history of this area (Memmott 1979: Ch.1).

Indigenous 'law' recounts the travel of various ancestral beings through the sea. Ganggalida oral traditions tell of the route taken by Shark Dreaming westwards from 'Dumbarra country' (in Estate I as shown on Figure 7:4), eventually arriving at a site known as Manangurra in Yanyuwa country (see Bradley 1988). During such travels the Dreamings performed specific activities at particular places. According to the Lardil perspective, Shark Dreaming (which is associated with the origin of Cycad trees throughout the region) travelled along the entire northwest coast of Mornington Island planting the seeds of this spe- cies of tree. Evidence of this mythic activity are the groves of Cycads which now grow at specific places. Similarly, on the southeast coast of Mornington Island a party of largely marine mythic animals and birds travelled along the coast, stopping at various rocky islets, reefs, and spits and tidal flats. A further example is Dingo Dreaming whose travel route connects the coastal mainland with both the North Wellesley Islands and distant inland areas.

Such travel lines can be encoded as a series of public and secret songs (known as *kujiga*) that are sung during male initiation ceremonies. While these ceremonies stopped being performed from around the 1930s on Mornington Island (and have not been performed in coastal Ganggalida country for a long time), they were revived on Mornington during the 1970s and now constitute a regular activity that is important in the reproduction of indigenous identity. Initiation ceremonies involving circumcision are part of the cultural traditions of all language group in the region (e.g. Evans 1995: 22–3).

Among Lardil people, there is a general body of sacred knowledge of particular significance as it deals with the mythic history of *Thuwathu*, the Rainbow Serpent, and explains its potent presence and powers throughout the seas today. Rainbow is believed to continue to exert strong influence on the well-being and health of humans. Rainbow can inflict a sickness known as *markirii* (Memmott 1982). The presence of this major Dreaming extends into the littoral domain, including those more elevated parts inundated only during very high tides. Some groups believe that cyclones, waterspouts and rainbows are manifestations of *Thuwathu*.

Throughout the region the spiritual features of 'saltwater country' are generally entwined closely with traditional resource gathering activities in coastal domains. The socioeconomic importance of the sea and coastal land systems, especially on the islands, complements the intensive bodies of religious knowledge that also pertain to 'saltwater country'. This aspect of indigenous cultures in this area can be referred to locally as 'Sea Law' or 'Saltwater Law'.

Issues of Native title

The Wellesley groups have commenced a joint native title application over their sea country.[5] In part, this action has been precipitated by the threat during recent decades to the customary control of their sea from non-indigenous fishermen. The latter persons at times harvest fish, dugongs, turtles and crabs, in a way that causes considerable distress amongst traditional owners, particularly when they use dynamite and/or netting practices that kill too many animals and are regarded locally as threatening the survival of certain species. Also of concern has been a proposal to build a slurry pipeline which would extend from an inland mine to a port either on the mainland coast or on an off-shore island.[6]

In making application for a marine native title determination, the Wellesley peoples have encountered a conceptual challenge in nominating how far to claim out to sea, given that no fixed boundary lines exist under customary marine tenure. A fairly common view amongst the claimants is that all seas within visual range of the shore are most certainly part of their sea country; this range may be about 20km but varies with the height of the viewer, the elevation of their observation point, tides, wave action, weather and general conditions for visibility. Visibility of the land from the sea was extremely important for

---

5   A separate Magistrates Court case has involved a particular Ganggalida man defending a charge of taking a protected animal on the grounds of his native title rights to do so according to Aboriginal law. As well as the defendant's evidence, the Magistrate accepted the results of ethnographic research and archaeological findings demonstrating Aboriginal occupation of a coastal Ganggalida estate (Eaton vs Yanner, No. 1692 of 1995, Mt Isa Magistrates Court).

6   The slurry pipeline from Century Mine was finally routed away from the immediate Wellesley Islands area to Karumba some considerable distance to the east. However, concerns about initial plans for it to run into coastal Ganggalida country and then out to Sweers Island caused much tension and concern among traditional owners of these areas (see Trigger 1997).

traditional marine navigation. Conversely, surveillance of the sea from the land is a constant preoccupation for those with a marine economy and cosmology.

While traditional customary use of the seas prior to European colonisation was limited by the available watercraft technologies, and while the South Wellesley islanders in particular faced a substantial degree of isolation, there was constant use of the seas in this area of the southern Gulf of Carpentaria. Furthermore, tenure over the sea should not be conceived solely in terms of waters that were available for physical use.

It should be clear from the results of intensive ethnographic research presented in this paper that expansive areas of the sea are regarded as owned because of their intellectually recognised properties as well as their economic significance. With the adoption of motor driven watercraft local Aboriginal people can now more safely use broader expanses of their sea country for resource-obtaining and other activities. This change wrought through processes of colonisation has involved a gradually increasing use of seas further out from coastal camps. However, we would argue that this represents an increased use of seas that were always regarded as customarily owned. A final comment on this matter is apposite.

Because of the relationship between coastal/offshore story places and meteorological phenomena, many cloud, tide and wind events which occur within visual range out to sea, are believed to be causally linked to the activities of humans at story places. The visual range of clouds in the sky, of course, extends beyond the limit of the horizon, but just how far is still under investigation. It has been calculated that a Morning Glory cloud travelling from the east at an elevation of about 1000m can be seen on a very clear day at a distance of about 112 km from Sweers Island.[7] Rising cumulo-nimbus clouds in summer storms[8]

---

7   These figures have been provided to the Carpentaria Land Council by Ms Cathy Robinson, Department of Geography and Environmental Science, Monash University, December 1995. Ms Robinson was requested to research this matter. For meteorological analysis of the 'Morning Glory' cloud, see Neal et al (1977).

8   Called *thaldija* or 'tower-up' clouds in Kaiadilt (Evans 1995: 769).

can probably be seen at significantly longer distances. Yet Aboriginal claimants will maintain that such phenomena can be controlled or influenced from nearby places in the seas surrounding the Wellesley Islands. There is thus a notion that Saltwater Law, as practised through customary behaviour, extends out into this wider territorial marine domain. In this sense, the notion of native title rights and interests in sea country should be understood as potentially extending much further than solely over the waters used customarily for traditional hunting and fishing.

References

Bradley, J. 1988. *Yanyuwa country: the Yanyuwa people of Borroloola tell the history of their land*. Richmond: Greenhouse Publications.

1991. 'Li-maramaranja': Yanyuwa hunters of marine animals in the Sir Edward Pellew Group, Northern Territory. *Records of the South Australian Museum* 25 (1): 91–110.

Evans, N. 1995. *A grammar of Kayardild, with historical-comparative notes on Tangkic*. Berlin: Mouton de Gruyter.

Keen, S. 1983. 'Yukulta'. In *Handbook of Australian languages* v.3 (ed) R. Dixon. Canberra: Australian National University Press. Pp. 191–304.

Memmott, P. 1979. Lardil properties of place. Unpublished PhD thesis. Brisbane: University of Queensland.

1982. Rainbows, story places, and Malkri sickness in the north Wellesley Islands. *Oceania* 53:163–182.

1983. *Social structure and use of space amongst the Lardil. In Aborigines, land and land rights* (eds) N. Peterson and M. Langton. Canberra: Australian Institute of Aboriginal Studies. Pp. 33–65.

1986. Lardil ethnography: the Aboriginal geography of place in the north Wellesley Islands. *Man-Environment Systems* 16(5 and 6): 218–226.

Neal, A., Butterworth, I. and Murray, K. 1977. *The Morning Glory*. Canberra: Department of Science, Bureau of Meteorology. Technical Report 23.

Robins, R., Stock, E. and Trigger, D. 1997. Saltwater country, saltwater people: geomorphological, anthropological and archaeological investigations of coastal lands in the Gulf Country of Queensland. *Memoirs of the Queensland Museum (Cultural Heritage Series)* New Series 1:1.

Tindale, N. 1962a. Geographic knowledge of the Kaiadilt People of Bentinck Island, Queensland. *Records of the South Australian Museum* 14(2):259–296.

1962b. Some population changes among the Kaiadilt people of Bentinck Island, Queensland. Records of the South Australian Museum 14(2):297–319.

1977. Further report on the Kaiadilt people of Bentinck Island, Gulf of Carpentaria, Queensland. In *Sunda and Sahul: prehistoric studies in Southeast Asia, Melanesia and Australia*, (eds) J. Allen, J. Golson and R. Jones. London: Academic Press. Pp.247–273.

Trigger, D. 1987. Inland coast and islands: traditional Aboriginal society and material culture in a region of the southern Gulf of Carpentaria. *Records of the South Australian Museum* 21(2): 69–84.

1992. *Whitefella comin': Aboriginal responses to colonialism in northern Australia*. Cambridge: Cambridge University Press.

1997. Reflections on Century Mine: preliminary thoughts on the politics of Indigenous responses. In *Fighting over country: anthropological perspectives* (eds) D. Smith and J. Finlayson. Canberra: Centre for Aboriginal Economic Policy Research, Australian National University. Pp. 110–128.

8

'We always look north': Yanyuwa identity and the maritime environment

John J. Bradley

> I look across the expanse
> of the open sea:
> The high waves in the north
> are at last calm.
> (Short Friday Babawurra)

The short piece of song-poetry given above was composed by a Yanyuwa 'saltwater man' while surveying the sea that he wished to travel upon. His descendants sang this and other song during the 1940s, 50s and 60s while working on cattle stations on the vast, wind-blown Barkly Tablelands and others, to remind them of the sea country which was there waiting for them. Today the Yanyuwa people live in and around the township of Borroloola some 1000 kilometres southeast of Darwin, and some 60 kilometres inland from the sea (Figure 8:1). Despite the effects of enforced relocation to provide a part of the labour force on the cattle stations and issues arising from various welfare polices, the sea has remained as an important point of identity for the Yanyuwa people.

It was Stanner (1965) who commented that within the anthropological literature there had been far too much emphasis on the inland Central Australian arid zone, primarily because it was perceived that the Aboriginal people of such areas had been isolated for the longest period of time from European influence, and therefore their social patterns and economies were felt to be still among the most traditional in Australia. There have been few major studies undertaken where the resources and environments of the coastal people of northern Australia have been explored. Chase and Sutton (1987) rightly argued, in relation to the coast, that this imbalance must be set right, as the coastal regions of northern Australia represent some of the most diverse in Australia, encompassing an area where the marine and the terrestrial environments come together. They (Chase and Sutton 1987:69) commented that:

> The northern tropical coastline of Australia presents an area where Aboriginal hunter-gatherers operated within such habitats, and the complex patterns of plant communities, marine environments and animal life in these tropical areas provide opportunities for resource exploitation which can hardly be exceeded elsewhere on the Australian continent.

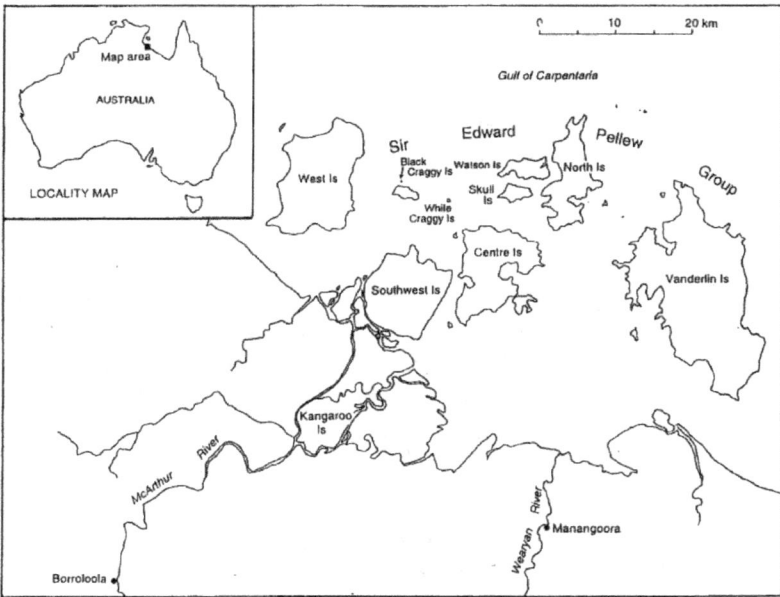

Figure 8:1 Southwest Gulf of Carpentaria, Borroloola and the Sir Edward Pellew Islands

The Sir Edward Pellew Islands and the immediate coastal areas provide a case where there is an interesting balance between mainland, sea and islands. Baker (1989) notes that the shallow nature of the sea in this area of the Gulf, the shape of the islands, and the complex maze of creeks and channels which make up the mouths of the rivers entering the Gulf, all produce a great length of coastline for quite a small amount of land. This large area of shallow water and long coastline has enabled the Yanyuwa to develop an economy and traditions which focus heavily on its marine and nearby terrestrial resources.

The island and coastal geography

The islands which comprise the archipelago of Sir Edward Pellew Group span out to the north and northeast across the mouths of the McArthur River, Wearyan River and Carrington Channel (Figure 8:1). These islands range in size from approximately 264 square kilometres (Vanderlin Island) down to isolated rocks of a few square metres. Arnol (1983:165–166) estimated that the group consists of eight large islands, more than fifty small sandy islets and approximately twenty reefs.

The dominant habitats on the islands are open eucalypt woodland, stunted monsoon forest, sandstone heath, salt marsh, dune communities, freshwater wetlands on Vanderlin Island, mangrove communities and, moving into the sea, sea grass beds. The sea grass beds surround the southerly coastal regions of the islands, and are therefore an important element of the total maritime ecology. This is especially the case in relation to a Yanyuwa perception of this environment (Arnol 1983; Ygoa-McKeown 1987; and Johnson and Kerle 1991).

Winds are an important factor in access to the sea and the sea grass beds and they decide whether or not people will be able to cross or hunt. During the mid to late dry season southeasterly winds blow at their most intense, the shallow waters of the Gulf become choppy and dirty as the water becomes clouded with sediment, thus reducing visibility through the water dramatically, and making it virtually impossible to hunt for dugong and sea turtle. Such sediment-filled water is called *yurduwiji*, 'being with dust', and is differentiated from *manginy*, sediment disturbed by feeding dugong and turtle. The analogy between dust storms on land and the 'dusty sea' for the Yanyuwa is very close as the term *yurduwiji awara* or a 'country being with dust' is used for both land and sea.

The Yanyuwa categorise their physical landscape in a manner which we would recognise, that is, divisions according to various land units, whereby the combination of vegetation, soils and topography provide distinct areas. The notion of distinctive land units recognised by Aboriginal people has also been explored by Jones (1980, 1985) in his research with the Gidjingali people of north coastal Arnhem Land, Williams (1982) with the Yolngu of North East Arnhem Land, and Chase (1980) and Chase and Sutton (1981) with Aboriginal people of Cape York Peninsula. Baker (1989) also discussed, in a general way, the notion of recognised land units amongst the Yanyuwa.

Such a sense of land units as discussed by the Gidjingali and the Yanyuwa people approximates a system developed by the CSIRO in 1953 (Christian *et al.* 1953, 1954; and Speck *et al* 1960). Briefly, it may be said that western biogeographers classify the land into units so as to reflect what they regard as objective ecological realities.

While the system of land units as devised by the Yanyuwa and the CSIRO may be broadly comparable, their functions are somewhat different, deriving from the very different ways in which knowledge is embedded within cultural structures and processes. That the Yanyuwa and the biogeographers end up with similar schemes is not that surprising, because both schemes relate to a commonly perceived 'real' environment, but the Yanyuwa scheme is nonetheless richer and more animated in its conception.

The Yanyuwa consider the sea and sea grass beds to be part of these geographic land units. The sea and tidal mudflats and coastal saltpans are often described as being 'open country', where one can see a great distance, whilst the mainland and the islands are sometimes described as 'closed country' where one's view is hindered by trees, hills and other geographical features. In the Yanyuwa language, the sea is often further divided into *antha*, which usually refers to that sea which is familiar and often travelled on during hunting and fishing, whilst the larger expanses of open sea and ocean are termed *warlamakamaka* or *malabubana*. These latter two terms connote a sense of caution necessary when travelling on them.

The term *kunjurrkunjurr* conveys the notion of sea that is so far away that people would be indeed rash to say they would travel there: it is unknown, dangerous and not within the realms of normal human activity.

The known sea is further divided into the sea grass beds and the sea above them and can be seen as a unit: this is the 'underwater country', named and known. The term *na-ngunantha* is used to describe the home or 'camp' of the dugong and sea turtle, and carries the same *na-* arboreal prefix which the Yanyuwa use for other types of 'homes', whether human or animal, such as *na-wungkala*, a flying fox 'camp', or *na-alanji*, a human camp'.

The sea and underwater country of the Yanyuwa is, as with the mainland, often called by the term *awara*. It is a word which conveys a large number of meanings, such as earth, ground, place, country, camp, sea, reefs and sandbars. The term highlights the Yanyuwa concept that the sea and the underwater country are known places, that they are named. As such, it is perfectly reasonable to ask for the name of a stretch of sea, reef, sandbar or sea grass bed. Often the sea grass beds, for example, are seen to be an extension of the mainland and carry the same name as a section of the coast. In other cases the sea grass beds and the reefs have their own names by which they and the surrounding area of sea are known (Figure 8:2).

These sea grass beds are the 'home' or 'camp' of the dugongs and sea turtles. A more common term used for describing the sea grass beds is *ki-maramanda*, which means 'the place with the sea grass'. Because these sea grass beds and reefs are seen to be country which is identifiable by name and therefore known, they are owned. The underwater country has semi-moiety/patriclan association, and thus it too is intertwined within the complex social workings of the *jungkayi* (guardian)—*ngimarringki* (owner) system, which in many respects is an expression of material, territorial and economic rights. Some of the sea grass beds and reefs are important sites due to the activities of the Spirit Ancestors, and many of them have song cycles travelling over them which are still sung during ceremonial performance. The Yanyuwa names given to the sea grass are also celebrated in these song cycles. Western scientific research has shown that the underwater country of the Yanyuwa is rich in sea grass species (Poiner *et al* 1987).

In Yanyuwa the term *maraman* is used to to describe all sea grass species. A distinction is then made between those sea grasses that they perceive to belong to the major sea grass beds which follow the coastline and some of which are exposed at low tide. The sea grasses which are found there, which also represents the most favoured hunting areas, are called by the term *ma-Lhanngu*. The Yanyuwa then make a distinction between the sea grasses which are found on inshore and on offshore reefs. The sea grasses found on reefs are said to be the 'proper' food for sea turtles, though it is acknowledged that dugong will eat them also. The term *na-wirralbirral* is used for inshore sea grasses. The term *na-julangal* is used for those species of sea grass which are found on offshore reefs.

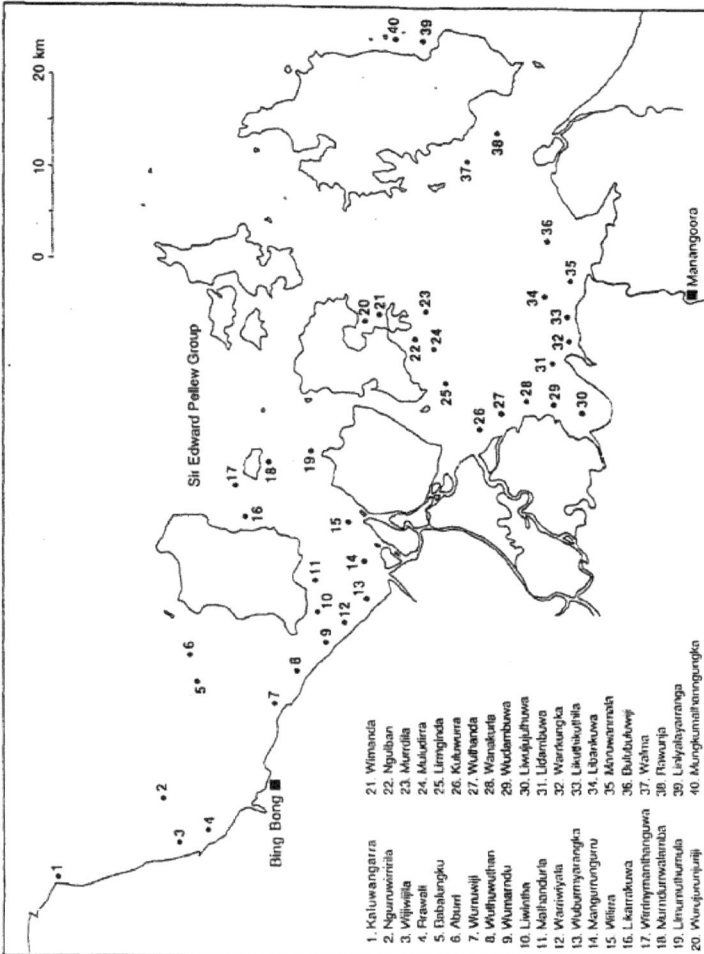

Figure 8:2 Sea grass beds and reefs known and named by Yanyuwa dugong and turtle hunters

1. Kaluwangarra
2. Ngurruwirrirla
3. Wijiwijila
4. Rawali
5. Babakungku
6. Aburi
7. Wurruwiji
8. Wudhuwudhan
9. Wumarndu
10. Liwintha
11. Malhandurla
12. Waariwiyala
13. Wuburrnyarrangka
14. Mangurrunguru
15. Wilirra
16. Lkarrakuwa
17. Wirrinymanthanrguwa
18. Murndurrwalarrala
19. Lirrurruthurrurda
20. Wundjurunjiji
21. Wirrandla
22. Ngulban
23. Murrdila
24. Muludirra
25. Liringinda
26. Kuluwurra
27. Wulhanda
28. Wanakurla
29. Wudambuwa
30. Liwijujulhuwa
31. Uddambuwa
32. Waarkungka
33. Likudlukuthila
34. Libankuwa
35. Manawarrmala
36. Buldukuwy
37. Walma
38. Rawurja
39. Liwiyalrayarranga
40. Mungkumalhanngurangka

Sir Edward Pellew Group

Bing Bong

Manangoora

20 km

The Yanyuwa perceive that there is a close relationship existing between the varying sea grasses and the dugong and sea turtle as, for example, in the expression *walya nyiki-nganji ki-maramanngku*, or 'the dugong and sea turtle are kin to the sea grass' (pers. comm. Charlie Miller 1980). A key word in Yanyuwa ethnoecology is the word *nganji* which, when accompanied with pronominal prefixes, conveys the meaning of kin, mate or established relationships. When unmarked by pronominal prefixes, the term means 'stranger' or 'enemy', in much the same way that host and hostile in English are related to each other. However, the word is multivocal and is dependent on context for full meaning. One of the implicit meanings of *nganji* when accompanied with pronominal prefixes is that of a perceived co-dependency of those entities to which the term is applied. The dependency is often associated with a hunter-prey relationship, where the hunter is always kin to the hunted. Many animals, plants and people are described using this term. For example, the Yanyuwa are kin to the sea, dugong hunters are kin to the dugong, while the dugong is kin to the sea grass beds. The term is used extensively in relation to the coastal seabirds; they are described by the Yanyuwa as being kin to the fish upon which they are said to feed. On a much more basic level, the term can be used to describe similarity, such as two yams which share the same soil type, two similar colours or a group of relatives (see also Chase and von Sturmer 1980 and Nash 1981). The term can also be used to make a detailed reference to someone's association with a particular place, or to a group of people who hold knowledge concerning a particular ceremony. The term *nganji* may be highlighting what the Yanyuwa perceive to be a mutual interest in each other's development.

Humans engage in a 'killing' dialogue with a number of animal populations which they pursue, kill and feed upon. Humans also have faculties which allow them to ponder the meanings of such bonds between themselves and the other species they observe. Such a view may provide one of the reasons why Yanyuwa hunters, both men and women, often express sorrow or pity when they are killing or butchering an animal. It is said by the Yanyuwa, obviously enough, that without the sea grass there would be no sea turtles, in particular, green turtles, or dugong: but likewise it is said that without the dugong and sea turtle, there would be no sea grass, as their feeding upon it keeps it healthy. In Yanyuwa ecological terms the death of dugong and sea turtles is seen to be important to the maintenance of the sea grass beds.

This belief echoes that of Heinsohn (1981:92) who suggested that 'the destructive feeding [of dugong] may help to maintain a diversity of species in sea grass communities by producing a large number of seral stages' and confirmed by Helene Marsh and Tony Preen (pers. comm. 1996).

The sea as country

There is a tendency amongst some Yanyuwa people, especially those of the older generation, to say that the mainland begins at the extreme inland limit of the coastal saltpans and mudflats. The reasoning for this is that these areas also contain small sandy 'islets', which are often covered in sparse vegetation. During the period of the king tides in the later half of the year and tidal surges caused by cyclones, these flats are inundated, leaving the small islets standing dry, quite isolated and surrounded by water. This landscape in Yanyuwa is classed as *narnu-ru-luruluwanka*. Trigger (1987:72), in his work with the Ganggalida people to the east of Yanyuwa country, has also found a similar perception that the mainland begins on the inland limit of the coastal salt pans and mudflats.

The Yanyuwa are at home in these lower 'saltwater' coastal regions, and while they hunt in the inland 'freshwater' limits of their country, they describe it as *jibuburula* which is usually translated as 'dry country'. The word is based on the root *jiburu*, which means unpleasant, unpalatable or even worn-out or broken; it is the country of the Garrwa and Gudanji people. The irony of the term 'dry' in this context is that it begins where the McArthur and Wearyan River systems are permanently fresh and not under the influence of the tides.

Such inland country is also called 'scrub country', and people describe it as country where it is not possible to get a breeze on one's face. This thought is highlighted in the following song composed by Elma Brown a-Bunubunu on her return to the coast from the Barkly Tablelands:

> I stand and feel the sea wind,
>
> it refreshes my face; for too long
>
> I have been a woman of the inland 'scrub country'.

People such as the Garrwa and Gudanji see Yanyuwa country as being very distinct from the mainland. It is a country which fits the Yanyuwa people who are known as 'saltwater people', while the Garrwa and Gudanji are called the 'freshwater people'. Gudanji and Garrwa people travel into this country, usually in the company of Yanyuwa people. These trips by the 'mainlanders' usually only take place during the more pleasant times of the year such as the cool part of the dry season, and they do not bother with such country during the mosquito-ridden, intensely humid pre-wet season period.

The Yanyuwa, however, see the coastal areas as being special in terms of their geography, the food sources that are available and as an environment that distinguishes them from the other Aboriginal groups in the area. The thought of their coastal country sometimes moves people to high levels of emotion. It is the sea more than any other geographical feature which the Yanyuwa use as a metaphor for their existence and their identity. The most common of these terms is *li-Anthawirriyarra*, which means 'those people whose spiritual and cultural heritage comes from the sea', but which in everyday English speech is rendered as 'the people of the sea'. Another term *li.Karinguthundangu*, means, 'those people who come from the coastal and sea country' and *ll-Kannuthundangu* means 'those people from the north', which is a shorthand reference to the sea and islands. Perhaps one of the most explicit references to this association with the sea is expressed in the saying *nganu li-Yanyuwa kaninyambu-ngka ki-anthaa*, meaning 'we Yanyuwa people have our origins, (or we originated), in the sea'. Young Yanyuwa people who do not speak Yanyuwa will describe themselves as 'saltwater people', or as an 'island man or island woman', and then often derisively add that they are not freshwater mainland people. The strength of this attachment to the sea has meant that Yanyuwa descendants who may have had little or no association with the sea and islands will proudly proclaim themselves as 'belonging to the saltwater country of the Gulf'.

The sea, as with nearly all other geographical features and phenomena in the Yanyuwa environment is a Spirit Ancestor. The sea, which is masculine, belongs to the Rrumburriya semi-moiety, while the waves are feminine and are also associated with the Rrumburriya semi-moiety. Both the spiritual essences of the waves and the sea are said to be located on Cape Vanderlin or Muluwa. The tidal patterns of the sea are associated with an area of beach of the central east coast of Vanderlin Island called Wabuwa. This locality is associated with the activities of the Dugong Hunter Spirit Ancestors. The waves are associated with the activity of a seasnake called, in Yanyuwa, *a-wirninybirniny (Lampemis hardwickii)*. The waves, *a-rumu*, which the snake creates, are feminine, as are the crests of the waves, *nanda-wuku*, literally 'her back', or the sea spray *nanda-rayal*, 'her sputum', *nanda-minymi*, 'her condensation from the mouth', which is the fine sea spray which results from waves pounding on the rocks. The sea snake is described as being *rrankunganji rru-rumungku*, or as 'one which is kin to the waves and sea'.

Similarly, many of the currents found around the islands are associated with the residual power of various Spirit Ancestors. These currents are generally called *wayikuku*, while the term *arrayalya* is applied to a point where two tidal streams come together, where Spirit Ancestor paths cross. The presence of two currents coming together is often evidenced by the existence of flows of tidal rubbish known in Yanyuwa as *janjirlkirri*.

As with many other Spirit Ancestor entities, knowledgeable people can use the spiritual power associated with the sea and tides for either negative or positive purposes. People can 'sing' the sea snake and cause waves to form, or cause the sea to become calm. Likewise, knowledgeable people can sing the tide, as Jemima Miller Wuwarlu describes:

> The old men and women can sing people, they can sing them
> to the sea, as the tide goes out people become dry, they are
> tired, listless, not well, then later as the tide comes back up
> they are refreshed, they feel happy again. Such people have
> songs which make the sea theirs.

Such songs are sung by 'jealous' people who are envious of people getting dugong, sea turtle and other sea foods, or by angry relatives who
have been left out of hunting trips or journeys to other places on the
islands. In 1992 during the process of the land claim on the Pellew
Islands, a number of people said they felt very tired and worn out. They
did not put it down to the intensity of the land claim process in which
they were involved, but rather, they said, someone had sung the tide
and it had made them weak. When I inquired as to why someone would
sing the tide on them, the reply was universally that other people on
the mainland were jealous that they, the Yanyuwa sea people, still knew
their country and were fighting to get it back.

The sea, as with the land, is not beyond influence, for there are those
who know how it can be used to the detriment or betterment of others.
The sea is still seen to be a mysterious place, but this is not to say it is
feared. It is respected, and people will choose the right time to travel
over the sea. It is common, when people are about to embark on a journey across a stretch of sea, or after having completed a journey, to recall
previous journeys or speak of their ancestors who had completed the
same journey in dugout and bark canoes.

The Yanyuwa are well aware that a life centred on the sea is far
riskier than one based totally upon the mainland, and in the past there
was a higher mortality rate associated with the sea. A number of stories are still told of drownings by overturned canoes, and of bark and
dugout canoes that literally fell apart mid-journey (see Timothy (Jnr)
in Bradley 1989:1 82; Timothy (Snr) in Bradley 1991:88). A number of
log coffin and bone bundle burials on the islands contain the remains
of people who died because of accidents at sea. In addition to this, a
number of special memorial stones over the islands represent people
whose bodies were never recovered. People were also born in canoes

and died in canoes. However, having said this, the Yanyuwa people's association with the sea has conferred on them certain unique benefits in terms of food sources, technology and ceremonies, and has given the Yanyuwa a very powerful status in relation to other language groups in the area of the Gulf. They are not, as they often put it, 'scrub dwellers of the mainland'.

The seas around the islands can become rough quite suddenly: squalls can hit without much warning. There are sharks, jellyfish, and stonefish as well as dugong, sea turtle and fish. Yanyuwa people respond to all this with great care, sometimes by the use of magic or 'power' and just as effectively, with great familiarity. For all the hardship that the sea can provide, it is still a familiar place. People accept the complex tides and currents and the, at times, unpredictable nature of the sea. Even when two people were involved in an incident where their dinghy capsized in rough weather when it hit a sand bar, the occupants were not overly concerned. It happened to the old people, and therefore it will happen to them, and as an added aside, maybe 'something' caused it to happen—an angry Spirit or human ancestor could just as well have done it. The dangers that the sea can provide for travellers are not spoken of as such. They are not even called risks: rather they are described simply as, 'that's just the kind of life we have on the sea' (pers. comm. Johnson Timothy 1982).

Such an acceptance of the dangers that the sea can provide is also expressed in the following song. It was composed after two women were caught in a westerly squall while paddling a dugout canoe and tells of how the two women felt during the experience:

> We may yet be able, to cross westwards,
>
> But we may be thrown eastwards, by these waves.
>
> (Suzanne Jujana and Darby Muluwamara)

The sea has represented for generations of Yanyuwa people a point of unity with the natural environment. It embodies for these people a place of origin. It provides metaphors by which they describe themselves. It is important to note that they do not often call themselves island people, they are 'sea people or saltwater people'. The reason for such self-description becomes obvious when one travels with the Yanyuwa people to the relatively shallow areas of sea, under which grows the seagrass that the dugong and sea turtle feed on.

Dugong and sea turtle

> The dugong and sea turtle they are sea creatures of authority, they belonged to our ancestors and they belong to us ... they are like the fruit of the cycad food as it too is a food of authority. (Nora Jalirduma 1988)

Within the Yanyuwa classification of the environment, the dugong, the green sea turtle and the fruit of the cycad palm *(Cycas angulata)* are all classed as being food sources of *wurrama* or 'authority'. They were in past times considered to be those food sources which were essential for the physical as well as the spiritual survival of the Yanyuwa people. At the present time, the cycad palm fruit is rarely gathered and processed, although when people speak of it, their voices still resonate with a degree of emotion, highlighting the importance that this food source has in the historical view of the Yanyuwa environment and their place in it (see Bradley 1988: 1–29; McDinny in Bradley 1989: 215–235).

The dugong and sea turtle are still important. They represent for the Yanyuwa an important focus which demonstrates a continuity with the past, and in times which are rapidly changing, an affirmation of the ability to maintain the links with the past. This is demonstrated not only by the hunting of these creatures but also in other knowledge associated with them, which seeks to explain their behaviour and their place within the marine environment (see Bradley 1991: 91–110). Yanyuwa men and women say that such creatures as the dugong and sea turtle have their own Law, their own culture, their own way of being. The view that the various species have their own culture is also evidenced in that they have their own favoured food sources and localities and that they behave in certain ways. Because of the strong links between people, living things and sites on the landscape, it is also felt that all life forms such as animals, plants, insects, fish and birds have the ability to make perceptions about the environment they live in. They can evaluate a given situation within themselves, and ultimately, they are seen to be totally conscious and responsible beings. Furthermore, just as human beings observe and interpret the actions of other living things, it is also felt that living things observe and interpret the actions of human beings. As such, they too are part of the established Law which began when their own Spirit Ancestors first moved on the landscape. Thus, the Dugong Spirit Ancestor not only provides the basis by which human beings can try to understand dugong, but the original Dugong Ancestor is also seen to provide the reasons why dugong behave like dugong. In this instance, the term Law is being used to describe the various habits of other species, and the word Law is being used as a paradigm for the biological traits which each species possesses.

Thus, the understanding of animals and other species having Law means that actions such as mating, giving birth to young, the laying and hatching of eggs, feeding habits, growth and eventual death are seen to be elements which express the eternity of the order which is simply called the Law. Such processes as alluded to above are a continual restatement about how things were in the very beginning, and how it is hoped they always will be. However, the contemporary world shows that outside influences can dramatically change the perceptions of this Law. For example, professional fishermen set nets which run over the sea grass beds, dugong get caught in them and drown. The question, 'Why don't the dugong learn about nets?' could be posed. The knowledge of nets, however, is not a part of dugong Law: it is a part of human Law. Humans, therefore, have to act on behalf of the dugong to try and preserve them. This should not be seen as just good environmental or ecological sense: rather, it is the way that kin should treat each other because of a shared genesis, dugong and Yanyuwa people are relatives.

Likewise, the activities of tourists, miners and other unknowledgable people over the sea and coast all worry the Yanyuwa in regard to their relationship with the other species which inhabit the environment. The death of large numbers of dugong in gill nets set by professional fishermen over the sea grass beds causes immense grief and anger amongst the Yanyuwa.

A general principle of Yanyuwa ethno-classification is a division between what are considered coastal-marine and island species as opposed to inland-mainland species. This categorisation is not rigid, and depending on circumstances, some creatures and plant species will move between the maritime environment and the mainland. Usually such examples have more to do with individual perception of the species involved, and in group discussion such differences in opinion can be the source of lively debate. Thus, any species seen to be associated with the sea, islands and coast are called *wurralngu*, a term meaning literally 'being for depths of the sea'; by extension, however, the term is also used to describe any creature which is perceived to belong to the marine and island environment. Yanyuwa people, too, are included in this category.

Dugong and sea turtle are of course labelled as *wurralngu*, but are more commonly referred to as *walya*. This term *walya* has no direct English translation, but it is generally translated as 'dugong and sea turtle'. The basis for such a category is probably twofold: firstly they are the only creatures in the sea which feed extensively on sea grass; secondly, they are the largest marine animals hunted and are culturally significant.

Hunters in the marine environment

Our hair is strong, tightly coiled and heavily oiled;

For we are inhabitants of the sea country

We are dugong and sea turtle hunters of excellence

(Jack Baju 'Akarrunda')

The above song is still sung by older Yanyuwa men and women. It was composed in the mid 1920s when a visitor from one of the linguistic groups neighbouring the Yanyuwa suggested that the closest relative of the Yanyuwa people was the black saline mud of the sea country, and that this mud could always be seen clinging to the bodies of Yanyuwa people. In response Jack Baju composed this song; it is bold and boastful and it speaks of meanings and understandings for the Yanyuwa people that words alone cannot convey.

The song is important for both Yanyuwa men and women. The key words in the Yanyuwa original are *li-wurralngu* which literally means 'the people, all people, who are inhabitants of the sea' and *li-marama-ranja*, which is best translated as meaning 'those people who are dugong and sea turtle hunters of excellence'. In the song Jack Baju has is stressing the importance and centrality of this activity to the Yanyuwa people, expressing it as a means by which they truly demonstrate their selfperceived uniqueness.

So strong is this bond between sea, dugong, sea turtle and being Yanyuwa that one elderly man once commented to me and a gathering of Yanyuwa men and women that:

> The old people spoke Yanyuwa, they were always talking Yanyuwa,
>
> we are here speaking Yanyuwa because we are dugong and sea turtle
>
> hunters of excellence, we are those people who desire to harpoon them
>
> (Tim Rakawurlma, field diary 1984).

For this old man and the assembled men and women, who added their own self-affirming comments, the fact that they speak Yanyuwa is also intimately associated with the activity of hunting sea turtle and dugong. The term *maranja* and the group term *li-maramanja* for skilled hunters are terms not used just for someone who is able to kill a dugong and sea turtle, although in the contemporary sense, it is more often becoming so. Rather, it is and was reserved for those people who also knew the Law associated with the sea, the sea grass, dugong and turtles, as well as knew the spiritual significance of the activity.

To become a *maranja* involves training, an apprenticeship, and finally, after some time, the term is awarded to an individual who has showed that he had absorbed all of the teachings associated with the activity and can demonstrate the knowledge in all its areas, from hunting, butchering, and distribution of meat to also knowing the more esoteric spiritual matters associated with the way of dugong and sea turtle hunting. In the past and, to some extent today, the training of young men to become hunters, and of young men and women to understand the Law associated with hunting, butchering, cooking and distribution involves quite strict procedural steps. There are certain rituals which are designed not just to increase the efficiency and discipline of the hunt but also to create respect for the roles played by the individuals involved in the actual hunt and by members in the community waiting for the return of the hunters.

Over the last hundred years, or perhaps more, the activity of hunting dugong and sea turtle has changed dramatically. New technology such as aluminium dinghies have replaced bark and dugout canoes, steel harpoon points, nylon and hemp ropes, and polystyrene floats have all changed the visible aspects of hunting. But other things have changed too. The time spent hunting, the necessity to hunt and who is available to hunt have all had an impact upon Yanyuwa dugong and sea turtle hunting.

Some factors associated with the activity of hunting have been relatively stable. They are the more esoteric things, and they continue to have importance for the Yanyuwa. They are part of the means by which the continuity from past hunters to contemporary hunters is preserved. One of the important ways this continuity is achieved is by the Spirit Ancestor narrative of the the *li-Maramaranja*, which the Yanyuwa simply call the Dugong Hunters, but which, as mentioned above, could be translated as the 'Dugong and Sea Turtle Hunters of Excellence'.

The narrative and song of the Dugong Hunter Spirit Ancestors are associated with the island Rrumburriya semi-moiety, and the path of these Spirit Ancestors crosses the breadth of the Pellew Islands from Vanderlin Island in the east to West Island in the west. All of the other semi-moieties have groups of spirit beings on their own country which are sung in their song cycles and which are also designated as dugong and sea turtle hunters. They are not creative beings in the sense that the

Dugong Hunter Spirit Ancestors are; rather, they are spirit beings who were sighted by other Spirit Ancestors as they journeyed.

For example, in the Wuyaliya song cycle associated with the Groper Spirit Ancestor, groups of spirit being dugong hunters are encountered on the northwest tip of South West Island at a locality known as Mawarndarlbarndarl. In the Wuyaliya song cycle associated with the Dingo Spirit Ancestor, spirit being dugong hunters are found at the mouth of the Crooked River. The Sea Turtle Spirit Ancestor of the Wurdaliya semi-moiety sings of spirit being dugong hunters at Mamadthamburru, or Crocodile Point, on the southwestern tip of West Island; and the Rock Cod Spirit Ancestor of the Mambaliya-Wawukarriya semi-moiety sings of dugong hunting spirit beings on Sharkers Point or Jarrka. It can be seen from Figure 8:3 that while there is a major Dugong Hunter Spirit Ancestor which crosses the islands, each semi- moiety has associated with it various tracts of their country where spirit beings engage in dugong and sea turtle hunting. Thus in a sense, these spirit beings and the Dugong Hunter Spirit Ancestors infuse the entire geography of the islands and the sea with that activity which the Yanyuwa see as of prime importance. Many of these locations, mentioned in the song cycles as having dugong and sea turtle hunting spirit beings, are now favoured as overnight or base camps from which contemporary hunters depart to hunt dugong or sea turtle.

The narrative of the Spirit Ancestor Dugong Hunters may be viewed, like many similar narratives, as just a list of named places through which they passed, or it may be interpreted as an act of creation, the effects of which are still resonating within the Yanyuwa environment, still capable of having a profound impact on the Yanyuwa community in contemporary times. One of the most important factors about the narrative is that the Dugong Hunter Spirit Ancestors, in many respects, represent the immediate and material reality of the present-day Yanyuwa dugong and sea turtle hunters. They travel in boats, they carry harpoons and ropes, they pursue dugong and turtle and it is at this level that the narrative provides very common ground with a contemporary reality. The boundary between Spirit Ancestor times to the everyday contemporary situation is not great.

219

The appeal of this Spirit Ancestor narrative to contemporary Yanyuwa people is that it does not deal with fish, birds, wind or insects being Spirit Ancestors; instead, the Dugong Hunters are seen as a group of men hunting, and although they perform some rather amazing feats on this journey, they are at all times primarily human. As some Yanyuwa people have commented, this narrative, more than any of the other Spirit Ancestor narratives, is 'like real history' (Don Miller with Johnson Timothy 1985).

The journey of the Spirit Ancestor Dugong Hunters, their 'mythic' journey, is the true reality; and the present and historical moments of hunting dugong and sea turtle achieve their full meaning and reality because of the repetition, recitation and reenactment of what occurred in the time of these Dugong Hunter Spirit Ancestors. It does not take set ritual performance and song to re-create the actions of these Spirit Ancestors: the mere fact of being in a boat, standing with a harpoon, turning the dugong to face the sea before butchering and cooking dugong flesh are all re-creations of the Dugong Hunters' reality. It should be added that there are actual religious ritual actions also associated with the Dugong Hunters, but on a day-to-day secular level, historical and present Yanyuwa hunters and cookers of dugong and sea turtle have experienced and are experiencing the 'true time' (Yerushalmi 1954; Eliade 1965) of the original activities and archetypes associated with the Spirit Ancestor Dugong Hunters.

In such a 'mythic' conception of time, everything continually recurs in the lifetime of those Yanyuwa people who pursue the hunting of dugong and sea turtle. The narrative and the song of the Dugong Hunters can be seen as a metahistorical story that can happen over and over again. A Yanyuwa person who hunts dugong or visits the sites scattered over the Pellew Islands associated with these Spirit Ancestors thus encounters the 'myth' directly and human history, which cannot be repeated, is replaced with the primary reality of dugong and sea turtle hunting and of being a Yanyuwa 'saltwater person'. Finally, the humanity of the Dugong Hunter Spirit Ancestors means that there are no real surprises, no actions that cannot be repeated. What has been, is now, and will hopefully be the future. The people who undertake the actual activities of hunting will change, but the essentials of the drama recounted in the narrative will always remain the same. Thus, things will end in the way they began, with people travelling in boats, being aware of the tide, carrying their harpoons and ropes in the hope they will achieve the aim of all such hunters, a dugong or sea turtle.

The account of the Dugong Hunters' journey appears to follow a linear path across the islands from east to west (Figure 8:3). The Yanyuwa tellers of this story speak of a group of people travelling in bark canoes over a much wider path and area. At its most basic, the narrative, which describes the journey of the Dugong Hunters, emphasises why Yanyuwa people are different from mainlanders. Yanyuwa people are not hunters of kangaroo and emu, although they sometimes do that, but their own self-perception and other people's perception of them is as hunters of dugong and sea turtle and as a people who are ecologically, economically and technologically distinct. There are still great contrasts between the life and economics of the Yanyuwa people who inhabit the coastal mangrove country, the saline flats, islands and sea, as opposed to those, who Tindale (1974:121–122) calls 'the scrub covered upland dwellers', a sentiment with which the Yanyuwa would no doubt agree.

Conclusion

People from mainland language groups such as the Garrwa, Gudanji and Wambaya show a degree of amazement that the Yanyuwa actually do travel to the sea and capture dugong and sea turtle and that the sea and the marine environment in general, is capable of sustaining human life.

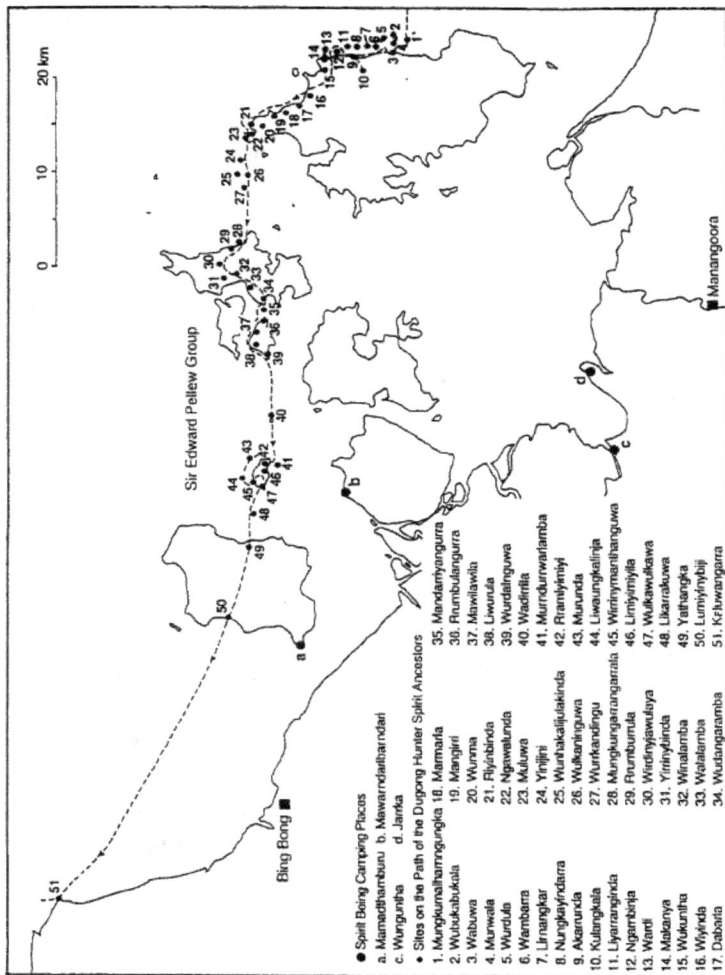

Figure 8:3 Paths and camps of the Dugong Hunter spirit ancestors over the Pellew Islands

The Yanyuwa term *nganji* ('kin') provides a key to explore one of the ways by which the relationship with the sea is sustained. The term connotes the enduring relationships that exist within the maritime environment that the Yanyuwa share with many species of plants and animals. In an environment where people describe animals as being kin to each other, such as sea birds being kin to the fish, or hunters to dugong, dugong to sea grass, there is also a belief that such relationships are beneficial to each other. If a hunter does not hunt a dugong, then the dugong numbers will decrease, which will be bad for the Yanyuwa. If seabirds do not hunt fish, then both the fish and bird will suffer. This aspect of Yanyuwa classification is also an implicit directive for action (putting classification into practice) that is, preying upon the creatures so linked as kin.

Amidst such discussions, people reflect also on a less intimate but no less important relationship between creatures and environment. As Annie Karrakayn has commented concerning the sea birds, 'they make me think about my country, my island, the sea, my mother, poor thing'. What is being demonstrated in such a statement are the deep and enduring emotional links between people, sea-country and many of the creatures which inhabit the area. This in itself is not unusual. It is spoken of continually in the media and in books and popular writings about indigenous peoples' relationships to their country, but when people make statements such as the one above, they are highlighting an evocative and emotional attachment of 'things' to people. This provides reference points which allow a phenomenological rendering of the Yanyuwa environment and it moves away from a presentation of dry empiricism to one which expresses the true consciousness of the people, including their belief in the consciousness of their environment.

Such an exploration does give rise to the idea of indigenous people being 'at one with the environment', rather than being separate, and in this there is nothing new. It gives a richer substance to the notion of 'being at one'. The Yanyuwa people stand within an ecological system, dominated by thoughts of the sea, which has as a part of its integral components human agents and spiritual beings one of which is the sea and special knowledge and power.

Note

I acknowledge with gratitude the large number of Yanyuwa men and women who have, over the years, been responsible for sharing the deep knowledge about the sea country. Many are now dead but amongst those who are still alive and should be thanked are Dinah Norman, Annie Karrakayn, Jemima Miller, Roddy Harvey, Mussolini Harvey, Tom Friday, Eillen McDinny, Steve Johnson and Mavis Timothy.

References

Arnol, J 1983. *McArthur River catchment management (NT)*. Melbourne: Monash University, Graduate School of Environmental Science.

Baker, R. 1989. *Land is life: continuity through change for the Yanyuwa from the Northern Territory of Australia*. Unpublished PhD thesis. Adelaide: Department of Geography, University of Adelaide.

Bradley, J. 1988. *Yanyuwa country: The Yanyuwa people of Borroloola tell the history of their land*. Richmond, Melbourne: Greenhouse Publications.

1989. Keeping up our language: a collection of Yanyuwa texts and articles dealing with Yanyuwa language and society. Unpublished manuscript. Canberra: Australian Institute for Aboriginal and Torres Strait Islander Studies.

1991a. 'Li-Maramaranja', the Yanyuwa hunters of marine animals in the Sir Edward Pellew Group, NT. *Records of the South Australian Museum* 25(2):91–110.

1994. Some Yanyuwa songs. In *Little Eva at Moonlight Creek and other Aboriginal song poems* (eds) Martin Duwell and R.M.W. Dixon. St Lucia, Queensland: University of Queensland Press. Pp. 3–67.

Bradley, J. and J. Kirton 1992. *Yanyuwa Wuka*, language from Yanyuwa country: a Yanyuwa dictionary and cultural resource. Unpublished manuscript. Canberra: Australian Institute for Aboriginal and Torres Strait Islander Studies.

Chase, A. and J. von Sturmer 1980. Anthropology and botany: turning over a new leaf. In *Papers in Australian linguistics No.13; contributions to Australian linguistics* (eds) B. Rigsby and P. Sutton. Canberra: Pacific Linguistics. Pp. 289–299.

Chase, A. and P. Sutton 1981. Hunter-gatherers in a rich environment: Aboriginal coastal exploitation in Cape York Peninsula. In *Ecological biogeography of Australia* (ed.) A. Keast. The Hague: W. Junk and Co. Pp. 1817–1852.

1987. Australian Aborigines in a rich environment. In *Traditional Aboriginal society, a reader* (ed.) W.H. Edwards. Melbourne: MacMillan. Pp. 68–95.

Christian, C. 1952. Regional land surveys. *The Journal of Australian Institute of Agricultural Science* 140–146.

Christian, C.and G.Stewart 1953. *General report on survey of Katherine-Darwin region 1946*. Land Research Series No.1. Melbourne: CSIRO.

Christian, C. and L. Noakes 1954. *Survey of the Barkly region, Northern Territory and Queensland, 1947–48*. Land Research Series No.3. Melbourne: CSIRO.

Eliade, M. 1965. *Cosmos and history*. New York: Harcourt, Brace.

Heinsohn, G. 1981. The Dugong in the seagrass system. In *The Dugong* (ed.) H. Marsh. Proceedings of a seminar/workshop held at James Cook University, 8–13 May 1979, pp.125–129.

Johnson, K. and J. Kerle (eds) 1991. *Flora and vertebrate fauna of the Sir Edward Pellew group of islands, Northern Territory*. A report to the Australian Heritage Commission and Conservation Commission of the Northern Territory. Wildlife Division. Conservation Commission of the Northern Territory. Alice Springs. 22.

Jones, R. 1980. Hunters in the Australian coastal savanna. In *Human ecology in savanna environments* (ed.) D. Harris. London: Academic Press. Pp. 107–146

1985. Ordering the landscape. In *Seeing the first Australians* (eds) L Donaldson and T. Donaldson. George Allen and Unwin. Pp. 181–209.

Nash, D. 1991. Comparative flora terminology of the central Northern Territory. In *Archaeology and linguistics: Aboriginal Australia in global perspective*. (eds) P. McConvell and N. Evans. Melbourne: Cambridge University Press Pp. 187–206.

Poiner, I., D. Staples and R. Kenyo 1987. Seagrass communities of the Gulf of Carpentaria, Australia. *Australian Journal of Marine and Freshwater Research* 38:121–31.

Speck, N. 1960. *The land and pastoral resources of the north Kimberley area*, WA Land Research Series No. 4. Melbourne: CSIRO.

Stanner, W. 1965. Aboriginal territorial organisation: estate, range, domain and regime. *Oceania* 36:1–26.

Tindale, N. 1974. *Aboriginal tribes of Australia, their terrain, environmental controls, distribution, limits and proper names.* Canberra: Australian National University Press.

Trigger, D. 1987. Inland, coast and islands: traditional Aboriginal society and material culture in a region of the southern Gulf of Carpentaria. *Records of the South Australian Museum* 21(2):69–84.

Williams, N. 1982. A boundary is to cross: observations on Yolngu boundaries and permission. In *Resource managers: North American and Australian hunter-gatherers* (eds) N. Williams and E. Hunn. Colorado: Westview Press. Pp. 131–154.

Ygoa-McKeown, R. 1987. *An assessment of the conservation significance of the Sir Edward Pellew group of islands.* Darwin: Environment Centre, NT.

Yerushalmi, Y. 1982. *Zakhor: Jewish history and Jewish memory.* Seattle: University of Washington.

9

Customary marine tenure at Groote Eylandt

Kingsley Palmer

In 1983 the Northern Land Council in Darwin agreed to prepare a submission for a closure of the seas, under the *Aboriginal Land Act 1978 (NT)*, for areas adjoining Aboriginal land on Groote Eylandt. The provisions of the Act afforded potential for limited control over access to closed seas and were also seen as a means of regulating unauthorised entry onto Aboriginal land via the sea, which had been noted as a problem on Groote Eylandt by the Aboriginal traditional owners. The claim was lodged on April 30 1994, but was not proceeded with and the Groote Eylandt people subsequently formed their own Land Council. However, the research has relevance to this volume in that it specifically addressed rights to the marine environment, rather than to land, which already enjoyed protection under the *Aboriginal Land Rights Act 1976 (NT)*. The system of tenure described illustrates clearly that Groote Eylandt people owned and occupied both land and sea and exercised a clearly identifiable customary marine tenure over the latter.

At the time I undertook the research I was working as an anthropologist for the Northern Land Council and did the fieldwork necessary for the application. This resulted in a 'claim book' (Palmer 1985), which contained ethnographic data relevant to the application. While the report addressed a number of issues quite specific to the application, much of the ethnography was relevant to the system of marine tenure and the relationship that existed between the claimants and the sea and much that was in it. While the ethnography was checked prior to the preparation of the final report, it should be noted that the fieldwork was conducted some thirteen years prior to the time of writing this chapter and some local circumstances may have changed. However, I doubt that the fundamentals of traditional land and sea rights and tenure have changed at all. It is hoped that this present chapter may be of use to both the Groote Eylandt people and other indigenous groups seeking to have their rights in the sea recognised by Australian law and so give effect to their concerns and responsibilities as owners of real property.

The original proposal to make application to close the seas around Groote Eylandt over a decade ago was seen as a huge task. Consequently, it was agreed at meetings with the traditional owners on Groote, that it would be wise to undertake the claim in several stages. Only the field-work for the first stage was completed and it forms the basis for what follows. Consequently, the ethnography on which this paper is based focuses on the northern and northeastern coast of the island. Reference is also made to two outstations which were established in this area: Mukmuntja and Marble Point where I stayed while undertaking the research.

Local organisation

Local organisation on Groote Eylandt has many similarities with mainland groups and is founded on a strong belief in spiritual principles which are invoked to legitimate title to bounded areas. Territoriality and related matters that sanction ownership encompass the domains of land and sea. In addition, intermediate zones where land and sea meet (e.g. tidal flats, reefs and sandbanks) have considerable economic importance recognised in the language, which has a special set of terms for these areas. Not only does territoriality comprise the marine as well as land environments, but there is an emphasis on the former rather than the latter in all matters that link people to territory and to the spirituality implicit in the relationship between the two.

The Groote Eylandt people recognise the existence of patrilineal lineages which they most usually call 'clans' in English, a term I adopt here. Each clan is differentiated by its local and religious associations, and its name. Recruitment to a clan is by patrilineal descent and membership is automatically accorded on the birth of an infant.

A clan consists of a man, his siblings and all their children in the male line. Each clan is named, and the names are used today rather like English surnames. A clan owns a specific area, which is often referred to by the name of an important location within the clan country. Territory and land are talked of synonymously, and the substitution of a clan name for a country name is usual, even if confusing for some (see Moore 1972: 14–16; Waddy 1988: vol 1, 111). For example, the clan with rights to the country around an outstation which is located in the north of the island called Marble Point is named Barabara, but the inclusive term for the territory and people who own it and are a part of it is Wangwarmalangwa (i.e. the people of Armalangwa). Similarly, the Bara clan is known as Wangwatarpulangwa.

The territory in which a clan has patrilineally inherited rights of ownership is an estate (*angalya*), and includes both land (*ajurungka—* Waddy 1988, vol 1: 52 notes *ariba*) and sea (*mukata*). For the Groote Eylandt people it is the whole complex of sea, seabed, rocks, reefs, offshore islands and land that is designated by the use of the clan name. The estate is bounded by reference to geographical features, though the extent of an estate offshore is more vaguely conceptualised by reference to practically useable seaways.

Traditionally, the Groote Eylandt people divide themselves into two exogamous moieties. The moieties are egocentrically designated. Ego calls his own moiety *yiranikapura*, which means literally 'our mob'. Ego calls members of the moiety other than his own, *wuranikapura*, which means literally 'the other mob'. As a result of interaction with the mainland, people designate clans as either *dhuwa* or *yirrija*, and these sociocentric terms are now in common use on Groote. Turner (1974: 220) noted the use of the southeast Arnhem Land terms. There is also a general acceptance of the principle of moiety exogamy. A man must marry a women from a clan of the moiety opposed to his own and to do otherwise would be considered incestuous. Consequently, a man has a mother from one clan and a father from another, and possibly a father's mother and a mother's mother from different clans again. Through marriage members of different clans have specifiable relationships with one another. Turner (1974) also demonstrated that Groote Eylandt kinship terminology is based on a recognition of cognatic and lineal relationships predicated upon clan estates.

It is not the personal identity of an individual or of his mother or father that determines his kinship identification. Rather it is the fact that a particular individual belongs to a particular local group (Turner 1974:33). How a man calls another person is then determined by his actual or putative relationship to that man's clan, rather than to the genealogical system that European Australians follow. Since clans are inseparable from land, it is correct to state that kinship on Groote is an expression of a series of relationships among people and between people and land. Turner (1974:33) calls this concept the 'local group family'.

A man inherits rights in his father's estate, which is called *nungarrkalang angalya*. A man is responsible for sites and areas of importance in that estate and jurisdiction over the land and sea is his. Ideally, members of the patriline must be consulted in ritual matters relating to the estate and they must grant permission before others may visit the estate, hunt, fish or forage over it. However, these rights and duties are not exercised by the patrilineal descent group without reference to others. Offspring of female members of the clan, who call the country *tuntirrkalangwa*, have a managerial role in the country and are called to help out when there is trouble and decisions about ritual or development cannot be taken without reference to them. These managerial rights are referred to by the southeast Arnhem Land term *junkayi*, and it is likely that this is a result of influence from the Nunggubuyu people, whose territory is on the mainland around Numbulwar, who are introducing their terminology and perhaps their concepts.

A man has rights of residence in his wife's country, which he calls *tatingiyarrka langwa angalya*, and may be consulted in matters relevant to it under certain circumstances. A man also has authority in the country of his mother's mother, which is called *anguwarrka angalya*.

Economic relationship to the clan territory

A review of the economic relationship with the clan territory provides an understanding of the substantially maritime orientation of the Groote Eylandt people. Consequently the delineation of their estates is as much, if not more, about the marine component as it is about the land component. This is reflected in the traditional owners' concept of territory as comprising land and sea together and in the spiritual preoccupations of owners, which reflect a marine bias.

When Worsley worked on Groote Eylandt in 1953, he found the Anindiliyakwa an 'essentially coastal people'. He (Worsley 1961: 156) went on:

> It has been pointed out that the main population of the whole of Arnhem Land has always been concentrated on the coast, with its rich supplies of marine products, and its more abundant water resources and vegetation. This is particularly true of Groote Eylandt, which has a rocky and fairly barren interior, with large areas of sandy soil and stringy bark forest.

Worsley (1961:157) also claimed that linguistic usage reflected the importance of the coast since he noted that directional terms in the language assumed the sea as the point of reference. Although much has changed on Groote since Worsley worked there, the substance of his observations remain valid. Similar observations about the relationship between people and the sea have been made by a number of other writers (see Meyers *et al.* 1996: 3–17 for a summary).

Waddy (1988, vol 1: 119–128) notes the extensive list of natural species associated with the Groote Eylandt clans. Some 87 of the over 200 listed (or over 40%) represent marine species, further confirming the important link between the traditional owners and the marine environment.

Groote Eylandt is a low-lying rocky island with coastal dunes and saline flats. Apart from some areas south and east of Central Hill, however, the island is covered with medium dense forest of stringybark

(*Eucalyptus tetrodonta*) and woollybutt (*Eucalyptus miniata*). There are small areas where the soil is rich enough to support dense rainforest, and these are termed locally 'jungles'. In coastal regions and particularly around creeks or billabongs there are swamps, some of which dry out completely in the dry season. Vegetation here is dominated by paper-barks (*Melaleuca sp*) and ground cover consists of speargrass and other grasses, ferns, low thorny shrubs and a variety of vines and creepers (see Levitt 1981:6, plates 87–92; Waddy 1988, vol 1:51).

The open forest, while accessible, does not provide an easy environment for travel. Undergrowth is often quite thick and the vines and thorny bushes impede progress. Walking is a little easier when the bush is regularly burnt. However, the ground is often rocky and the forest is sheltered from cooling breezes, and particularly during the hotter months, it harbours hordes of unpleasant mosquitoes. The residents of the outstation at Marble Point formerly tried to establish their settlement several kilometres from the coast at the south of North West Bay. Mosquitoes subsequently drove them to camp on the beach and away from the forest before they relocated the outstation close to the beach.

My informants did, however, demonstrate that the bush may be used as a convenient means of access to the littoral zone, when it is not otherwise easily accessible on foot. The residents of Marble Point carefully burnt the bush in a small valley to the north of their settlement to enable them to walk to a large beach north of Finch Island. Burning the bush was said to be an accepted and desired practice on several occasions, and is regarded by local land owners as being an important part of maintaining the land. However, it was apparent that the inland areas were often regarded as convenient corridors to provide access to a beach or a shoreline rather than as hunting and gathering environments *per se*.

The beaches and shoreline are quite different from the forest. Sand below the high water mark provides relatively firm and uninterrupted passage, making walking easier than along the dunes, which in turn are also easier to traverse than the forest. Moreover, in the northern areas of the island, where there are no permanent creeks, water is best obtained from soaks dug in open sandy areas immediately behind the beach (see

Turner 1974:162). The residents of both Marble Point and Mukmunja obtained their water supplies from soaks dug in dunes behind the beach. The marine environment is a valuable source of food, and it was apparent during my stay with the Groote Eylandt people that their interest was primarily in the sea and the seashore. Visits were made to the interior of the island, but not as frequently as were visits to the sea and the shore. People did give me lists of land animals which they caught and ate: wallaby, goanna, frill-neck lizard and bandicoot along with wild honey, which is much prized for its sweetness. At Mukmunja, people told me that the last wallaby they had eaten was during the previous wet season. Wallabies, the major source of non-marine food, are agile and difficult to both see and shoot in the forest. However, there is a variety of other vegetable food available from the forest as is noted by Waddy (1988, vol 1: 51–52). On the other hand, the sea provided a much wider range of foods, including many varieties of fish, turtle, eggs, shellfish and crabs, most of which are easy to obtain in abundance and available all year round (see Palmer 1984:454).

For example, turtle eggs are collected in some numbers during the winter months of July and August from known sandy beaches on off-shore islands round the north of the main island. These represent an important supplementary food source and are much prized because of their limited seasonal availability and comparative scarcity. Oysters can be gathered from the rocks at low tide all year round. Stingray can be speared in the shallows, along with other in-shore fish, like mullet, while those with ready access to boats trawl well known reefs for the copious fish to be found in the bays and straits of the coastal region. The food-providing areas of the littoral zone and off-shore reefs are clearly identified in the local language. The rocky reefs (*awunta*) provide clams, oysters and fish. The sandy shore (*imingyila*) provides various bivalves, gastropods and crabs, while the mangroves (*anuma*) are home to a variety of other shell fish. There are other areas identified in the language as well: the open water within bays; the deep water beyond the headlands; the dunes; the sandy areas behind the dunes before the forest commences. Each is known for its particular food resources and exploited accordingly.

Movement and subsistence are executed by reference to the two distinct environments. Since plentiful supplies of water and food, and the opportunity to move easily and freely, are better afforded by coastal rather than hinterland areas, it is hardly surprising that traditional owners move around the coast by boat or on foot more frequently than they do the inland areas. It is also not surprising then that their religious beliefs and preoccupations are also predominantly marine in emphasis. The sea, shore and littoral zone forms the focus for Aboriginal life and thought and also constitute an area of priority in a range of socio-religious values.

Religious system

In outline, the traditional religious belief system of the Groote Eylandt people is similar to that recorded elsewhere in Arnhem Land. The clans and their territories are believed to have been created and ordained during the period of the Dreaming (*amutiyurrariya*). The spirituality which was and is manifest as a consequence of this time is known generally as *mardayan*. During the creative era, ancestral beings roamed the land and sea, creating natural features, modifying the existing sea and landscape, and endowing them with spirituality. This spirituality is also believed to be contained in special ritual objects, paintings, designs or songs, or to be extant at specific locations within the landscape or sea. People believe that they are connected to the natural world, and this is articulated as comprising relationships between people and ancestral beings, the majority of which are now believed to be sea creatures. The paths or tracks followed by these creator beings extend across the sea and are now believed manifest either in the sea, across the seabed or in the rocks and islands emerging from it.

The ancestral beings defined the clan estates, and their travels are now used by traditional owners as a reference to identify spiritual principles within the landscape or in the sea. The patrilineal clan is deemed to be both a human expression of, and the protector and a guardian of, the spirituality which is considered to be the essence of all life. When two clans share similar beliefs and myths about ancestral beings, they are said to be 'of one blood' and may form an alliance for the administration of their land, rituals, paintings and songs associated with it. This alliance is termed 'company' in English or *wurruwilyapama* (literally 'one lot, in a heap'). The company relationship is not arbitrarily formed, and those in company must be of the same moiety and share the same Dreamings. Above all, agreement has to be reached between clansmen that the arrangement is proper. Those who form a company relationship retain their primary rights to the estate of their patriclan, which they term their 'number one country' (*awilyapama angalya*). The country for which they have a company relationship is called their 'number two country' (*ampilyima angalya*). Waddy noted that pockets of territory lying within one clan's country could be 'owned' by a second clan as a consequence of totemic affiliations. The same writer also indicates that this provided potential for some flexibility in the attribution of the nature of and extent of rights of owners over such territory (Waddy 1988, vol 1: 136–137).

Owners of local estates

There were three principal estates in the area which was studied. The approximate boundaries of these estates are shown in the map which is Figure 9:1. The first, known generally as Barabara, extends from the southwest corner of North West Bay to the eastern portion of the peninsula south of Chasm Island and includes a number of adjacent offshore islands, as well as the more distant Wedge Rock and Hawknest Island, the reefs, sandbanks and shoals and offshore waters. The estate is *dhuwa*, by mainland moiety conventions, and is owned by the Barabara clan. The same clan name is also used for Chasm Island, an area of great importance both for this clan and for all other people living on Groote Eylandt.

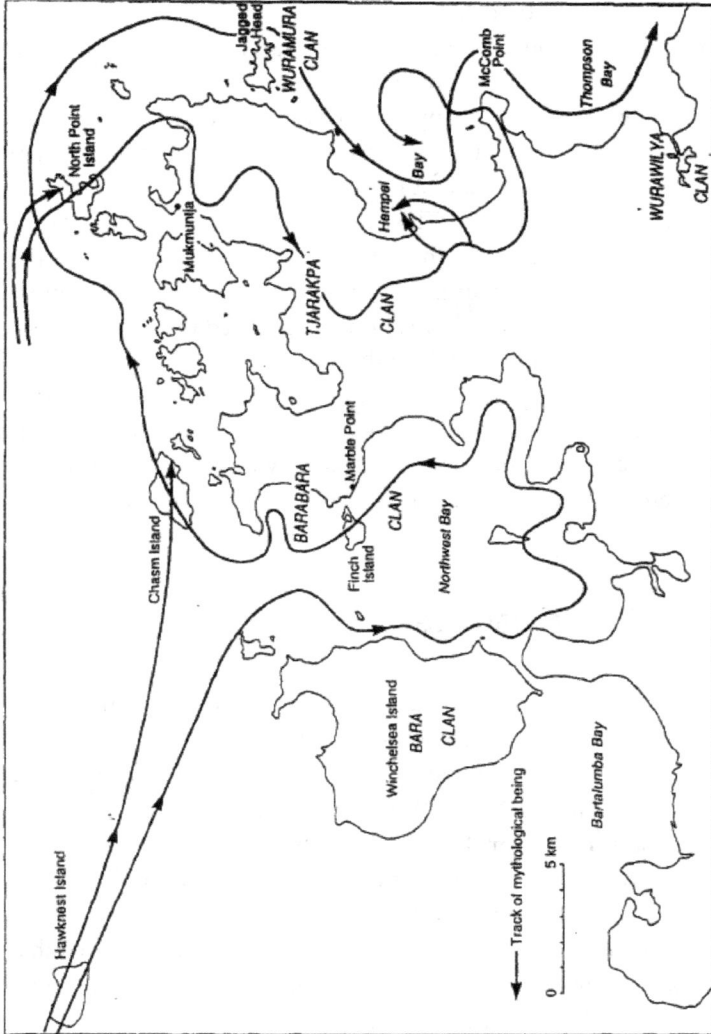

Figure 9:1 Northern Groote Eylandt estates

The second estate, referred to as Jarakpa, borders the first and lies to the east. It extends from Barabara territory round to Northpoint Island and south to the southern part of Thompson Bay. Once again, the estate includes numerous islands, reefs, bays and all the useable sea beyond the shore. This estate is *yirrija*. Jagged Heads belongs to a third clan, Wuramura, and is *dhuwa*. This estate comprises islands, reefs and sea, being separated from the main island by a narrow channel.

Details of the owners and these three estates were clearly set out by community members during the period of field work. Genealogies demonstrated the continuity of the patrilines over several generations, while company relationships were also indicated. Rights of matrikin were also recorded. Clans were also noted as having special spiritual relationships with the natural world. For example, the Barabara people were cited as having a special spiritual association with pearlshell, turtle, porpoise and tiger shark, and some areas of importance in their estate are linked in mythology to these species.

By mutual agreement, the care of Jarakpa land and sea had passed to a fourth clan, who were considered to be 'in company' for the estate because at that time the surviving members of the Jarakpa clan did not feel able to fulfil their obligations to their estate.

The third clan, Wuramura, has its principal estate on Bickerton Island and it has designated another clan (Mamarika) to look after the relatively small area.

Marine tenure

For the Groote Eylandt people, then, major religious beliefs are associated with the sea, being identified at a series of sites, where particular incidents are believed to have occurred, linked by well-known 'tracks' which were followed by the creator beings. These spiritual principles link the traditional owners to the marine environment and serve to define the extent of their estates. Owners have a series of customary rights within their estate, including a responsibility to ensure that the land and sea is correctly looked after, that sites and tracks are protected from abuse or harm and that strangers do not inadvertently stray into the area causing damage to themselves and perhaps to others. Finally, owners are responsible for the spiritual renewal of the land and sea through the practice of ritual, the maintenance of ritual objects and the singing of songs and performance of ceremonies. The customary marine tenure system for the Groote Eylandt people, then, comprises a series of rights, duties and responsibilities which extend over both land and sea, but which have as their primary focus and legitimating spirituality the latter rather than the former.

This is best illustrated by examining a number of narratives and tracks relevant to the area. The Groote Eylandt people with whom I worked provided details of the activities of the creator beings, their journeys and interactions. Most beings traversed the sea and bays, dwelling at key locations which are now of special significance because of the spiritual associations that developed at that time. The sea territory of the local groups is considered to be constituted of the spirituality of the ancestral beings who endowed the sea, the sea bed, coastline, reefs and other marine features with their fundamental being. The owners regard their rights of ownership to derive from the ordaining activities of these creative beings which designated sea territory. The land, in contrast, while not devoid of such sites and tracks, receives significantly less attention. Two examples of these travels and activities illustrate the point further. The narratives cited here are public versions, with no restriction on audience.

Barabara: shark and porpoise

This is a major narrative complex which links the mainland, Wedge Rock, Hawknest Island, Chasm Island and the coast from North West Bay around to Umbakumba. The narrative tells of the travels of Tiger Shark, who travelled from a site on the mainland via Wedge Rock and Hawknest Island and then down Northwest Bay. He created all the features of the present coastline as he travelled, emerging from the north

238

eastern corner of North West Bay at Chasm Island. The sweeping action of his swimming was responsible for the many rounded bays and inlets in this area. At Chasm Island he met Porpoise, who had also travelled from the mainland, following much the same course as Tiger Shark, then attacked Porpoise and bit him in half, and the Porpoise is now represented as a rock at the eastern end of Chasm Island. Shark then swam on round the island, forming more bays and natural features, until he reached Umbakumba. Here he chased two mullets and in so doing, created the lagoon on which Umbakumba is situated. He then travelled on to the southern areas of the island.

Another part of this narrative links Porpoise to Chasm Island, where there is a site of utmost significance, one generally feared by all Groote Eylandt people and members of other communities living elsewhere. They believe that any interference with the place will result in events of apocalyptic proportions.

Jarakpa: Yiningpuna (the Snake) and Kunkuna (Trevally)

Snake and Trevally were brothers who travelled from the mainland north of Blue Mud Bay. Both are considered to be spiritually potent and to have created or ordained areas that are now physically dangerous. Snake landed on a beach on the north of North Point Island (Namukumanja) and made the rocks and bays there. Trevally is now a large slab of rock on the northern point of the island. An area of sea off the north of the island is associated with Trevally, and, it is believed, any boat crossing the water there is likely to capsize and its occupants be drowned.

Snake continued across the northern peninsula of Groote Eylandt, where it was responsible for making all the trees across the land. These trees cannot be cut today because the person doing so will become sick and sores erupt all over his body.

Snake went on to a low rocky hill in the centre of the peninsula which takes its name from him. He met a local Jarakpa woman there whom he married. They had many children. All then went east to

Hempel Bay and the children are now submerged rocks in the bay. They now represent a spirit place for unborn children, known as *wurralau-taarra*. Snake is now represented at McComb Point, and the woman as a rocky headland in the middle of the Bay called Yitarrikimanja. Snake now lives in the deep water in the bay, and is potentially very dangerous.

While these two narratives and associated sites and tracks represent a very small part of the rich mythology of the region, they do serve as excellent examples of the fundamental spirituality which links people to their estates. Not only are estates perceived of as comprising both land and sea, but the narratives relating the activities of the Dreaming beings emphasise the marine environment. The sites, for which owners have primary responsibility, are considered sacred, inviolable and sometimes potentially dangerous. Beneath the narrative complex lies an extensive set of ritual and ceremonial responsibilities that extend to maintenance of objects and ritual performance.

Customary marine tenure: rights and duties

The Dreaming narratives define the extent of the estate owners' territory and designate the nature and extent of the customary rights and duties that are a component of tenure. The fundamental marine emphasis of the spirituality and its links to people today also defines a set of enduring relationships between people and both land and sea country. Owners have rights and duties that are commonly recognised in relation to both domains of land and sea which, in this case, constitute the clan's estate. This system of marine tenure can be identified and its component parts described.

Owners' rights are inherited from the father and the owners comprise a patrilineal group. Matrifiliates also have an interest in the estate and act to ensure the duties of the owners are respected and exercised with all due care.

Owners also have the right to use, enter and exploit the land and seas within their estate. They have the right to take, consume and exploit the natural produce of the land and sea that comprises their country. The Groote Eylandt people stated that known kin as well as members of other clans may freely traverse the estate as well as fish or forage within it, although there is a protocol for ensuring that the senior owner is aware of the activity and formally, at least, has the opportunity to comment on or to direct the proposed activity. However, strangers (and this includes non-indigenous people) are not afforded this right. This is a consequence of two factors. First strangers are not a part of the owners' known universe. There exist no kinship or affinal links such as might be expected to exist between an owner of one estate and the owner of another. Second, however, owners have a responsibility to ensure that no harm comes to the country and the sea as well as to individuals, even if they are strangers. It is the owners' responsibility to ensure that areas where Dreaming spirituality (*madayan*) is believed to be extant are protected from physical harm or trespass by unauthorised or ritually unqualified persons, who themselves might suffer real physical harm as a consequence. Failure to meet these obligations can result in severe censure from fellow clansmen and from matrikin, whose managerial rites include the duty to ensure that the members of the patriline fulfil their obligations properly.

Harm may result from unauthorised access and ignorance. The harm may come to the stranger, or because the sea is so potent, to all inhabitants of Groote Eylandt or beyond. For the men and women with whom I worked, this duty found principal expression in a fear that 'strangers' might do irreparable harm. In particular, fishing boat crews had a reputation for being intrusive, insensitive and likely to land on the reefs and beaches and perhaps interfere with sites. I was shown evidence of barbeques on the beach close to the dangerous site on Chasm Island. So great was the concern that the clansmen had come to an understanding with a sympathetic employee who worked for the mining company on the island (Groote Eylandt Mining Company or GEMCO). In return for 'policing' the islands and bays on their behalf, he was given free access to the areas which he had been instructed were safe and he was trusted to keep well away from the places known to be spiritually dangerous.

Further examples demonstrate how individuals may come to harm and how owners have a responsibility to ensure strangers act appropriately at all times. While camping at Namukumanja, I unwittingly broke a small branch from a tree beneath which I was camping in order to make a hook upon which I might hang my billy. An owner, who was with me, expressed grave concern and told me of the prohibition on breaking branches from the trees. He also apologised for not telling me of the danger. He felt responsible for my well-being. I was also told of a number of instances when non-Aboriginal people had traversed dangerous areas of the sea and suffered dire consequences as a result. For example, the community advisor at Umbakumba had taken the Outstation Resource Centre boat too close to a dangerous area and it had hit a reef and sunk. Fortunately, all the passengers and crew clambered ashore and no one was injured. Similarly, the fate of trawlers that hit reefs was explained by the indiscretion of their captains in entering seas when ignorant of the spiritual potency and attendant dangers of the area.

Owners also have the right to be consulted about any activity that is to be conducted within their estate. This includes development activity as well as casual visits and access. My helpers commented that the Macassan trepangers had always asked for this permission and that it had usually been granted (see Egan 1996: 6). Modern-day fishermen are not so conscious of this requirement. While the rights of owners to control access is well accepted, and indeed generally enforced with respect to the hinterland areas of estates (which are Aboriginal land under the *Aboriginal Land Rights Act 1976 (NT)*), this is not the case with the sea and littoral zones. There is little or no impediment to members of the mining community or to professional fishermen to entering waters, fishing, anchoring boats, having parties on shore and generally regarding the seas, channels and bays as lacking owners who have rights and duties in these waters. The result is a high level of anxiety on the part of owners that they are unable to properly exercise their concomitant duties because they have no recognised authority over non-Aboriginal people who enter their sea estates.

Owners also have the right to direct and to be consulted about ceremonial activity which directly relates to their land. This may involve the way in which ritual is to be performed (including song and dance) the holding of sacred objects, the use of body designs and so on. The concomitant duty is expressed as a responsibility to ensure that any ceremonial activity is carried out correctly according to conventions and traditions.

Conclusion

The Groote Eylandt people have clearly defined territory which consists of both land and sea. Consistent with their economic exploitation of the region, which has as its focus the use and exploitation of a marine environment, religious and spiritual associations are predominantly marine in emphasis. The owners have customary rights, duties and obligations in relation to their land and sea country. These can be specified and constitute a system of customary marine tenure which has endured over generations because its integrity resides in a patriline which endures across the generations. The narratives and associated spiritual beliefs (which find expression in ceremonial practice) are situated mainly within the marine environment. The delineation of estates is founded upon the concept that the Dreaming defines the parameters of an owner's property, both in terms of the estate and the duties that accompany it. It remains a fundamentally unsatisfactory state of affairs that indigenous tenure of sea country is unrecognised by Australian law, and the jurisdiction of the owners is consequently limited. While rights to landed parts of the estates are realised through current legislation, the majority of the estate and those parts that are spiritually the most vibrant, as well as potentially the most problematic, remain beyond the owners' effective control. It is a matter that needs to be addressed.

Note

The author wishes to thank the traditional owners of the areas discussed in this paper who provided the materials upon which this work
is based. The traditional owners also gave their time and hospitality at
Umbakumba, as well as at the outstations of Mukmuntja and Marble
Point. The Northern Land Council funded the research and coordinated
the preparation of the original document supporting the application for
a closure of the seas and their permission to use original material is
acknowledged. All material was endorsed by the members of the local
communities prior to the completion of the documentation.

References

Egan, T. 1996. *A justice all their own*. Melbourne: Melbourne University
Press.

Levitt, D. 1981. *Plants and people*. Canberra: Australian Institute of
Aboriginal Studies.

Meyers, G.D., M. O'Dell, G. Wright and S.C. Muller 1996. *A sea change
in land rights law: the extension of native title to Australia's offshore areas*.
Canberra: Australian Institute of Aboriginal and Torres Strait Islander
Studies.

Moore, C. 1972. Groote Eylandt families. In *Groote Eylandt stories* (ed) K.
Cole. Melbourne: Church Missionary Historical Publications. Pp. 12–22.

Palmer, K. 1984. Ownership and use of the seas: the Yolngu of north-east
Arnhem Land. *Anthropological Forum* 5(3): 448–55.

1985. *A report prepared in support of an application to control entry onto
seas adjoining Aboriginal land, north Groote Eylandt, Northern Territory*.
Corrected with addendum. Darwin: Northern Land Council.

Turner, D.H. 1974. *Tradition and transformation*. Canberra: Australian Institute of Aboriginal Studies.

Waddy, J. A. 1988. *Classification of Plants and Animals from a Groote Eylandt Aboriginal Point of View*. Darwin: Australian National University, North Australian Research Unit. (2 volumes.)

Worsley, P. 1961. Utilization of natural food resources by an Australian Aboriginal tribe. *Acta Ethnographica* 10:153–90.

10

Gapu Dhulway, Gapu Maramba: conceptualisation and ownership of saltwater among the Burarra and Yan-nha<u>ng</u>u peoples of northeast Arnhem Land

Geoffrey Bagshaw

Although a considerable body of literature now exists on aspects of customary marine tenure and/resource usage in the Blyth River—Crocodile Islands region of northeast Arnhem Land,[1] little has been written about the ways in which the local Burarra and Yan-nha<u>ng</u>u peoples actually conceptualise saltwater and articulate concomitant relations of sea ownership. Ultimately, and perhaps inevitably, this lack of focus upon indigenous conceptions of saltwater has resulted in the promulgation and uncritical acceptance of certain ethnographically inaccurate representations of regional sea tenure patterns and principles. Foremost among these (mis)representations is the widely held view that traditional patterns of land and sea tenure in this region are, to all practical intents and purposes, identical (cf. Davis 1984a; Davis and Prescott 1992; Cooke 1995:9–10; Keen 1984–85:433; see also Northern Land Council 1992:1, 1995:2,4–5). Deriving from this perspective are the equally erroneous, if often less explicitly articulated, assumptions to the

---

1   See, for example, Aboriginal Land Commissioner (1981); Bagshaw (1979, 1991a, 1991b, 1991c, 1995a); Cooke (n.d.[a], n.d.[b], 1995); Davis (1981, 1984a, 1984b); Davis and Prescott (1992); Dreyfus and Dhulumburrk (1980); Keen (1977, 1981, 1984–85); Meehan (1977a, 1977b, 1977c, 1982, 1983); and Ritchie (1987). Similar material from neighbouring parts of Arnhem Land can be found in Aboriginal Land Commissioner (1988); Davis (1981, 1982); Ginytjirrang Mala/ADVYZ (1994); Hiatt (1982); Keen (1982, 1983); Northern Land Council (1992, 1995); and Palmer (1984–85).

effect that saltwater elements of local estates constitute little more than spatially contiguous offshore projections of relatively well-defined land areas and, further, that for the purposes of estate ownership and delineation, saltwater is indistinguishable from other contiguously located marine features such as sites and seabed.[2]

In order both to counter such views and to contribute to the development of a more comprehensive ethnographic base for future work on customary marine tenure in this region, the current paper presents the first detailed account of Burarra and Yan-nhangu concepts of saltwater and its ownership.[3]

Burarra and Yan-nhangu

The Burarra and Yan-nhangu peoples[4] traditionally own adjoining territories on and near the Arafura Sea coast of northeast Arnhem Land. Broadly speaking, Burarra territory extends inland for varying distances from points west of the Blyth River to Cape Stewart and nearby islands in the east, while Yan-nhangu country encompasses most of the Crocodile Islands group (Figure 10:1). Despite marked differences in language and social organisation—Burarra speak a prefixing non-Pama-Nyungan language (cf. Glasgow and Glasgow 1985) and subscribe to an Aranda-like system of kin classification (Hiatt 1965), whereas

---

2 Both assumptions clearly inform Davis' mapping of local estates (see Davis 1984a:89–90).

3 Being an initial ethnographic statement the paper does not attempt to explore the complex theoretical issues (e.g. the logic of moiety classification, the constitution of patrifilial groups, the relationship between patrifiliation and consubstantial identification with country, competing claims of sea ownership and trans-regional 'communal title') to which it sometimes refers. It is hoped that at least some of these issues will be the foci of future studies.

4 Burarra and Yan-nhangu are locally employed sociolinguistic designations. The Burarra are also called Gidjingali by Hiatt (1965)

Yan-nhangu speak a dialect of the suffixing Pama-Nyungan Yolngu-matha language (Zorc 1986) and classify kin asymmetrically (Keen 1994)—the two peoples characterise themselves as 'close' (B: *yi-gurrepa*; Y: *galki*)[5] and maintain high levels of sociocultural interaction (including intermarriage).

Local estates (B: *rrawa*; Y: *wanggala*) within both domains (Stanner 1965) are identified with, and owned by; small, exogamous patrifilial groups (Bagshaw 1991c, 1995a; Keen 1994). Called *yakarrara* by Burarra and *baparru* by Yan-nhangu,[6] each such group bears a proper name and is affiliated to one or another of two named, exogamous patri-moieties (B: *Yirrchinga* and *Jowunga*; Y: *Yirritja* and *Dhuwa*). In all cases, estates and their associated religious resources (*madayin*)[7] are believed to have been created by, and inherited from, eternal, moiety-specific supernatural entities known as *wangarr*, who shaped the world in the far distant past (*baman*). Consubstantial identification with a particular *wangarr*, or group of *wangarr*, and possession of related sacra (cf. Hiatt 1982:14) constitute the principal ontological

---

5 Burarra terms are rendered here according to the standard Glasgow and Glasgow (1985) orthography. Yan-nhangu terms are based on the Zorc (1986) orthography. Certain terms (e.g. *wangarr, madayin*) are common to both languages.

6 *Baparru* is a polysemic term which also refers to several other types of social formations and metaphysical categories (cf. Shapiro 1981, Williams 1986, Keen 1994, 1995). Although variations of the same term (e.g. *baparrurr* and *baparru*) are also used by Burarra-speakers (cf. Hiatt 1965), the term *yakarrara* more precisely designates the patrifilial estate-owning group. Partly as a result of their relatively small size and partly as a result of the fact that all but one of them possess a single onshore estate tract, Burarra *yakarrara* appear to be much less labile in terms of their constitution and estate identification than the Yolngu *baparru* recently described by Keen (1995).

7 As other observers have pointed out, *madayin* variously connotes 'greatest value [... and ...] beauty' (Williams 1986:243), 'sacred law' (Morphy 1991:170) and 'sacra, [a] category of things and events associated with *wangarr* ancestors, [including] sacred objects' (Keen 1994:308).

and material bases of estate ownership. Collectively, the members of each *yakarrarra* or *baparru* are referred to as 'country leaders' (B: *rrawa walang*) or 'country holders' (Y: *wanggala watangu*) in respect of their estates.

Complex ritual connections based on the journeys and activities of *wangarr* link different estates and estate-owning groups within and between domains (Hiatt 1965; Keen 1978, 1994; Davis 1984a). Variously expressed in terms of shared *madayin* and concomitant notions of shared identity, and/or immutable kinship relations between estates (e.g. sibling, spouse and MM-fDC/ZDC relationships), such mythologically inscribed linkages confer a range of collectively held rights and interests in the estates of other groups (see Bagshaw 1995a:11–12 for details).

Significant individual rights and interests in other estates are also conferred by actual kinship relations. For Burarra and Yan-nhangu alike, the most important kintypes in this regard are ZC and ZDC, with persons in the former category being termed 'breast-related group' (B: *ngamanbananga*) or 'breast possessors' (Y: *ngamani watangu*) and those in the latter 'MM-related group' (B: *aburr-mari*) or 'MM possessors' (Y: *wayirri watangu*). Among other things, initiated males in both categories are charged with the custodial care of their maternal and MM estates and the performance of associated ceremonial duties (Hiatt 1965; Keen 1991; 1994, Bagshaw 1995a).[8]

---

8 Persons in the former category in particular are sometimes referred to as 'guardians' (B: *jaga an*-gugana; Y: *jagay*) of the relevant estates and associated *madayin*. Keen (1991, 1994) notes that in the Yolngu region (of which the Yan-nhangu domain is generally considered to form a part) *waku-watangu* or 'MMM-related group' also have significant rights and interests in their MMM estates.

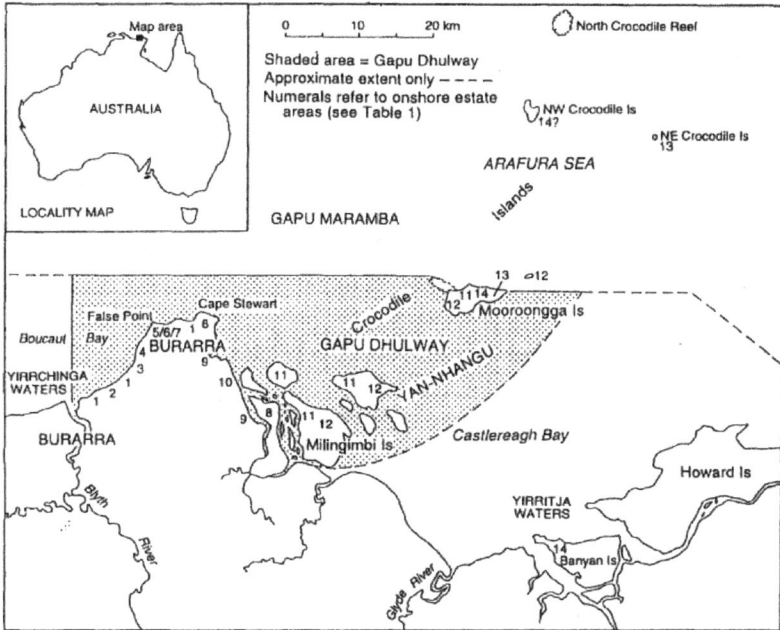

Figure 10:1 Blyth River—Crocodile Islands region

Coastal estates

Some eleven Burarra *yakarrarra* and four Yan-nhaŋu *baparru* are identified with coastal estates in the immediate Blyth River—Crocodile Islands region.[9] Of these, three Burarra groups (or two, according to

9   Owing to the fact that they share major religious resources with a Yan-nhaŋu *baparru*, the members of two predominantly Burarra-speaking *yakarrarra* also identify themselves as Yan-nhaŋu speakers (see also main text below). In addition to their proper names, most of the of the patrifilial groups referred to here are identified by broad, and in some cases moiety-specific, designations which expressly denote the coastal setting of their estates. Among these 'district' designations are Gurridhay ('coast'; both moieties), Gulala or Gulalay ('mangrove pod'; Yirritja moiety

251

at least one of my principal informants) are often considered to jointly own a single estate, while another is extinct.[10] Like the latter, all of the remaining *yakarrara* and *baparru* are identified with distinct estates. The general locations of their onshore territories are shown on Figure 10:1. The proper names of the relevant estate-owning patrifilial groups, together with their patri-moiety affiliations, approximate populations and socio-linguistic affiliations are set out in Figure 10:2.

Burarra and Yan-nhangu coastal estates incorporate both onshore and offshore areas.[11] In the Burarra domain, onshore estate areas usually consist of a single mainland tract (sometimes with adjacent small islands) encompassing numerous named sites (B: *rrawa*).[12]

In contrast, all of the island-centred Yan-nhangu estates consist of two or more geographically disparate tracts and associated sites

---

only) and Maringa ('coast'; Dhuwa moiety only). Such terms are common to both the Burarra and Yan-nhangu languages. Additional Burarra estates are located on the coast west of the Blyth River mouth (see Hiatt 1965:18, 1982). However, like the two Dhuwa moiety Jinang estates (Gangal, Manharrngu) and the two Yirritja moiety Wulaki estates (Mildjingi, Baytjimurrungu) in and around the Crocodile Islands, these are not considered here.

10 The Jowunga moiety Maljikarra, Marrawundi and Balwarra *yakarrara* are often considered to be joint owners of a single estate in the vicinity of *Inanganduwa* (False Point). I have, however, also recorded information which indicates that each group may be primarily identified with distinct, albeit adjoining, sites and territories. One of my principal informants alternatively maintains that Maljikarra and Marrawundi are one and the same *yakarrara*. The Jowunga moiety Gaburrburr *yakarrara* is extinct. Its estate is variously managed by the Liralira (Burarra, Jowunga moiety), Gamalangga (Yan-nhangu, Dhuwa moiety) and Warrawarra (Burarra, Yirrchinga moiety) groups (cf. Davis 1984a:52). Liralira, Gamalangga and Gaburrburr share the same principal *madayin*, while Warrawarra owns a neighbouring estate defined as 'spouse country'.

11 I include all permanently exposed islands (B: *bamara*; Y: *dhakal*) in the former category.

12 The sole exception to this pattern is the Gamal estate, which includes discontinuous tracts in the vicinities of Boucaut Bay and Cape Stewart.

(Y: *wanggala*).[13] In both domains, tracts identified with neighbouring coastal estates are usually partially demarcated by environmental 'boundary markers' (B: *rrawa gu-gorndiya* ['country it-cut self']; Y: *wanggala gulthana* ['country cut']) such as vegetation, beaches and gradients (cf. Davis 1984a:60–4; Keen:1994:105). and are generally (but not invariably) owned by *yakarrara* or *baparru* affiliated to opposite patri-moieties. The latter circumstance has prompted some observers to speak of a 'checkerboard' (Davis 1984a:43; Williams 1986:77) pattern of alternating moiety affiliations among estates on the coast of northeast Arnhem Land. Quantitative data compiled by Davis (1984:106–10) indicate that the majority of Burarra and Yan-nhangu coastal estates in the immediate Blyth River—Crocodile Islands region have total land areas (i.e. land above high-water mark) of between 13 and 53 sq.km.[14] Offshore estate areas in the Burarra and Yan-nhangu domains consist either of permanently submerged or tidally exposed sites and adjacent seabed, on the one hand, or, on the other, of sites, seabed *and* the surrounding saltwater. As described in greater detail later in the chapter, this previously unrecorded distinction in the constitution of coastal estates (i.e. inclusive or exclusive of saltwater) is closely linked to local conceptions of the sea as two separate bodies of water, that is, as physically and mythologically distinct zones of inshore and open sea water.

Marine sites (B: *rrawa gu-bugula*; Y: *wanggala gapunga*) include specific topographic features such as rocks, reefs, sandbars and mudbanks, all of which are explicitly construed as 'land'. Like onshore sites, these features are differentially associated with a variety of *wangarr* and are interpreted as focal points of noumenal activity and/or presence (cf. Keen 1984:433). Whilst some marine sites can be approached by persons irrespective of age or gender, others are only accessible to initiated men.

---

13 Estate-specific tracts in both the Burarra and Yan-nhangu domains are generally named after prominent sites therein (i.e. each tract is known by a single 'big' place name, cf Davis 1984a:57–8; Keen 1994:104).

14 The figures referred to here exclude the 222sq.km of Gamalangga territory on Banyan Island (*Garuma*) to the south and south-east of the Crocodile Islands (Davis 1984a:107).

Figure 10:2 Burarra yakarrarra and Yan-nhangu baparru with coastal estates

No.[1]	Name	Patri-moiety	Population[2]	Affililiation
1	Gamal	Yirrchinga	91	Burarra/ Yan-nhangu
2	Guwowura	Jowunga	11	Burarra
3	Yemara	Jowunga	4	Burarra
4	Bindararr	Yirrchinga	10	Burarra/ Yan-nhangu
5	Maljikarra[3]	Jowunga	11[4]	Burarra
6	Marrawundi	Jowunga		Burarra
7	Balwarra	Jowunga	12	Burarra
8	Barlaytjina	Yirrchinga	10	Burarra
9	Warrawarra	Yirrchngga	60+	Burarra
10	Gaburrburr	Jowunga	0	Burarra
11	Gurryindi[5]	Dhuwa	36+	Yan-nhangu
12	Ngurruwula	Yirritja	6	Yan-nhangu
13	Malarra	Dhuwa	34	Yan-nhangu
14	Gamalangga	Dhuwa	34+	Yan-nhangu

Notes to Table
1. Numerals refer to onshore estate areas; see Figure 10:1.
2. Approximate 1996 population.
3. The Maljikarra, Marrawundi and Balwarra *yakarrarra* are generally considered to be joint owners of a single estate.
4. Combined 5 and 6.
5. Although Gurryindi is a Dhuwa moiety *baparru*, many of its members are personally affiliated to the Yirritja moiety as a consequence of intra-moiety marriages.

Others still, are regarded as extremely dangerous (B: *gun-bachirra*; Y: *mardangarrangarr* or *rrathangu*) and are carefully avoided. Details of numerous marine sites in the Blyth River—Crocodile Islands region have been recorded in the course of sea-closure and /or site-protection research (see Bagshaw 1979, 1991a, 1991b; Davis 1981; Dreyfus and Dhulumburrk 1980; and Meehan 1983).

Seabed, which is locally referred to as 'earth' (B: *jel*; Y: *munha-tanga*), primarily includes all tidally exposed areas around and between marine sites. As previous authors have noted, such areas are also explicitly regarded as 'land', with the Lowest Astronomical Tide (LAT) level effectively delineating the exploitable limits thereof (cf. Davis 1984a:78; Davis and Prescott 1992:50). Although such 'land' is also generally thought to underlie continuously inundated inshore areas, Burarra and Yan-nhangu have no elaborated concept of permanently submerged seabed in deep water zones.

According to Davis (1984a:60–7; Davis and Prescott 1992:46), estate-specific offshore areas in this region are demarcated in much the same ways as, and often with reference to, onshore areas. Watersheds, river channels and onshore vegetation are said to be of particular significance in this regard (Davis 1984a). While my own data partly confirm this observation, they also clearly show that whereas an estate's marine sites and seabed are usually contiguous with its onshore area(s) and are generally interpreted as spatial extensions thereof, saltwater elements invariably extend well beyond the lateral onshore boundaries of the relevant estates (see section on saltwater ownership and moiety-specificity for further details).

With respect to the northern (i.e. seaward) extent of marine sites and seabed, one of my principal informants unequivocally maintains that Burarra estates do not incorporate such elements beyond the recognised junction of the two bodies of inshore and open sea water referred to above. (Specific details of this junction are given in the following section). This observation is fully consistent with the marine site survey work I have undertaken in and around the Boucaut Bay—Cape Stewart area since 1979 (see Bagshaw 1979, 1991a, 1991b). Within the Yan-nhangu domain, however, at least three (and possibly four) estates include sites and/or seabed beyond the recognised confluence of inshore and open sea waters.[15] It should be added that the results of a recent aerial survey of major marine sites to the north of Murrungga (Mooroongga Island) strongly suggest that no estate-specific Yan-nhangu sites and seabed are located beyond the outermost reefs of *Gunumba [1]* (North Crocodile Reef).[16]

In their concerns to represent the regional marine environment as a locus of diverse, site-specific *wangarr* activity and/or a key resource base most previous studies have perfunctorily conflated sites and seabed with saltwater, construing all three as indivisible elements of 'sea country' (cf. Northern Land Council 1992; Cooke 1995) Whilst undoubtedly justified at a broad socio-ecological level, this conflation has nevertheless consistently (if unwittingly) obscured the distinctive cultural status of saltwater, both in metaphysical terms[17] and in terms of its traditional ownership. I shall therefore devote much of the balance of the paper to a detailed consideration of this status.

---

15   Relevant estates include those of the Gurryindi, Malarra and Ngurruwulu *baparru*. Members of the Gamalangga *baparru* also claim to have such interests in this area (see also main text below).

16   I conducted this survey in August 1995 with a now deceased senior male member of the Malarra *baparru*.

17   A limited exception is the Ginytjirrang Mala/ADVYZ (1994) document (see also footnote 25 below). Typically, even among those who, like the Aboriginal Land Commissioner in the Castlereagh Bay/Howard Island sea closure case, acknowledge that '[t]he land and water of an estate is conceived of as the substance of the ancestral beings ('wangarr'), which inhabit it' (1988:3), there is no clear recognition of saltwater itself as such a being or beings. In the instance just cited, saltwater (i.e. 'water') appears to be interpreted as a medium that is somehow consubstantial with the other *wangarr* 'which inhabit it'. It should also be noted that in all of their extensive writings on customary marine tenure in and around the Crocodile Islands (see footnote 2 above), neither Keen nor Davis makes mention of the fact that saltwater itself is accorded *wangarr* status.

Gapu dhulway, gapu maramba

Burarra and Yan-nhangu view the Arafura Sea in the immediate Blyth River—Crocodile Islands region as two distinct bodies of saltwater (B: *bugula gunbachirra* ['water bitter']; Y: *ganitjirri rrathangu ['water bitter']). Commonly termed gapu dhulway and gapu maramba (gapu* being a wider Yolngu-matha noun for water[18] which is also used in this particular context by Burarra and Yan-nhangu), these two bodies of saltwater respectively comprise all shallow (B: *gun-delipa*; Y: *gulku-rungu*), turbid (B: *burul*; Y: *ritji*) inshore waters within the region and all deep (B: *gu-lupa*; Y: *dhulupurr*), clear (B: *rrewarrga*; Y: *garkuluk*) waters of the open sea.[19]

Like other mythologically related waters to the east (see below), *gapu dhulway* and *gapu maramba* are both construed as moiety-specific noumenal entities (*wangarr*) endowed with creative power (*marr*) and active agency—attributes which are deemed to be manifest in their movement, sound and changing form (cf. Davis and Prescott 1992:52).[20] Such natural phenomena are, in fact, themselves interpreted as quintessential aspects of the two *wangarr* and are accorded highly specific ritual names known as *bundurr* (see below). At a more colloquial (and also more general) level, the dynamic form and nature of the *gapu dhulway* and *gapu maramba wangarr* are underscored and affirmed

---

18   Zorc 1986:122.

19   *Gapu dhulway* is said to contain or flow over mud (B: *gapurra*; Y: *djudum*). It is also explicitly associated with floating mangrove leaf debris (*gaylinjil*). *Gapu maramba*, on the other hand, is said to flow over rock reefs (B: *gun-gurrema*; Y: *dhungupal*) and is associated with floating seaweed (B: *gapalma*; Y: *jiwul*).

20   Constant movement of water (B: *bugula gu-gakiya gu-workiya*; Y: *gapu bayngu walngan*), constant sound of water (B: *bugula gu-weya gu-workiya*; Y: *gapu bayngu wanga*), constantly changing form of water (B: *bugula gu-ngukurdanyjiya gu-workiya*; Y: *gapu bayngu bilyun*). The Yan-nhangu term *bayngu* 'habitually' should not be confused with the identical Yolngu-matha word for 'none / nothing'.

through the use of anatomical referents for various saltwater features.[21] Examples of such usages include 'knees' (B: *menama gu-jirra*; Y: *bun*) for waves, 'teeth' (B: *rrirra gu-jirra*)[22] or 'mouth' (B: *ngana gu-jirra*; Y: *dha*) for the shoreline edge of the sea, 'abdomen' (B: *gochila gu-jirra*; Y: *gulun*) for moderately distant waters [i.e. relative to land]), 'chest' (B: *gumbach gu-jirra*; Y: *miriki*) for distant sea and 'lower back' (B: *barra gu-jirra*; Y: *mundaka*) for far distant waters. In a similar conceptual and linguistic vein, the constant crashing of beach surf and of inshore waves is described as saltwater 'habitually speaking' (B: *gu-weya gu-workiya*; Y: *bayngu wanga*). In like manner, the more distant (and therefore less clearly audible) waters of the open sea are said to perpetually 'rumble' or 'growl' (B: *gumurrijinga gu-workiya*; Y: *bayngu murriyun*).[23] Finally, laterally flowing bodies of saltwater (see below) are usually described as 'habitually walking' (B: *gu-bamburda guworkiya*; Y: *bayngu garama*).

The designations *dhulway* and *maramba* are locally characterised as *baparru* names (cf. Shapiro 1981, Williams 1986; Keen 1994, 1995), meaning (in this context at least) that they are regional-level appellations connoting both the geographical horizons and distinctive cosmological identities (including patri-moiety affiliations) of the two saltwater *wangarr*. To the extent that *gapu dhulway* is exclusively identified with the *Yirritja* (called *Yirrchinga* in Burarra) patri-moiety and *gapu maramba* with the *Dhuwa* (called *Jowunga* in Burarra) patri-moiety, the appellations *dhulway* and *maramba* appear to correspond to the broad, moiety-specific names *manbuynga* and *rulyapa* as used in respect of the same and other similarly classified waters by peoples in the Galiwin'ku (Elcho Island) region (cf. Ginytjirrang Mala/ADVYZ 1994; Northern Land Council 1995).[24] Although versions of these

21 The use of anatomical referents is a basic feature of Burarra and Yan-nhangu modes of classifying form and space. Terms of the this kind are also applied, *inter alia*, to onshore topographic features and material goods.

22 I am told that there is no equivalent Yan-nhangu expression.

23 See also footnote 32 below.

24 According to Ginytjirrang Mala/ADVYZ, however: Our names for

latter names (i.e. *manbuyma* and/or *manbuynga* and *ruljaparr*) are also employed by Burarra and Yan-nhangu, their meanings and usages are generally more restricted (see below).

Gapu dhulway is held to flow on an east-west axis from points in the general vicinities of Mooroonga Island (Murrungga; to the north-east) and the mouth of Darbilla Creek (southeast) to the mid-channel of the mouth of the Blyth River (Angartcha wana 'big river', west). Surface bubbles (B: *mun-janajana*; Y: *dhangngurr* or *mulmul*) in or near the Blyth River mouth are said to indicate the western limit of this body of water.[25] Despite marked seasonal fluctuations in the degree and extent of inshore turbidity, its permanent seaward limit—and thus also its boundary with *gapu maramba*—is defined as a conceptual line projecting east and west from two mythologically inscribed locations in the immediate vicinity of Murrungga. These locations are Galidjarra reef (east) at co-ordinates 11.55.45S, 135.07.43E and Budha reef (west) at co-ordinates 11.54.34S, 135.01.46E (see Figure 10:3). The physical junction of the two bodies of water along this plane is characterised in Burarra as *bugula galamurrpa gubirri-gataji* ('water[s] / meeting / they two to it-there standing in line') and in Yan-nhangu as *balaytjini dhamanarpana ganitjirri* ('they two/ together/ water[s]'). All saltwater north of this recognised confluence is construed as *gapu maramba*.

---

the seas off our homelands are Manbuynga and Rulyapa. Manbuynga ga Rulyapa are the names of the two elemental forces or currents in the Arafura Sea. These are the most important names for the sea and Yolngu law arises from their journey. There are also named waters which arise in the bays and elsewhere along our coast. But those names stop in inshore areas. All water ends up as Manbuynga ga Rulyapa. Only these two names extend out into deep water (1994:3).

25   Although inshore waters immediately to the west of the Blyth are also identified with the Burarra Yirrchinga patri-moiety, they are considered to be mythologically unrelated. Further research is needed to fully establish the eastern limits of *gapu dhulway*. In view of the posited mythological relationship between *gapu maramba* and separately owned Yirritja moiety waters located near Howard Island to the SSE of *Murrungga* (see main text below), it is likely that *gapu dhulway* does not extend very far beyond the eastern tip of *Murrungga*.

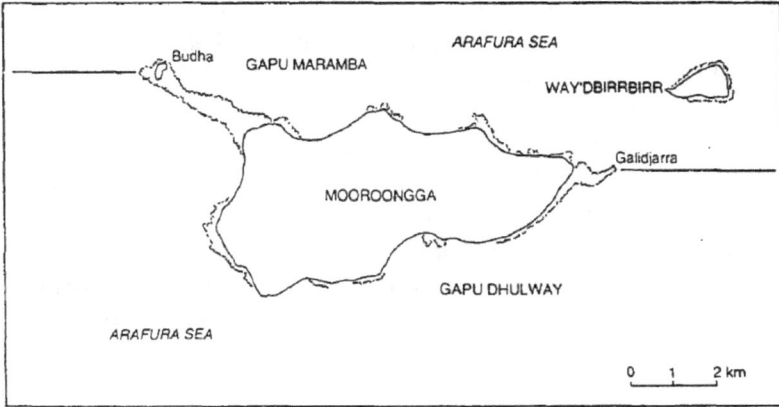

Figure 10.3 Junction of gapu dhul way and gapu maramba at Mooroongga Island

Gapu maramba (which is also colloquially known in Yan-nhangu as *gapu mundaka* 'lower back of the water'; i.e. distant sea) is believed to commence at an unspecified location far to the west of the Blyth River—Crocodile Islands region and to flow east to *Gukurda*, a reef near *Galiwin'ku* (Elcho Island) owned by the now extinct Gunbirridji *baparru*. Still further to the east the same body of water becomes known as *wulamba* and is primarily identified with the Djapu *baparru* (cf. Berndt 1951, 1955; Williams 1986).[26] From a Burarra and Yan-nhangu perspective, the western waters of *gapu maramba* include seas in the vicinity of the Goulburn Islands (175km WNW of Murrungga) and Croker Island (270km WNW of Murrungga). The far distant northern waters of *gapu maramba*, which are also variously termed *wulan, gurri* and *dhawal*,

26 According to Williams (1986:67–8):*Balamumu* and the contextually linked term *Wulamba* are names that refer to specific characteristics of waters off the shores of Blue Mud Bay in the Gulf of Carpentaria: rough water and foaming white caps as the strong trade winds ... come from myth-related lands to the south and lash these waters. *Balamumu* is a name in the category*baparru* names that belongs to the Djapu clan, and a number of other groups of the Dhuwa moiety may symbolise their relationship to the Djapu through the *Balamumu* (or *Wulamba*) *baparru*.

260

are said to extend to the shores of the island of New Guinea, known to Burarra and Yan-nhangu as *Bapua* (cf. Ginytjirrang Mala/ADVYZ 1994:5). The approximate horizons of *gapu dhulway* and *gapu maramba* within the immediate Blyth River—Crocodile Islands region are shown on Figure 10:3.

In both cases, important mythological linkages are held to exist with other waters to the east. These latter are, in fact, explicitly construed as direct physical and metaphysical extensions of *gapu dhulway* and *gapu maramba* and, as such, are often respectively characterised as 'one water' (B: *bugula gu-ngardapa*; Y: *ganhaman gapu*). *Gapu dhulway* is thus connected to *Yirritja* moiety inshore waters in the vicinities of Darbilla Creek (Mildjingi *baparru*), Howard Island (Wobulkarra *baparru*) and Cape Arnhem (Wangurri) *baparru*),[27] while *gapu maramba* is, as previously indicated, similarly connected to *Dhuwa* moiety open sea waters near Galiwin'ku (Elcho Island, Gunbirridji *baparru*) and the Yirrkala region (Djapu *baparru*).[28] In effect, therefore, local *yakarrara* and *baparru* identified with either *gapu dhulway* or *gapu maramba* form part of two much wider, moiety-specific sets of saltwater-owning groups. At the broadest social and geographical levels, it is these maximally inclusive sets which collectively hold what may be termed 'communal title' in respect of Yirritja and Dhuwa waters (cf. Ginytjirrang Mala/ADVYZ 1994; see also below).

Gapu maramba is further characterised as the mother's brother (B: *jachacha*; Y: *gaykay*) of inshore waters around Howard Island, to which

---

27 Similar connections may also exist with waters in the vicinities of Gananggarngur Island (Baytjimurrungu *baparru*) and the mainland near Elcho Island (Guyamirrilili *baparru*).

28 Contrary to the trans-regional dichotomy of Yirritja moiety inshore waters and Dhuwa moiety open sea assayed here, McIntosh (1994:129) refers to a line from a 'camp song' associated with the Yirritja moiety Warramiri *baparru* from the Wessel Islands in which it is stated: 'Ngayum Djangu Golula. I am the open sea'. As Palmer (1984–85) further refers to both Dhuwa and Yirritja land and sea estates in the Wessel Islands area, it may well be the case that patterns of sea tenure in the Wessel Islands differ substantially from those in the Burarra and Yan-nhangu region.

(according to local mythology) it carries *rrambala*, the mangrove-wood *wangarr* most closely identified with the latter area. Although mutual kinship statuses are less commonly ascribed to *gapu maramba* and *gapu dhulway* (but see Addendum), the two are certainly believed to inter-act—most notably in the context of tidal action, which is thought to result (in part at least) from both entities 'knocking' each other forward (incoming tide) and back (outgoing tide).[29]

Like other *wangarr* in the Burarra and Yan-nhangu cosmos, each body of water is also associated with a set of more specific ritual names (*bundurr*) connoting its distinctive features and/or characteristics (cf. Keen 1994:103–4). *Jawurrjawurr* (sound of inshore water), *bulurrbulurr* (fast, tumbling waves), *nyirdawuku* (mid-section of waves), *manbuyma* (high waves also pronounced *manbuynga*), *gularri* (rough, bubbling sea), *gulaynyingga* (whitecaps) and *makalama* (cold sea breeze) are among the many *bundurr* associated with *gapu dhulway*. Some of the *bundurr* associated with *gapu maramba bundurr* include *dhawunuwunu* (far distant sea), *balawurru* (high waves), *mirikindi* (sea horizon), *rul-japarr* (distant open sea), *jingamurriyun* (sound of distant sea) and *dhangarrngarr* (sea 'biting' land).

Publicly invoked in certain ceremonial contexts,[30] saltwater *bundurr* names figure in 'coastal' (as distinct from the 'hinterland') verses of song-cycles (*manikay*) such as Wulumungu (associated with *gapu dhulway*) and Murrungun (also called Malarra after the *baparru* of the same name; associated with *gapu maramba*).[31] Like the related designs

---

29 Tidal action is also the subject of more highly elaborated mythologies. Owing to their culturally restricted nature, however, these mythologies will not be discussed here.

30 E.g. mortuary rites and circumcision rituals.

31 Other regional *manikay* also contain references to saltwater (see also footnote 42 below). In performances of the Wulumungu and Murrungun *manikay*, the sounds and relative distances of *gapu dhulway* and *gapu maramba* are evoked through particular styles of singing: the inshore water verses of the Wulumungu *manikay* are clearly articulated and sung 'with the mouth' (B: *ngana aburr-jirra*; Y: *dha dhana bayngu milama*),

depicted in sacred and secular art, these names and song cycles constitute some of the basic religious resources (*ma_dayin*) of the various patrifilial groups (B: *yakarrarra*; Y: *baparru*) most widely considered to own either *gapu dhulway* or *gapu maramba*. Indeed, identification with, and possession of, such resources (particularly the relevant *bundurr*) is locally construed as a primary index of saltwater ownership.

Consubstantial identification and associated possessory rights in saltwater

For Burarra and Yan-nha_ngu, the customary ownership[32] of *gapu dhulway, gapu maramba* and associated *ma_dayin* is primarily predicated upon consubstantial identification with the relevant saltwater *wa_ngarr*. Articulated at both the individual level and the level of the *yakarrarra* or *baparru*, such identification is principally mediated by patrifiliation.[33] In this connection, members of most of the *yakarrarra* and *baparru* generally considered to own either *gapu dhulway* or *gapu maramba* explicitly state that they were begotten by, *inter alia*, their human genitors (B: *ngun-anya nguna-bokamarra* 'to me-father / to me-begat'; Y: *ngarrana walkur milaynha* 'to me / male line / begotten-procreated') *and* the body of water which forms part of their respective estates (B: *bugula nguna-bokamarra* 'water / to me-begat'; Y: *gapu ngarrana bukmana* 'water / to me / begat').[34] Thus designated as 'rightful holders' of the relevant

whereas Murru_ngun verses pertaining to the more distant waters of *gapu maramba* are deliberately muffled and sung 'with the throat' [B: *gu-lorr aburr-jirra*; Y: *gurak dhana bayngu milama*).

32 By 'customary ownership' I mean that certain *yakarrarra* and *baparru* traditionally hold a specific and inalienable set of possessory rights in respect of either *gapu dhulway or gapu maramba* (see also main text below).

33 Adoption into a relevant *yakarrarra* or *baparru* may also confer *de facto* consubstantial status.

34 Similar statements are also made in relation to the totality of a

saltwater *waŋgarr* (B: *waŋgarr an-/jin-gurrimapa*; Y: *waŋgarr wataŋgu*) and its associated ritual names, such individuals are sometimes given saltwater *bundurr* (see above) as personal names and may be addressed or referred to as '(salt)water' (B: '*bugula*'; Y: '*gapu*').[35]

For the persons and groups so related, consubstantial identification confers a particular range of inalienable possessory rights in *gapu dhulway* or *gapu maramba*. Collectively constituting the indicia of customary ownership, these rights are corporately held, though for the most part individually exercised, by the members of each of the appropriate *yakarrarra* and *baparru*. In cases where more than one *yakarrarra* or *baparru* are consubstantially identified with the same body of water, the relevant possessory rights are jointly held (i.e. held in common) by all of the patrifilial groups concerned.

Although, as previously indicated, other groups to the east of the Blyth River—Crocodile Islands region also hold similar rights in saltwater and thus form part of wider constellations of 'title holders' in respect either of Yirritja and Dhuwa waters, it is only the members of the relevant Burarra and Yan-nhaŋgu patrifilial groups who are considered to hold and exercise all local-level possessory rights in *gapu dhulway* and *gapu maramba* within the area under consideration.

Following Sutton (1996 and pers.comm.), I group local-level possessory rights in *gapu dhulway* and *gapu maramba* into three broad categories: (1) identification and representation, (2) access and (3) use.

---

person's estate (i.e. including the land component). In the Burarra context, the concept of actively engendering phenomenal existence (i.e. 'begetting') is further elaborated to include a notion of reciprocal begetting (-*boka-marrachichiyana*) between members of the same *yakarrarra*. However expressed, the concept of begetting invariably connotes an equivalence of identity between the begetter(s) and the begotten. Among the Burarra and Yan-nhangu groups most widely identified with saltwater, the only one which is sometimes not regarded as being consubstantial with saltwater is Bindararr (for further details see main text and footnote 44 below).

35 Saltwater *bundurr* may also be used as personal names by second-descending generation matrifiliates (B: *aburr-mari*; Y: *wayirri wataŋgu*) and their offspring.

In that same author's (slightly amended) terms, the rights within each category include:

(1)(a) The right to publicly assert that the body of water concerned is part of one's own estate.

(b) The right to speak for and about that body of water (and its associated religious resources) as property (i.e. to *represent* it in both senses).

(c) The right to hold, assert and concretely exercise responsibility for the spiritual and physical welfare of that body of water.

(d) The right to perform (as distinct from merely participate in) rituals related to that body of water.

(2)(a) The right to be asked for permission to enter the specified body of water.

(b) The right to control movement within or around that body of water.[36]

(c) The right to enjoy unfettered access to that body of water (subject to the observance of customary restrictions upon gender, site avoidance, etc.).

(3) The right to hunt (turtle, dugong, rays, etc.) and fish on and in that body of water.

While many of the rights enumerated here (notably 1c, 1d, 2b, 2c and 3) are also extended to persons who are not themselves members of the *yakarrara* and *baparru* considered to own saltwater (see above), it is only the latter who possess the full complement.[37] This is most clearly

---

36 Matrifiliates may control movement within or around a body of water. Ideally, however, only members of the owning *yakarrara* and/or *baparru* may give permission to enter that body of water (i.e. to persons other than matrifiliates in the first or second descending generations).

37 The former, non-exclusive, rights in saltwater are perhaps most appropriately termed rights of possession or association. Davis (1984a:78–84), variously characterises such rights as complementary or subsidiary rights and goes on to point out that a number of authors have distinguished between 'primary and secondary rights' (Peterson *et al* 1977) or 'primary [/] presumptive and subsidiary rights (Williams 1983:103).

apparent in relation to those rights (e.g. 1a, 1b and 2a) which expressly allude to the ontological basis of identification with saltwater (i.e. consubstantiality). Apart from certain very limited exceptions (as in 1c, 1d, and 2b), such rights are the exclusive preserve of the owning *yakarrarra* and *baparru*.[38]

Full possessory rights may also be claimed or asserted by members of patrifilial groups other than those considered to be consubstantially identified with the relevant saltwater *wangarr*. In one such case discussed later in the paper, a senior Yan-nhangu man asserts that his own *baparru* holds exclusive rights of ownership in respect of *gapu maramba* as a result both of its identification with certain non-saltwater religious resources (*madayin*) believed to be shared with a now extinct group of saltwater owners and the fact that further mythological connections link its estate to particular sites located within *gapu maramba*. This claim, and the bases on which it is made, are, however, vigorously

---

38   Aside from the members of the owning *yakarrarra* and *baparru*, the only persons at the local-level who formally hold rights 1c, 1d and 2b are matrifiliates in the first and second descending generations. It is possible (but not yet firmly established by my research) that members of other patrifilial groups identified with saltwater in areas to the east of the Blyth River—Crocodile Islands region may also be entitled to exercise right 1d. The argument of Verdon and Jorion (1981) concerning the relationship between 'ontological distance' from an ancestral being and degrees—or, as they put it, the 'intensity' of land ownership—is highly relevant here. According to these authors: ' [the] ontological distance which governs access to the various levels of religious knowledge is also used as a scale to measure a 'gradient of rights of ownership' which stem, to a certain degree, from occupancy and use of the land surrounding the totems [...] all who exploit the land 'own' it, in the sense that they enjoy a privileged access to it, but some own it more than others. Those who own it the most with respect to the criterion of occupancy are, at the same time, those ontologically closest to the ancestor whose sites are located on that land, and who can therefore claim to have occupied the the land since its creation.' (1981:100). Unlike these authors, however, I maintain that, in this area at least, there are indeed specific, identifiable estates and *corporately* held rights therein. In this last respect, I also differ from Keen (1995).

contested by members of another patrifilial group who maintain (with general public concurrence) that they themselves are the sole owners of *gapu maramba* by virtue of consubstantial identification.

It may also be the case that joint ownership of a sea-specific song-cycle (i.e. of a song-cycle which is also owned by consubstantially identified groups), together with a direct identification with other closely related *wangarr* and the possession of a land estate directly abutting the relevant body of water, are regarded as sufficient conditions for the members of a non-consubstantially identified patrifilial group to hold and exercise full possessory rights in saltwater. I say 'may' because it is not entirely clear to me whether one of the groups generally recognised as a co-owner of *gapu dhulway* is consubstantially identified with that body of water or whether it is merely associated with inshore water on the terms just described (see below for further details).

Saltwater ownership and moiety-specificity

Earlier in the paper I observed that *gapu dhulway* is exclusively identified with the Yirritja (called Yirrchinga in Burarra) patri-moiety and *gapu maramba* with the Dhuwa (called Jowunga in Burarra) patri-moiety. Consistent with the totalising logic of moiety affiliation and differentiation which informs all aspects of Burarra and Yan-nhangu social, local and religious organisation, each body of water is owned by correspondingly identified *yakarrarra* and/or *baparru* (i.e. *gapu dhulway* is owned by Yirritja moiety patrifilial groups and *gapu maramba* by Dhuwa moiety groups [or rather, as I indicate below, a single Dhuwa moiety group]).

It follows from this moiety-specific pattern of ownership that no Yirritja patrifilial groups own the open sea water (i.e. *gapu maramba*) abutting their terrestrial estates and no Dhuwa groups own similarly situated inshore water (i.e. *gapu dhulway*). In actual terms, the former situation applies only to the Ngurruwula *bapurru*, the sole Yirritja moiety group with an estate tract north of the confluence of *gapu*

267

dhulway and *gapu maramba* (see above, also Figure 10:1). The latter situation, however, variously applies to the An-mujolgawa Guwowura, Yemarra, Maljikarra, Marrawundi, Balwarra and Gaburrburr *yakarrarra*, all of which possess land estates directly abutting inshore water. It also partially applies to the Gurryindi, Gamalangga and Malarra *baparru*, being groups with some estate tracts abutting *gapu dhulway* and others adjoining *gapu maramba* (see Figure 10:1).[39] Contrary to much of the literature, therefore, the so-called 'checkerboard' pattern of alternating moiety affiliations typically associated with neighbouring onshore estate areas (Davis 1984a, Williams 1986) is not transposed onto saltwater.[40] Instead, a much broader, regional-level moiety dichotomy is used to define and distinguish two physically and metaphysically discrete bodies of water.

Moreover, since *gapu dhulway* and *gapu maramba* are both conceived of as discrete, spatially continuous regional entities (see above), the fact that they are differentially identified with *yakarrarra* and/or *baparru* of a single (i.e. corresponding) moiety only means that the saltwater associated with each such group's estate invariably extends well beyond the lateral horizons of its (i.e. the group's) 'land' territories. This is because the water concerned also abuts or covers the land and seabed owned by neighbouring (or at least proximate) groups of the opposite moiety. The immediate question, then, is: which patrifilial groups are identified with either *gapu dhulway* or *gapu maramba*?

Saltwater yakarrarra and baparru gapu dhulway

Although some individuals broadly characterise *gapu dhulway* as 'shared (or common) water' (B: *bugula gun-ganawa*; Y: *gapu dhamanar*)

---

39 Available evidence suggests that one of the latter tracts which is presently claimed by the Gamalangga *baparru* is, in fact, Gurryindi territory.

40 Keen (1994:105) contests the notion of alternating patrimoiety estates along the coast. In my own view, such patterning constitutes a general, though by no means universal, feature of local territorial organisation.

conjointly owned by all Yirritja moiety groups within the region, the most detailed local exegeses I have recorded indicate that this body of water is specifically identified with, and exclusively owned by, certain patrifilial groups which also jointly own the Wulumu<u>ng</u>u *manikay*, the regional song-cycle most closely associated with inshore water (see above).[41]

Respectively named Gamal, Bindararr, and <u>N</u>gurruwula, these 'common *manikay*' (B: *manikay mun-ganawa*; Y: *manikay dhamanar*) groups variously hold onshore territories in the Burarra (Gamal and Bindararr) and Yan-nha<u>ng</u>u (<u>N</u>gurruwula) domains. (By way of acknowledging their joint ownership of the Wulumu<u>ng</u>u *manikay* and, indeed, the language in which this song-cycle is phrased, members of the Gamal and Bindararr *yakarrarra* often describe themselves as Yan-nha<u>ng</u>u-speakers.) Since the three groups are also collectively known as Walama<u>ng</u>u (a semantically related near-homophone of Wulumu<u>ng</u>u [Sutton pers.comm.]),[42] the inshore water with which they are identified is often referred to as 'Walama<u>ng</u>u water' (B: *Walama<u>ng</u>u gun-nika bugula*; Y: *nhan'kubi Walama<u>ng</u>u gapu*).

---

41 The more general characterisation of *gapu dhulway* as shared Yirritja moiety water may be related to the fact that most, if not all, Yirritja moiety patrifilial groups also have saltwater verses in their respective *manikay*. As I understand it, however, the saltwater *bundurr* (ritual names) within these latter *manikay* directly refer to, and are exclusively identified with, the estates of patrifilial groups which own the Wulumu<u>ng</u>u *manikay*. Accordingly, only these latter are actually considered to own the relevant *bundurr*.

42 As I have pointed out elsewhere (Bagshaw 1995b:123), Walama<u>ng</u>u is often mistakenly given as the name of a single *baparru* (Warner 1937:51; Davis 1984a:110; Davis and Prescott 1992:57; Keen 1978:24). The Gamal and <u>N</u>gurruwula groups and estates are held to exist in a permanent, totemically defined sibling relationship. The Gamal and Bindararr groups and estates are, however, respectively defined as MM/MMB-fDC/ZDC. Surprisingly, therefore, the <u>N</u>gurruwula and Bindararr groups and estates are also defined as siblings.

There appears to me, however, to be some uncertainty as to whether members of the Bindararr *yakarrarra* are consubstantially identified with that body of water, or whether their status as co-owners of inshore water actually derives from a combination of other factors such as their joint possession of the Wulumuŋu *manikay*, their identification with certain *wangarr* deemed to be closely associated with saltwater[43] and the physical location of their offshore 'land', which both adjoins Gamal territory and is overlain by *gapu dhulway*.[44] (In this last connection, the Bindararr group and its 'land' holdings [including onshore terrtitory] are typically described as being situated in the immediate vicinity of saltwater or, to be more precise, on the 'flank of the land/coast' [B: *rrawa gerlk gu-jirra*; Y: *gali gurridhay*]—a description which is also applied to the Gamal and Ŋgurruwula groups and their respective terrestrial estates). At the local level, though, the issue of Bindararr consubstantiality with saltwater seems to be rarely canvassed or even considered. It is certainly not a source of evident contention among the Walamaŋu groups.

---

43 The Bindararr *yakararra* is directly identified with the dingo (B: *gulu-kula*; Y: *wartu*) and northeast wind (*luŋgurrma*) *waŋgarr*. Both are held to be intimately associated with the incoming tidal movement of inshore water. Only the latter *wangarr*, however, is common to all Walamaŋu groups.

44 One of my principal Gamal informants contends that the saltwater verses of the Wulumuŋu *manikay* exclusively identify *gapu dhulway* with Gamal and Ŋgurruwula and, that as such, the Bindararr group is only linked to this body of water by virtue of its co-ownership of the *manikay* as whole, rather than by way of direct, consubstantial identification with the relevant saltwater *waŋgarr*. The Bindararr connection to *gapu dhulway* is thus said to be purely 'song-based' (B: *manikay wupa*; Y: *manikay bam*). Although I cannot say how widely this opinion is shared by other Burarra and Yan-nhaŋu people, it does appear that, for all practical purposes at least, the group concerned is generally regarded as a legitimate co-owner of inshore water (see also footnote 49 below). Since the death of the most senior Bindararr man at Milingimbi in August 1995, I have not had the opportunity to obtain any Bindararr perspective on the matter.

Walamangu (and, in particular, Gamal and Ngurruwula) identification with *gapu dhulway* is explicitly enunciated in saltwater verses of the Wulumungu *manikay*. In one such verse, for example, inshore waters in the vicinities of *Milinginbi* (i.e. Milingimbi; Ngurruwula *baparru*) and *Bunbuwa* (Gamal *yakarrarra*)[45]—that is to say, waters at or near the eastern and western extremities of *gapu dhulway*—speak as localised aspects of a single *wangarr*, variously and inclusively identifying themselves as Gulalay (a regional-level appellation applied only to Ngurruwula and Gamal), as Mandjikay (a much broader, predominantly Yolngu totemic aggregate to which Ngurruwula and Gamal belong) and as Walamangu.[46] As the following excerpt[47] from this particular verse illustrates, the two waters also specify some of their *bundurr* names which are indicated by asterisks.

Transcription

    [...] gulalay / mandjiridjirra / ngalipi / walamangu

    Gulalay / Mandjikay / we two / Walamangu /

    'mangrove-pod group'/ 'sandfly group'/ inclusive

    manbika / nyirdawuku* / gulaynyingga* / bulurrbulurr* /

---

45 The principal focus of the complete verse is upon the waters in the Bunbuwa area.

46 Variously referred to as a 'phratry' (Warner 1937) or 'clan-aggregate' (Keen 1978), Mandjikay is a Yirritja moiety 'totemic union' (Shapiro 1981:23) based on common identification with rock and mangrove wood *wangarr*. According to Keen (ibid:24–5), its constituent groups include: Gulalay/Gamal, Walamangu/Ngurruwulu, Wangurri, Lamilami, Golumala, Wobulkarra, and Ngurruwula also form part of a much broader totemic aggregation called Mandjikay. Guyamrirrilili/ Galngdhuma/Liyalanmirri. McIntosh (1994:98) also refers to 'a Mandjikay clan from Howard Island [called] Golpa'. This latter group may be the same as Wobulkarra. Keen (1995:515) adds that 'perspectives on which Yirritja moiety groups were Manydjikay [sic] people, linked by the journeys of Rock and Mangrove Log ancestors along the coast, differ'.

47 My transcription of this excerpt omits certain stylised features such as extra and/or extended final syllables in some words. The excerpt itself constitutes less than half of a single saltwater verse.

271

high waves / mid-section of waves / whitecaps / fast, tumbling waves /

stylised form of manbuynga˙

djalnyirr˙ / galkalmiyangu / milinginbi / bunbuwa /

lines of foam bubbles / waves heaping shells / Milinginbi area/ Bunbuwa area /

i.e. Milingimbi)

galarrawuya˙ / dhalarrbunungu.

I halt here / (sea) breaking on shore.

Translation

'(We are) Gulalay and Mandjikay, we are both Walamangu. (Our) rough waves heap beach shells in the Milinginbi area and the Bunbuwa area, where my (i.e, the Bunbuwa area) waters terminate, breaking onto the shore'.

While localised stretches of *gapu dhulway* (cf. references to *Milingimbi* and *Bunbuwa* area waters in the Wulumungu verse just quoted) are ultimately conceptualised as aspects of a single, spatially continuous and collectively owned entity, the fact that such geographically disparate waters are differentially associated (be it mythologically and/ or physically) with particular Gamal, Bindararr and Ngurruwula sites and/or areas means that they are also frequently characterised as distinct, estate-specific features. Accordingly, saltwater in the general area called *Bunbuwa* (common name) or *Dhawukula* (*bundurr* name) is typically identified with the Gamal *yakarrara*, while inshore waters in the *Munungurrumba* (common name) or *Marrambirpirl* (*bundurr* name) area and the *Walamarrana* (common name) or *Girrkirra* (*bundurr* name) area are usually respectively identified with the Bindararr *yakarrara* and the Ngurruwula *baparru*.[48] Available evidence suggests

48 The *Bunbuwa / Dhawukula* and *Munungurrumba / Marrambirlpirl* areas are both on the east coast of Boucaut Bay. The *Walamarrana / Girrkirra* area is situated on the east coast of *Rapuma* (Yabooma Island). Several other named sites and areas are either directly or indirectly linked to *gapu dhulway*. Of those mentioned here, only the *Marrambirlpirl /* Munungurrumba appears to have no explicit connection to saltwater in

that there may, in fact, be some environmentally-referenced delineation of the waters associated with such estate-specific areas. In this regard, at least one Burarra individual has told me that frothy surface bubbles (B: *mun-janajana*; *dhangngurr* or *mulmul*) mark the junction of waters overlying the Gamal and Bindararr offshore areas.

Saltwater yakarrarra and baparru gapu maramba

According to my principal Yan-nhangu and Burarra informants (a Malarra man and his Gamal wife), *gapu maramba* is directly identified with, and currently solely owned by, Malarra, a Yan-nhangu *Dhuwa* moiety *baparru* which possesses the Murrungun (also known as Malarra) song-cycle associated with the open sea (see above). Although additional Jinang and Burarra groups also share the same *manikay*,[49] the fact that none of them possess territory directly abutting (or even close to) *gapu maramba* (cf. the Bindararr estate vis-a-vis *gapu dhulway*; see above) means that the sea-specific references within the Murrungun song-cycle are invariably and exclusively associated with the Malarra estate.[50] As far as I can discern, it is for this reason that my informants do not regard the former groups as co-owners of *gapu maramba*.

The same informants also maintain that this body of water was once jointly owned by the Yan-nhangu-speaking *Mukarr* or

the Wulumungu *manikay* (cf. footnote 45 above) It should be noted, however, that the *bundurr* name *Marrambirlpirl*—which also features in the Wulumungu *manikay*—primarily denotes an area of tidally exposed flats and is thus indirectly connected to inshore water.

49   Other patrifilial groups said to share this *manikay* include Bargatgat (Jinang), Gangal (Jinang), Maljikarra (Burarra), Yemara (Burarra) and Guwowura (Burarra).

50   The Murrungun or Malarra *manikay* appears to be the same song-cycle as that called Goyulan by Hiatt and Wild (in Wild ed. 1986) and Clunies Ross (in Dixon and Duwell eds. 1990). Several of the 'Goyulan' themes mentioned by these authors directly refer to Malarra-owned territory in the Crocodile Islands.

Gurrmirringu—the semi-mythical *Dhuwa* moiety inhabitants of *Gurriba* (northwest Crocodile Island) who are said to have been annihilated by warriors from Murrungga and other locations. With their demise, it seems, sole ownership of *gapu maramba* passed to the Malarra *baparru*.

This latter perspective is, however, challenged by a senior male member of the Yan-nhangu-speaking Gamalangga *baparru*, who asserts that his own Dhuwa moiety group holds exclusive ownership rights in respect of the open sea.[51] His assertion appears to be largely based on the conviction that Gamalangga members shared (or perhaps inherited) certain religious resources (notably the *rrirakay* or clapstick *madayin*) with (or from) the now extinct *Mukarr* inhabitants of *Gurriba* (northwest Crocodile Island) and *Gunumba* [1] (North Crocodile Reef), and that as such, responsibility for the latter's land and sea territory is now legitimately held and exercised by the Gamalangga *baparru*. At the same time he also emphasises connections to the general *gapu maramba* area via the *mulunda* (booby) *wangarr* which links Gamalangga territory at *Manbengur* on Banyan Island (*Garuma*) with the important Gurryindi reef site at *Ngaliya*, some distance offshore from Murrungga, and the *yerrpany* (wild honey) *wangarr* which links sites on Banyan Island and Murrungga. To the best of my knowledge, though, he does not assert that Gamalangga members are consubstantially identified with the open sea, as Malarra people and the deceased *Mukarr* beings are (or were) generally held to be. In this last connection, his reasons for overlooking (or at least failing to acknowledge) the Malarra group as joint owners of *gapu maramba* are not entirely clear to me, although I suspect that they may well pertain to a long-standing territorial dispute (centred mainly on Gurryindi land and sites) between Malarra and Gamalangga members (see also Davis and Prescott 1992:51–2).

Whatever the case may be, the Gamalangga claim—and the apparent bases on which it is made—are categorically rejected by my main

---

51 As he put it to me in a mixture of Burarra and English: '*Yi-gurrepa Bapua* blue sea, still *gun-ngaypa* ... Gamalangga *gun-nika*, ngika company': 'The open sea close to [i.e up to] New Guinea is still mine ... it belongs to Gamalangga, it's not jointly owned'.

Malarra and Gamal informants. As I understand their objections, they variously maintain that the open sea is not a Gamalangga *wangarr*, that the Gamalangga song-cycle (called Djambidj) does not specifically refer to the open sea itself (i.e. in the sense of citing the actual *bundurr* names of *gapu maramba*), that assertions of connectedness to particular sites cannot be legitimately extended to include saltwater itself and, finally, that the person making the claim to *gapu maramba* is 'coming from [a] long way' (i.e. from Banyan Island [*Garuma*], approximately 34km SSE of Murrungga and 57km S of *Gurriba*), both in physical and metaphysical terms. As Keen (1994:124–25) indicates, differences of this sort are not uncommon in estate-related matters.[52]

Since limitations of space preclude any sustained analysis of this particular situation, I round off the present discussion with the general observation that in contexts where competing and mutually exclusive claims to the ownership of saltwater arise or, more precisely, are openly asserted, it is the claims of persons who are widely regarded as being consubstantially identified with saltwater that are, irrespective of any other social and political considerations,[53] the ones most likely to be

---

52 According to Keen (1994:124–25), people in this general region: 'argued about at least four aspects of relations to land and waters: the extent of a group's country, the group identity of a particular place, the ranking of groups who possessed the songs and ceremonies about a place and succession to a deceased or dying group's country'.

53 Cf. Keen (1994:129): 'Certain matters were widely agreed. The general location of named places and their spiritual significance were widely known, although there were disagreements and variation in the depth of knowledge about details. Under many circumstances such matters could remain ambiguous. Where they had to be resolved, what counted was being able to act on one's version of ownership; to enact the prerogatives due to a land-holder or *dja:gamirri* (one who 'looks after'), which include control of access to the ... land and use of the country, such as to establish an outstation, and performance of the related ceremonies. The size of the group was important for such abilities, but so was one's place of residence. Those who lived at or near a disputed country, who had the more detailed knowledge of it, and could muster the most support, were at an advantage.

acknowledged by the majority of the Burarra and Yan-nhangu jural public. This is because it is that same modality of identification which constitutes and expresses the most fundamental basis of relatedness to country for all Burarra and Yan-nhangu people.

Summary

To close the paper I will briefly summarise its key findings. In my own view, these findings collectively provide an essential frame of reference for any future ethnographic work on customary marine tenure in the Blyth River—Crocodile Islands region. They may also be of some assistance in the conduct of similar work elsewhere in northeast Arnhem Land and perhaps (albeit in a far more general way) in other parts of coastal Aboriginal Australia as well.

Burarra and Yan-nhangu people conceptualise saltwater within the region as two distinct, moiety-specific noumenal entities (*wangarr*). Respectively termed *gapu dhulway* and *gapu maramba*, these entities are considered to be physically manifest as separate bodies of inshore water and open sea water. *Gapu dhulway* is exclusively affiliated to the Yirritja (called Yirrchinga in Burarra) patri-moiety and *gapu maramba* is exclusively affiliated to the Dhuwa (called Jowunga in Burarra) patri-moiety.

All coastal estates in the region incorporate marine elements such as sites and/or seabed. Only certain estates, however, are said to incorporate saltwater. Where this occurs, the saltwater elements of an estate invariably extend well beyond the lateral horizons of the estate's onshore, site and seabed territory. For the purposes of estate delineation, therefore, saltwater is distinguishable from both onshore elements and other marine elements.

No Yirritja moiety estates incorporate open sea water (*gapu maramba*) and no Dhuwa moiety estates incorporate inshore water (*gapu dhulway*). As such, regional sea tenure patterns differ markedly

Sheer physical force, related to group size and demographic structure may also have been a factor'.

from the alternating pattern of moiety affiliations often associated with neighbouring onshore estate areas.

Saltwater in the region is most clearly identified with and owned by four patrifilial groups (B: *yakarrarra*; Y: *baparru*). The inshore water of *gapu dhulway* is thus identified with the Gamal, Bindararr and Ngurruwula groups (collectively known as Walamangu), while the open sea water of *gapu maramba* is identified with the Malarra group. In each case consubstantial identification and/or (cf. the Bindararr group's possible status in relation to *gapu dhulway*) the ownership of sea-specific religious resources (*madayin*) are locally cited as the principal criteria for such connectedness.

It is also the case that the onshore estates of the groups most closely identified with either *gapu dhulway* or *gapu maramba* directly abut the relevant body of saltwater.

Claims to the ownership of saltwater may also be made on other grounds, including estate-succession and mythological connections to sites and land in or near the relevant body of saltwater. Such claims, however, tend to lack the ontological force of claims made by consubstantially identified persons and groups and may well be contested by the latter. A case in point is the claim made to the ownership of *gapu maramba* by members of the Gamalangga *baparru*.

Consubstantial identification with saltwater is primarily mediated by patrifiliation, and is articulated at both the individual level and the level of the *yakarrarra/baparru*. As the principal basis of customary ownership, such identification confers upon the members of relevant *yakarrarra* and *baparru* a particular range of inalienable, local-level possessory rights in the particular body of saltwater with which they are identified. While many of these rights are also extended to other members of Burarra and Yan-nhangu societies, whether on the basis of kinship relations or of cosmologically inscribed connections between patrifilial groups, it is only the owning groups which possess the full range thereof.

The Burarra and Yan-nhangu patrifilial groups identified with either *gapu dhulway* or *gapu maramba* also form part of more extensive,

277

moiety-specific constellations of 'title holders' in respect of saltwater. In both social and geographical terms, these constellations extend well beyond (i.e. to the east of) the immediate Blyth River—Crocodile Islands region. It is, however, only members of the relevant Burarra and Yan-nhangu groups who can speak with authority in relation to the local waters of *gapu dhulway* and *gapu maramba*.

Addendum

I have since learned that Burarra and Yan-nhangu also regard *gapu dhulway* and *gapu maramba* as gendered bodies of saltwater, with the former construed as female (B: *gun-gama*; Y: *munhkangu*) and the latter as male (B: *gun-guchula*; Y: *marlaway*).[54] Moreover, the two stand in a mutual spouse relationship (B: *awurri-berrkuwa*; Y: *galay'manydji*) which effectively demarcates them from other, mythologically related, waters further east.[55]

The Burrara-speaking An-mujolgawa *yakarrarra* has been inadvertantly omitted from the lists of coastal estate-owning units. A Jowunga moiety *yakarrarra* (population 4), Anmujolga's territory includes at least one onshore coastal site located 1–2 miles east of the Blyth river and bordered on either side by on either side by Ganmal *yakarrarra* territory.

Notes

This chapter is partly based on a report prepared for the Northern Land Council on regional marine native title rights and interests (Bagshaw

54   54 I am grateful to Fiona Macgowan for suggesting this line of inquiry to me.

55   I have not yet ascertained whether the mixing of inshore and open sea water is metaphorically associated with sexual reproduction in the way that the intermingling of fresh and saltwater reportedly is among the 'Yolngu' (Keen 1994:211).

1995a). I thank Diane Bell, Peter Sutton and James Weiner for their comments on an earlier draft of the present document. I am also especially indebted to Lily Garambara and her late husband RR, to Kevin Jawunygurr and to Michael Marragalbiyana for the provision of much of the information recorded here. The paper itself is dedicated to the memory of RR.

References

Aboriginal Land Commissioner 1981. *Closure of seas: Milingimbi, Crocodile Islands and Glyde River area.* Darwin: NT Government Printer.

1988. *Closure of seas: Castlereagh Bay / Howard Island region of Arnhem Land.* Darwin: NT Government Printer.

Bagshaw, G. 1979. *Coastal sites: Blyth River Cape Stewart.* Report to Northern Land Council. Darwin: Northern Land Council.

1991a. *Report to the [Northern Territory] Aboriginal Areas Protection Authority on the registration of marine sacred sites at Wumila and Mirragaltja near Milingimbi Island.* Confidential report. Darwin: Aboriginal Areas Protection Authority.

1991b. *Report to the [Northern Territory] Aboriginal Areas Protection Authority on the registration of marine sacred sites in the eastern Boucaut Bay site complex.* Confidential report. Darwin: Aboriginal Areas Protection Authority.

1991c. *Burarra country: the socio-cultural context of sites in the Blyth River estuary.* Unpublished ms. Darwin: Aboriginal Areas Protection Authority.

1995a. Preliminary report on sea tenure and native title in the Blyth River Crocodile Islands region. Report to Northern Land Council.

1995b. Comments on S. Davis' map. In *Country: Aboriginal boundaries and land ownership in Australia* (ed.) P. Sutton. Canberra: Aboriginal History Monograph 3. Pp. 122–124.

Berndt, R.M. 1951. *Kunapipi: a study of an Australian religious cult*. New York: International Universities Press.

1955. 'Murngin' (Wulamba) social organization. *American Anthropologist* 57:84–106.

Clunies Ross, M. 1990. Some Anbarra songs. In *The honey-ant men's love song and other Aboriginal song poems* (eds) R.M.W. Dixon and Martin Duwell. St Lucia: University of Queensland Press. Pp. 70–103.

Cooke, P. n.d.(*a*). *A draft literature review concerning Aboriginal interests in submerged lands in the eastern Arafura Sea*. Report. Darwin: Northern Land Council.

n.d.(*b*). *Ethnographic pilot eastern Arafura Sea*. Report. Darwin: Northern Land Council.

1995. *Literature-based view of Yolngu marine interests*. Report. Darwin: Northern Land Council.

Davis, S. 1981. *A report on Aboriginal sites of significance in north eastern Arnhem Land* [Sections 1 and 2]. Confidential report. Darwin: Aboriginal Sacred Sites Protection Authority [NT].

1984*a*. *Aboriginal tenure and use of the coast and sea in northern Arnhem Land*. MA thesis: Melbourne: University of Melbourne.

1984*b*. Aboriginal tenure of the sea in northern Arnhem Land. In *Workshop on traditional knowledge of the marine environment in northern Australia*. Series No.8, Great Barrier Reef Marine Park Authority.

Davis, S.L. and J.V.R. Prescott 1992. *Aboriginal frontiers and boundaries in Australia*. Carlton: Melbourne University Press.

Dreyfus, M. and M. Dhulumburrk 1980. *Submission to Aboriginal Land Commissioner regarding control of entry onto seas adjoining Aboriginal land in the Milingimbi, Crocodile Islands and Glyde River area*. Unpublished Report. Darwin:Northland Land Council.

Ginytjirrang Mala/ADVYZ 1994. An indigenous marine protection strategy for the Arafura Sea. Report to Northern Land Council and Ocean Rescue 2000.

Glasgow, K. and D. Glasgow 1985. *Burarra to English bilingual dictionary*. Darwin: Summer Institute of Linguistics.

Hiatt, L.R. 1965. *Kinship and conflict: a study of an Aboriginal community in northern Arnhem Land*. Canberra: Australian National University.

1982. Traditional attitudes to land resources. In *Aboriginal sites, rights and resource development* (ed.) R.M. Berndt. Perth: University of Western Australia. Pp. 13–26.

1986. Rom in Arnhem Land. In *Rom: an Aboriginal ritual of diplomacy* (ed.) Stephen A. Wild. Canberra: Australian Institute of Aboriginal Studies. Pp.3–13.

Keen, I. 1977. Contemporary significance of coastal waters in the spiritual and economic life of the Aborigines. Submission to the Australian parliamentary joint select committee on Aboriginal land rights in the Northern Territory. *Official Hansard Report*, Tuesday 3 May 1977.

1978. *One ceremony, one song: an economy of religious knowledge among the Yolngu of north-east Arnhem Land*. PhD thesis. Canberra: Australian National University.

1981. *Report [to Aboriginal Land Commissioner] on the Milingimbi closure of seas hearing*. Typescript.

1983. *Report [to Aboriginal Land Commissioner] on the application to close the seas adjoining Aboriginal land in the Castlereagh Bay Howard Island region of Arnhem Land*. Typescript.

1984–5. Aboriginal tenure and use of the foreshore and seas: an anthropological evaluation of the Northern Territory's legislation providing for the closure of seas adjacent to Aboriginal land. *Anthropological Forum* 5(3):421–439.

1991. Yolngu religious property. In *Hunters and gatherers:* [Volume 2] *property, power and ideology* (eds.) Tim Ingold, David Riches and James Woodburn. New York/Oxford: Berg. Pp. 272–291.

1994. *Knowledge and secrecy in an Aboriginal religion.* Oxford: Clarendon Press.

1995. Metaphor and the meta-language: 'groups' in northeast Arnhem Land. *American Ethnologist* 22(3):502–527.

Meehan, B. 1977. *Submission to parliamentary joint select committee on Aboriginal land rights in the Northern Territory.* Typescript.

1982. *Shellbed to shell midden.* Canberra: Australian Institute of Aboriginal Studies.

1983. *Sites of significance at the mouth of An-gatja Wana (Big River) or the Blyth River in Arnhem Land.* Confidential report. Darwin: Aboriginal Sacred Sites Protection Authority [NT].

McIntosh, I. 1994. *The whale and the cross: conversations with David Burrumarra MBE.* Darwin: Historical Society of the Northern Territory.

Northern Land Council 1992. Submission to the Resource Assessment Commission Coastal Zone Inquiry, June 1992. Darwin: Northern Land Council.

1995. Marine protected areas: a strategy for Manbuynga ga Rulyapa. Unpublished report.

Palmer, K. 1984–5. Ownership and use of the seas: the Yolngu of northeast Arnhem Land. *Anthropological Forum* :448–455.

Ritchie, D. 1987. *An-gatja Wana site complex: attempts by Aboriginal custodians to protect the area from intruders.* Report to Aboriginal Sacred Sites Protection Authority [NT].

Shapiro, W. 1981. *Miwuyt marriage: the cultural anthropology of affinity in northeast Arnhem Land.* Philadelphia: Institute for the Study of Human Issues.

Stanner, W.E.H. 1965. Aboriginal territorial organization: estate, range domain and regime. *Oceania* 36(1):1–26.

Sutton, P. 1996. *The robustness of customary Aboriginal title under Australian pastoral leases.* Draft paper, version 13 May 1996.

Verdon, M. and P. Jorion 1981. The hordes of discord: Australian Aboriginal social organisation reconsidered. *Man* (N.S.) 16(1):90–107.

Warner, W.L. 1937. *A black civilization: a study of an Australian tribe.* New York: Harper.

Wild, S.A. (ed) 1986. *Rom: an Aboriginal ritual of diplomacy.* Canberra: Australian Institute of Aboriginal Studies.

Williams, N.M. 1986. *The Yolngu and their land: a system of land tenure and the fight for its recognition.* Canberra: Australian Institute of Aboriginal Studies.

Zorc, R.D. 1986. *Yolngu-Matha dictionary.* Batchelor NT: School of Australian Linguistics

11

Ownership and resource use on islands off the Liverpool River, Northern Territory

Peter Cooke and Gowan Armstrong

During 1995 and 1996 the Northern Land Council (NLC) Native Title Unit commissioned preliminary surveys of Aboriginal interests in seas and submerged lands at a number of locations along the coast of the Northern Territory. In May 1996, Peter Cooke provided the NLC with a draft report covering an area extending eastward from de Courcy Head, on the eastern boundary of the current marine native title claim lodged by people at Minjilang (Croker Island) to the mouth of the Blyth River in Central Arnhem Land. From de Courcy Head to the Blyth River mouth is a distance of about 200km in a straight line. However, the length of coastline between those two points (including the coastlines of North and South Goulburn Islands) is about twice that distance.

The first part of this chapter summarises the results of archival and field research undertaken by Cooke, while the second focusses on a predominantly marine estate in the mouth of the Liverpool River. Complex arrangements for access and resource use under local customary law are described and discussed, drawing on data collected by Armstrong during the 1960s and early 1970s and by Cooke during the 1996 survey.

Aboriginal people have been in Australia a minimum of between 40,000 and 30,000 years BP and less conclusive evidence points to site dates as early as 60,000BP (Bowdler 1993:60). Between 26,000 and 11,000 BP the sea level was between 65 and 130m lower than today: the lowest levels are estimated at 18,000 years BP (Smith *et al* frontispiece). When these lower sea levels are plotted on modern marine charts the dynamic nature of the coast becomes apparent: the coastline has retreated landward more than 100km over the last 10,000 years.

Within the oral history of this region are stories, framed in mythological terms, which may relate to these geological/hydrological events that happened thousands, rather than hundreds, of years ago. At Goulburn Island there is a mythologically interpreted record of the separation of Weyra and Warruwi, or North and South Goulburn Islands. At Maningrida, ancestral beings are deemed responsible for the separation of Entrance Island from the mainland. A large freshwater swamp on the former 'land bridge' connecting it with the mainland is now shallow sea where fresh water rises to the surface from submarine springs.

Defining the seaward extent of marine tenure

Defining the seaward extent of Aboriginal marine territories is not straightforward. Of the generalised descriptions put forward by various Aboriginal people interviewed during the survey that advanced by Ralph Gurmurdul, a principal Aboriginal consultant, seems to deal best in a comprehensive way with this issue. Gurmurdul says Aboriginal people's sea territory extends to:

1. Those places where they go hunting or travelling.
2. Those places for which Aboriginal owners have names.
3. Those places known to Aboriginal people as being inhabited by ancestral beings.

The seaward limits for travel by dugout or bark canoe are not clear. However, during the survey Albert Wurrdjal (Worrdjol), an experienced canoesman, indicated that it was not uncommon for people to travel by canoe in a straight line from the mission at Warruwi (Goulburn Island) to around Cuthbert Point, a distance of about 45km. The midpoint of this journey is about 12km from the coastline.

Of sites named during the survey, the most distant from shore would appear to be Wulurunbu and Lingardji, regarded by people from the Goulburn Island area as islands inhabited by the spirits of the dead. These islands, which are said to remain hidden under the sea by day and emerge by night, are regarded as 'real' places. Some older people can indicate the direction of the islands from various points along the coast. A rough 'triangulation' of those directions suggest that they may be a large area of shoal at about 5–6 fathoms lying about 20km east of North Goulburn Island in waters generally at 13–15 fathoms.

While camped near Cuthbert Point, the survey party watched lightning visible far out to sea. Senior Aboriginal consultants said this lightning indicated the presence of a particular spirit being and they interpreted the westward movement of the lightning activity as the movement of that spirit being across the sea.

During the 1996 survey, 350 named coastal and marine locations were mapped between the Blyth River and de Courcy Head.

Identifying owners of marine territory

Aboriginal people within the 1996 survey area asserted that there are no differences between owning land and sea. Estates and interests on land extend into adjoining seas and an estate may be comprised of mainland terrestrial, littoral, marine and insular components. These elements make up a single area which is usually known by what is referred to in English as a 'big name'. Such a big name is often that of a pre-eminent spiritual site within that territory, although it might also derive from a focal occupation location, such as a modern outstation. Sites of spiritual significance may be found in any of these ecological zones within an estate.

Aboriginal people in the survey area usually indicate land ownership by identifying a group defined by patrilineal descent as having primary responsibility for a named estate. These patrilineal groups are known by a number of different names — *yuwurrumu, kunmukurrkurr, namanamadj, yákkarrarra and bábburr. Nguya* is a more generalised word for 'group' used often in most western Arnhem Land languages as a synonym for one of the more particular names for a patrilineal group, locally referred to in English as a 'clan'.

Although the more specific words are to an extent associated with particular languages and locations, they are also known and used interchangeably and widely throughout the region. This is particularly so along the coast. Cooke and other researchers working for the NLC have found the word *namanamadj* most commonly used at Minjilang for the patrilineally defined primary land owning group. Armstrong (1967) found the word *namanamadj* used by Kunibidji (Gunavidji) people from the Liverpool River in a way in which the meaning of the word signified not only the landowning group but also their estate. A Kunibidji man might speak of a particular named section of Kunibidji territory, with its known boundaries and which is owned by his father's father/father' father's sister, his own father/father' sister and brothers/sisters and all relatives traced in the patriline, as his *namanamadj*.

Elkin, Berndt and Berndt (1951) translate *namanamadj* loosely as 'follow my father' and this seems apt. Children normally belong to the patrilineal descent group to which their father belongs. However, only males can pass this affiliation on. Women of the group bear children who 'follow their fathers' from other *nguya*. In special cases where a woman may have had husbands belonging to different *nguya*, the children may identify with their biological father, or perhaps accept bestowal of membership of the group of a stepfather. Similarly, children who may have been the result of a liaison rather than a marriage, may, as they grow up, choose between the *nguya* of their biological or social father. People may be adopted into a *nguya* without it involving a sexual relationship between their mother and a man of a particular *nguya*. This is the case in one instance, where a childless man, the last of his descent group, decided to bestow membership of his group on another man's children. In this case and others, a person may follow two fathers — claiming affiliation with two *nguya*, through biological or social paternity, including adoption. Dual affiliation is certainly possible, but it may provide the grounds for other people to suggest unreasonable opportunism, particularly if the dual membership brings financial gain.

The survey identified 32 named, patrilineally defined descent groups with primary claim to estates along the 400km of coastline surveyed. Information on some 1200 living and deceased members of these groups was entered onto a genealogical database file (Reunion software) enabling easy formatting of lineages from apical individuals or purported siblings. Data was drawn from field recording, the NLC Land Interest Reference and 1979 printouts from the (then) DAA Aboriginal Population Record database. Most of these genealogical charts extend back to individuals born about 1900 but in some cases they extend perhaps as far as the mid nineteenth century.

About half of the 32 groups have a distinctive *nguya* name with a primary interest in one estate. In the other cases the same *nguya* name, or a cognate term, may apply to a number of lineages associated with separate estates. In one case in 1996, three slightly different versions of one name were recorded for lineages associated with five separate estates. In another case, a second name is used in addition to a common *nguya* name to distinguish amongst four lineages with primary interests in four separate estates. Armstrong (unpublished field notes) observed that it is common in the Liverpool River area for a group to have a 'big name' and a 'small name'. There seems reasonable grounds to suggest that in some cases at least, a second name preserves the name of an extinct group whose territory has been subject to succession.

Thus, as the coastal physical environment is dynamic, so too is the coastal social and cultural milieu. People must deal with the decline and extinction of groups and find ways to accommodate long term 'migrants'. Armstrong (unpublished field notes) observed that there is evidence that some *yákkarrarra* (patrilineally defined groups) merge and that in situations when the members of a *yákkarrarra* all die, their estate is incorporated into the territory of another *yákkarrarra*. The 1996 survey recorded five estates where the processes of succession were at various stages. Some cases are straightforward andthe new owners easily and quickly find acceptance locally, but in other situations, succession may be contentious and may take decades to be resolved.

Lamilami (1974:136) noted that connections between same (and similar) named groups associated with different languages and different estates are widely recognised. He talked about his coastally situated Maung group, Maiirwulidj and the similar-named Neinggu (Kunwinjku) inland group, Mairrgulidj and also a Yiwaidja group of the same name. As he observed: 'I think they must have been related way back in their ancestors'.

In some cases ancestral connections between same-name groups with separate estates may be remembered clearly and this may lead members of the two groups to assert shared interests in one another's lands. One lineage may assert seniority within such an aggregation of people and estates but over time a 'subordinate lineage' is likely to assert its own independent identity and rights of decision-making in respect of its particular estate.

Nguya with quite distinctively different names and separately named estates may also propose that they regard these estates as held in common to some degree at least. Such arrangements are widely referred to in western Arnhem Land as 'company'. In one example from the 1996 survey, the basis for a strong company arrangement between adjacent, same moiety *nguya* was that senior members of both *nguya* had the same mother. She had been married first to a man from *nguya* A and then after his death she married a man from *nguya* B. A senior member of one of these two groups identified the implications of this company arrangement as:

1. Both groups discuss proposals affecting either parcel of land and make decisions, as a group, but recognising to a degree separateness of interest in each parcel.
2. One partner clan does not make a decision on major issues by itself for its own land or for the other 'half' of company land.
3. Each party recognises the right of the other group to be asked for access to their land.
4. Members of the clans share equally in income derived from either parcel.
5. Members of both clans have free access to each other's lands for normal resource use.

This example also perhaps demonstrates one way in which matrifiliation may strongly influence land ownership, despite the acknowledged primacy of patrifiliation in land ownership matters. While the patrilineal descent approach realistically represents the primary contemporary determinant for land ownership in Western Arnhem Land, behind that lies a complex web of other factors which may ultimately decide an issue where a patrilineal connection is not completely straightforward. It is difficult to generalise about such situations because the parameters of legitimate process in the Western Arnhem Land system of tenure are broad and allow many paths for a person to press a claim where there is no clear and extant nexus between a patrilineage and an estate.

People in Western Arnhem Land generally talk about who country belongs to by reference back to focal ancestors who lived on the land and were associated with it in a mundane way, as well as also celebrating its spiritual attributes in ceremony. Descendants of the male line can call this 'my country' and hold the broadest range of rights. The descendants of the women of the group also enjoy considerable rights.

While it is difficult to compare or categorise in a hierarchical way the rights of the patrilineal sons and daughters of a clan and the descendants of women of that clan without inadvertently freezing ongoing social process, it is possible to identify various incidents of native title for descendants of the earliest recalled members of the land-owning *nguya*, whether the connection be through mother or father. These incidents are mediated by various factors, not the least of which are age and gender.

Some rights and responsibilities of the patrifiliated recorded during the 1996 survey include:

1. A member of an owning group has the right to be asked for permission for someone to enter his or her land or sea country. A senior person has the right to expect that they, rather than a junior member of the group, would be asked.
2. Members of an owning group have the right to grant or refuse a person permission to enter or stay on land or seas within their estate (again seniority is relevant).
3. A senior member of a group has the right to expect to be offered a share of any resources harvested in, or income derived from, land or sea

within their group's estate. Where non-traditional activites are involved, it may be that all members of the group are entitled to a share, i.e. 'royalties' or 'clan money'.

4. Members of an owning group have the right to be inducted into the religious life of their group and to be a joint holder of the group's sacred property, such rights being mediated by age, experience and gender.

5. Members of an owning group have rights to free access to their lands and waters, constrained at times only by temporary closures to some members of a group because of ceremonial activity or because some sites may be 'too dangerous' for their owners to approach.

6. Senior members of an owning group have the right to close all or part of seas and land within their estate after the death of important people and subsequently, the right to open access again.

7. Senior members of an owning group have the right to allocate names associated with their estate to members of their own group or to people in more distantly related groups.

8. Members of an owning group have a responsibility to see that their country and the spirits of that country do not harm visitors on the country.

9. Members of an owning group have a responsibility to pass on knowledge of their clans' physical and spiritual resources to their descendants.

Some rights and responsibilities which operate through the sons and daughters of women of a clan include:

1. A responsibility of men in particular, but also women, to progressively learn the ritual associated with the land and sea country of their mothers and mother's brothers and to assist members of that group to perform ritual associated with the country.

2. A responsibility as above in respect of sacred sites on mother's and mother's brother's sea and land country.

3. A right to free use and access to resource in one's mother's and mother's brother's sea and land country. These use rights extend but with diminishing strength to more distant matrifiliates.

4. A right to challenge strangers found on ones mother's and mother's brother's sea and land country and demand to know who has given

them permission to be there. A right to insist that such people leave the estate if they have not been authorised to be there by appropriate members of the patrilineal group.

5. A right to speak up for one's mother's and mother's brother's sea and land country in contentious issues such as succession, with an expectation that one's views will be respected in any outcome. Again strength of interest is strongly mediated by age.

Rights in one's mother's mother's country are strengthened by the fact that (conventionally) it is of the same patrimoiety as one's own country. The major contemporary ceremonies of Kunabibi and Yabburddurrwa, each have strong prohibitions against 'mixing up' moiety determined roles. Unconventional marriages which result in fathers and children being of opposite moiety therefore present some problems in the ritual sphere. However, the increasing regularity of performances of these ceremonies in the survey area shows that such problems are not insoluble. At the time of writing, a Kunabibi was in progress at Minjilang, two more near Maningrida as well as a Yabburddurrwa near Maningrida. As many as a thousand people may attend the conclusion of such events in this region.

In the east of the survey area there is a greater tendency for people to emphasise the importance of intra-clan patrimoiety homogeneity than there is in the west where there is more emphasis on correctness of matters relating to matrimoieties and the matrilineal semimoieties, although not so great as to override the importance of patrilineally defined local groups in land matters.

As well as identity within a language group and within a patrilineally defined *nguya*, people also belong to social groupings which are somewhat more difficult to define. Lamilami (1974) discussed a number of these, in some cases using the word '*wara*' in connection with a name. These names often mean 'mob from such and such a place'. They do not refer only to members of the particular landowning group from that place and it appears they are usually names which might apply to groups which come together in particular places during the seasonal cycle, often to pursue some joint economic strategy, whether fishing or hunting geese or so on. Some examples of these words are: Maindjinaidj (Manjdjinadj), a very extensive coastal grouping; Muwamal, people from the coast inside Junction Bay who moved to around Hall Point in the wet season to escape mosquitoes; Mabárnad, coast dwelling Ndjébbana-speaking clans; and Márro, coast dwelling Nakkara-speaking clans. They do not say much about land and sea tenure except perhaps that they indicate groups who shared access to one another's lands and sea estates on a regular basis and therefore established fairly persistent rights of access and use.

Some groups may use one word in respect of both a people and their language, e.g. Maung language, Maung people. In other areas, different terms are used for people and for their language, e.g. the Kunibidji people from the Liverpool River area speak Ndjébbana[1] and the Márro people on the coast to their east speak Nakkára, while the Warlang to the west of the Kunibidji speak Kunbarlang. Within the region, language may be an important qualifying factor in various issues, including succession. Some people might, for example, propose that a patrilineal owning group with the same name as an extinct group might succeed to that extinct group's estate. Other people might oppose the succession on the grounds that those people are from 'too far away, different language', if the genealogical connections between the two groups are lost in time and the distant group has little experience or knowledge of the land and sea country under succession.

Language is also an important factor in defining individuals and groups with resource rights associated with particular areas of land. Speaking the 'right' language for a place is not just of mundane importance — it is central to the relationship between people and the ancestral spirits of their estates and the land and sea resources within those estates. Amongst the Ndjébbana-speaking Kunibidji of the Liverpool River, these ancestral spirits are known as *múya* (singular)

---

1 Graham McKay (pers. comm.) points out that Kunibidji is not a Ndjébbana word, but is what others call the people who speak Ndjébbana. However, it is not uncommon for Ndjébbana speakers to refer to themselves as Kunibidji, particularly when talking with non-Aboriginal people.

or *barramúyiba* (plural) and are associated with particular estates and *nguya*. The Kunibidji believe that these spirits are watching over their country and the actions of people on the country and that they have the power to affect outcomes in everyday life, particularly failure or success in hunting. They can be persuaded to be generous with natural resources, but only if asked in their own language.

The lúrra fishing expedition

Armstrong was the first to document the ritualised fishing expedition called *lúrra* amongst the Kunibidji. The primary qualification for participation in this ritual is language.

The *lúrra* takes place within the estate of the Wúrnal *nguya* who, in company with Karddúrra and Malandjárridj, are the owners of a large area of sea country in and off the mouth of the Liverpool River—see Figure 11:1. The Malandjarridj primary interest is on the mainland, east of Ndjúdda (North East Point), the Karddúrra primary interest around Ndjúdda and Kabálko (Entrance Island), while the main Wúrnal terrestrial interests are the two islands, Kabálko and Ngarráku (Haul Round Island). Kabálko is the larger of these islands, about 1.5km along the east-west axis and about the same north-south. On the northern side are a series of stone fireplaces the Macassans, used for processing trepang, until they were prevented by legislation from continuing their trade with Australia in 1907.

There are 11 Kunibidji *nguya* extant, all speaking Ndjébbana language. Eight coastal *nguya* speak a *njárlkkidj* (hard) form of Ndjébbana and three inland groups speak *marndálangurrnga* (soft) Ndjébbana. The coastal groups refer to their language as 'seagull language' or *malamaldárra* (generic name for tern) language. There also seem to be minor differences between *djówanga* (*duwa*) and *yirriddjanga* (*yirridj-dja*) moiety speakers (Graham McKay pers. comm.). There are six clans regarded as *djówanga* and five clans regarded as *yirriddjanga*. However,

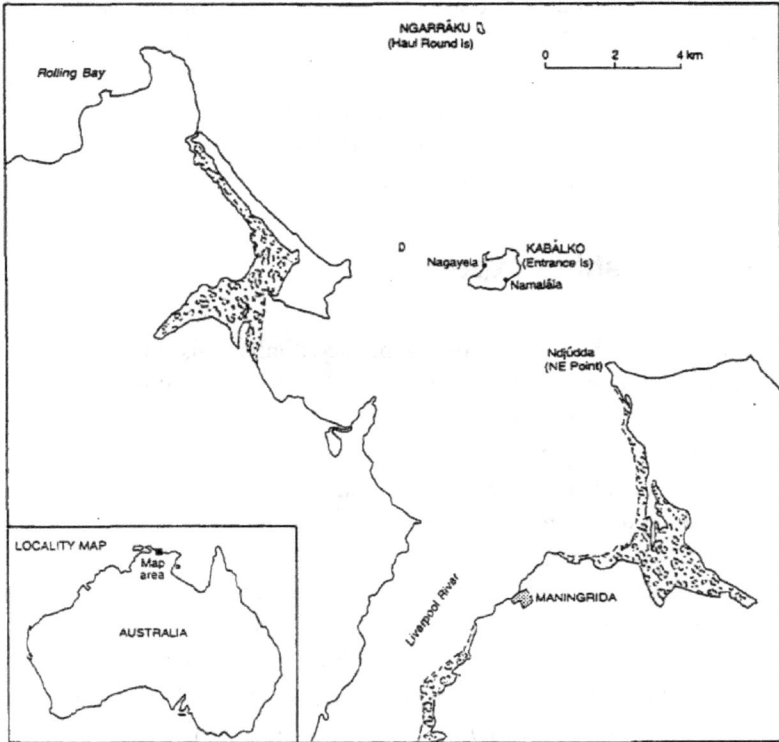

Figure 11:1 Liverpool River estuary

Gowan Armstrong was at Maningrida when the last lúrra took place at Kabálko and made this record of it:

There are two main qualifications for participation:

1. The men had to speak the 'sea language' dialect of Gunabidji (Kunibidji). Men from southern/inland clans whose dialect had affinities with Gungaragone (Gungurrgoni) and other inland groups were excluded—unless their mothers came from a 'sea language' speaking group and had transmitted their mother tongue to their sons. A certain Gunwinggu (Kunwinjku) man and a Walang (Warlang) man were able to qualify for this reason.

2. Only fully initiated youths and men could participate, and for a youth this usually meant being present at three sacred ceremonies. Among other things *lúrra* was an age grading ceremony.

The ceremony takes place in *duwa* (*djówanga*) territory but men from *yiritja* (*yirridjdjanga*) country have an active role in helping to organise it. The senior *yiritja* men choose a period toward the end of the wet season (April in 1964) and others listen for them to ask, 'you like fish?' In 1964 Mangiru (Dúkurrdji leader) talked to everybody and 'pushed' them. Five 'new men' participated for the first time. Four older men who were eligible to go, and were by no means incapacitated, did not go and stayed in the camp.

The men travelled from Maningrida Settlement to Juda Point (Ndjúdda) where they began collecting the black berries or 'plums' from the malayman (*marlémarla*) trees (*Diospyros calycantha*).[2] They also gathered paperbark, which they bound together to make torches (*djit* [*djird*]).

Late that afternoon they loaded the dilly bags full of berries and the bark torches into their canoes and travelled in line 'level' across to the beach Namalála on the eastern side of Entrance Island Gabalgu (Kabálko). Two other possible sites for *lúrra* could have been Nagayela or Ngaraku (Ngarráku, Haul Round Island). In 1964 at Namalala the men told me that they smeared their bodies with mud, and kept their eyes closed as they hammered the berries with hammer stones to protect themselves from the burning effects of the juice. The hammering broke the skin of the berries to release the juice. The berries treated thus were put into dilly bags.

As darkness fell the men were seated on the sand and the new men in particular were seated on one side of the rocky area where the hammering was done and told not to talk or laugh. They had to sit with legs outstretched and with their hands on their knees. They were told the *múya* (the Dreaming one, [*múya*]) listens and if he hears the new men speaking he will not give fish. They were permitted to use sign language.

2　A more recent botanical evaluation identifies these trees at Ndjudda as *Diospyros maritima* (Carolyn Coleman, pers. comm.).

Fires were also lit on the sand. When the tide began to go out, they would listen for the calls of the sea birds. When birds began to call, a leader would say 'oh, we are lucky. A lot of fish. You young men, don't talk'.

One man with firestick in hand would then be sent into the knee deep water, ringed by rocks, looking 'like a billabong'. As he confirmed that the fish were there everyone took up either a dilly bag full of broken berries or a triangular fish net or a *djit* which he lit. They moved forward 'like *balánda* (white men) quick march'. As they entered the water the dilly bags were immersed and whirled about to spread the toxic juice, moving particularly around the sides of the rocky depression. As the fish were paralysed and gathered into the nets, they were placed in the dilly bags. When the leaders are satisfied that all the fish have been taken, they are brought back to the rocks where the berries were crushed and spread out. The older men then addressed the new men 'You people can talk now. The *muyu* spirit belonging to this country hears you now'. The older men give some fish to the younger ones to cook and eat. They say, 'the people of this country are one relation'. Presently the fish are loaded into the canoes and taken across to the women waiting at Juda Point. They are happy and say 'plenty fish'.

Men told me that if someone was present who could not speak the sea language of Gunavidji the fish would not come and the men would return empty handed.

A *lúrra* ceremony was carried out 'in Mr Drysdale's time', possibly 1958 and in our time in 1964 when we could see the red flares of the torches across on Entrance Is around 8pm. Another was planned for 1965 but because of continuous rain it was postponed and finally not held. A couple of older men complained that European staff people were going out to Entrance Island to fish and would sometimes camp out overnight. Because of the possibility of Europeans being on the island they were reluctant to plan the ceremony.

No singing or dancing are involved in the *lúrra* ritual. Jimmy Borwarg and Johnny Godawa's (Garduwa) son said, 'We born from Juda

Point. We talk like seabird Mula-mulara (*malamalárra*): I believe this to be one of the terns (Armstrong, fieldnotes).

During the 1996 survey, Cooke identified ten men who did participate in *lúrra* and who are still alive. Two of these men, Albert Wurrdjal and Peter Marralwanga were interviewed and provided descriptions of *lúrra* generally consistent with Armstrong's report.

Wurrdjal, in particular, stressed the importance of the 'language test' for participation.

> But some people they're not going. Some *djówanga* and some *yirriddjanga* (moieties). My language, I'm talking really Ndjébbana. Really soft one Ndjébbana orright. My wife (from inland), or even her brother they not allowed. ... This is very danger(ous). Like ceremony one. If someone (does) wrong you get trouble, same as *marddáyin* (highly sacred and dangerous ritual). No allow *balánda*, no allow Nakkara, no Kunbarlang, no some Kunibidji. Only Kunibidji from here (seaside). ... They (spirit beings) can't put fish if wrong people. If they see nother blokes, all the devil will say, 'different blokes, we can't put that fish'. Boss people talk to all the spirit. They tell them about that new man, 'you saw him (when he was) little boy, him here now, we show him here tonight'. ... New man can't talk (uses whistles and tongue clicks only). We had to be very quiet otherwise that *djówanga* debil from there (Kabálko) and Ndjúdda come out. He comes from jungle way on the point and two points and looks after the lighthouse (on Ngarráku). He belongs to that country.

Wurrdjal's recollection is that the young men were still prohibited from speaking until after fish had been cooked and eaten. When some of the fish have been cooked and eaten by the young men, the leader asks them if they are getting full. He asks again, 'Full?' and then takes off the prohibition on speaking by wiping sweat across their mouths.

The main *lúrra* site is in a 'pocket' on the northern side of Kabálko where rocks make a natural enclosure at the right tidal elevation. Peter Marralwanga says the *lúrra* was held on a full moon towards the end of the wet season, while the grass was still long and standing.

The full moon is accompanied by a spring tide rising during the night. Towards the end of the wet season, large schools of a number of species of mullet come in around the island. Of these Wurrdjal says the main target species in the *lúrra* was the large mullet *barrábarrakabulúyara*, which has a darkish body and eyes reflecting red in the light from paperbark torches. This is probably the diamond-scaled mullet, *Liza vaigiensis*, although other mullet species were also caught. The diamond-scaled mullet has been recorded up to 4.5kg in weight (Grant 1982:517). Wurrdjal and Marralwanga say 'might be hundreds' of fish were caught.

After participation in a *lúrra* young men were then allowed to participate in egg harvesting on Ngarráku, Haul Round Island.

Sea bird egg harvesting on Haul Round Island

At high tide Haul Round Island is perhaps half the size of a football oval. There are no trees—only patches of long grass, tangles of *Ipomea* vine and areas of the prickle caltrop (*Tribulus sp*). Jagged rocks appear from the sea over a large area to the east and north as the shelf of ironstone on which the sand island sits emerges on the falling tide. Five years ago biologists from the Parks and Wildlife Commission of the Northern Territory began to collect information on seabird breeding on Haul Round Island as part of a larger project across north Australian coastal waters. Ray Chatto, the principal biologist involved, has made five or six aerial surveys of the island and three or four ground visits. His records indicate that during the breeding season (late wet, early dry) there are many thousands of bridled terns, more than 5000 roseate terns, more than 30 pairs of silver gulls and small numbers of crested and black-naped terns on the island. Pied cormorants breed on a rocky reef/island with mangroves which is only a few hundred metres from the sand island. This is one of only six or eight such sites known in the Top End. The breeding population of roseate terns is regarded as being of international conservation significance (Chatto 1996:pers com).

Not surprisingly, the island and its resources are also regarded as highly significant by the local community. Even before people had the tools and technology to make dugout canoes they used folded and sewn canoes of stringybark (*Eucalyptus tetrodonta*) to travel to Ngarráku, six kilometres north of Kabálko, which in turn is three kilometres from Ndjúdda. From the coast around Hawkesbury Point to Ngarráku is about nine kilometres. The stability and efficiency of these canoes was noted by Thomson (1952:3):

> A large canoe made from a single sheet of bark, which I saw at Rolling Bay on the north coast of Arnhem Land in 1943, had an overall length of 15 feet and measured 12ft 9 inches along the keel. This canoe had a beam of 3 feet and a maximum depth inside the hull of 1 foot 11 inches. It carried a crew of four men comfortably and made journeys at least two or three miles out into the sea even under choppy conditions without any difficulty. One such bark canoe under actual test made better time in a choppy sea than a ship's dinghy driven by two experienced men each using two oars.

The oldest living male Kunibidji today is Johnny Naliba, from the coastal clan adjoining that of Wúrnal and Karddúrra. In 1926, while Naliba was still *in utero*, his father and his father's cousin went to Ngarráku to gather sea eggs, travelling by bark canoe from Kabálko. They never returned and it is presumed the canoe broke up and they drowned. Older people today assert that someone must have sabotaged the canoe or they would never have been lost: such experienced seafarers don't just drown! The dangerous nature of the journey is one obvious reason why women and children were not allowed to go to the island.

Hunting pressure on the island escalated astronomically with the growth of the government 'settlement' at Maningrida after it was established in 1957 and with the coming of dinghies and outboard motors in the early 1970s. The patrol officer Gordon Sweeney noted about 130 Kunibidji at two locations east of the Liverpool in 1939. One might presume the usual presence of, say, a maximum further 70–100 people on the western, Warlang side of the estuary. In 1960 the population at

Maningrida was 485 and by 1965 it had risen to 800 as more groups were drawn into the new settlement. By 1972 there were about 1100 Aboriginal people and more than 150 non-Aboriginal staff and their families. In 1996 the Maningrida clinic carried health records for more than 2200 people but with the return to country since 1970 the population of Maningrida in the dry season is now about 800 Aboriginal people, rising to perhaps 1200 in the wet season. As well as the Kunibidji, the more or less permanent population now includes close countrymen such as Gungurrgoni, Nakkara, Warlang and some Kunwinjku speakers. More distant groups with longterm residential association include Maung, Rembarrnga, Dangbon, Djinang, Burarra and Gun-nartpa, as well as a smaller number of families from further east.

Non-Aboriginal staff brought with them western notions of the sea as a commons belonging to everyone and they generally ignored the traditional ownership of sea country. Similarly a Government-sponsored fisheries project in the late 1960s introduced Aboriginal people to this exotic philosophy and gave encouragement to unregulated use of the seas and island resources.

By the second decade after settlement, Burarra people from the east had attained a fairly dominant position at Maningrida in terms of jobs and of political power within the village council. However, from the early 1970s the Kunibidji people began to reassert their traditional authority for country, reminding people that Maningrida was not a Balánda (non-Aboriginal) town, nor a Burarra town, nor a Djinang town.

During Armstrong's time at Maningrida, the Wúrnal man George Yarlmurr was the senior leader for his group and the territory around the two islands. After his death and the later death of his brother, the Wúrnal were without senior adult members. A senior Karddurra man became the principal spokesman for the two groups and to an extent Karddurra became the senior clan in the 'companyship'. This man died two years ago and the senior Wúrnal, now in their late 30s and 40s, reasserted their primacy for the islands and surrounding waters.

A few longterm non-Aboriginal workers at Maningrida have set a better example to new staff by making a point of asking permission to fish or camp in various places and have honored the principle of sharing catch with estate-owners. Although not all non-Aboriginal people show respect in this way, the situation is vastly improved over that through the 70s and early 80s.

It has been somewhat more difficult for the Wúrnal and Karddurra to control pillaging of the egg resource on Ngarráku. Dissatisfaction about egg harvesting and a general lack of respect for traditional owners led to a 'showdown' over the issue about 1990. The senior Karddurra man, Billy Yirinyin (Yírrkin, since deceased), and Yarlmurr's daughter Helen Williams addressed a large crowd of people gathered for the unloading of the Maningrida supply barge and stated their demands as traditional owners, particularly in respect of the egg resource. Helen Williams also later made a video broadcast over the local BRACS system and arranged for a sign to be placed on the island. She said:

> I spoke in public to the people who had boats. Next time whoever got boats must come and ask us before they go and collect eggs off the island. That way, we'll know who is going out there. 'We want eggs too', I told them. 'You guys have got boats and we haven't. But next time come and ask us'. Long time ago people shared lots. A little bit here, little bit there. And I told people there's gotta be a limit. Leave some eggs to breed. The reason why it upset me was that when I walked around the camp every afternoon I could see shells. 'Heh! How many eggs have this mob taken?', I thought. 'How come they don't come and tell us or remind us or bring some to us, this family, landowners?'. That's how I started to realise some aren't sharing. Countrymen too, I don't care.[3]

---

3   In June 1997 David Bond, who has been visiting Ngarraku for more than 20 years, reported that he had never seen so many young birds on the island as this year. This perhaps indicates that the wishes of the landowners are again being respected, one small but significant victory for culture and conservation.

During the 1996 survey, a number of the Aboriginal consultants, in particular Albert Wurrdjal, Jockey Bundubundu and Johnny Nalíba provided previously unrecorded information about the traditional arrangements concerning the egg harvest. Wurrdjal confirmed Helen Williams' statement that the owning clan should collect the first eggs 'to open the season'. This would be done in consultation with the senior person to call the island 'mother's country'. These principal Aboriginal consultants also described the division of egg gathering rights amongst eight clans, the Wúrnal, Karddúrra and six other clans whose estates abut the Wúrnal/Karddúrra estate. These comprise seven *djówanga* clans and one *yírriddjanga* clan. Five are Ndjébbana speaking clans and three are Kunbarlang speaking.

The survey party visited Ngarráku in March 1996 early in the egg laying season. Johnny Nalíba and Jockey Bundubundu walked around the island indicating discrete boundaries between areas of the island where each of these clans had exclusive rights to gather eggs, except for Wúrnal and Karddúrra, who shared one area. The allocation of rights appears to follow proximity to country in most cases, that is, each clan's egg gathering area was situated on the part of the island closest to the land of their home estate. The exception was one clan whose estate is due west of the island but whose egg gathering rights are on the north-eastern side of the island, but from which the land of the clan's estate is visible across the low elevation of the island. There are no physical markers marking the boundaries. Yet as Nalíba walked around indicating boundaries, he appeared to be taking bearings on various parts of the mainland before providing an unequivocal position for a boundary.

The Aboriginal consultants say emphatically that the apportionment of egg gathering rights does not carry with it ownership of the land from which the eggs are gathered. The island, the reefs and water surrounding it are all for Wúrnal and Karddúrra. As Albert Wurrdjal says, 'all that *nguya*, that just for egg. That island for Wúrnal and Karddurra properly'.

The Wúrnal and Karddurra seem to have slowed the free-for-all pillaging of eggs since they aired their grievances in 1990. A quick survey of likely hunters with boats suggests that there were only a few egg gathering expeditions in 1996. The landowners gathered a few hundred eggs during our survey of the island and later in the season a senior Kunibidji man, camped near Rolling Bay, also paid a visit.

Notes

Ndjébbana words are written with an accent on the syllable which carries the main word stress. In this paper the authors have attempted to follow the locally established Ndjébbana orthography and are grateful for the advice of linguists Dr Graham McKay and Carolyn Coleman on this and other matters in the paper. Where words are quoted from written text or where an 'official' spelling differs from Ndjébbana conventions, the conventional spelling appears in brackets afterwards.

References

Armstrong, G. 1967. *Social change at Maningrida*. Unpublished thesis for Diploma in Anthropology. Sydney: University of Sydney.

Bowdler, S. 1993. Sunda and Sahul: a 30 kyr culture area. In *Sahul in review* (eds) M.A. Smith, M. Spriggs, and B. Fankhauser. Canberra: Australian National University. Pp. 60–70.

Cooke, P. 1996. *A sea of meaning: a preliminary survey of Aboriginal interests in seas and submerged lands along the central and western Arnhem Land coast*. Unpublished confidential report. Darwin: Northern Land Council.

Elkin, A.P, R.M. and C.H. Berndt 1951. Social organisation of Arnhem Land, 1. Western Arnhem Land. *Oceania* 21:253–307.

Grant, E.M. 1982. *Guide to fishes*. Brisbane: Department of Harbours and Marine.

Lami Lami, Lazarus 1974. *Lami Lami speaks*. Sydney: Ure Smith.

Smith, M.A., Spriggs, M. and B. Fankhauser (eds) 1993. *Sahul in review*. Canberra: Australian National University.

Thomson, D. 1952. Notes on some primitive watercraft in northern Australia. *Man* 52:1–5.

12

The Sandbeach People and dugong hunters of Eastern Cape York Peninsula: property in land and sea country

Bruce Rigsby and Athol Chase

Thomson (1933:457) described the Sandbeach People of eastern Cape York Peninsula as 'a very distinct type of Australian [A]borigine ... essentially fishermen and dugong hunters, and ... often great seafarers ... skilled canoe builders and navigators ... [who] make adventurous voyages among the coral reefs and sand banks of the Great Barrier Reef, in search of dugong and turtle, and the eggs of turtles and sea birds'. Thomson (1933, 1934) made much of their marine orientation and he wrote of their outrigger canoes, harpoon technology and beach-based camps in which they spent much of the annual seasonal round.

In their indigenous languages, they indeed describe themselves with phrases such as Umpila *pama malngkanichi* and Uuk-Umpithamu *ma-yaandhimunu* 'people who own the sandbeach'. [1]Thomson (1934:238) noted that their homelands extended from 'the shallow waters of Princess Charlotte Bay almost to Cape York', and he (Thomson 1933:458, 1934:237) identified them as the tribes[2] which he called 'the

---

1 The linguistic forms in this paper are from Rigsby's fieldwork on the Sandbeach People's languages and from Thompson (1988). We write the single Umpila and Kuuku Ya'u rhotic, a tap-trill, here as *rr* so as to use the same inventory of characters for all the languages. Our spellings are given in a conventional Australianist practical orthography where *th* is a laminodental stop, *ch* a laminopalatal stop, etc.

2 The term 'tribe' has a long history in anthropology and in the study of Aboriginal society and culture, but since the publication of Service (1962), the term usually signifies a type of social organisation that is non-hierarchical and lacks formal political institutions and structures. In Service's

Koko Ompindamo, the Yintjingga, the Ompeila, the Koko Ya'o and the Wutati' (in south to north order). Together, these 'tribes' of Thomson's Sandbeach People account for over 300 km of coastline and associated waters, northward from the bight of Princess Charlotte Bay. We too write of the cultural bloc of Sandbeach People, but building upon Thomson's work, we identify them somewhat differently and we distinguish their contemporary social organisation from its classical antecedent. As well, it is plain that there were and are many similar maritime-orientated Aboriginal groups along the coasts of the continent.

The Sandbeach People

The Lamalama people are the southernmost Sandbeach People. Their territory extends along the coast some 70 km from Goose Creek, near

---

evolutionary typology, tribes are more complex than bands, but less so than chiefdoms and primitive states. But from the 1970s, there has been a concensus amongst Australianist anthropologists that tribes as well-bounded units did not exist in classical Aboriginal social organisation. See Dixon (1976:232–235) for a brief historical review of Australianists' definitions of the tribe, including Howitt, Spencer, Radcliffe-Brown, Elkin and the Berndts. As Peterson (1976b:50) notes, Tindale and Birdsell's working definition of the tribe derives from Radcliffe-Brown, who wrote (1918:222): 'By a tribe I mean a collection of persons who speak what the natives themselves regard as one language. the name of the language and the name of the tribe generally being one and the same.' Thomson also used the term in its Radcliffe-Brownian sense.
More recently, Rumsey (1989, 1993) has argued that 'tribe' is usefully employed to label the language-named groups that have emerged as land-owning groups in the recent period. Rigsby and Hafner (1994a, 1994b) used the term in the same way in the Lakefield and Cliff Islands National Parks claim books, noting that it corresponded closely to the claimants' usage—see also Rigsby (1995). However, contemporary indige-nous usage of terms such as 'nation,' 'tribe,' 'mob' and the like have variable reference by context, etc., so we caution that our technical use of 'tribe' here is not always exactly paralleled by local usage.

the heel of Princess Charlotte Bay, where the sandbeach gives way to mangroves and saltpans, northward to the Massey River vicinity—see Figure 12:1. They are the direct descendants of many of the people whom Thomson worked with at Port Stewart in 1928–1929,[3] the people whom he (Thomson 1934) called 'The Dugong Hunters of Cape York'. They live mainly at Port Stewart, having reestablished a community there in the late 1980s after people were removed from there in 1961 (Rigsby and Williams 1991:11; Hafner 1995; Rigsby 1996a). Under Aboriginal law and custom, they own an estate of land and sea country that includes most of the Princess Charlotte Bay and surrounding coastal region. Under Australian law, they own 2100 ha of land at Port Stewart which they acquired by transfer under the state *Aboriginal Land Act 1991*. With neighbouring groups, they made a successful claim under the 1991 Act to Lakefield National Park (Lakefield Report 1996) and on their own, under the same Act, they successfully claimed the Cliff Islands National Park (Cliff Islands Report 1996). They await the Minister's decisions whether to follow the Land Tribunal's recommendations to grant the lands on the grounds of traditional affiliation. The remaining terrestrial part of the Lamalama estate is on Lily Vale Station, Running Creek Station and Silver Plains Station. The state government currently owns Silver Plains, but its future as national park and Aboriginal homelands is unclear.

The Lamalama are a language-named tribe: see footnote 3. Their identity as a distinct people or tribe is based upon their ownership of particular land in the region (Chase *et al.*, 1995), upon common close genealogical relationships, upon a common cultural heritage and upon a common history over the past century. The Lamalama emerged as a distinct group over the past century through the amalgamation of people from upwards of forty patriclans, perhaps five indigenous languages, an unknown number of local groups and their transformation into a language-named tribe made up of over a dozen cognatic descent groups.

---

3   Hale and Tindale (1933–1936) visited Port Stewart for a fortnight in January–February 1927, and they met and worked with some of the same people that Thomson encountered a year later.

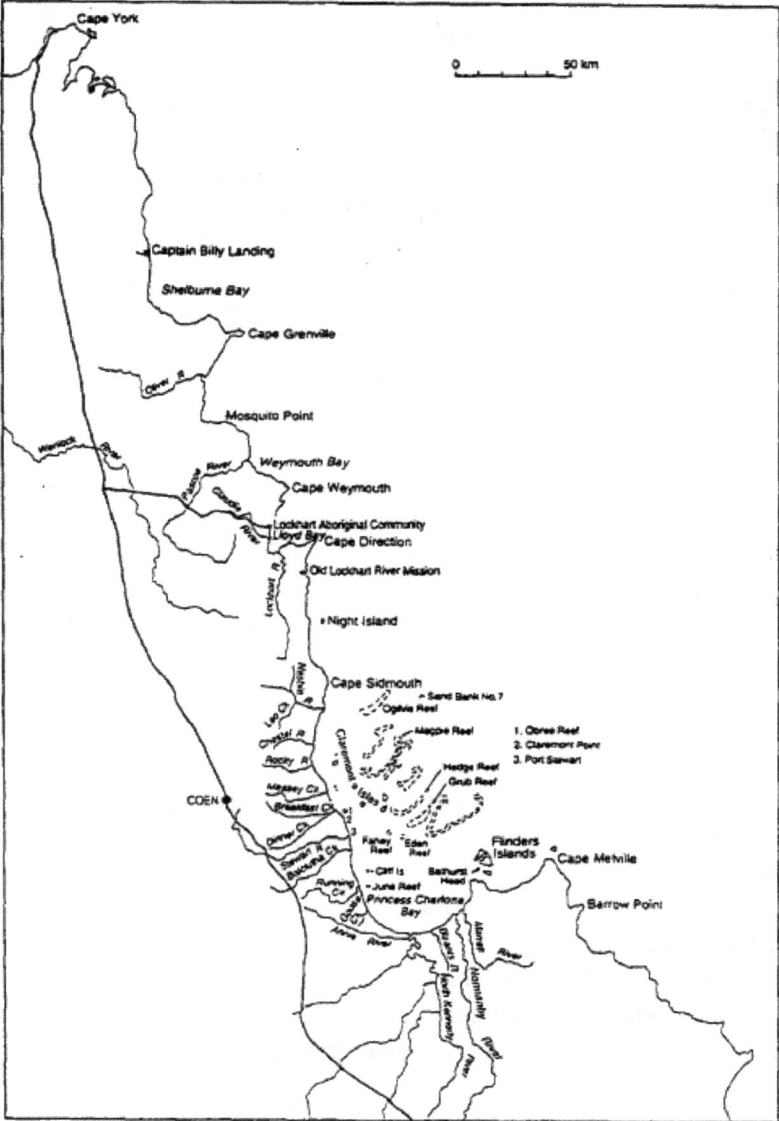

Figure 12:1 Lamalama and related peoples, sea country

The Umpila, Uutaalnganu[4], Kuuku Ya'u and Wuthathi peoples are also organised as language-named tribes, but the first three groups, as contrasted with the Wuthathi and the Lamalama, have retained strong knowledge of the more distinctive clan estates which comprise the language territories. This is no doubt in part due to their long residence at the Lockhart River Mission (the 'Old Site' at Bare Hill), in Uutaalnganu territory. From there, people travelled constantly up and down the coast while employed on lugger boats and for bush 'holidays' away from the Mission from 1924 until the late 1960s, as outlined below. Throughout the period, the Umpila, Uutaalnganu and Kuuku Ya'u people were never out of visiting range for their countries. They now live mainly at Lockhart Aboriginal Community, near Iron Range in the Lloyd Bay area, but some Wuthathi people live at Injinoo, formerly Cowal Creek, in the Northern Peninsular Region (Sharp 1992). Under Aboriginal law and custom, these groups own estates of land and sea country that extend eastwards from the coastal ranges, across a narrow littoral plain and out to the Great Barrier Reef. The Umpila, immediately north of the Lamalama, extend some 55 km to the vicinity of Friendly Point, and northward of the Umpila, and the Uutaalnganu territory encompasses the coastal area for approximately 70km to the mouth of Lockhart River. Further north are the Kuuku Ya'u, whose coastal territory ends around the Olive River (about 90km), and beyond them are the Wuthathi, who have land and sea country along another 70 km or so of coastline to Captain Billy Landing. Under Australian law, the Aboriginal people who live at Lockhart Community, whose core are Umpila, Uutaalnganu and Kuuku Ya'u people, own the former Reserve lands by a Deed of Grant in Trust. All four groups also have land claims active under the state *Aboriginal Land Act 1991* and under the *Native Title Act 1993*, for example the Ten Islands claim, the Iron Range National Park claim, the Mungkan-Kaanju National Park (formerly, Rokeby-Kroll National Park), and the Night Island claim. The Umpila people have also lodged a native title claim to their sea country and part of the adjacent mainland,

---

4   However, the Uutaalnganu more often call themselves and are called the 'Night Island mob.'

and the Lamalama people have accepted their invitation to join them in an extended sea claim. The inland Kaanju (linguistic congeners of the Umpila, Uutaalnganu and Kuuku Ya'u) have also lodged a native title claim for land.

The four coastal groups north of the Lamalama have a somewhat different contact history. They were much more involved in the marine and sandalwood industries, which dominated European intrusion into this area from the 1870s to the outbreak of WW2, and for about 40 years most of them were missionised (Chase 1980:87–132; Thompson 1995). The Anglican Church established a mission at Orchid Point in Lloyd Bay in 1924, but shifted it south the next year to Bare Hill, on the coast 15 km south of Cape Direction, remaining still within Uutaalnganu territory. The gazetted Lockhart River Reserve took in all of the Uutaalnganu land, the southern portion of Kuuku Ya'u territory, and a large portion of the Kaanju country which lies inland behind the coastal area. During the 1920s–1930s, the state native affairs department and missionaries removed children and adults from along the coast and the interior and shifted them to live at (Old) Lockhart River Mission. Numbers of people from all the Sandbeach groups were removed to Lockhart, as were also people from Flinders Island and the coast nearby in the 1930s. For a period during the Second World War when Japanese invasion seemed imminent, the missionaries were evacuated and people were told to avoid the mission and set up new bush camps. The Lamalama and Flinders people walked home and resumed bush life along the coast, and other groups returned to key locations in their homelands along the coast. During the early 1960s, the state government took control of the Lockhart River Mission from the Church and made plans to shift people from the Bare Hill site to Bamaga. A small group accepted relocation there in 1964, but the majority strongly rejected the resettlement plans. The people remaining at Lockhart River Mission were persuaded to accept a new site, close to Iron Range airstrip, about 3 km inland. By 1969, they were resettled, and the state native affairs department administered the community with a stern hand until the 1980s. Since then, the Lockhart Reserve has been made into the Lockhart DOGIT (Deed of Grant in Trust, a form of tenure), and an elected Council having new powers and a new sense of its independence has governed Lockhart Community. However, there have been homelands movements at Lockhart since the mid-1970s, and currently, there are outstations located at the old Bare Hill mission site, at Portland Roads, inland on the Wenlock river and at Chinchanyaku on the coast opposite Night Island. Others are planned.

North of the Lockhart DOGIT lands, the tenure status (under Australian law) of the land up to Shelburne Bay varies, ranging from special leases, pastoral leases, occupation licences and national park lands. To the south, the Lockhart DOGIT lands abut Silver Plains Station and a Timber Reserve, where the southern Umpila and Kaanju homelands are situated. During the development boom years of the 1980s and early 1990s, the Lockhart-based groups successfully resisted plans for silica mining (on Wuthathi land), a satellite launch site (on Kuuku Ya'u and Wuthathi lands), a large resort (on Kuuku Ya'u land), a resort village (on Kuuku Ya'u land) and various mining activities (on Umpila and Uutaalnganu lands). The Kuuku Ya'u people are currently challenging in the Land Court another resort development proposed for one of their islands.

The Sandbeach People have extensively intermarried among themselves, as well as with their inland neighbours, such as the Kaanju, Ayapathu, Wik Mungkan, Olkola (formerly spelt Olkolo in the literature) and Kuku Thaypan peoples, and with Torres Strait Islander people.

Classical and contemporary social organisation

In the classical social organisation of the Sandbeach People, the land-owning groups were patriclans, exogamous and perpetual corporations of people who acquired membership by patrifiliation. The clans were named; in fact, they often had names in several languages. The clan names often identify the group as having a particular Story or totem or as owning or coming from a particular country; in some cases, the clan names are those of human ancestors. As well as property in land and sea country, the clans also owned particular ceremonial and religious knowledge, songs and bodypaint designs. While the old clan-based organisation has virtually disappeared among the Wuthathi and the Lamalama, the other tribal groups have retained it for much of their coastal estates. This retention has been, in part, a function of anthropological recording. Chase and others carried out detailed territorial mapping work with Umpila, Uutaalnganu and Kuuku Ya'u people during the 1970s when considerable numbers of older bush-born people were still alive. Young people and children accompanied them on these visits which took place at a critical time in the history of the Lockhart River community. Active older people were much concerend about the possible loss of knowledge, and they were anxious to have it recorded. In May 1997, the Umpila people drew upon Chase's recorded information when they revisited Umpila territory in order to reacquaint themselves with specific estates and their sites.

While people's knowledge of their families' estates may be very attenuated in parts of the Sandbeach Region, some people know that they are primarily connected to particularly well-known sites and locations. The vagaries of survival among older knowledgeable people is clearly a factor in the retention of knowledge, as also are the historical facts of settlement and residence at the Lockhart River Mission and at Port Stewart. Among the Wuthathi, all knowledge of clan estates has disappeared, and they regard themselves as a single land-owning 'tribe' (Chase 1996).

The estates of all the clans from the Normanby River to Massey Creek have passed into Lamalama tribal ownership through the operation of traditional law and custom (but see next paragraph). In at least one case, a sisters' sons' clan inherited the estate of their mother's fathers' and brothers' clan, and the combined estates have passed to tribal ownership. More commonly, the estates of clans that otherwise died out without obvious heirs were looked after by members of neighbouring clans and became part of the larger tribal estate.

These same processes of succession sometimes give rise to disputes about land where two modern tribes border each other, for example the Lamalama and the Umpila contest which of them owns the land between Massey and Breakfast Creeks (and similar potential disputes can be found around language border areas further north). In the classical system, say, of 1930, the estates of two clans covered this area. The estate of the Morrokoyinbama clan (whose indigenous language was a coastal Ayapathu variety) included Dinner Creek, Breakfast Creek, the Silver Plains homestead area and the upper Massey Creek, while the Morrindhinma[5] clan (whose indigenous language is an Umpila variety) clan estate centred on the lower Massey Creek and adjacent coast. It is unclear how the Lamalama and the Umpila will resolve their differences at the tribal level, but the senior descendants of the two clans recognise one another's rights and interests in their respective estates.

In the contemporary system, the language-named tribes are, as we have seen, the landowning units for the Wuthathi and Lamalama, but among the Lamalama, the contemporary cognatic descent groups also continue some of the old clans in that their members regard themselves as having special relationships with the estates of the clans of their founding ancestors. In the Lakefield and Cliff Islands National Parks claim books, Rigsby and Hafner (1994a, 1995b; see also Hafner 1995) described the classical and contemporary social organisation of the wider claimant group, who included the Lamalama. They labelled the cognatic descent groups there as 'families' before they recognised that these are cognatic descent groups—see Ackerman (1994) and Sutton (1996b). Among the Kuuku Ya'u, as well as an emphasis on clan estates for key areas, there are two intermediate cognatic 'countryman clusters' (Thompson and Chase 1997), which group together families originating from the old clans whose estates adjoined in the classical situation.

People and (thus also) clans belonged to named moieties. The

5 Morrokoyinbama and Morrindhinma are the Morrabalama language names of these clans; they are Mangulthananhu and Uukinhu, respectively, in Uuk-Umpithamu. We have not recorded their own names for themselves.

moieties, like the clans, were sociocentric, exogamous groupings. The moiety organisation cut across clan and local group insularity and provided some basis for regional organisation. Moieties played a role in ceremonial life, and the landscape and seascape was a checkerboard of estates of the moieties—for example see the text and maps in Chase (1984:110–11). Thomson (1934:493–499, 1946:160–161) noted that the complex of custom relating to tooth evulsion makes reference to moiety membership. At or about puberty, young people underwent evulsion of an upper incisor tooth (right incisor for righthanded person, etc.). The operator came from mother's (i.e. the opposite) moiety, and they called out the personal names and totems of members of that moiety. When the tooth broke off—in Creole and Aboriginal English, people say that it 'jumps out'—that was a sign. If it broke at the calling of a personal name, its bearer would give one of their clan totems to the young person. If it broke at the calling of a totem, then that totem was given to the young person. Such totems were not called *puula* 'father's father', as one's own clan totems were, but they were called *ngachimu nguunthachi* 'mother's father having-the-vital force' (from *ngachimu* 'mother's father' and *nguunthal* 'fontanelle, breath or 'wind', i.e. vital force'). They were the objects of taboos, for example one should not kill or eat them, and they were associated with the animating part of the spirit (*nguunthal*), which leaves the child when the frontal suture closes and goes to live in the mother's country. At death, the *nguunthal* spirit reunites with the *mitpi*[6] spirit, the part of the person's spirit which travels during dreams, etc. We speculate that these maternal clan totems also conferred non-transferrable rights and interests in one's mother's clan land—see Sutton (1996a). Some older people still alive underwent tooth evulsion, but the custom is no longer practiced.

The moieties were still operative at Port Stewart when Thomson worked there, but contemporary Lamalama people say that they are a feature of Lockhart people's law and custom, not of theirs. When Chase worked at Lockhart in the 1970s, the recognition of people's moiety

---

6 *mirrpi* is the southern Umpila variant of the word. The terms in this section are all Umpila and Kuuku Ya'u.

membership was very strong and exogamy remained a cardinal rule, and people said that they could identify people's moiety affiliations by their physical features. Likewise, the physical attributes of 'countries' identified their moiety affliations too (Chase 1980). But among young people and children there today, moiety recognition has all but disappeared.

The moieties are called Kaapay and Kuyan in the Ayapathu, Umpila, Uutaalnganu and Kuuku Ya'u languages, and they are Aparra and Urrana, respectively, in Uuk-Umpithamu.

Sharp (1939:259) said the Wuthathi lacked named moieties, but Thomson (1972:24) recorded them as *o'waiya and o'garra*, respectively. There are no moiety names recorded in Lamalama, Morrabalama and Rimanggudinhma, and speakers say there were none in the past. The dual division between the Kaapay and Kuyan moieties is symbolised by mythic oppositions between Dugong and Wallaby Stories, and Emu and Cassowary Stories, respectively (Chase 1980:140). The absence of moieties and moiety names among people of the Lamalama-, Morrabalama- and Rimanggudinhma-speaking clans is perplexing because most, if not all, of their neighbours have or had moieties in the past. Among the Olkola-speaking people, they are associated with Elar 'mopoke owl' and Akabakab 'owlet nightjar'/ 'carpenter bird' (Philip Hamilton, personal communication). Although Hale and Tindale (1933–36:79) reported moieties among the people of the Flinders Islands and adjacent mainland, where Owaimini and Ungawu are equivalent to Kaapay and Kuyan, Sutton (pers. comm.) doubts that the Flinders people had moieties, on the basis of his deeper ethnographic and linguistic work. Terwiel-Powell (1975:114–118) and Haviland (1979:213–215) reported moieties among the Guugu Yimithirr-speaking people, where they are associated with the nightbirds, Mirrgi 'mopoke owl' and Wambal 'owlet nightjar', and with Nguurraar 'black cockatoo' and Waandaar 'white cockatoo'. The moieties are also associated with short-funnel and long-funnel[7] native bee species, but we do not know the details.

---

7 These terms describe the shape of the entrance to the hives.

Kin terminology and classification in the languages of the classical system were quite similar. They distinguished relatives of one's own side or moiety (e.g. siblings and parallel cousins, father and father's brothers, father's sisters, man's children and brother's children) from those of the other side or moiety (e.g. cross-cousins, mother and mother's sisters, mother's brothers, woman's children and sister's children). All the languages distinguish older brothers and older sisters from younger siblings, and the same distinction was made among the children of parent's older and younger same-sexed siblings, e.g. father's older brother's daughter is classified as older sister and mother's younger sister's daughter is classified as younger sister. There was similar recognition of senior and junior cross-cousins, the children of opposite-sexed siblings. The prescribed marriage partner was a cross-cousin. The Lamalama people say that their old law and custom was for marriage with a first cross-cousin—Thomson's and more recent genealogies provide a number of instances of first cross-cousin marriage—but their new law is for marriage with a classificatory cross-cousin. Some of the Umpila and Port Stewart Ayapathu genealogies that Thomson recorded also showed evidence of generational skewing of the Omaha type, where mother's brother's children were classified upward with mother's brother and with mother, while father's sister's children were classified downward with sister's children (see Thomson (1955:40) and comments by Scheffler in Thomson (1972:4, 6, 46–47). Chase (1980:399–402) reported upward skewing in the recognition of children of cross-cousins for the Umpila and their northern neighbours. Thomson (1955:40) observed that only first cross-cousins were designated by the reciprocal senior and junior cousin terms, while other cross-cousins were designated by the appropriate affinal terms. Thomson (1972:28) recorded no cross-cousin terms in coastal Ayapathu—he called it Yintjingga, after the indigenous name of the Port Stewart area—and Rigsby has never recorded them in Lamalama, Morrabalama or Rimanggudinhma. It remains unclear in the latter languages whether cross-cousins were designated by generationally skewed terms or by affinal terms.

Kin classification and terminology in contemporary Creole and Aboriginal English basically maintain the same semantic distinctions. People at Lockhart and Port Stewart still use many of the indigenous Umpila / Uutaalnganu / Kuuku Ya'u terms, but they also use terms of English origin, but with indigenous semantics, for example, people address parallel cousins as 'brother' and 'sister', but refer to them as 'cousin-brother' and 'cousin-sister', respectively, which distinguishes them from siblings and cross-cousins. As in the classical systems, people address and refer to relatives of the great-grandparents' generation with the children's generation terms, and in return, relatives of the great-grandchildren's generation are designated by the parents' generation terms. Like the earlier situation that Terwiel-Powell (1975) reported for Hopevale, children at Lockhart and Port Stewart have lost the knowledge and use of some traditional kin and affinal terms. For example, they have collapsed the senior and junior cross-cousins into a single category, realised as *ngami* in Umpila and 'cousin' in Creole.

Thomson (1935, 1972) described some of the behaviours customarily associated with kin dyads, and some of these continue in similar form, for example, in-law avoidance, adult brother-sister avoidance and joking between classificatory grandparents and grandchildren. Again, the finer traditional distinctions in these behaviours are now disappearing. Similarly, older people observe traditional restrictions on who can share food with whom, or perhaps these are better stated in terms of who can eat food produced by whom. Parents cannot eat food from their children, nor can a father's younger sister or mother's younger brother (who are potentially spouse's parents), but grandparents, father's older siblings and mother's older siblings can.

Local groups or bands in the classical social organisation included men and women of different clans. The focal male leaders of local groups centred their residence and group movements on lands of their own clan estates, for example, Thomson's notes and genealogies identify the focal men of the Yintjingga local group in 1928–1929 as several older Mbarrundayma[8] clan men and their resident sisters' sons of the

---

8 This is the Lamalama language name for the clan. It is called

Mumpithamu clan—see also Cliff Islands Report (1996:54). It was during the wet season that local groups were at their largest and most sedentary. There was plenty of fresh water available on the coast then and the weather was good for marine hunting; the northwest monsoon replaces the southeast tradewinds, many mornings are without wind and the waters are calm.

Households[9] were the smallest groups based on common residence and commensality in the classical social organisation. In past days, households were based upon a married couple and their dependents who together maintained a separate hearth and aggregated with other households to form bands. Today, households are larger (see Jolly 1997), they typically domicile themselves in permanent houses or semi-permanent tent-under-tarpaulin structures, and they aggregate to form permanent communities, as at Coen, Port Stewart and Lockhart.

Religion

Thomson's writings (especially Thomson 1933) on the Sandbeach People made much of what he regarded as a distinctive religious cult, organised around 'tribal totemism' and functioning to initiate young men into manhood. This cult was in Thomson's view, Melanesian-influenced in its ritual and ceremonial paraphenalia, and its 'tribal totemism' represented an intermediate stage between Australian and Melanesian social systems. Such evolutionary perspectives on change are clearly dated, but his work does correctly emphasise the permeability of the classical Australia—Melanesia boundary.

Sandbeach People say that in the beginning, before there were Pama (*pama*[10] 'Aboriginal person, people'), in the beginning, the animals,

---

Thookopinha in Uuk-Umpithamu.

9 Thomson (1932:197–198) called households 'families'.

10 *pama* is from the Umpila, Uuutaalnganu, Kuuku Ya'u, Kaanju and Ayapathu languages, and it is known throughout the Sandbeach Region. People recognise *bama*, pronounced with a voiced stop, as its Guugu

birds and fish were like human beings, like Aboriginal people. These spirit people are what Pama call Stories (elsewhere, Dreamings). The Stories made the landscape with all its features, they named the places on the land and they established Aboriginal Law on it during the Story-Time (elsewhere called the Dreamtime).[11] Contemporary Pama are descended from the Stories, who still live in and on the land in their own places. As well, the spirits of the ancestors, the Old People, still live on the land because when Pama die, their spirits return to their homelands. The Old People also include the recently dead, whom living people know and remember, and they continue to take an interest in the living and how they live their lives. The Old People may bring good fortune and luck to the living in their various endeavours (e.g. fishing, hunting, gathering, etc.), but when the living transgress Pama Law, the Old People may express their displeasure by bringing misfortune, illness and bad luck.

The Stories put the different indigenous languages in their proper countries on the land, and it is from their own languages that the tribes get their names—see footnote 3. The Lamalama tribe is unusual in that its predecessor clans owned and spoke five or so indigenous languages, only one of which gave its name to the whole group. Many younger

---

Yimithirr equivalent. Other indigenous Sandbeach languages have undergone sound change and their speakers pronounce cognate forms as *mba* (Lamalama), *apma* (Morrabalama), *ama* (Uuk-Umpithamu) and the like. Lamalama people more often use the word Murri (*mari*), which ultimately originates in a central Queensland coastal language, when they speak Creole and Aboriginal English. Peter Sutton (*personal communication*) speculates that Biri might have been the source for Murri as they travelled early as Native Mounted Police, among other things.

11   In the southern part of the Sandbeach Region, prominent people often had traditional personal names that signified the names of significant places in their estates. Old Man Monkey Port Stewart's 'Murri name' was *Aakurr Yintyingga* 'Yinjingga Country', and Old Lady Emma Claremont was *Ngaachi Yalmarraka* 'Yalmarraka Country' or just *Yalmarraka*. Old people also recall that Emma used to shout out '*Yalmarraka!*' when she was so moved.

Lamalama people are not familiar with this complex sociolinguistic history.

Children usually take their tribal membership and particular land interests from their fathers, they remain connected with their mother's tribe and they take land affiliations from their mother too. Where a child's father is non-Aboriginal, the child always takes its identity from its Pama mother.

Pama have a dual relationship to both the spiritual and material worlds. This can be expressed simply in the propositions that the Pama belong to the land and the land belongs to the Pama. In the first instance, the Pama belong to the land because they share a spiritual essence in common with it. Pama men and women beget and birth children as men and women do everywhere in the world, but Pama children are not simply made up from flesh and blood. All Pama have a spirit counterpart[12] or alter ego, which comes from the land and from the Old People. That is, a person's spirit does not come into existence from nothing, but it comes from spirit that has always existed in and on the land, and it enters the embryo at or sometime after conception. Moreover, a person's spirit does not just come from anywhere; it comes from a specific country or place. In this way, each Pama person incarnates a spirit that indissolubly connects them with a country of origin, even though there are no reports in this region of specific conception sites, as found elsewhere in Australia.

---

12   We use *spirit*, rather than *soul*, in line with regional Creole and Aboriginal English usage. The words for 'spirit' differ in the several indigenous Sandbeach languages. In contemporary Umpila, Uutaalnganu and Kuuku Ya'u, it is *mitpi*, but *puuya* 'life essence, heart (in the metaphorical sense)' and *nguunthal* 'fontanelle, wind or breath' are closely connected. In Uuk-Umpithamu, the word is *nanga* 'spirit, wind or breath, lungs,' while it is *anga* in Lamalama and Morrabalama with the same glossing. The term signifies much the same entity that Christians call the soul, but Pama believe that the spirit returns to its home country after death, lives there for the most part and visits and otherwise makes itself known to living people.

This is why we say that the Pama belong to the land. They are a part of the land just as a person's head is a part of their body. The late Professor Stanner (1969:4) spoke of this relationship as one *in animam* 'in spirit'. It is a spiritual relationship because spirit connects people to their land. Linguists would describe it as a relationship of inalienable possession, the relationship of a part to its whole.

Pama also have a material relationship to the land. It is a relationship *in rem* 'in a thing'. People's rights *in rem* to country derive from their spiritual relationship to it *in animam* and depend upon it. This provides the root of their traditional title to land. There were no written title deeds to record that so-and-so acquired such-and-such land by purchase or grant of the Crown. Instead, Pama know and tell how the Stories fashioned a specific landscape and in a number of locations[13] 'sat down' there to remain for all time metamorphosed into rock or other material features. Their title derives from the creative acts of the ancestral Stories in the Story-Time and from the unbroken links of spirit among the land, their Old People and themselves. Pama also say that it was not just during the Story-Time that the Stories lived and acted. They still live in and on the land, as do the spirits of the Old People, the long dead and the recently dead alike.

This is why we say that the land belongs to the Pama. They own the land: that is, they have rights *in rem* to the land and the sea. Phrased differently, we can say that specific groups of people have specific rights in specific tracts of land 'as against the the world'. These include rights to live on the land, to use and enjoy it in various ways, to speak of and present themselves as its owners and to exclude others in various ways from exercising the same rights. Linguists would describe this as a relationship of alienable possession, the culturally constituted and socially sanctioned relationship which we conventionally call 'ownership'

---

13   In Umpila and its congeners, placenames for these special locations often are compound words built with -muta as their second element. It signifies 'pereneum', which metonymically is the 'sit-down place' of the body. For example, *Kampalmuta* is a place not far south from Port Stewart whose meaning might be translated as 'Where Sun Sat Down'.

in English. Since the Mabo No 2 decision of June 1992 and the federal *Native Title Act 1993*, the common law of Australia recognises Aboriginal rights and interests in land arising from indigenous law and custom where they have not been extinguished by Act of the Crown or adverse act. But so far as Pama are concerned, their traditional title cannot be extinguished by the acts of others.

The Stories not only fashioned the material world to be as it is, but they also instituted law and custom which stipulate how Pama should live their lives and which define the dimensions of the proper social world. In Standard English, we distinguish among law, custom and tradition (Rigsby 1996b; also Rigsby and Hafner 1994a). Laws compel people's behaviour because they have the backing of the state and its courts and police, while customs operate to guide people's behaviour informally. Traditions, for their part, seem simply to be old customs, but on closer examination, traditions also have a normative character which gives them greater force than mere customs. Their age and their connection with ancestors sanctify them and give them greater value.

In Aboriginal English and Creole, Pama speak of 'Pama Law' and 'Pama way' in ways that parallel some of the distinctions above, and in ways which are seen as imperative. When people say that some way of doing things is 'the Law' or 'Pama Law', we believe that they are in effect saying that it has the moral force backed by the weight of sanctions that we associate with tradition, i.e. it is traditional. When people say that a particular way of doing things is the 'proper Pama way', we take that as a statement that it is customary—a 'proper' way of behaving which respects local etiquette, but does not necessarily have a spiritual sanction.

For example, Pama say that it is Pama Law for people to 'warm' or 'smoke' a house with burning ironwood boughs to send away the spirit of the dead person and make it leave the world of the living behind. It breaks Pama Law for the head of a family not to have the warming ceremony performed, and the aftermath of such a breach may may bring down illness or misfortune on the lawbreaker and other members of the family. By way of contrast, among many Pama on eastern Cape York Peninsula, it is customary to use knives and forks when *parra* or whitefellows[14] are present, but more often, when alone or in a small family group, for example, people generally eat with their fingers and not with cutlery. To insist on eating with knife and fork when one's family and mates are eating with their fingers is to chance being called 'flash', like a whitefellow, not like a Pama. It is not the Pama way, but it does not break Pama Law.

Pama learn Pama Law and Pama ways mainly by observation and experience. People often tell us that it was not their way to ask their old people why they performed ceremonies or observed particular customs. Instead, they learned to wait until their old people told them to do whatever and not to question them or ask them why. Nonetheless, adults do instruct younger people in such matters as the proper use of kin terms, the behavioural prescriptions and proscriptions appropriate to specific places, and so on, for example, Lamalama people do not fish at the Running Creek waterfall nor at the Moon Story-Place at the Rocky Creek crossing for their Law proscribes it.

Many, if not most, Sandbeach People are Christians, and many consider that their indigenous religious traditions and Christian belief and practice are compatible (Thompson 1995). Chase (1988) described a fusion of Christian and traditional spiritual elements in the way that people regard and use 'holy water' and 'holy oil'[15] from the church sacristry, and Thompson (1985) reported the commonalities that people draw between the Christian and Sandbeach rituals and beliefs.

---

14 Whitefellows are called *parra* in Umpila, Uutaalnganu and Kuuku Ya'u, and *waypala, ngarr* and *akngarr* in Uuk-Umpithamu, Lamalama and Morrabalama, respectively. The latter two words also signify the malevolent spirits that are called 'devils' and 'quinkans' in English; *awu* is their Umpila, Uutaalnganu and Kuuku Ya'u equivalent in this sense.
In Creole and Aboriginal English, whitefellows are often called *migolo*, a word whose specific southern origins are unknown.

15 Also called 'blessing oil' in Creole.

Thomson (1933) described many features of classical Umpila, Uutaalnganu and Kuuku Ya'u religious belief and practice, but he focused on Kuuku Ya'u beliefs and practices of the hero cult complex centring on *Iwayi* 'Old Man Crocodile'. He also described similar ceremonies which he witnessed at Port Stewart in late 1928. More recently, Laade (1970) and Chase (1980) outlined related ceremonial complexes for the Uutaalnganu and Umpila. Throughout the east coast of the Peninsula, people call these ceremonies 'Bora' and say they have to do with 'inside business', i.e. restricted esoteric knowledge and practice. Thomson proposed that the cult provided the basis for tribal integration, but we believe it better to speak of regional integration here—see also Hiatt (1996:108–109). The complex is more widely distributed than just among the Sandbeach People, and it drew together men and women from different clans and language groups over the wider region.[16]

Indigenous languages

The geographical and sociological distributions of the indigenous languages of the Sandbeach People have changed much over the past century. A hundred years ago, the patriclans antecedent to the Lamalama tribe owned and spoke five or six indigenous languages (Rigsby 1980a, 1980b, 1992; Rigsby and Hafner 1994a). The estates of the Lamalama- and Rimanggudinhma-speaking clans just touched on the Sandbeach Region. The estates of two Morrabalama-speaking clans were located along the coast at its very southern extreme, and they extended discontinuously to the Cliff Islands. The coastal estate of the single Uuk-Umpithamu-speaking clan was just to the north. The coastal strip from Running Creek northward to Breakfast Creek and the upper Massey Creek belonged to the estates of four Ayapathu-speaking clans[17] One

16 Roth (1898) observed similar Bora ceremonies on the North Kennedy River that were hosted by a Koko Warra local group.

17 One should not reify social categories defined by speaking the same language into social groups, such as tribes, without other warrant. The

(or two?) of them shared the Cliff Islands with the Morrabalama clan. On the lower Massey Creek and adjacent coast, the language variety of the Morrindhinma clan can be described or labelled in different ways. Umpila, Uutaalnganu and Kuuku Ya'u people regard it as distinctive and they call it Kuuku Yani (Rigsby 1992:358; West 1964). In contrast, the Lamalama people consider it simply to be Umpila and they do not recognise the Kuuku Yani name.

From south of Massey Creek northward to Friendly Point, Umpila is the indigenous language, and there are seven Umpila estates encompassing the coastal lowlands and the inner Reef waters. Uutaalnganu is the indigenous language from Cape Sidmouth to Cape Direction, and Kuuku Ya'u is situated from there north to the Wuthathi language area, which begins close to the Olive River, north of Temple Bay.

Today, language shift is well underway, and the indigenous languages have few speakers. Most Sandbeach People are vernacular speakers of a local Creole variety (at Lockhart and Port Stewart).[18] Lamalama has less than ten speakers, Morrabalama has perhaps three, Rimanggudinhma has perhaps three and Uuk-Umpithamu has perhaps a half dozen. The coastal Ayapathu dialect has no speakers. Umpila, Uutaalnganu and Kuuku Ya'u have perhaps several dozen good speakers left. Wuthathi has no speakers left, but a few older people remember words and phrases.

---

contemporary Ayapathu tribe, a language-named tribe based in Coen (Chase et al. 1995), does not include the extinct coastal Ayapathu-speaking clans, and their estates have passed to the Lamalama tribe by traditional succession. Thomson (1934:237, 239–240, 251) described the social distance of the Yintjingga local group, whose focal members were men of a coastal Ayapathu-speaking clan, from the inland Ayapathu-speaking people. The latter and their Kaanju neighbours were *kanichi* 'inlanders,' respected for their magical charms and feared for their potential for sorcery.

18   It is an interesting question whether the vernacular at Port Stewart is a creole variety or an Aboriginal English variety, and the answer hinges not so much on the empirical facts as on how the terms are defined formally and functionally.

Land and sea as environment and habitat

The homelands of the Sandbeach People are bounded by the Great Dividing Range in the west and the outer Great Barrier Reef in the east. They include complex mosaics of terrestrial and marine country. In the south, the Lamalama tribal estate extends westward from the Normanby River around the mangrove-lined Princess Charlotte Bay to north of the Stewart River. The mangroves fringing the lower Bay give way to open expanses of sandbeach a few kilometres south of Goose Creek, a few kilometres south of Running Creek. The Sandbeach Region with its open beaches, headlands and bays begins here and extends northward to Captain Billy Landing, where Wuthathi country ends. Its coast is punctuated by a number of short and swiftly flowing rivers and creeks, of which the Stewart, Lockhart, Pascoe and Olive Rivers are the largest. In the south, there is a wider coastal plain between the sandbeach and the Great Dividing Range, but north of Massey Creek, the Range (including smaller ranges) approaches the coast and the coastal land strip narrows to a few kilometres in depth.

The prevailing southeast trade winds and the terrain interact to produce a mosaic of lowland plant communities of great diversity and complexity. Vine forest, rainforest, dry sclerophyll, heathland, grassland, open and closed wetlands, mangrove forest and littoral dune thicket occur in many combinations, none of them dominant. The indented coastline, headlands, small hills and spur ranges also contribute to topographic and floristic variability (see Chase 1984:104–106; Chase and Sutton 1987:73–74). There are extensive saltpan systems and large wetland complexes (e.g. the Rocky River and Balclutha Creek swamplands) in the more lowlying, southern half of the Sandbeach Region. In former times, groups of men fished the saltpans with frame nets during the kingtides at the end of the year. Thomson photographed such a saltpan fishing sequence at Port Stewart in 1928. There were no stone fishtraps in the region. We have not recorded weirs in the Sandbeach Region, but

Logan Jack (1922:488) recorded what must been a weir[19] across a small tributary of the Normanby River, not far south around the Bay.

Above the estuaries, many of the short streams flow only during the wet season (roughly, January through April), but there are permanent pools in the watercourses, as well as fringing lagoons. The eastern-facing slopes of the uplands are clad in dense rainforest, and this habitat extends coastwards to form narrow galleries along the watercourses. It includes many desirable fruit trees and plant species, and provides habitats for bird and animal species, including cassowary and cuscus in the north. Sandbeach People fish today with handlines and the four-pronged wire spear. The Lamalama people use no saltwater gear or bait when they fish in fresh water, nor do they use freshwater gear or bait in the salt water.[20] As well as fish, people also take many freshwater turtles and crayfish. They dig and gather several yam species (including long yam *Dioscorea sativa* and hairy yam *Dioscorea rotunda*), which grow in the sandy soils along the streams and in the scrubs behind the beach dunes. They use rifles to hunt wallabies, kangaroos and emus in more open country, and feral pigs near swamps and waterholes, using dogs[21]

---

19   Logan Jack's party made their Camp 26 at a lagoon on the east side of the Normanby, and he (Logan Jack 1922:488) wrote: 'Half-a-mile above our camp there had been a NATIVE FISHING STATION last wet season. The mouth of the gully (still retaining a few water-holes) had been stopped by a fence of stakes and twisted branches. The blacks must have got a good many large barramundi, judging by the heaps of large scales lying about.'

20   The salt water/fresh water opposition extends to other behaviour as well. Under Lamalama Law, people should cook and eat mussels, whelks, oysters and other shellfish at the coast, and not take them inland to Coen, as they sometimes do.

21   People keep and use only dogs of European origin today, but in the past, they got dingo pups and tamed them as hunters and companions. Dogs had and have personal names, just as humans do. Some of the Lamalama dogs at Port Stewart have indigenous language names, e.g. Keith Liddy's dog is *Waymuwa*, the name of Goose Swamp, one of his clan countries.

to bail up their quarry. They also hunt ducks, geese and other birds in the large freshwater swamps and wetlands that are home to many species, some migratory and others not. They also gather scrub turkey, scrub fowl and goose and other eggs when available. From Umpila territory northward, people raid the close inshore islands in the dry season for Torres Strait pigeons, especially when the squabs are well-grown. People also forage the land to gather useful resources, for example, firewood, timber, several kinds of bark and gum, various bush medicines and palm fibre for string to make twine and netting (Rigsby and Williams 1991:13; Chase 1980:153–155).

The estuaries (including mangroves and channels) and sandbeach present other sets of habitats. People fish with handlines and spears for a range of species, favouring barramundi and salmon, but taking a dozen or more other fishes. We do not know whether people used shell fish hooks in former times, but they adopted metal fish hooks early in the contact period. Men previously made and used frame nets, but they no longer do so. Men and women hunt and forage along the water's edge and shallow waters, taking a variety of rays, crabs, fishes and shells. Of particular value are the large 'mudshell' bivalves (*mupa*) and the spiral whelks (*ayka*),[22] which can be easily gathered in the mangrove zone.

The reefs, cays and sandbanks of the outer Great Barrier Reef lie thirty and more kilometres offshore, and oral histories and archaeological evidence tell us that Sandbeach men made canoe voyages out there in the past. As well, many people worked in the marine industries along the coast from the middle 1860s, and the experience probably gave them (mainly men) the opportunity to visit and use their own and other people's sea countries out to the outer Reef more intensively and more often than previously. Today, Umpila men still go out occasionally for turtle to the outer Reef. The inner reef waters are studded with terrestrial islands, sandcays, smaller reef complexes and sea grass beds, which present another range of habitats and resources. The Umpila and the Kuuku Yau constantly hunt dugong and turtle in these waters

---

22 These species names are in Umpila.

around Lloyd Bay today, using modern aluminium boats with outboard motors.

Land, sea and resources as property

As noted earlier, it can be various combinations of contemporary language-named tribes, family-based estate groups, or regional groupings who assert primary control over the countryside and seascape, depending on the situation. People generally gain these rights from their father. Among the contemporary Lamalama tribe, other things being equal, any adult Lamalama person has the right to live on, camp on, visit and use the resources found on any part of their tribal estate. But some people have special rights and interests in subparts of the tribal estate that in the past belonged to their ancestors' clans; for example, the Liddys are recognised as having special rights and interests in the Port Stewart area that come to them from Grandfather Harry Liddy, who got them from his mother and her younger brother. Other people defer to them on matters relating to the area, but nonetheless, other Lamalama people live there as they wish and use its land and resources without having to ask permission. North of the Lamalama, among the Lockhart-based people, there is still strong adherence to a more differentiated estate model of control.

In past times, the sense of property was also well developed, and owners regularly monitored their land and sea country to see who was on it or had been on it. Outsiders were expected to present themselves to the resident owners and to make themselves and their intentions known. If they did not, the residents assumed that they were up to no good, that they were there to use resources without permission or to bring harm to someone. If owners discovered the tracks or signs of outsiders where they did not belong, they might then send a messagestick to the offenders and invite them to come give an account of themselves. Such a meeting could result in a spearfight. Failure to account for their actions could lead to a well-aimed spear without warning. If owners caught outsiders in the act of trespass and unsanctioned use of resources, they would throw spears at them both to drive them away and to punish them.

People also speak of fish and game as property even when it is free ranging and not under anyone's control or possession. Owners expect to be given a share of fish and game taken from their land or sea country, and the same pattern obtained in the classic situation. Some people were known to be quick to speak and use a spear to press their rights to a share of the product others got from their estates and to insist on what they considered to be a proper amount.

Local groups often include non-owners, but non-owner spouses and recognised partners have the right to reside on their partners' land and to use their resources. The same was true in the classic situation. Where a person's mother was from a different area, then that person can expect to visit their mother's people's estate and use its resources in the usual case, but they should seek permission and advise their intentions. And in fact, some people grow up with their mother's people and take their identity as primary. For example, the children of a senior Lamalama woman grew up among her people after their Olkola father's death, and they are regarded as Lamalama generally. However, they have not given up their Olkola rights and interests, and when Rigsby did Olkola family history work in 1995, they and their Olkola relatives made sure they were included on the list of Olkola people. There are two large Umpila families at Lockhart of siblings whose mothers were Lamalama, and when they and their descendants visit Port Stewart, they activate their rights and interests to camp and to use the resources of the Lamalama estate. Two of the main turtle and dugong hunters at Port Stewart in 1997 were young Umpila men; one was partnered with a Lamalama woman and the other was the son of a Lamalama woman.

There is also a distinction to be drawn between domestic space and public space that parallels the situation in the wider Australian society where a lessee may have rights of exclusive possession over a dwelling or a block that originate by contract with the lessor, who themself may be an owner or a lessee. The hearth and immediate living area or camp of a household is such domestic space and is not generally accessible to non-members unless they are invited in or they are acknowledged after they approach and signal their desire to enter by asking or otherwise. Thomson (1932:162–163) observed that hearth areas were private 'family' space, and he wrote:

> No man, married or single, ever approaches close to the fireside of another family when the women folk are present. Even the long discussions that take place at night are carried on by shouting from fireside to fireside, or at fires at which the men only forgather.

Within a camp, households have their own hearths and areas, and when guests come from elsewhere, the host owners direct them to a particular area with its own shade, which then enters the possession of the guests for the duration. They can also expect to use the same area when they visit again, and they may leave personal property, such as eel logs or boxwood bark baskets, there for later use. And when in occupation, guests or non-owners can be confident of their rights to control the space and exclude others. Peter Sutton (pers. comm.) tells of an exchange he witnessed during his work with Wik-speaking people where an angry guest spoke to his intruding host words to the effect, 'We may be on your land, but you're in my camp. Now get out!' The same sentiments and action would not be out of place among Lamalama people.

The rules, or patterns, of how people acquire rights and interests in land and sea country involve complexities and contingencies that we cannot examine further here, but suffice it to say that wherever we observe an Aboriginal person on and using land or sea country where they do not have primary rights, we can always identify a kin or affinal connection and/or an agreement or license permitting them to be there. At Lockhart River, the exception to this generalization is the 'public' area around the community, and the old mission site, as people regard both of these areas as communal areas as a result of longterm mixed occupancy. But even in these cases, the 'public' is the local Aboriginal one, and there are complaints when outsiders enter these areas. There is, for example, very strong objection to Torres Strait Islanders coming into local waters to exploit crayfish and trepang commercially, and there is also general objection to the considerable prawn trawling done in the region. The land and sea and their resources are property, not free goods for any and all to exploit and use at their will. The other side of the situation is that people attribute and recognise the same rights and interests in property to other tribes and groups beyond the Sandbeach Region, and they conduct themselves in the same manner that they expect others to act with respect to them. Property is not limited to things that are under human control and possession, but it extends to all things in which people are considered to have rights and interests as against others. And only owners, in whatever particular form this is defined, can properly present themselves as such and say 'Such-and-such place is my land' or 'Such-and-such island is mine'.

Marine hunting, fishing and foraging

In past times, Sandbeach men constructed dugout canoes, which they used to hunt dugong and turtle (preferably, green seaturtle, but also hawksbill and other species) and to transport people and gear to the islands, reefs and sandcays, as well as along the coastline.[23] In the north,

---

23 The large Princess Charlotte Bay is in the southern part of the region, and one can see the Flinders Islands, Bathurst Head and Jane Table Hill from Port Stewart at low tide on a clear day. However, people did not generally cross the Bay in their dugouts, but travelled around it close to the shore. Frank Salt, born about 1910, told Rigsby of a canoe trip his family made from the southwestern Bay to visit their relatives at Bathurst Head when he was a boy. On the other hand, Florrie Bassani told Rigsby of people sailing by dugout and dinghy from Flinders Island to Port Stewart in a later period.
People also used floating logs, got on the spot, to cross rivers and other stretches of water. They call these *floting wud* in Creole. One old Lamalama man was known for swimming across rivers in preference to using a canoe or floating log.

they fitted their dugouts with double outriggers, while in the south, they used a single outrigger.[24] Thomson observed both canoe types at Port Stewart in 1928 and 1929, and he (Thomson 1952:2) said that Claremont Point,[25] a few kilometres north, 'marks the division between the two forms of outrigger'. Hale and Tindale (1933:118, 120–121) also observed both kinds of dugout at Port Stewart in 1927. They said that people south of Running Creek did not make the double outrigger type, but Port Stewart was the northernmost occurrence of the single out-rigger type. Thomson (1934:242–243) earlier reported that the Koko Ompindamo tribe (our Mumpithamu clan) around Running Creek and their southern neighbours made only single outrigger canoes, whereas their northern congeners made double outrigger ones.[26] Men powered both types of canoe with spatulate paddles and poles in the main, but they also used sails made from cloth or the large fan-shaped leaves of cabbage trees, *Corypha elata*. It is unclear whether they used sails before contact with Europeans, but it seems that Torres Strait Islanders did, and the latter sometimes raided and traded down along the east coast into the sea country of the Sandbeach People. Hale and Tindale (1933:121) speculated that both types originated from outside the region and that the single outrigger type came later. The double outrigger type is said to be more manoeuvrable and seaworthy in rougher seas. These features no doubt accounted for its popularity among most of the Sandbeach People.

People also began to use wooden dinghies for hunting, fishing and transport by the 1930s, powering them by rowing and sailing, but men

---

24   At Port Stewart, Jimmy Kulla Kulla taught his older daughter and younger son how to make dugouts. Women helped men in making canoes.

25   Claremont Point is not local usage. Aboriginal people call it 'Man-o-War Point' or 'Four-Mile (Point).'

26   Davidson (1935) used material from Roth (1910) and Hale and Tindale (by personal communication) on the distribution of the two outrigger-types and concluded that 'a southward diffusion... [was] taking place during the past quarter century, if not for a longer period'.

continued to make and use outrigger dugouts at Port Stewart until the 1961 removal, and at Lockhart River until the 1950s.

Thomson (1934:242) described the plan of an Umpila or Kuuku Ya'u double outrigger canoe (*tangu*) and its usual three crew positions. The canoe owner (*tangukunchi*), when he takes his canoe hunting, was generally also the harpooner (*wataychi*), the most skilled of the crew. At sea, the harpooner directed the helmsman when they sighted their quarry, but generally the crew each knew their roles well and carried them out with little detectable leadership. The title of *wataychi* was and is a valued one, and Thomson (1934:250–253) said that harpooning skill was rare and he wrote that men supplemented their ability with magic and charms (best obtained from the inland Ayapathu and Kaanju peoples) and followed certain prescriptions and proscriptions intended to maximise their chances of success. The coastal graves of prominent *wataychi*[27] were marked with the bones of their prey, the dugong skulls being placed at the head of the grave, and the rib bones arranged below it (Thomson 1934:254, and see Plate XXXI, Fig. 2. This may have been the grave of Harry Liddy's father, who died shortly before Thomson's arrival). As late as the 1970s these graves could still be seen along the coast as far north as Temple Bay, although today the bones have mostly leached away.

There were two harpooners active at Port Stewart when Thomson was there. Willie Webb (*Waarrathu*) was the older, and Thomson (1934:251, 255) described the younger man, Harry Liddy (*Nongorrli*), as 'by far the most expert harpooner that I have seen'. Some men at Port Stewart and southward were able to 'sing' dugong so that they could be more easily speared and would tire quickly. Thomson (1934:252) also noted that the *Ukaynta* (Bora) ceremonies among the Kuuku Ya'u people included a special rite at its end that made the initiand 'good for turtle' hunting. The old men also told him that the ceremonial eating of human flesh, usually calf muscle, conferred special prowess in hunting dugong. Thomson (1934:252) also recorded one Sandbeach clan that had a Dugong Story (totem). He saw the Kuuku Ya'u-speaking clan

---

27 The terms in this section are in Umpila.

perform an increase ceremony at its Dugong stone totemic centre at Mosquito Point. There is another major Dugong site, unrecorded by Thomson, in an Uuthalnganu estate near Lloyd Bay.

Men generally hunted dugong in daytime (Thomson 1934:245–246). They are found more often on their seagrass bed feeding grounds near reefs and in shallower waters. Sometimes men hunted on moonlit nights towards the end of the year when the southeast tradewinds had abated. The harpooner stood on the bow and directed the canoe silently to the dugong. When close enough, he struck forward and leapt overboard as he drove the harpoon home with the full weight of his body. He had to watch the rope carefully (so as not become entangled), he had to collect the long harpoon shaft (from which the head embedded in the animal had separated) and put it in the canoe and then get back aboard. He had to do all this before the fleeing animal ran out the length of the rope—Thomson purchased a locally made rope 199 feet in length—and got the craft under tow. When the animal tired and quietened, the crew passed a rope around its tail and held its head underwater until it drowned.[28] Then they towed it home. Kuuku Ya'u and Umpila men made a fine double outrigger canoe with the traditional ropes and harpoons in the 1970s for the University of Queensland Anthropology Museum.

Sometimes men hunted dugong at night from platforms built over shallow feeding grounds. Knowledgeable men could gain much information about the animal, its location and movement from the sounds and odour of its breathing spouts.

Men got turtle from a slightly wider range of places and further offshore. The introduction of metal harpoon heads (*kuyurru*)[29] doubtless

28 Men also drowned exhausted dugong by stuffing their nostrils open with dried grass (?)

29 *kuyurru* is the regional term in both the indigenous languages and Creole. Its origin is not known.

The acquisition of metal for harpoon heads must have increased the chances of successfully taking an animal after striking it. Previously, they were made of bone or hardwood. One type of head is made up from three made their capture easier, but sometimes a good swimmer could capture an animal by turning it on its back and taking it under control—we have both witnessed such captures, which are more easily done when the turtles are mating in close connection in October-November. The female with eggs inside is the favoured prey. Men brought and bring turtles alive back to shore, placing them on their backs until butchering.[30]

Hunting parties brought their catch back to specific places for butchering. These were on the coast or up mangrove channels, always away from the camp. Thomson (1934:247) said that the canoe owner, the harpooner or one of the old men did the initial butchering of dugong, cutting the animal into six or more named portions, which were apportioned to the crew, as well as the canoe owner, if he had remained ashore. Thomson (1934:249) wrote that he once intervened during butchering to say that he wanted a particular portion cut for himself. The owner balked, there was a heated discussion and the owner fell sullen. Thomson later realised that he had claimed most of a crew member's share and 'had practically forced the ... [canoe-owner] to give me that over which he had actually no control at all'. We interpret this as evidence that owner and crew had property rights in specific cuts of meat.[31]

---

pieces of nail or wire bound together, but it is not as efficient as one made up from a piece of three-cornered file. One day in May, 1997, hunters from Port Stewart struck three turtles near Cliff Island using the former type of head, but it failed to hold any of them.
Thomson (1934:264, Plate XXIX, Figs. 4 -9) provides illustrations of harpoon heads and their mode of fitting and rigging.

30　Thomson did not describe the method of killing turtles in his time, but today Sandbeach men dispatch overturned turtles by striking them on the nose (Lockhart) or on the windpipe (Port Stewart) with the blunt edge of an axe. David Claudie drew Rigsby's attention to this difference in custom.

31　Mrs Florrie Bassani, Harry Liddy's eldest daughter, told Rigsby that canoes were the personal property of their maker-owners. A borrower had to ask and get permission to use a canoe and its gear, and the person who took another's canoe without asking could expect to have a spear thrown

After the initial butchering, the men cut their portions into long narrow strips and boiled them in bailershell cooking vessels. Such cooked meat keeps up to the third day. Men also butchered and shared out turtle in named portions, and they collected the oil rendered from cooking dugong and turtle and used it for other cooking and for mixing with hard gums and resins to make them workable. Once meat was cooked, men took it back to their households, and people then redistributed it widely throughout the community. Today, Sandbeach men continue to hunt dugong with harpoons (*waap*)[32] fitted with metal heads both day and night, though outboard powered dinghies have replaced dugout canoes. Indeed, taking one's first dugong is an important event for a young man, and proficiency at hunting dugong and turtle provides high status throughout the region. People redistribute and share raw meat, according to particular kin and affinal links (see Chase 1980: 259–265) and traditional patterns of butchering and using bush medicines (charms) still apply.

In former times, people say that only senior men (*chilpu* 'man with grey hair and beard') ate dugong,[33] and young men and women were not allowed to eat it at all. Thomson (1934:255) reported that people had

---

at them with no warning. The borrower also had to give a substantial share to the owner. Pikers and stinters could also expect a spear.
Other gear, such as spears, firesticks, axes and dillybags, were also personal property. Husbands and wives shared each other's gear, but otherwise, men and women made and used their own. Today, close relatives may borrow gear from one another, but some individuals are known to be particular and touchy about their gear, so no one asks them nor dares to use their gear without asking.

32   The origins of this Creole word lie outside the Sandbeach region in Torres Strait, where it is found in the Western and Central Torres Strait Island Language, Meryam Mir (the indigenous language of Murray, Stephen and Darnley Islands) and the indigenous languages around Daru at the mouth of the Fly River.

33   Thomson took a series of photographs in 1928 of the mature men at Port Stewart feasting on a dugong they had cooked in an earth oven. He called such occasions 'gorges.'

already changed these rules when he first visited Port Stewart in 1928, but that women were not permitted to eat dugong killed by a younger man. That worked some hardship because the younger resident harpooner was the more productive hunter. In the 1970s, older Lockhart people told us that people changed the rules at the old mission in the 1920s to allow women and children to eat dugong; this was done in response to food shortage (Chase 1980: 260). In former times, there were no similar taboos on eating green seaturtle, but pregnant women and male initiands could not eat hawksbill turtle.

The offshore islands vary in the opportunities they offer their traditional owners. Some islands are the home of Stories who require quiet respectful demeanour, for example, a powerful Wind Story inhabits the largest of the three islands of the Cliff Islands group. Apparently, only small groups of people visited these islands, and they camped only on the smallest one.

A few islands have a fuller suite of floral and faunal species, but they are often known for some particular resource, such as fish, turtle eggs, seabird eggs, flying fox camps and Torres Strait pigeon rookeries (where carpetsnakes usually live too). People also collected birds' eggs and turtle eggs on some sandcays.

Men hunt turtle on some reefs, and in the past, they collected bailershells (*Melo sp.*), giant clams and other shell species on reefs. They used bailershells as cooking vessels and water containers, and they fashioned and shaped clam shells into adze blades for canoe manufacture. In past times, some food, such as shredded stingray, mixed with the oil of its liver, was cooked only in bailershells (Thomson 1934:250) and not in metal saucepans. Men also worked bailershell into the ovoid pieces that form the counterweight on the local woomera type. As well, inner nacre from the striped nautilus shell provided small pieces for necklaces. Thomson (1933:540, Plate XXIX) published photographs of people wearing ornaments made of reef shells. The man in his Figure 1 wears a pendant made from the base of a large cone shell (*Conus millepunctatus*)[34], the man in Figures 2 and 3 wears a pendant made from

---

34 See also the entry for 'piti'widi' in Thomson (1933:527). *pitiwiti*

mother-of-pearl shell,[35] and so too does the woman in Figure 4. Large trumpet shells provided ridged strips which were used for nose ornaments. Sandbeach men traded bailershells and woomera weight blanks, as well as stingray-barbed spears, with their inland trading partners in the regional exchange system, which was part of the wider continental system of interregional trade.

Fishing with hook and line was and is a more routine activity than marine hunting, and it surely provides greater amounts of food and calories over the subsistence year. People go out to fish in the nearby interior and coastal waters frequently. At Lockhart, people more often go out to fish when they are free from work or other commitments, but at Port Stewart, people fish even more frequently. The arrival of the large migratory threadfin fishes just after the wet season spurs increased fishing activity. The ablebodied person who does not go out to fish when the weather is good and there is little fish in the camp freezer or household larders is likely to be remarked upon. Whenever people go to places they visit infrequently or have not been to for years (e.g. reefs and remote waterholes), they always take fishing gear and try their luck. Barramundi and salmon are preferred saltwater species, while fat jewfish from fresh water make a rich broth (called 'soup' in Creole). Generally people catch and eat most any species they can, especially when they are down on their luck. They also prize the longnecked turtles they catch by handline in fresh water.

Final remarks

There is a general ethic today among Sandbeach People that people should take only as much of a resource as they and their fellows can use, and when people trangress this ethic, their fellows comment upon it critically. Sandbeach People contrast themselves positively with

signifies both the species and the ornament in Umpila and its congeners.

35 The species and the ornament are both called *piirra* in Umpila and its congeners.

whitefellows when they observe the latter leaving fish and other animals to rot and waste, especially species which do not appeal to the European taste, like rays and barracuda. As well, people also observe an ethic of sharing and general reciprocity which insures that meat and fish are widely distributed within local communities. Some items, such as the wild yams and plant foods, are shared more narrowly within households or closely related households. People produce a substantial amount of their own subsistence, and they value bush tucker (including marine produce) more than purchased food. They believe that the traditional foods are more nutritious and taste better, and many thoughtful adults say that it is important to exercise the knowledge and skills they acquired from their old people and to 'keep them going' by teaching them to children and young people. In the 1970s at Lockhart, there were renowned hunters who boasted that they would not waste money by purchasing meat, and that their spears 'fed' them. People also express considerable disdain for Torres Strait Islanders who, they say, sell dugong meat to their relatives to make money. However, women rarely prepare the old labour-intensive staples, such as mangrove pod or cheeky yam porridge and wild rice or lilyroot damper. They have replaced them with white flour, prepared as damper and fried bread, and with rice. But Sandbeach People's subsistence production, exchange, sharing and gifting rests squarely upon their property rights and interests in land and sea country. Sandbeach People produce much of their subsistence from resources they own using their own labour and tools that they own, and the items they exchange, share and gift among themselves are also items of property. If we wish to analyse, describe and understand Sandbeach culture and society in all its richness, we cannot ignore the institution of property any more than we can ignore kinship and religion.

It is clear from our discussion that traditional connection to land and sea and the use of their resources remains strong among the Sandbeach People, despite the vicissitudes of early contact and later European disruption and domination. It is now well-recognised that the continuity of tradition involves change, sometimes in dramatic form, as is evidenced here by language shift, reformulated views of group/territory connection in someparts of the region, and in the multiplex ways that people recognise and use country. But in the Sandbeach Region, we can discern certain core cultural values which seem to hold constant, and around which changes are fashioned. One of these is the perceived regional unity which impressed Thomson (1934:238) so strongly when he wrote, 'They are a splendid seafaring people—great adventurers and great fighters'. The Sandbeach identity was, and is, based principally upon the possession of a shared and related set of mythic beliefs and the initiation ceremonies which came from them, a common pattern of territorial recognition which took in coastal land, sandbeach and the inner reef waters, a marine technology which centred around the seaborne hunting of dugong and turtle, patterns of intermarriage, and in recent history, a common pattern of European intrusion and engagement, particularly by the lugger industries.

These core beliefs and experiences override any forces of separation which have occurred, for example, the concentration of Umpila, Uutaalnganu and Kuuku Ya'u people on the old Lockhart River Mission and the later government settlement, and the enforced removals of the Lamalama and the Wuthathi to other places. It is not of major concern to the Lamalama and the Wuthathi that their particular ceremonial practices disappeared some time ago—it is enough for them to know they existed in the past. The spiritual relationships of people to land and sea still exist. Through these connections they also see strong links to other Sandbeach People. With the recent decisions by the High Court regarding native title, the Sandbeach People now have new fora within which to assert their common connectedness, and it is perhaps fitting in this case that their first major native title action is over their sea territories. Whatever the outcome from mediation or later court action, the very process of engagement over their joint sea territories will be important in re-affirming and strengthening their traditional ties of interconnectedness.

Notes

We dedicate this paper to the memories of Isaac Hobson and Billy Brown.

Isaac Hobson, or Chalpi, died tragically at Port Stewart on 23 November 1996. He was a grandson of Tommy, Donald Thomson's good mate, and he was an Umpila man and a dugong man—a proper Sandbeach man. Kylie Tennant (1959) wrote of him:

> 'Who is the most intelligent boy in the school?' John [Warby] asked.
>
> 'Isaac Hobo [Hobson],' I replied promptly.
>
> 'Isaac?' John was disappointed. 'He chases girls. I've never seen any signs of intelligence in Isaac.'
>
> 'The others watch me in class, but Isaac's eyes are glowing with joy, and he watches me more carefully because at night in the village he is going to do a splendid imitation of me teaching. I wish,' I said wistfully, 'I could see him do it.'

Billy Brown passed away in March, 1997 after massive renal failure. He was an Umpila man, one of a fast dwindling set of old people who were born on their own country and grew up in the bush. His country was on the Nesbit River, and for years he had struggled to re-establish his family back on their homeland. His knowledge of Umpila country was encyclopaedic, and he is sorely missed by younger generations anxious to learn about the traditions of their Umpila countries.

We also thank Peter Sutton for helpful comments and suggestions.

References

Ackerman, Lillian A. 1994. Nonunilinear descent groups in the plateau culture area. *Ethnology* 21(2):286–309.

Chase, A.K. 1996. *Wuthathi:Ten Islands land claim*. Cairns: Cape York Land Council.

1988. Lazarus at Australia's gateway. In *Aboriginal Australians and Christian missions* (eds) Tony Swain and Deborah Bird Rose. Adelaide: Australian Association for the Study of Religions. Pp. 121–139.

1984. Belonging to country: territory, identity and environment in Cape York Peninsula, northern Australia. In *Aboriginal landowners* (ed) L.R. Hiatt. Oceania Monograph 27. Sydney: University of Sydney. Pp. 104–122.

1980. *Which way now? Tradition, continuity and change in a north Queensland Aboriginal community.* Unpublished PhD Thesis. St Lucia: Department of Anthropology and Sociology, University of Queensland.

Chase, A. and P. Sutton. 1987. Australian Aborigines in a rich environment. In *Traditional Aboriginal society: a reader* (ed) W.H. Edwards. Melbourne: Macmillan. Pp. 68–95.

Chase, A., Martin, D., Rigsby, R. and Sutton, P. 1995. The Aboriginal people of Coen and surrounding region. In *Culture and bush tucker of Coen* (by) Coen Kindergarten Association Incorporated. Coen: Coen Kindergarten Association Incorporated. Pp. 5–7

Cliff Islands Report. 1996. *Aboriginal land claim to Cliff Islands National Park. Report of the Land Tribunal established under the Aboriginal Land Act 1991 to the Hon. the Minister for Natural Resources. April, 1996.* Brisbane. 140 pp.

Davidson, D. 1935. The chronology of Australian watercraft. *Journal of the Polynesian Society* 44(1):1–16; 44(2):69–84; 44(3):137–152; 44(4)193–297.

Dixon, R.M.W. 1976. Tribes, languages and other boundaries in northeast Queensland. In *Tribes and Boundaries in Australia* (ed) Nicolas Peterson. Social Anthropology Series No. 10. Canberra: Australian Institute of Aboriginal Studies. Pp. 207–238.

Hafner, Diane. 1994. Lamalama 'One mob' for land: The Port Stewart Lamalama community. In *CYPLUS Land Use Program: indigenous management of land and sea project and traditional activities Project.* St Lucia: Community Resource Management Program, Department of Anthropology and Sociology, University of Queensland. Pp. 9–1—9–22.

Haviland, John B. 1979. How to talk to your brother-in-law in Guugu Yimidhirr, In *Languages and their speakers* (ed) Timothy Shopen. Cambridge, Massachusetts: Winthrop Publishers. Pp. 160–239.

Hale, Herbert M. and Tindale, Norman B. 1933–1936. Aborigines of Princess Charlotte Bay, north Queensland. *Records of the South Australian Museum* 5:63–116, 117–172.

Hiatt, L.R. 1996. *Arguments about Aborigines: Australia and the evolution of social anthropology.* Cambridge, New York, Melbourne: Cambridge University Press.

Jolly, Lesley. 1997. *Hearth and country: the bases of women's power in an Aboriginal community on Cape York Peninsula.* Unpublished PhD thesis. St Lucia: Department of Anthropology and Sociology, University of Queensland.

Laade, Wolfgang. 1970. Notes on the boras at Lockhart River Mission. *Archiv fuer Voelkerkunde* 24:273–308.

Lakefield Report. 1996. *Aboriginal land claim to Lakefield National Park. Report of the Land Tribunal established under the Aboriginal Land Act 1991 to the Hon. the Minister for Natural Resources. April, 1996.* Brisbane. 364 pp.

Peterson, Nicolas (ed). 1976a. *Tribes and boundaries in Australia.* Social Anthropology Series No. 10. Canberra: Australian Institute of Aboriginal Studies.

Peterson, Nicolas. 1976b. The natural and cultural areas of Aboriginal Australia: a preliminary analysis of population groupings with adaptive significance. In *Tribes and Boundaries in Australia* (ed) Nicolas Peterson. Social Anthropology Series No. 10. Canberra: Australian Institute of Aboriginal Studies. Pp. 50–71.

Radcliffe-Brown, A.R. 1918. Notes on the social organisation of Australian tribes. Part I. *Journal of the Royal Anthropological Institute* 48:222–253.

Rigsby, Bruce. 1996a. Appendix 1. In *Yalga-binbi Institute for community development, Port Stewart Lamalama community development plan 1996.* Cairns: Yalga-binbi Institute for Community Development Aboriginal and Torres Strait Islander Corporation. Pp. 27–40. [This is a reprinting of Chapter 6, written by Rigsby on the history of the Port Stewart region and extracted from Bruce Rigsby and Suzette Coates, *'Murri been 'ere before!': An Historical and Anthropological Investigation of Factors Affecting the Deaths in Custody of Two Port Stewart Lamalama Men.* Unpublished report prepared for the National Aboriginal and Islander Legal Services Secretariat and submitted to the Royal Commission into Aboriginal Deaths in Custody, February, 1991. 32pp.]

1996b. Law and custom as anthropological and legal terms. In *Heritage and Native Title: Anthropological and legal perspectives* (eds) Julie Finlayson and Ann Jackson-Nakano. Canberra: Native Title Research Unit, Australian Institute of Aboriginal and Torres Strait Islander Studies. Pp. 230–252.

1995. Tribes, Diaspora people and the vitality of law and custom: Some comments. *In Anthropology in the native title era* (eds) Jim Fingleton and Julie Finlayson. Canberra: Native Titles Unit, Australian Institute of Aboriginal and Torres Strait Islander Studies. Pp. 25–27.

1992. The languages of the Princess Charlotte Bay region, In *The language game: papers in memory of Donald C. Laycock* (eds) Tom Dutton, Malcolm Ross and Darrell Tryon. Pacific Linguistics, C–110. Pp. 353–360.

1980a. Land, language and people in the Princess Charlotte Bay area. In *Contemporary Cape York Peninsula* (eds) N.C. Stevens and A. Bailey. Brisbane: Royal Society of Queensland. Pp. 89–94.

1980b. The language situation on Cape York Peninsula: past, present, future. In *Reef rainforest mangroves man* (eds) J. Wright, N. Mitchell and P. Watling. Cairns, Queensland: Wildlife Preservation Society. Pp. 5–7.

Rigsby, B. and Williams, N. 1991. Reestablishing a home on eastern Cape York Peninsula. *Cultural Survival Quarterly* 15(2):11–15.

Rigsby, B. and Hafner, D. 1994a. *Lakefield National Park land claim: claim book*. Cairns: Cape York Land Council on behalf of the claimants. [In three parts].

1994b. *Cliff Islands National Park Land Claim. Claim Book*. Part A (Chapters 1, 2, 3, 5 and 7). Cairns: Cape York Land Council on behalf of the claimants. [In three parts].

Roth, Walter E. 1910. Transport and trade. North Queensland Ethnography Bulletin No. 14. *Records of the Australian Museum*. 8(1):1–10.

1898. On the Aboriginals occupying the 'hinter-land' of Princess Charlotte Bay. A Report to the Commissioner of Police. Cooktown. 81 pp.

Rumsey, Alan. 1993. Language and territoriality in Aboriginal Australia. In *Language and culture in Aboriginal Australia* (eds) Michael Walsh and Colin Yallop. Canberra: Aboriginal Studies Press. Pp. 191–202.

1989. Language groups in Australian Aboriginal land claims. *Anthropological Forum* 6(1):69–79.

Service, Elman. 1962. *Primitive social organization: an evolutionary perspective*. New York: Random House.

Sharp, Nonie. 1992. *Footprints along the Cape York sandbeaches*. Canberra: Aboriginal Studies Press.

Sharp, R. L. 1939. Tribes and totemism in north-east Australia. *Oceania* 9(3):254–275.

Stanner, W.E.H. 1969. The Yirrkala case: some general principles of Aboriginal land-holding. Unpublished manuscript.

Sutton, Peter. 1996a The robustness of Aboriginal land tenure systems: underlying and proximate customary titles. *Oceania* 67:7–29.

1996b. *Families of polity: post-classical Aboriginal society and native title*. Discussion paper published by the National Native Title Tribunal. 77 pp.

Tennant, Kylie. 1959. *Speak you so gently*. London: Victor Gollancz.

Terwiel-Powell, F. J. 1975. *Developments in the kinship system of the Hope Vale Aborigines*. Unpublished PhD thesis. St Lucia: Department of Anthropology and Sociology, University of Queensland.

Thompson, David A. 1995. *'Bora belonga white man': missionaries and Aborigines at Lockhart River Mission*. Unpublished MA thesis. St Lucia: Department of Anthropology and Sociology, University of Queensland.

1988. *Lockhart River 'Sand Beach' language: an outline of Kuuku Ya'u and Umpila*. Work Papers of SIL—AAIB, Series A, Volume 11. Darwin: Summer Institute of Linguistics.

1985. *'Bora is like Church'*. Sydney: Australian Board of Missions.

Thompson, D. and Chase, A. 1997. *Kuuku Ya'u land claim to Iron Range National Park. Cairns:* Cape York Land Council.

Thomson, Donald F. 1972. *Kinship and behaviour in north Queensland: a preliminary account of kinship and social organisation on Cape York Peninsula*. Australian Aboriginal Studies No. 51. Canberra: Australian Institute of Aboriginal Studies. Foreword, Afterword and Editing by H.W. Scheffler

Thomson, D. F. 1952. Notes on some primitive watercraft in northern Australia. *Man* 52:1–5.

1946. Names and naming in the Wik Monkan tribe. *Journal of the Royal Anthropological Institute* 76:157–167.

1935. The joking relationship and organized obscentity in north Queensland. *American Anthropologist* 37:460–490.

1934. The dugong hunters of Cape York. *Journal of the Royal Anthropological Institute* 64:237–262.

1933. The hero cult, initiation and totemism on Cape York. *Journal of the Royal Anthropological Institute* 63:453–537.

1932. Ceremonial presentation of fire in north Queensland: a preliminary note on the place of fire in primitive ritual. *Man* 32:162–166

West, LaMont, Jr. 1964. Alphabetical first name list of Lockhart River Mission residents and kin. Unpublished manuscript.

13

The Sea of Waubin:
the Kaurareg and their marine
environment

Michael Southon and the Kaurareg Tribal Elders

In attempting to reconstruct the social institutions surrounding owner-ship and control of the marine environment of the Kaurareg,[1] it should be born in mind that the Kaurareg have experienced an extreme degree of social and cultural dislocation since the arrival of Europeans in the Torres Strait in the 1870s. As a result of the massacre of the crew of the *Sperwer* at Wednesday Spit between Wednesday Island and Hammond Island in 1869 (Sharp 1992:30), the Kaurareg on Prince of Wales Island (Muralag) were in turn massacred, almost to the point of extinction (Sharp 1992:70; Singe 1979:169). It was later discovered that the killing of the *Sperwer's* crew was carried out not by Kaurareg but by the Kulkalgal of Naghi island (Sharp 1992:72; Singe 1979:168). But by this time only a handful of the Muralag population were left. The survivors were moved to Hammond Island (Kiriri). Kiriri was subsequently chosen as the site of a Roman Catholic Mission and in 1922 the Government moved the

---

1 The paper focuses on the Kaurareg living on Narupai (Horn Island). There are smaller numbers of Kaurareg living on other islands in the Torres Strait: Moa Island (at Kubin), Thursday Island, Hammond Island, and Friday Island. On the mainland there are Kaurareg living at Injinoo, Bamaga, Weipa, Townsville and Darwin. Some of the words in this report are not Kaurareg but belong to other language groups to the north and east. The Kaurareg language has close affinities with Australian lan-guages (Haddon 1935:290) and indeed Kaurareg themselves refer to it as 'Aboriginal' in contrast to 'Torres Strait language'. As a result of the forced removal from Hammond Island to Moa, Kaurareg people lost some of their own words and adopted words from the people of Moa.

Kaurareg at gun point to Moa island.² The Kaurareg lived on Moa island until 1947 when one of the Kaurareg elders, Elikiam Tom, attempted to move back to his country on Kiriri. Upon his return to Kiriri, however, Elikiam Tom was told by the Catholic Father in charge of the Catholic Mission on Kiriri that he could only stay on the island on the condition that he converted to Catholicism. Not wishing to do this, Elikiam Tom moved to Horn Island (Narupai) where he was soon joined by other Kaurareg elders from Moa, who, on their own initiative, started building a 'model village' at the site now known as Wasaga village. In 1950 the Government decided to move the Kaurareg away from Narupai for the same reasons 'that had led to the forced removal of the Kaurareg from Hammond Island' in 1922 (Sharp 1992:116). The Department of Native Affairs proposed to resettle the Kaurareg at Red Island Point on the mainland but this time the Kaurareg stood their ground and they remained on Narupai (Horn Island) and they continued to use their traditional land and sea country in the region.

Customary marine tenure

CMT is taken to refer not only to the ownership or control of areas of the sea, but also (and perhaps more importantly) to the ownership or control of marine species: an important issue in sea tenure is that the sea is not the resource itself but merely the medium in which the resource moves (Southon 1989:367).

The traditional use and control by the Kaurareg of their marine environment can only be understood in the context of their beliefs about ancestral spirits and the supernatural order. Central to Kaurareg marine tenure is the mythological figure Waubin, whose exploits provide the charter for Kaurareg tenure of both land and sea. Waubin was a warrior

2 The removal from Hammond Island reflected a general tightening of racial segregation following the First World War, and was part of the 'betterment scheme' whose purpose was to save 'the native' from 'hopeless contamination' through 'complete segregation' (Sharp 1992:110).

352

and a giant who came from mainland Australia to the island of Muralag which was already inhabited by a number of other mythological figures, also warriors. Waubin either killed these individuals or chased them out to sea, acquiring their wives in the process. Waubin was turned into stone and his metamorphosed body lies off the northeast end of Hammond Island as a rock named Waubin (Hammond Rock). There, as an outpost of Hammond Island, Waubin protects the islands to the south from intruders. He sends a strong current through the Prince of Wales channel which is said to discourage outsiders from venturing further south into the Kaurareg area. This deep channel, which runs along the north side of Hammond Island, is known as Waubinin Malu, or 'The Sea of Waubin'.

Though Waubinin Malu refers specifically to this channel on the north side of Hammond Island, Kaurareg people also use the term in a more general sense to refer to the whole Kaurareg sea territory. During his battle with the warriors on Muralag, Waubin encountered Badhanai, a warrior of very small stature, who darted between Waubin's legs and sliced off his right leg with the bamboo knife *upi* (Sharp 1992:105). The blood from Waubin's leg was carried by the currents throughout the waters surrounding the Prince of Wales group of islands. Wherever the blood from Waubin's leg was taken became Waubin's territory; thus it is that the whole sea enclosing the Kaurareg islands is called Waubin in Malu.

Though there is ambiguity about the extent of the traditional Kaurareg sea territory (see Figure 13:1), some points are clear. In the north the Kaurareg sea extended as far as the channel between Warar (Hawkesbury Island) and Dollar Reef (which belonged to the people of Moa). On the south side of Hawkesbury Island is a rock which represents Pithulai, a warrior who fled Muralag Island, driven by the ever-jealous Waubin. On the west side of the island lies another rock which represents Ibibin, another warrior who fled Muralag for the same reason. These two mythological figures are said to mark the northern extent of the Kaurareg sea territory:

He (Waubin) sent them (Pithulai and Ibibin) out to the island, they in that place, that's identification for Muralag ... that Pithulai and Ibibin (Billy Wasaga, Kaurareg tribal elder).

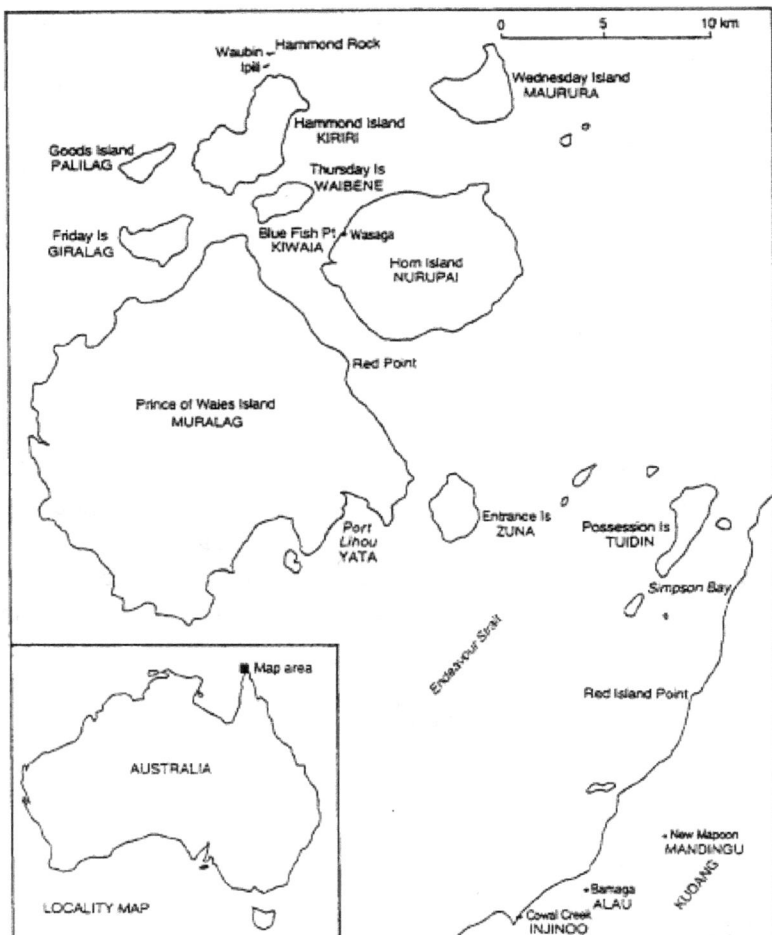

Fiure 13:1 Muralag and adjacent islands

In the west, Kaurareg sea extended as far as Booby Island where there is a rock that represents Ngiyangu, another warrior who was chased off Muralag by Waubin. Billy Wasaga described the role of Ngiyangu as a boundary marker:

> That what he stand there for, stop there, that's Kaurareg district, let the other people know that as a far as boundary, you know, for this way boundary.

The southern boundary of Waubinin Malu is less clear, perhaps reflecting the fact that Kaurareg traditionally had much better relations with their southern neighbours than with Islander peoples immediately to the north (Singe 1979:164). For example, informants state that the turtle hunting grounds on the islands south of Muralag, though they belonged to the Kaurareg, were shared with the Gudang people of the mainland.

Though Kaurareg conceived of their boundary as a number of significant sites rather than as a line, informants say that Kaurareg people always knew whether or not they were in their own sea territory or that of a neighbour. For example, people state that Kaurareg traditionally would not fish or hunt north of Hawkesbury Island, and would kill anyone from the north without traditional rights who fished or hunted south of Hawkesbury Island.

Within the Kaurareg sea there appear to have been no further spatial divisions governing ownership of the marine environment. Rather, the 'Sea of Waubin' was held in common by all the related clans inhabiting the Kaurareg islands. Each clan had a chief or *mamus*[3] but there was also an overarching *mamus* for the whole Kaurareg people. By some accounts this chief *mamus* governed the use of the fishery. For example, he would use sorcery to call up dugong and then allocate a certain number of dugong to be taken by each community. Communities which took more than the quota assigned by the chief *mamus* were punished. There was a strong ethic of taking from the sea only what was required

---

3 Mamus is not an indigenous word. Its ultimate origins are unknown, although it appeared in the pidgin English used in Torres Strait in the past century.

to satisfy immediate needs. Indeed, a principle of Kaurareg marine lore is that one can only fish or hunt successfully when one is hungry. There were strong sanctions, enforced both by the elders and by the clan leaders, against extravagant exploitation of species.

The use of magic to call up species was an important element in the Kaurareg management of their marine environment. This practice can be considered an aspect of marine tenure, since it involved the control of access to marine resources. As well as dugong, turtle were also called up by the use of sorcery. Amongst the people of Moa, who like the Muri Islanders were part of the Kaurareg, a rock in the shape of a turtle's back was used to call up turtle during the mating season. It was said that within five minutes of the ritual being performed, turtles would start coming ashore at a nearby beach.[4]

The calling up of species is still an important feature of Kaurareg hunting and fishing. It is often said that only people who know how to 'talk to the country'—whether on land (*murrup*) or sea (*malu*)—are able to hunt or fish successfully in a given locality.

Kaurareg people state that the waters within the Kaurareg sea territory were regarded as a common resource to be shared by all Kaurareg. However, the institution of *gangar* shows that on an informal level there was (and is) some kind of individual tenure of the sea. A *gangar* is a fishing spot where a particular individual regularly fishes. Some *gangar* are closely guarded secrets and are handed down to a man by his father, together with a spell or magic formula that ensures good fishing. A further example of marine tenure below the level of Waubinin Malu was the ownership of stone fish traps. There were at least two stone fishtraps in Kaurareg waters: one in the Bay of Siziri on the north side of Hammond Island and another at Thaniu buthu (*butu*, 'beach') on the south side of Hammond Island.

---

4   While I was on Horn Island, news arrived from Moa that this stone had been bulldozed into the sea by the local Government Authority to make way for a housing development.

Traditional knowledge of the marine environment

One of the most important institutions in Island society was the initiation, or *Kernge*, whose function was the transmission of mythology and traditional knowledge about the marine environment from elders to young men. The main informant for this chapter, Billy Wasaga, did not become an initiand as the *kernge* had already ceased to operate by the time he was a young man.[5] However, his father did go through *kernge* and passed on some of his knowledge to Billy. Billy also said on a number of occasions that his knowledge of the stars and tides and the behaviour of marine species is only a fraction of what it would have been, had his people not been removed from Hammond Island:

> These people in this area, they studied water and tide, that's what I tell you about *kernge*, they know which place to go to in which time, that's why they study them two, for that sort of thing. They lived on the water! Their life, that was their food, in the water!

The elders taught the *kerngeli*, the young men, by instructing them to go out and catch certain species from certain places at certain times of the year. Informants say that the young men would always find what they had been told to catch at the specified location: such was the knowledge of the elders who taught them. However, they had to bring back the exart number or quantity of the species which the old men had specified, or face punishment. As Billy said:

> .. they (the elders) send him (the kerngeli) out, they see that tide and after they tell him alright you go and get some fish, alright, and they tell him don't spear any fish, only one fish they send him for spear that one, they don't kill lot, just one kind, and if he can't find that one...but he will find it, because

---

5   The initiation ceremonies seem to have fallen into abeyance at the time of the forced removal from Hammond Island. Billy Wasaga says that at the time of the removal a number of young men were undergoing initiation; Lou Bagie (now deceased) had completed part of the initiation while Jimmy Kaur was a candidate but had not yet entered.

they send him at the right time, the tide is there, the fish will come on top, they get it, ... for the dugong same thing again, send him out at night, 'You take one, not more than one', they go out, get it, bring him home, they say 'one' or 'Get more than one', well, they get it, but they get the number, the figure, how much they bring him in, got to bring the same figure, not more not less, exactly what they said, its a training.

Tides and currents

Johannes and Macfarlane (1991:16) note that tides in the Torres Strait Islands are 'complex, pronounced, unusual and unpredictable'. They go on to observe that 'Numerous reefs, banks and islands accentuate the tides' effects, generating swift, complex currents that strongly influence the Islanders' choice of methods for fishing and for hunting dugong and turtle'. This fact of the marine environment is reflected in a well developed Kaurareg vocabulary for tides and currents.

Kaurareg people distinguish amongst at least six different kinds of tide: *gath* (very low), *seisam* (low), *koei wur* (high), *silel badh* (very high) and *yabagar* (highest). *Yabagar* occurs only during the northwest monsoon or Kuki. Between *seisam* and *silel badh* is another tide whose name people could not remember. *Seisam* is a particularly good tide for collecting crabs as the roots of the mangrove trees are left exposed for about a week.

Tides which flow with the wind and against the wind produce different surface conditions. When the tide is running in the same direction as the wind, it is known as *kuulis*, when it is flowing in the opposite direction to the wind, it is known as *guuthath*. The interval between tides when the water becomes temporarily still is known as *kas*.

An example of how the Kaurareg used detailed knowledge of the tides in the exploitation of the marine environment concerns the catching of turtles on Kathainab reef. From a hill on the south side of Hammond Island called Zangaitha (Bruce Point), Kaurareg elders had a clear view of Kathainab reef, the first of the three reefs lying on the north side of Hammond Island. Inside Kathainab reef is a lagoon called Dhudhun Li (lit. 'Dhudhun's basket'). A certain tide would take turtle into this lagoon and then leave them stranded there when it receded. From their vantage point at Zangaitha, Kaurareg elders would observe the tide and at the right moment would send young men in canoes around Hammond Island to Dhudhun Li, knowing that by the time they arrived the tide would be down and the turtles trapped.

A senior elder explained that tides are of general importance in the catching of turtle. When they find themselves in strong tides or currents, turtle always seek the security of reefs or islands to avoid being taken too far out to sea. Certain reefs and islands between Muralag and the mainland are known to be good places to find turtle when certain strong tides are running.

Knowledge of tides is also essential for catching fish. As is discussed below, Kaurareg have a repertoire of places known to be good for catching certain species of fish marked by *gangar*. But this knowledge is not sufficient in itself for each spot is associated with an optimal tide: it is knowing the combination of place and tide that determines success in fishing.

Off the northeast of Kiriri (Hammond Is.) lies a group of rocks called Ipili ('the wives', see Figure 13:1), which represent Waubin's wives. Some distance further out to sea lies a single rock which is the metamorphosed body of Waubin. When the tide is flowing southeastwards past Hammond Island towards Horn Island, a current is generated which acts as a backwash, flowing from Ipili around the eastern side of Waubin. When the tide is running in the other direction (i.e.. flowing northwestwards from Horn Island to Hammond Island), the same phenomenon occurs in reverse; a current runs from Ipili around the western side of Waubin. This current which always flows out from Ipili to Waubin, is called Muibubu ('inner current'). Its origin is grounded in mythology. Waubin placed his wives at Ipili and then he himself went and stood out to sea forming Hammond Rock. Waubin, known for his jealous guarding of his wives, so positioned himself that anyone wanting to see his wives would have to encounter him first. Thus it is, Kaurareg people explained, that whichever way the tide is flowing, a 'back current' will always take you back out from Ipili to Waubin.

As can be seen from the above account, currents are thought to be caused by ancestral spirits. In some cases, currents can be slowed down by making offerings to the spirits associated with them.

Just off the northeast corner of Muralag (Prince of Wales Island) is an oblong rock named Kiwain. In the narrow gap between Kiwain and Thursday Island the sea boils up, probably the result of the meeting of several different currents. Kaurareg say that in the days when heads were an important item in the trade between Torres Strait and New Guinea, the victims of Kaurareg headhunting raids were beheaded on this rock. Their bodies were thrown into the sea, thereby 'feeding' the current and slowing it down.

Somewhere between Hammond Island and Moa Island is an area of sea which Kaurareg people describe as being 'boxed-in' by currents on all four sides. Kaurareg people still placate the spirit of this potentially treacherous patch of sea by throwing bread into the water or by lighting a cigarette and throwing it into the sea.

The seasonality of resources

Kaurareg divide the year into two main seasons: *Sager* and *Kuki*. *Sagerau thonar*, the 'time of the southeast winds', lasts from the end of March through to November, while *Kukiyau thonar*, the 'time of the northwest winds', lasts from December to March.

During *Kuki* or 'northwest time' the Kaurareg traditionally concentrated on dugong and avoided eating most species of fish. A species of jellyfish appears during the northwest monsoon and is eaten by turtle and by many species of fish. Eating the flesh of these species causes the skin to swell up and become itchy. The herbivorous dugong which feeds exclusively on seagrass, are unaffected by the jellyfish. Some species of fish, especially those living in creeks and swamps, do not feed on jellyfish and are therefore targetted in December, January and early February. These are the file stingray (*thukmul*), two species of mullet (the silver mullet, *maker*, and the big-scaled mullet, *muragudal*), leatherjacket (*karmui*), grunter (*zaram*), bonefish (*kube*), garfish (*zaber*). During the northwest season Kaurareg would also gather and eat mangrove seed pods (*biyu*).

In the middle of the northwest season, in the month of January, two stars appear in the early morning. These stars represent the mythological figure *Dhogai*, a devil-woman who 'gathers every tucker from the sea and puts him in one place'. The appearance of Dhogai signals that the jellyfish are gone and that it is safe again to eat fish. After these stars appear, shallow waters are said to be teeming with fish and other marine life. However, though the jellyfish are gone, the waters are dirty from March to April, making it difficult to spear fish.

Towards the end of February another group of stars, (*zugubal*), appears in a certain position in the southern sky, indicating that the southeast winds are imminent. This takes the form of a shark (*baidam*). When the shark stands on its tail, the *Sager* season is about to start. *Sager* lasts from April through to October and is said to be a time of plenty: all species of fish are 'fat', as are crabs, mussels and bailershells. The water is clear, and at the same time there is abundant 'bush tucker'. Many plant species, whose shoots appeared in October of the previous year, are now ready to harvest. In particular, two species of yam, *kuthai* and *sawur*, are harvested in the months following April.

In August the southeast winds abate and the weather turns fine. In September the winds become northeasterly (*naigai*). This is known as the period of 'hot sun'. From the end of August to the beginning of November is the turtle breeding season or *soeulal*, when mating pairs of turtle are found floating on the surface in 'fast'. *Soeulal* is a good period for turtle hunting since the turtles are less alert than they normally are and therefore easier to catch. Furthermore, the females are considered particularly good eating at this time of the year as they have started to produce eggs.

In November the winds become squally again and a constellation of stars called Dagul (lit. 'thunder') drops towards the horizon in the southern sky. This constellation consists of five stars which take the form of a fishing spear. The falling of this constellation below the horizon is known as Dagul sisari (lit. 'the coming down of the Fishing Spear'). Dagul sisare is associated with various other natural phenomena. Firstly, as soon as Dagul drops into the sea, the thunder and lightning of the wet season begin. It is said that as long as the 'thunder stars' are in the sky, there is no thunder or lightning. Secondly, the disappearance of Dagul below the horizon brings on the rains of the northwest monsoon: it is said that Dagul falls into the sea with a big splash, causing a downpour of rain on the islands. Thirdly, the disappearance of Dagul signals the end of the turtle breeding season; the 'sliding' of Dagul below the horizon is linked to the sliding of the male turtle off the female turtle's back. This time is known as *waru sisanthari* (*waru* 'turtle', *sisanthari* 'to slide'). Fourthly, as soon as Dagul drops into the sea, various species of fish—in particular the file stingray (*thukmul*), make for shallow water where they are easy to spear. Dagul is said to be like a person who chases the fish towards the creeks and mudflats.[6]

The transforming effect of Dagul is evident not only on sea but on land as well. Dagul is said to shake up the land, causing rapid growth in all plants, leading to the abundance of bush tucker, particularly wild yams, in the following season of *Sager*.

Specific locations for hunting and fishing

Kei Yelubbi and Meggi Yelubbi were nesting grounds for green turtle as were Dumaralag Island, Woody Island and Red Woody Island. The last two islands, in addition to being turtle hunting grounds, were also places where three species of bird eggs were gathered: *kangan, sara* and

---

6 One Kaurareg person, attempting to explain the transforming effect of Takul, offered a modern analogy: the falling of Takul into the sea, he said, is like dropping a toaster into a bathtub.

sialwal. Dugong were hunted in the mouth of Kuipidh creek on Horn Island. A reef on the northeast side of Horn Island called Taigwata was known as a place to hunt hawksbill turtle. On Tharilag and Zuna islands there were several known fishing spots. Between Horn Island and Thursday Island there is a reef called Thoerigani which is known as a good fishing site. On the south side of Horn Island is a place called Puwapun, a large rock with a reef around it, which was a main fishing place in former times. Between Yelubbi and Tuidin (Possession) Island are some rocks which is a place known for catching hawksbill turtle.

The contemporary fishing economy on Horn Island

Fishing amongst the Kaurareg of Horn Island can broadly be divided into two categories: small-scale handlining and spearing from the rocks, beaches and jetties of Horn Island, and the more intensive fishing, cray-fishing, and hunting of turtle that is done from aluminium dinghies powered by outboard motors, of which there are about twenty on the island. There are five full-time Kaurareg fishermen on Horn Island. These men fish for crayfish on the islands of Muri (Mt. Adolphus) and Warar (Hawkesbury) and on the three reefs north of Hammond Island (Kathainab, Dadatiam and Giyai Moeza). There are a further nine men who are part-time fishermen.

In 1990 there was an attempt to start a trochus gathering enterprise on Muri Island. The project employed a number of young Kaurareg men from Horn Island and was part of the CDEP program. It foundered shortly after its inception and has not been revived.

For most Kaurareg people on Horn Island, fishing is a way of sup-plementing income derived from various forms of social security such as pensions and unemployment benefit. One informant explained that many households on Horn Island find their cash income is only suffi-cient to meet rent and non-food bills; by the second week of the pension period they have no money left for food and therefore they engage in subsistence fishing.

Beyond its purely economic significance, exploitation of the marine environment is closely bound up with Kaurareg social organization (Beckett 1994:5). One example of this is the role of dugong and turtle meat in Kaurareg feasts, held at 'tombstone openings', weddings and funerals. At a more fundamental level, the activities of fishing and marine-hunting are the basis of Kaurareg self-identity.

The Kaurareg fishing economy and the fisheries of the Torres Strait

The Kaurareg seas lie within two different fisheries management regimes. A small area in the north of the Kaurareg seas lies within the Protected Zone and is therefore under the jurisdiction of the Torres Strait Protected Zone Joint Authority (TSPZJA). The remaining area of Kaurareg seas (to the south) lies within Queensland jurisdiction and is thus under the management of the Queensland Fisheries Management Authority (QFMA). The main fisheries within the area of the TSPZJA are prawn, lobster, mackerel and live pearl shell, while the main fisheries in the area of the QFMA are trochus shell, beche-de-mer, and cultured pearls.

Figure 13:2 Indigenous involvement in each of the Torres Strait fisheries

	Share of catch%	
	Islander	Non-Islander
TSPZJA Fisheries		
Prawn	0	100
Lobster	70	30
Mackerel	3	97
Live pearl shell	100	0

QFMA Fisheries		
Trochus shell	100	0
Beche-de-mer	100	0
Cultured pearls	0	100

(Source: Altman, Arthur and Bek, 1994:11)

There are a number of characteristics regarding indigenous involvement in Torres Strait fisheries. Firstly, there is no indigenous involvement in prawn trawling. This can be attributed partly to the high capital costs of entering this fishery as well as high operating costs. Another important barrier to indigenous involvement in prawn trawling may be the conditions of employment: '...the demands of employment in the commercial prawn fishery do not make this fishery attractive for Islanders owing to the need to work long continuous shifts for several months at a time' (Altman *et al.* 1994:12). Secondly, there is a high indigenous participation in the lobster fishery. This is attributable to the low capital costs of entering the fishery (the cost of an aluminium dinghy and outboard engine) and the extremely high profit margins (1994:13). Thirdly, the fisheries that have the highest incidence of indigenous involvement—trochus and pearl shell collection—are those in which Islanders have had long-standing involvement and expertise (1994:12). Overall indigenous participation in Torres Strait commercial fisheries is slight; the prawn fishery—which alone accounts for 78% of the total value of Torres Strait commercial fisheries (1994:7)—is completely in the hands of non-indigenous people.

Kaurareg sea country, like the Torres Strait as a whole, could sustain a much higher fishing yield than it does at present. Johannes and MacFarlane state that 'coral reef, seagrass, sand bottom complexes, such as those in the Torres Strait' could produce a sustainable yield of 4 to 5 tonnes per square kilometre (1991:198). On the basis of a much more conservative figure of 1 tonne per square kilometre, they calculate that the region could sustain a yield of 5.5 kg of seafood per day per capita. Yet the total quantity of prawns, crayfishes, and finfishes exported from the Strait at present amounts to no more than 0.3 kg per day per capita. Altman et. al. also argue that present fisheries production in the region is significantly below maximum sustainable yield. They estimate that the total value of the commercial fisheries in the Torres Strait could be increased by $13.3 million, from $26.7 million to $40 million (Altman *et al.* 1994:8).

One issue of great concern to Kaurareg is the recognition by other Islanders of Kaurareg traditional ownership of the reefs to the east of the Muri (Mount Adolphus Island). These reefs traditionally belonged to the Muri Islanders who are part of the Kaurareg people. The four reefs to the east of Muri are currently being exploited by other Islanders without regard to Kaurareg ownership of these marine resources.

The centre-piece in the Kaurareg view of the future of their fishery is a plan to put Kaurareg Rangers on all the seventeen islands which lie within the Kaurareg traditional sea country. This is seen not only as a way of creating employment for Kaurareg people, but also as the most efficient way of managing their marine resource. These Rangers would police fishing regulations and would also pass on information to Coastwatch about drug-running activities. Because of their local knowledge, Kaurareg argue that these Rangers would be in a much better position to detect such activities than European government officers.

Notes

This is a modified version of a paper that was prepared as part of a project funded by the Queensland Department of Economic Development and Trade. It is republished here with permission. We thank Rod Mitchell for assistance in spelling Kaurareg words and phrases and for some thnographic advice.

References

Altman, J. C. and W. S. Arthur, H. J. Bek. 1994 *Indigenous participation in commercial fisheries in Torres Strait: a preliminary discussion*. Discussion paper No. 73/1994 Centre for Aboriginal Economic Policy Research (CAEPR). Canberra: Australian National University.

Beckett, J. 1994 A historical perspective: Torres Strait Islanders and the Sea. In M. Mulrennan, N. Hansen and the Island Coordinating Council *Marine Strategy for Torres Strait: Policy Directions*. Darwin: Australian National University North Australia Research Unit and the Torres Strait Island Coordinating Council.

Haddon, A. C. 1935 *Reports of the Cambridge Anthropological Expedition to Torres Straits*, vol 1. Cambridge: Cambridge University Press.

Johannes, R. E. and J. W. Macfarlane 1991 *Traditional Fishing in the Torres Strait Islands*. Hobart: CSIRO.

Sharp, N. 1992 *Footprints Along the Cape York Sandbeaches*. Canberra: Aboriginal Studies Press.

Singe, J. 1979 *The Torres Strait: People and History*. St. Lucia: University of Queensland Press.

Southon, M. H. 1989 Competition and Conflict in an Ecuadorian beachseine fishery. *Human Organization* 48(4):365–369.

14

The promise of native title and the predicament of customary marine tenure

Sandra Pannell

There seems to be no doubt in the minds of many lawyers that native title in Australia 'extends to the sea' (Bartlett 1993a:17).[1] More specifically, a number of lawyers have argued that native title applies to the seabed and sea fisheries, and includes both coastal waters and territorial seas (Bartlett 1993a; Bergin 1993; Behrendt 1995; Kilduff and Lofgren 1996; Storey 1996). As such, native title extends from the territorial sea baseline for a distance of two hundred nautical miles, covering the area now referred to as the Exclusive Economic Zone (EEZ) (Kilduff and Lofgren 1996; Storey 1996).[2] This still seems to be the predominant view amongst the legal fraternity even in the face of the argument that the common law does not exist outside the colonial boundary of the low water mark. This is a strange argument indeed for it appears to acknowledge that in all other situations it is possible for the Crown to extend the limits of its sovereign rights over time, but insists, in this instance, on freezing native title at that moment in history when the doctrine of *terra nullius* first came into effect in Australia.

While the legal status of native title over offshore places and seas seems clear in the minds of many, this is certainly not the case

---

1 As Sharp (1996:205) points out, even those individuals and organisations ideologically opposed to native title concluded that 'rights to the sea [are] inherent in the High Court's decision'.

2 The Exclusive Economic Zone incorporates those areas of the sea which were previously known at the 'Contiguous Zone', the 'Continental Shelf' and the 'Australian Fisheries Zone'. In those cases where the continental shelf extends past 200 nautical miles, the outer limit of the EEZ is taken as the edge of the continental shelf to a maximum distance of 350 nautical miles.

regarding the anthropological evidence for native title over these areas. The basis of this particular expression of native title is often spoken of by anthropologists in terms of 'customary marine tenure' (CMT). Just as a system of land tenure underpins the observation of native title on land, CMT is posited as encapsulating the fundamental principles, or laws and customs, which inform native title over waters, seas, sea bed and fisheries and to which native title conforms to. The investigation of CMT is not confined to the discursive practices of anthropologists nor is it restricted to the area of native title. In this regard, CMT is also of considerable interest to those working in the related areas of resource management, environmental protection, and sustainable development. In anthropology, and in other disciplines such as geography, marine science and law, CMT is spoken of as something which has a discernible, empirical reality and thus as something which is a legitimate object of study. Following on from this, CMT is also seen as something which has disciplinary value as a theoretical concept. This has not always been the case, however, and it is correct to say that CMT has only achieved this status in the last twenty five years or so. Before this time, CMT, as an acknowledged area of inquiry within the discipline of anthropology, did not exist.

The discipline of anthropology is historically characterised by the making, unmaking and remaking of its object of study. For example, this century we have seen the abandonment of 'primitive thought', the rise and fall of totemism, a gradual disenchantment with kinship, the decline of culture and its recent rediscovery in postmodernist writings. Often this ebb and flow of inquiry is associated with the fortunes and misfortunes of schools of thought within the discipline, such as structural functionalism, and/or with the slings and arrows of politically-driven, social changes.

If totemism represents one of the disappearing objects of anthropology then, conversely, it could be said the Customary Marine Tenure or CMT constitutes one of the rapidly emergent artefacts of the discipline; one which is also exported (or imported) to other disciplines. The broad appeal and cross-disciplinary employment of CMT suggests a shared understanding of the value and content of this concept. Yet, it is evident from the literature that CMT is used to speak of often widely disparate things. In this respect, and as I demonstrate in the following sections of this chapter, current discussions of CMT have much in common with the previous anthropological treatment of totemism.

The obvious question to ask here is how useful a concept is CMT in demonstrating proof of native title over the sea, and to what extent can the anthropological record on CMT be called upon to support these claims? If we ask the question, as I do in this paper, what is CMT, the answers, as we shall see, represent a multitude of often conflicting definitions. If this is the case, then perhaps it is more productive to ask what is accomplished when the concept of CMT is invoked, and who really benefits from its invocation?

Tenure and native title

It could be said that until the advent of federal land rights legislation in Australia in 1976, anthropological interest in the subject of Aboriginal tenure, particularly land tenure, was on the decline. It is probably true to say that it never, independently at least, reached the dizzying anthropological heights that totemism, Aboriginal religion, kinship or social organisation did—evidence of which is reflected in the fact that between 1935 and 1971 more than 40% of the articles printed in *Oceania* were devoted to these subjects. As this suggests, more often than not, discussion of Aboriginal systems of land tenure was subsumed within an examination of what had become the staples of anthropology in Australia. There are exceptions, of course, and, in this respect, the continent-sized undertaking of Tindale (1974) and the more localised work of Piddington (1971) and Pink (1936) spring to mind.

It is not entirely clear whether these references to systems of land tenure within the context of religion, social organisation and kinship intentionally reflected the interpenetration of these themes in Indigenous cultures or whether this conjunction was a product of its

371

time, conforming to the requirements of holistic ethnography (Marcus and Cushman 1982; Clifford 1988). What is apparent, however, is that in the post-land rights era in Australia, a number of ethnographic works devoted primarily to the subject of land tenure (and land rights) were published (see Peterson and Langton 1983; Hiatt 1984; Myers 1986; Peterson and Long 1986; Williams 1986).

In this period, the previous works of anthropologists were (and are) often called upon to corroborate land claim findings, and their use in this supportive role functioned to stamp these findings with the authenticating mark of time and anthropological tradition. The same can be said of anthropological research in the era of native title where the work of anthropologists and others in a particular region arguably takes on an even greater significance than under the federal *Aboriginal Land Rights (NT) Act 1976*.

Under the *Native Title Act 1993*, the former writings of ethnographers, missionaries and explorers now function to not only corroborate present-day forms of social and territorial organisation, but they also serve as evidence of the distinctiveness of native title-holding communities and their laws and customs (a role they are rarely called upon to perform under land rights legislation). These texts and other sources are also invaluable in demonstrating continuity of occupation, of connection between the native title applicants and the previous occupiers and of connection between the applicants and the area covered by a native title application. And where they do not fully support existing laws, customs, and social forms, they often provide some indication of indigenous processes of transformation and succession.

Anthropologists are not the only ones to appreciate the importance of these materials in the determination of native title, especially in a Federal Court situation. Lawyers have pointed to the need for documentary sources in providing proof of native title (Bartlett 1993b; Fitzgerald 1995), while Aboriginal and Torres Strait Islander Representative Bodies recognise the crucial role of historical records and texts and have begun the process of document acquisition and the establishment of native title research collections. Furthermore, indigenous peoples are not only aware of the significance attached to these documents by lawyers and anthropologists in the native title process, but they also acknowledge the meaning some of these sources have for them at a more personal level.

While there appears to be a general acceptance amongst those involved in the preparation of native title documents of the requirement to engage historical and, in particular, anthropological sources, there has also been some criticism of these texts. At one level, previous commentaries on Aboriginal and Torres Strait Islander land tenure have the potential to become, in a largely uncritical manner, the base-line of tradition in native title hearings. A situation similar to that which existed in the first decade or so of the *Aboriginal Land Rights (NT) Act 1976* could easily prevail under the native title regime. This time, however, conformity is expressed with respect to the codifications found in previous writings rather than in terms of the model found in the legislation. This problem is all too evident in the constant recourse to Tindale's tribal map of Australia (although not necessarily recourse to the book which the map accompanies), which often presents a situation where the map precedes the territory to the point where it becomes its own referent (Baudrillard 1983). For some anthropologists, then, the challenge in the post-Mabo era is to 'expound the fundamentally different meaning of *land* and of relationships with *land* which exist in Aboriginal Australia [emphasis added]' (Kondos and Cowlishaw 1995:12).

As this last comment suggests, the focus of anthropologists and of anthropological texts is (and has been) upon land and land tenure systems. If we look to the anthropological record in Australia, we find that, up until the late 1970s, references to the sea are strangely muted, if not absent, in the writings of anthropologists. Let me illustrate this statement with specific reference to the Kimberley region of Western Australia.

To the islands: the north-west Kimberley region

The area of the north-west Kimberley I have in mind includes the fiord-like coastline from Wyndham to Derby, the thousands of islands and reefs congregated into archipelagos and groups located off-shore, and the hundreds of thousands of square kilometres of coastal waters and territorial sea encompassed within this region. Some of the most prominent figures in the discipline of anthropology undertook research in this region. Anthropologists such as Basedow (1918), Elkin (1930a; 1930b; 1931–2; 1933), Kaberry (1939), Tindale (1953; 1974), Birdsell (Tindale 1953), Lommel (1952) and Petri (1954), not to mention missionary ethnographers such as Reverend J. R. B. Love (1917; 1927–40; 1935a; 1935b; 1939) and Reverend Gribble (1930). Even Sir James Frazer (1937) refers to this region in the supplement to his *magnum opus* on taboo and totemism. All these anthropologists worked with people who had a long tradition of coastal and marine occupation and lived within close proximity of the sea. It was also the case that at the time they conducted their research in this region the only effective means of transport between the towns of Derby and Wyndham and the missions established in more remote places, such as Kunmunya or Forrest River, was by lugger or other sea-going vessel. And yet, for all of this, there is barely a mention of the sea or anything to do with it in their writings, let alone any discussion of Aboriginal systems of marine tenure and the possibility that areas of sea could be owned by Aboriginal peoples in a proprietary sense.

Elkin (1930a:349), for example, writing about the Aboriginal inhabitants of the Forrest River Mission, briefly mentions that the tides experienced in Cambridge Gulf are caused by the actions of 'Lumiri', a 'large, salt-water snake'. This is the closest Elkin gets to talking about Aboriginal laws and customs in relation to the sea. For the most part, his comments on the sea or the coast are confined to stating the territorial location and extent of various tribal groups. For instance, Elkin (1931–32:312) states that the 'country of the Ungarinyin, Wurara and Unambal tribes ... extends from the north-western shore of King Sound up the coast some little distance north of the Prince Regent River, and inland about one hundred miles at most'.

Elkin's efforts are easily surpassed by Petri (1954), even though Petri mainly worked with people, the 'Ngarinjin', who were considered to be a 'land-locked tribe'. Not only does Petri give the coastal locations of various tribal territories, he also provides some details about the mythological creation of Walcott Inlet and the origin of the tides, the use of shells as trade items and the construction and use of catamarans and canoes amongst neighbouring 'tribes'. None of this, of course, even approximates a discussion of indigenous systems of marine tenure.

These comments of Elkin and Petri, and others such as Kaberry and Lommel, amount to nothing more than a form of ethnographic curio collecting. This kind of data collection often characterised earlier anthropological objectives, which was the compilation of an ethnographic compendium on a particular 'tribe' or 'society'.

Of the ethnographers who worked in this region prior to the 1970s, Tindale provides the most detailed descriptions of Aboriginal occupation of coastal and marine environments, even though the time he spent in the area was limited to a number of months only. However, given Tindale's pre-occupation with setting the record straight on Australian Aboriginal tribes, their proper names, terrains, distribution and their use of the environment, much of what he has to say in his fieldnotes and published work is driven by these objectives. For example, comments about tribal terrains, such as 'along the coast to the north of the Worora are the Wunambullu, who extend from Mt Trafalgar to Cape Voltaire' (Tindale 1953:81), are quite common. He also (Tindale 1953:83–85) remarks about the composition of tribes:

> the remnants of a small tribe whose headquarters are the Montgomery Islands are the Yaudjibaia, [who are] now rapidly being absorbed into the Worora, but [are] men of a distinct physical type.

There are also numerous references to Aboriginal exploitation of marine environments and the use of sea-going vessels. For instance, Tindale (1953:865–867) writes that the Laiau clan of the 'Wunambal':

used wooden canoes to visit all the islands from Cape Voltaire to Cassini Island and Long Reef. They have visited these
areas for as long as present day people remember ... Dugong,
turtle eggs and cockles were obtained on these trips, which
were made in the wet season when there is water on the islands; in dry times they visited waters on the mainland.

Or, in a passage which seems to encapsulate most, if not all, of
Tindale's anthropological concerns, he (1974:147) writes that:

In the island-dotted northern half of King Sound, the Buc-
caneer Archipelago, and the Montgomery group, there were
four ... peoples—the Jaudjibaia, Umede, Ongkarango and
Djaui—all of whom were dependent on rafts for gaining the
greater part of their subsistence. Of these the Umede and
Ongkarango were in part mainland based and exploited
some inland products; the Jaudjibaia ... of the Montgomery
Islands ... were completely island based.

While Tindale's material contains some valuable references to
Aboriginal occupation and exploitation of marine areas and resources
in this region, nowhere does he talk explicitly about Aboriginal possession of waters, seas, sea bed and resources. As such, there is no
discussion of what might today be identified as a system of 'customary
marine tenure'. The closest Tindale comes to this is in his discussion of
the location and extent of clan and tribal territories which, in a number
of instances, includes the littoral, off-shore islands and, on one occasion
where he describes the tribal territory of the 'Jaudjibaia', 'reefs' (Tindale
1974:242).

Much of what Tindale observes for the various 'tribes' occupying
the north-west Kimberley coastal region is also found in Blundell's
(1975) doctoral thesis on the 'Worora'. Written some twenty years
after Tindale's fieldwork in the Kimberley, Blundell also describes
Aboriginal use of marine resources (although in more detail than
Tindale), their occupation of coastal and offshore places, the production of marine-based technology, trade in marine products, the location
and limits of 'tribes' in the region and, more specifically, the estates of

particular Worora clans. While Tindale's material indicates that for one tribe at least, Aboriginal people possessed exposed and submerged reefs, Blundell suggests that the estates of two Worora clans include coastal waters. According to Blundell (1975:97), the Be:waninawaja clan owns 'the large bay called George Water', while the Umbrewewul clan is said to have 'owned Doubtful Bay and the immediately adjacent coast from the mouth of the Sale River, south around Doubtful Bay to Raft Point'. Blundell also differs from Tindale in that she provides information about the cosmological significance of the land and some offshore islands, and as such, presents a more detailed discussion of Aboriginal land tenure in this part of the Kimberley. Notwithstanding these details, it is not clear from her ethnography whether the system of social and territorial organisation she describes also applies to sea areas. And, certainly on the subject of marine tenure, Blundell is silent.

I should point out here that in both Tindale's and Blundell's work, discussion of Aboriginal occupation and use of marine environments is by no means coherent or concentrated, but is scattered, largely as passing references, throughout the text. This is also the case for the other works I referred to earlier in this section.

The historical paucity of published material on Aboriginal maritime use and occupation is not unique to this region, and has been commented upon by a number of researchers working in other areas in Australia (see Johannes 1988; Palmer 1988; Cordell 1991a, 1991b, 1999c; Bergin 1993). Of these researchers, Kingsley Palmer is one of the few who have attempted to offer an explanation for this situation.

Palmer suggests that one of the possible reasons for the lack of documentary information derives from the consequences of European settlement. According to Palmer (1988:4), 'many of the coastal cultures were among the first to disappear from the face of the newly settled land'. While this argument may be more applicable to other parts of Australia, it does not adequately explain present-day continuity of occupation among coastal peoples (e.g.. Bardi and Jawi peoples living at One Arm Point and Lombadina on the Dampier Land Peninsula) who have a long history of contact with other societies, including Europeans.

Palmer is perhaps more correct when he states that the lack of information on Aboriginal maritime cultures is a product of European perceptions and orientations. In this respect, he (Palmer 1988:4) identifies the preoccupation of anthropologists with 'myth ... religion, material culture, ... kinship and social organisation' and the settler's economic focus on land as the major causes for these omissions.

This is partially the case in the northwest Kimberley region which, thanks largely to Elkin, became one of the recognised sites for research on Australian Aboriginal totemism. This part of the Kimberley was also internationally acknowledged as the home of 'Wandjina' paintings, and a considerable proportion of the literature on this region is devoted purely to the examination of this particular form of rock art (e.g. Elkin 1930b; Love 1930; Schulz 1956; Lommel 1961; Crawford 1968; Capell 1971; Blundell 1974). As a result, the significance of Wandjina in local tenure (both land and sea) systems was largely overlooked in the ensuing European obsession with the image itself.

As for Palmer's argument that Europeans were oblivious to Aboriginal use of the sea because of their own emphasis upon land-based economic activities, it is difficult to sustain this proposition historically with respect to the northwest Kimberley region. Europeans had long exploited the marine and offshore resources of this area. From the 1860s, Europeans were actively harvesting pearl shell and pearls from the reefs of the region. In addition, American whaling ships operated in the area, and a number of the offshore islands were exploited for their guano and mangrove bark resources. Other Europeans commercially collected trepang and trochus shell, and exploited turtle and dugong populations. In many of these endeavours, Aboriginal people were contracted, in part, because of their expertise and local knowledge and, in part, because they were seen as expendable.[3]

---

3 An article on the 'Northwest Pearl-Shell Fishery' in *The Inquirer*, dated March 1875, reports that 'no dark man's life is valued in the economising of that life, but the utmost of diving must be sucked out of that man, kill him or not; for who knows who will be his owner next season'.

The operation and continuation of European commercial activities in the coastal waters of this region was facilitated by the marine equivalent of the doctrine of *terra nullius, mare nullius*. The sea was (and still is) envisaged by Europeans as common property, where individuals enjoy unrestricted access to what are seen as inexhaustible public resources.[4] For Europeans, this vision of unlimited, infinite resources is not muddied by the actualities of localised resource depletion. In the case of the Kimberley and elsewhere in Australia, when this situation arose, users simply shifted their efforts to another area and 'discovered' a hitherto unexploited shell bed or fishery stock. A similar attitude applied to the use of 'native labourers', with European pearlers travelling to different parts of Indonesia (Kupang, 'Makassar', Endeh, the Kei Islands and Solor), Singapore and north Australia to pick up divers to replace those who had been exhausted or killed by the activity.[5] If the sea was *mare nullius*, then non-Europeans were definitely *homo nullius* (Pannell 1996). This kind of shifting cultivation on the part of the Europeans, more correctly referred to as 'resource raiding' (Bennett 1976), not only relied upon the concept of *mare nullius*, but it usually went hand-in-hand with the expansion of colonial frontiers.

One of the paradoxes of this kind of exploitative strategy is that it tends to downplay or ignore the fact that exploitation of marine areas and resources is predicated upon quite specialised knowledge of species and environments. This is still the case today where recreational and even some commercial fishing, for example, is casually spoken of in terms of the alternating operation of luck and misfortune and yet this kind of fishing is underpinned by a long history of angling lore as well

---

4   In an 1894 editorial in the *Nor' West Times*, entitled 'Our Pearling Industry', the writer declares that 'facts and figures prove that the supply of shell is practically inexhaustible, and is being renewed each year...' (1894:2).

5   An advertisement in the 17 October 1891 edition of the *Nor' West Times* placed by Galbraith and Co. describes the services they offer. In the words of the advertisement: 'Coolies, boatmen, divers and goods imported from Singapore, and produce sold there to best advantage' (1891:2).

as a multi-million dollar information industry. The upshot of this is that fishers and those who exploit the sea and its resources are seen as the marine equivalents of hunter-gatherers, occupying and using the sea in a largely arbitrary fashion.

While *mare nullius* and its associated assumptions informed the prevailing ethos, the reality, however, was quite different. Off the Kimberley coast, for example, productive pearling grounds were jealously guarded by Europeans, as were reefs and banks stocked with trepang and trochus shell.

The fact is that even historically the sea was far from the propertyless or ownerless expanse it is commonly believed to be. In this connection, many writers, including anthropologists (Ruddle and Akimichi 1984; Sharp 1996), are quick to cite the 'freedom of the seas' (*mare liberum*) case argued by the Dutch attorney Hugo Grotius on behalf of the Dutch East India Company in 1604, as the source of the common property view of the sea (see Sharp this volume). However, as the historian Leonard Andaya (1993:41) points out, the notion of *mare liberum*, and the concept of free trade that was associated with it, was rejected by the Dutch in their mercantile operations in Asia. To acknowledge a 'policy of open seas' would have placed Dutch interests at a severe disadvantage in the already 'well-entrenched Portuguese and Asian trade networks'. Another historian, Simon Schama (1988:341), even goes so far as to refute the idea that the Dutch were actually advocating an open seas policy, and argues that Dutch mercantile colonialism was predicated on an 'elaborate and extensive system of protection'. As this indicates and, as Cordell (1989:12) rightly points out, the concept of 'freedom of the seas' is inextricably linked to the idea of privatisation. It is this contradiction between public property and private profits which largely contributes to the 'tragedy of the commons' (Hardin 1968).

Strange as it may sound, it is from the paradoxical crucible of the 'tragedy of the commons' that 'customary marine tenure' emerges in the early 1970s. The motivating force behind the appearance of this concept was not purely a moral or ethical one driven by the need to recognise the long overlooked proprietary rights and cultural interests of indigenous peoples in seas and resources. Rather, it was more an economic one, powered by the pressing industry requirement for alternative strategies for managing over exploited marine fisheries.

The 'solution': CMT

It became apparent in the early 1970s that there was a 'crisis in the world's fisheries' (McGoodwin 1990:1). Simply stated, 'there [were] too many people chasing too few fish' (McGoodwin 1990:1). However, there was more to the crisis than just an imbalance between fish and people. As McGoodwin (1990:72–74) points out, part of the problem stems from the models upon which the modern management of fisheries is based.

For the past forty years, the most prevalent management strategies for fisheries have been based on bio-economic modelling, that is, a combination of models to do with the biology of fish populations and models circumscribing the economic conditions of markets. Unfortunately, as experience demonstrated, formal bio-economic models work well in theory but never quite perform so well in reality. The problem is that these largely mathematical formulations assume a rational, steady-state and predictable world, both human and biological. As such, they are unable to adequately explain the emotional investment and social value of fishing for small-scale producers. Furthermore, these models are not very useful when trying to understand the political process of policy formulation in the fisheries sector (McGoodwin 1990).

One of the other major stumbling blocks in this 'crisis in the world's fisheries' was with the very identification of the 'root cause' of the problem. Many analysts pointed their finger at the common property, open-access status of fisheries and argued that the lack of regulation in this commons was the real cause of over-exploitation and over-capitalisation (McGoodwin 1990). While there a number of limitations associated with the somewhat deterministic 'tragedy of the commons' formulation of the problem (for an outline of these limitations, see McGoodwin 1990), one of the outcomes of this soul searching was an emphasis upon local management regimes. This emphasis is not just a recognition of the impact of small-scale producers on fisheries resources, but it is also an acknowledgment that local and, in many cases, indigenous, management practices could be used in large-scale fisheries to avoid the occurrence of the tragedy of the commons.

The notion that indigenous customs and behaviours could be incorporated into modern management practices and regional fisheries policy particularly captured the imagination of anthropologists, fisheries scientists and bureaucrats working in the Pacific in the late 1970s. And, thus, systematic work commenced on what, Ruddle (1994) calls, 'traditional community-based systems of marine resource management'. From these studies the concept of 'customary marine tenure' gradually emerged.

The recent emergence of CMT: the Pacific

Many authors comment upon the relatively recent emergence of CMT as an object of study, particularly in the Pacific. For example, Donald Schug (1995:17) observes that 'since the late 1970s, there has been a growing literature describing various systems of customary marine tenure in Oceania'.

Hand-in-hand with these statements about the recent appearance of CMT are comments relating to the paucity of materials on CMT. For instance, Ruddle and Akimichi (1984:5) talk about a 'dearth' of studies, 'scant literature', and 'relative lack of anthropological studies'. They (Ruddle and Akimichi 1984:4–5) identify one of the paradoxes of the anthropology of fishing when they state that 'compared with the large literature on agricultural societies there are far fewer anthropological and related studies of fishing communities. And more importantly, most such studies of fishermen concern their activities on land and not at sea'. This is a view also supported by Cordell (1989:5) when he describes how 'classic land tenure studies are virtually silent on the subject of sea tenure'.

While many writers are quick to point out the lack of material on CMT, few propose explanations for why this might be the case. Ruddle (1994:1) suggests that the nature of local CMT is not well known due to the 'fragmentary and commonly anecdotal nature of, and confusion of tenses in, the existing literature, the lack of ... fieldwork ... and the rapid decay and disappearance of such systems since Western contact'. In an earlier work, Ruddle and Akimichi (1984:5) argue, somewhat enigmatically, that the paucity of research can 'be attributed to ... methodological and operational problems ... [and is the] function of national priorities where developing countries... have directed their national development efforts at agriculturalists'. In the same work, however, they (Ruddle and Akimichi 1984:4) also observe that the passage of the United Nations Law of the Sea Convention 'has further obscured the preexisting and age-old 'Fishermen's Law of the Sea' or traditional sea tenure'. Apparently linked to this argument, Ruddle and Akimichi (1984:1) state that 'understanding of traditional systems of inshore sea tenure was hampered by the dominant Western theories of fish as a common property resource...'.

At the same time that authors bemoaned the absence of materials and talked about the recent development of CMT, many were able to refer to historical materials on indigenous relationships with the sea. For example, while Carrier and Carrier (1989) explicitly point to a dearth of published material on sea tenure, they cite works which refer to aspects of sea tenure going back to the turn of the century. The fact that they are able to do this is confirmed by Cordell's (1984:306) observation that 'generations of Western explorers and ethnographers have documented and often marvelled at the sophistication of indigenous nautical science and fishing in Oceania'. Nicholas Polunin (1984) is another author who provides numerous examples of what he calls 'sea tenure', taken from a variety of historical sources, many pre-dating more recent literature and some going back as far as 1840.

Contrary to the view of many, Polunin suggests that the lack of observations does not necessarily account for the apparent patchy distribution of marine tenure systems. He (Polunin 1984:269) argues that it may be the case that 'marine tenure never existed in certain areas, or, if it existed, it disappeared some time ago'. With regard to this argument, Polunin (1984:272) proposes that one of the reasons 'why marine tenure might not have developed more extensively than it appears to have done [is because] marine areas may not be worth owning in many cases: the resources may not be valuable enough'. Indeed, he (Polunin 1984:270) suggests that in many cases 'more reliable means of human sustenance were available on land' and that 'when faced with the alternative of land—or a sea-based livelihood, people seem in most cases more inclined to choose the former'. In this connection, Polunin (1984:271) cites the attitudes of the 'Balinese' and their reported aversion to the sea. He also talks about the uncertainty of the sea and the dangers associated with it, especially in relation to 'natural phenomena, such as tidal waves' and social factors such as the risk of slaving raids.

Now you see it, now you don't

Polunin's (1984) comments represent a cautionary tale against assuming the empirical and universal existence of CMT. And, yet, the appearance of CMT as a valid object of study is often spoken of as the discovery of this assumed reality rather than as a discourse that was produced at a particular place and moment in history. For example, Ruddle (1994:1) observes that '...only in the last two decades has it been realised that 'sea tenure' ... exists at all', while Ruddle and Akimichi (1984:1) declare that '... sea tenure—is one of the most significant 'discoveries' to emerge from the last ten years of research in maritime anthropology'. Viewing CMT as a discourse rather than as a discovery sheds some light on the different descriptions of what CMT is. In the literature on CMT in the Pacific, there seems to be less emphasis on indigenous proprietary rights in marine areas, which in some countries, such as Fiji, Vanuatu, Yap and Western Samoa, have, to varying degrees, been constitutionally or legally recognised, and more emphasis upon 'traditional', community-based management of fisheries resources, to the point where Bergin

(1993:22) is able to declare that 'CMT in the Pacific [refers to] systems of 'traditional resource management'. This observation becomes even more pertinent when we examine the representation of CMT in Australia.

It seems that at the very moment when Ruddle and others are celebrating the discovery of CMT, it threatens to disappear. Ruddle (1994:19) himself talks about 'the rapid decay and disappearance of such systems since Western contact' while Carrier and Carrier (1989:115) declare that 'traditional forms of sea tenure may be disappearing in Oceania'. Robert Johannes (1981:79) is even more pessimistic and talks about how 'the destruction of fishing tenure in the vicinity of district centres may be inevitable in Oceania [and concludes that] It has already occurred in many places'. In light of the constant reminders about the recent appearance of CMT and the paucity of historical materials on this subject, it is somewhat puzzling to ascertain the basis let alone the content of these comments. This situation is made even more puzzling by the fact that many of these same authors speak of the incredible 'heterogeneity in tenure traditions across cultures' (Cordell 1989:21). Not only variability but, as Gracie Fong (1994:1) points out, 'it has been said that the Pacific Basin probably contains the greatest ... complexity and adaptability in customary marine tenure systems'. If this is the case, it would seem then that the observation and identification of 'traditional' systems undergoing collapse or 'destruction' is a somewhat difficult, if not impossible, undertaking.

The 'decline', 'breakdown', 'disappearance' and 'loss' that authors such as Polunin (1984:270, 280), Ruddle and Akimichi (1984:4–5), Nietschmann (1985:144), Zann (1985:65) and Cordell (1989:301) and others talk of is said to result from 'commercialisation' (Cordell 1984:301) and the 'impact of Western marine management concepts' (Ruddle and Akimichi 1984:4). Again, these are strange remarks and appear to be oblivious to the *longue duree* of cross-cultural encounters in this region (cf. Sahlins 1981).

As a response to this situation of perceived loss and decay, a number of authors suggest a form of salvage anthropology, arguing that 'if not intensively studied soon, the opportunity to examine on a worldwide basis a phenomenon that is still scarcely known will be irretrievably lost' (Ruddle and Akimichi 1984: 5).

This is a familiar narrative in anthropology—a case of the 'pure products... going crazy' (Clifford 1988:5) upon contact with a dismembering and diseased modernity. Also familiar is the scenario of rescue and redemption through the salvage work of anthropologists. Both the story and the solution assume a certain fragility and passivity on the part of indigenous cultures and peoples. As Clifford (1988: 14–15) points out, 'the great narrative of entropy ... assumes a questionable Eurocentric position at the 'end' of a unified human history ... memorialising the world's local historicities'. One of the things this history does is to determine which peoples and which cultures will be relegated to the status of museum pieces and which will be redeemed as active, intact, coeval societies and practices. Judging from the literature on CMT in the Pacific, it seems that for some groups, at least, the writing (read, their future destinies) is already on the wall. The implications of this scenario for arguing native title over seas and offshore places in Australia is both politically obvious and ethically disturbing. Especially, when authors such as Johannes and MacFarlane (1984 and 1991) have already signalled the decline of 'traditional sea rights' in the Torres Strait.

CMT in Australia

As in the Pacific, CMT in Australia is said to be a recent phenomenon. Writing at the beginning of the nineties, Cordell (1991a:511) states that 'the rights and ownership customs of maritime peoples [in Australia] have not been widely documented until recently'. Notwithstanding this recent interest in CMT, Cordell (1991c:108) is still able to claim that 'Australian researchers are at the leading edge of work in documenting CMT systems and studying their management applications'. Unaware of the ironic truth of his statement, Cordell (1991a:514) even goes so far as to suggest that 'if sea tenure didn't exist it would probably have to be invented'.

Unlike the initial situation in the Pacific, the 'invention' of CMT in Australia is largely linked to the assertion and recognition of indigenous 'sea rights'. While there is some suggestion of the 'narrative of entropy' in operation—Cordell (1991a:514) talking about 'pockets or vestiges' of CMT, Williams (1994:39) on the 'decline' of customary fishing rights in the Torres Strait and, of course, Johannes and MacFarlane's (1991) comments on the same subject—many writers point to the historical, political, cultural and legal circumstances which resulted in the marginalisation or complete disavowal of indigenous tenure systems.

A much celebrated case in point is the Mabo No. 1 judgement, a precursor to the decision that signalled the abandonment of the notion of *terra nullius* and the recognition of native title in Australia. Here Sharp discusses Justice Moynihan's conclusion that the plaintiffs' claim to seas and reefs was not supported by the evidence and, in fact, their rights to these areas had been 'lost'. Sharp (1996:194) argues that Moynihan came to this conclusion because he assumed that 'rights must be exercised in order to keep them alive'. In other words, rights in an area are extinguished if that area is not continually used by the native title holders. Sharp (1996:194) remarks that this particular viewpoint amounts to a 'transference of western legal concepts and social values to the appraisal of an indigenous order'. The recent literature on CMT in Australia provides us with a number of other examples where the long-held doctrines and straight-out racism which inform *mare nullius* and its claims of universal applicability are exposed.

The common property assumptions of *mare nullius* represent one, particular expression of European marine tenure, a system of marine tenure which has been written about in some detail. If the common property model and its various permutations represent the predominant European marine tenure system in Australia, what then does customary marine tenure refer to in this context?

What's in a name?

One of the major problems encountered in assessing the materials on CMT in Australia (and elsewhere, for that matter) is terminology, or more precisely, variation in the terminology used by researchers and writers.

In part, this variation can be explained in terms of disciplinary differences, most notably, in the disciplinary differences between law and anthropology. Notwithstanding the legal origins of the concept of tenure, members of the legal profession tend to avoid using the term CMT and prefer to use other disciplinary terms. Terms such as, 'Aboriginal sea rights' (Bartlett 1993a:9), 'native title to the sea' (Bartlett 1993a), 'sea rights' (Allen 1993:53), 'Indigenous Peoples' rights over the sea' (White 1993:65), 'Indigenous sea rights' (White 1993:69), 'sea rights' (McIntyre 1993:107), 'Indigenous sea rights' (McIntyre 1993:112), 'fishing rights' (Bennion 1993:113) and 'customary or traditional fishing rights and interests' (Sutherland 1996:3). Even when lawyers do use the expression CMT, as in the case of Allen (1993) and Haigh (1993), they observe that it is a term customarily associated with the work of anthropologists and tend to rely on their definitions of CMT.

There is also considerable terminological variation amongst anthropologists (or those acting in this capacity) and, even at the level of individual anthropologists, there seems to be a lack of consistency in their use of terms. For instance, in addition to CMT, we find 'traditional customary fishing rights' (Williams 1994:39), 'ownership of the seas' (Palmer 1988), TURF ['Traditional Use Rights in Fisheries'] (Johannes 1988:33), 'marine traditional native property rights' (MTNPR) (Bergin 1993:31–33), 'sea country' (Bergin 1993:1), 'coastal landscapes', 'seascapes' and 'coastscapes' (Smyth 1993:25), 'sea property' (Sharp 1996:205) and 'sea tenure' (Davis 1988:68; Cordell 1991a:513 and 1991b:7), just to cite a few of the many appellations used. To add to the problem, a single author will not only use a number of different terms but will use these different terms as if they are interchangeable. For example, Cordell (1991a:511) uses the term 'marine property customary law' as interchangeable with 'sea tenure', which is also inter-changeable with 'customary territorial rights and arrangements'. In the same volume, Cordell (1991a:512, 514) also speaks of 'traditional marine tenure', 'home reef tenure systems' and 'community custody and territorial regulation of home reef economies'. Elsewhere he (Cordell 1991c:1–2) uses the expressions 'sea country', 'extended regional estates', and 'ancestral domains in the sea'.

While it is apparent that this variability can, at one level, be accounted for along professional lines, it is also probably the case that it stems, in part, from the nascent status of CMT as an object of study. However, the confusion which arises from the variable use of these terminologies is not alleviated by attempts to define these terms or describe what CMT is.

A system of tenure by any other name ... ?

Before I proceed with a discussion of the different definitions of CMT, I should point out that in a number of articles and volumes, the meaning of 'customary marine tenure' is often assumed. That is, writers often use the phrase without offering any details about its content. This said, there are many who do offer stock definitions of CMT.

A number of writers suggest that CMT refers solely to the own-ership of marine areas—an association captured by Haigh (1993:131) when he mistakenly glosses CMT as 'customary marine territories'. For example, Allen (1993:50) states that 'the general term employed to describe ownership of salt-water country is CMT'. In a similar vein, Keen (1984:431) observes that the 'formal systems of tenure of coastal peoples embrace the foreshore, seas, reefs, rocks, and sandbanks, as well as large and small islands'. This is a view reiterated by Mulrennan (1992:35–36) when she states that 'traditionally many nearshore water areas [in the Torres Strait] were owned or policed through native cus-toms and tenure ... '. Perhaps, Cordell (1991c:2) neatly summarises this particular approach to what CMT is when he states that:

> the range of group territories indigenous peoples have fash-
> ioned in the sea are dealt with under the rubric 'customary
> marine tenure'. CMT systems ... consist of collective or 'com-
> munal' domains—discrete, culturally-defined, territories,
> controlled by traditional owners.

Obviously, 'ownership' in the sense that it is used here refers to local or folk notions of possession as opposed to the common law under-standing of these concepts.

A number of authors argue that 'sea tenure is indivisible from land tenure' (Cordell 1991b:7), and it is apparent from their work that CMT is just an extension of 'exactly the same principles as land tenure' (Sharp 1996:197). As such, the units of local or territorial organisation recorded for Aboriginal land tenure systems are also advocated for CMT systems. Thus, while Cordell talks generally about 'traditional owners', there seems to be no doubt in the minds of many writers that areas of sea, reef and coast are 'owned' by either lineages, clans or both. For instance, Sharp (1996:197) writes that for the Meriam Peoples, 'the sai, reef flat areas and 'outside' or further out to sea to certain named fish-ing grounds, are the property of clans and lineages who resided within clan territories'. In the case of the Yolngu, however, Keen (1984:433) states that 'the sea is held by individual clans'. In the case of the Lardil people, these are 'patriclans' (Memmott 1983:44). Smyth (1994:21) sug-gests that in addition to the 'local clan', the 'coastal sea' is owned by the 'members of ... family group [who] have primary and even exclusive use and management rights'.

While these authors suggest that the sea-holding unit is a local-ised descent group, a clan or a lineage, others suggest that 'sea tenure' and 'sea rights' are organised according to systems of kinship (Beckett 1991:348; Cordell 1991a:513). This would suggest a more inclusive possessory group, which theoretically would consist of people from a number of so-called 'lineages' or 'clans'. This seems more in line with Cordell's (1991c:103) assertions that CMT refers to 'communal, or col-lectively-held coastal marine property' and is closely associated with 'cultural identity' (1991b:7).

While some authors talk of ownership of areas, in what seems to be a local as opposed to a legal reality, others define CMT as a 'bundle of rights' (Haigh 1993:131). Cordell (1993:161) also speaks of CMT in terms of rights when he remarks that 'CMT is the de facto communal form of property rights still practiced extensively by indigenous coastal groups and other traditional maritime communities'. Jackson (1995:91), on the other hand, jettisons the concept of CMT altogether and prefers to speak of 'sea rights' which, in her words, refer to 'the rights of indigenous people to own, use, exclude others, and manage their maritime estates and all contained within them (permanent or transitory), including the sea bed'. The 'bundle of rights' view of CMT is particularly noticeable in works published post-Mabo where the focus is upon the legal determination of native title wherein the Crown is recognised as holding radical title to lands and seas. In this connection, Sharp (1996:205) writes 'native title to the sea ... accommodates conceptions of the sea and 'sea property' embedded in the principles of customary marine tenure'. In these comments, the phrase 'native title rights' becomes a synonym for CMT or replaces the term altogether.

Michael Southon (1995:6–1) is critical of the 'sea rights' only perspective of CMT and argues that 'an important issue in sea tenure is that the sea is not the resource itself but merely the medium in which the resource moves'. In this connection, Southon suggests that CMT does not just refer to possession of marine areas but also includes exclusive possession of marine resources. Obviously, this is something different in his eyes than talking about rights in resources and areas.

There are a handful of writers who tend to describe CMT purely in terms of certain resources and specific associated activities. Most notably, 'traditional' fisheries and 'traditional' fishing. This view coincides with much of the writing on CMT in the Pacific. For instance, Williams (1994:39) states that '[Torres Strait] islanders had a system of traditional fishing customs under which different groups of people (usually clans) held clearly defined areas in which they could hunt and fish'. Cordell (1991a) is critical of the view which restricts CMT to the usage of fisheries and advocates, on this occasion at least, a more inclusive definition of CMT. For Cordell (1991a:513), 'sea tenure is closely bound up with kinship, sharing, traditional law and authority, and other structures which shape cultural identity...'

In this definition, CMT appears to know no bounds and, in the words of Cordell (1991a:513), also includes: 'the use of marine resources ... access to subsistence fisheries ... food preferences ... sacred seaspace ... social relations ... named story places ... a knowledge system'; 'myths, totems and taboos' (1991c:109); 'octopus holes, winds and currents, star clusters, an area of beach, the right to gather shells at certain times of year, rights of passage through reefs and between islands, landing places for canoes, and mythical islands' (1991b:5). A similar kind of definition is given by Davis (1988:68) who, in his examination of 'sea tenure', discusses the 'boundaries of clan estates, economic zones, sites and paths of ancestral activity, the location of residential and hunting camps and the knowledge and use of the sea and foreshore throughout the yearly cycle'.

One of the problems with this more inclusive definition of CMT, a problem also encountered by anthropologists in their attempts to nail down totemism, is that it tends to define CMT out of existence. CMT is now so broad in its scope and so encompassing in its subject range that it loses its power of discrimination.

This was also the fate of totemism. One of the fundamental problems with totemism was the disposition, on the part of anthropologists, to lump together quite disparate and unrelated phenomena into a single category which supposedly not only had an analytical veracity but also corresponded to an empirically observable reality. In those situations where it was apparent that a discrepancy existed between what was observed and the conceptual basis of totemism, a situation which it seems occurred quite frequently, anthropologists and others reverted to a series of secondary elaborations to smooth over the ruptures produced by the seeming contradictions. Elkin's dissection of totemism into a 'multiplicity of heterogeneous forms' (Levi-Strauss 1963:114) is a classic example of anthropological attempts to preserve the notion of totemism even in the face of overwhelming evidence to the contrary. These attempts led Levi-Strauss (1963:79) to conclude that:

> totemism is an artificial unity, existing solely in the mind of the anthropologist, to which nothing specifically corresponds in reality.

The desire to create unity where there is none is also apparent in the way that anthropologists and others make sweeping statements about the common features and functions of CMT. For example, Sharp (1996:204) states that 'customary marine tenures in coastal Australia have major similarities'. Cordell (1993:162–164) is far more ambitious and not only lists what are the 'essential features and issues' of CMT but also states that 'CMT systems can be viewed ... as an attempt by indigenous societies to deal with problems of managing resources by controlling and restricting access to territory' (1991c:108). These kind of generalisations about CMT abound, notwithstanding Cordell's (1991c:110) cautionary words to the effect that 'sufficient data do not yet exist, nor have adequate consultation procedures been instituted with indigenous groups, to definitively typecast peoples' land tenure much less CMT'.

And, yet, given all of this—the often inconsistent terminological variations, the differences in definition, and the sweeping generalisations—there still seems to be acceptance and acknowledgment of the theoretical and practical value of the CMT concept.

The theoretical and practical value of CMT

Customary marine tenure is often spoken of as if it were the anthropological equivalent of interferon and, in this respect, is often accorded quite amazing powers and properties. For example, Mulrennan (1992:35) declares that 'the concept of customary marine tenure is a particularly valuable marine conservation measure', while Cordell (1989:19–20) argues that 'sea tenure studies provide new insights into its [fishing conflicts] sources and may suggest new resolutions'. On another occasion, Cordell (1984:302) suggests that studies of CMT have 'produced a heightened appreciation of the nature, causes and consequences of human territoriality in the coastal marine environment'. Ruddle and Akimichi (1984:6), on the other hand, point to the economic and political benefits of CMT, and state that the study of 'traditional systems of sea tenure [will] enable policy-makers and planners to make better informed choices and to avoid repetition of past and often needless and tragic failures'.

Anthropologists and others are able to make these claims on the basis of what they perceive to be are the many positive functions of CMT. Some of properties attributed to CMT systems are summarised by Ruddle and Akimichi (1984:4) when they state that 'certain systems of traditional law prevented over-fishing and promoted resource conservation and a stable fishery by limiting access to a particular fishing ground or by enforcing temporal restrictions of various kinds'. In addition to their management functions, CMT systems are also said to preserve 'sacred sea space' (Davis 1984), alleviate 'uncertainty' (Cordell 1989:18), resolve conflict, ensure 'community survival', 'spread risk', foster 'equality', meet 'basic human needs', and avoid 'scarcity' (Ruddle, Hviding, and Johannes 1992).

While Cordell (1989) cautions against rashly asserting some of these claims, it is apparent from the way that anthropologists, marine scientists, geographers and lawyers speak of the features and functions of 'Customary Marine Tenure' that CMT is fast acquiring the status of a canonical truth in much the same way that ESD ('Environmentally Sustainable Development'), TEK ('Traditional Ecological Knowledge'), ERM ('Environmental Resource Management') and other popularised concepts have. In this connection, I would like to conclude by looking at the implications of invoking CMT.

The invocation of CMT

Levi-Strauss recognised the power of canonical truths when he spoke about what is accomplished by the invocation of totemism. Levi-Strauss saw how the idea of totemism became the yardstick by which it was possible to distinguish the 'savage' from 'white' Christian civilised society. This was accomplished not simply by placing 'primitive' societies in nature but by differentiating them according to their 'attitude towards nature' (Levi-Strauss 1963:70). As such, he concludes that totemism produced the very categories and beliefs it was said to reflect or be a study of.

Many of Levi-Strauss' insights relating to this aspect of totemism can be readily applied to the idea of CMT. CMT obtains its meanings from its inverted juxtaposition with non-indigenous, notably Western systems of tenure. A distinction is thus made between community-based, restricted property models of indigenous groups and the self-interested, open-access tenure models of Europeans. In this scenario, the roles ascribed to the actors in the colonial fantasy of *terra nullius* are reversed and it is the Europeans who now suffer the 'tragedy' of *mare nullius*.

These differences in tenure are used to mark a much wider range of differences between indigenous and non-indigenous practices and peoples. Positioned in this inversion, CMT also comes to signify what is traditional and tribal, what is caring and conservative, what is primitive and past, and what is sustainable and sensitive. In many respects, it is because CMT carries with it the political capital of authenticity that it is invoked by indigenous groups in their engagements with others, be it local agencies, national governments or multinational enterprises. In some cases in the Pacific, this has led to the legal codification of aspects of local CMT (Graham 1994).

The invocation of CMT, however, is not simply confined to the polarised playing field of indigenous and non-indigenous differences. Nor is it the case that those who claim CMT or are identified by others as 'having' it constitute a homogenous group. In the way that concepts such as 'tradition' and 'custom' have been used in Australia and Melanesia, CMT, as the literature from the Pacific and, closer to home, the Torres Strait indicates, is also invoked to authorise and refute claims amongst indigenous individuals and groups in relation to a specific location, region or resource (see Teulieres 1992; Ruddle 1995; Schug 1995).

Nothwithstanding these uses of CMT, the concept has the potential to become a marker of difference in the way that race, class and gender are often used. Moreover, because it gives the appearance of equally valuing other practices and beliefs, the invocation of CMT often masks the operation of discourses such as primitivism, racism, sexism and nationalism.

Like the concepts of race, class and gender, there is an assumption that CMT is or can be objectified. That it somehow exists separate from other arenas or aspects of social life, and that it is communally acknowledged as doing so. There is also a belief that it exists as real outside of any discourse. And, thus, CMT is presented as an empirical reality which innocently awaits circumscription rather than being seen as part of a discourse which requires critical retrospection.

What usually results from this kind of positioning is a discursive differentiation in terms of the who of CMT. A distinction is thus made between who has CMT and who hasn't. This further leads to qualifications as to what extent CMT is intact or to what extent it has 'broken down', as some would say. CMT in this sense constitutes a form of social distinction. However, it is not the content of CMT that serves to differentiate between social groups but its application. CMT thus singles out those 'endangered authenticities' (Clifford 1988:5) so beloved of classical anthropology and largely ignores those populations and practices viewed as contaminated by contact with the West or other 'outside' influences. In this respect, CMT represents another way of essentialising the Other. Rather than recognising and celebrating difference, the invocation of CMT can be seen as a continuation of the imposition of colonial categories of difference. It either maintains hierarchies or creates new ones. In this connection, CMT becomes a mechanism for marginalising the already marginal.

People are now defined not because they have a common culture or a common history of experience, but because they share CMT, even though this representation may not accord with the way they themselves view their collective identity. At the same time, however, CMT also represents a way of legitimating people's understandings and practices. But, as the example of CMT in the Pacific clearly demonstrates, this new-found respectability and rationality often derives from the desires of the West. Those peoples who possess CMT are said to have something which not only has been lost by the West but which also has the power to redeem and rejuvenate Western practices, particularly those concerned with fisheries and environmental management. In the Pacific, the so-called 'discovery' of CMT was triggered by these acquisitive needs. The paradox of this situation is that while CMT is often used to critique European discourses and management practices, its very appropriation serves to perpetuate these discourses and extend the ground for the articulation of difference and hierarchy.

Often propped up by out-dated concepts of culture and society, which valorise consensus, homogeneity, stability and corporateness, CMT has more to do with the aspirations of those who invoke the concept than those who are said to possess it. Discussion of CMT not only highlights the concerns of certain individuals but it promotes this concern as a universal phenomena. In doing so, it narrows the potential for other kinds of discussions.

CMT, I would argue, is more imagined than documented. CMT constructs its referents rather than reflecting them. But this does not make it any less real, and nor does it seem to lessen its appeal.

The predicament of CMT

The predicament of CMT, then, and the predicament for those practitioners working in the area of native title, is that behind the single concept of CMT lies the collective reality of unsubstantiated generalisations, a multitude of often conflicting definitions, a variety of often incommensurate terms, inconsistencies in terminological usage, limited field-based research, a paucity of published sources, an ignorance of the ontology of CMT, disregard for the effects of a discourse centred upon CMT and a largely uncritical use of CMT as a concept.

The problem is not, as Cordell (1993:166) suggests, the 'potential for misinterpretation and distortion of custom, particularly on questions of maritime boundaries, and in identifying traditional owners and the composition of communities of tenure-holders'. This is a problem which is not particularly unique to CMT and could easily characterise the kind of issues encountered in many areas of anthropological endeavour. The real predicament lies in the potential for CMT, like totemism, to become a victim of its own fetishization where in the end only the signifier (CMT in this case) remains, 'bereft of its erased significations' (Taussig 1992:118). It would seem then that without the caution derived from anthropological hindsight, CMT, like totemism, will collapse 'at the very moment when it [seems] most secure' (Levi-Strauss 1963:72). The looming tragedy for anthropology is that the 'misadventures' of CMT, like totemism, will serve as an allegory for the state of the discipline.

CMT and native title

So where does this leave CMT in the era of native title? I would suggest here that unless anthropologists and others develop, what McGoodwin (1990:80) calls, 'more rigorous methods of analysis in their studies' CMT will be left high and dry as an analytical category. However, as I have already indicated, the problem is not purely a matter of an absence of 'analytical rigour'. The problem is more fundamental than this, and derives from the ontological and epistemological foundations upon which the edifice of CMT rests. Until these issues are seriously debated and addressed in a reflexive and constructive manner, the legal and anthropological value of CMT as an element of proof in native title claims over seas, sea bed, fisheries and offshore places is extremely limited. This is not to say that CMT has little value in terms of its popular or political appeal. Far from it. And perhaps it is here, in the negotiation of policy guidelines, legislative and regulatory initiatives, environmental planning, management strategies, development agreements, conservation measures, heritage protection and social equity outcomes between indigenous and non-indigneous interests, that the real value of CMT lies.

Notes

The writing of this paper was made possible by an award of a Research Fellowship at the Centre for Resource and Environmental Studies, The Australian National University. Some of the material included here derives from archival research conducted for the Kimberley Land Council. I would like to extend my thanks to Nicolas Peterson for his subtle questions and gentle suggestions regarding the content of this paper.

References

Allen, David 1993. Some shadows of the rights known to our law. In *Turning the tide: conference on indigenous peoples and sea rights, 14 July–16 July 1993: selected papers*. Darwin: Northern Territory University. Pp. 53–64.

Andaya, Leonard Y. 1993. *The world of Maluku: eastern Indonesia in the early modern period*. Honolulu: University of Hawaii Press.

Bartlett, Richard 1993a. Aboriginal sea rights at common law: Mabo and the sea. In *Turning the tide: conference on indigenous peoples and sea rights, 14 July–16 July 1993: selected papers*. Darwin. Northern Territory University. Pp. 9–20.

1993b. The source, content and proof of native title at common law. In *Resource development and Aboriginal land rights in Australia* (ed.) R. Bartlett. Nedlands: University of Western Australian Press.

Basedow, H. 1918. Narrative of an expedition of exploration in north-western Australia. *Royal Geographical Society of Australasia, South Australian Branch*: 18: 105–295.

Baudrillard, J. 1983. *Simulations*. New York: Semiotext(e).

Beckett, Jeremy 1991. The eastern islands of the Torres Strait. In *Sustainable development for traditional inhabitants of the Torres Strait region* (eds) David Lawrence and Tim Cansfield-Smith. Townsville: Great Barrier Reef Marine Park Authority. Pp. 347–355.

Behrendt, Jason 1995. So long, and thanks for all the fish .... *Alternative Law Journal* 11–15.

Bennett, J. 1976. *The ecological transition: cultural anthropology and human adaptation*. New York: Pergamon.

Bennion, Tony 1993. Protecting fishing rights—recent fisheries settlements in New Zealand. In *Turning the tide: conference on indigenous peoples and sea rights, 14 July–16 July 1993: selected papers*. Darwin: Northern Territory University. Pp.113–130.

Bergin, Anthony 1993. *Aboriginal and Torres Strait Islander interests in the Great Barrier Reef Marine Park*. Townsville: Great Barrier Reef Marine Park Authority.

Blundell, Valda 1974. The Wandjina cave paintings of northwest Australia. *Arctic Anthropology* :213–223.

1975. *Aboriginal adaptation in northwest Australia*. PhD dissertation. Madison: University of Wisconsin.

Capell, A. 1971. Cave painting myths: northern Kimberley. *Oceania Linguistic Monographs*. No. 18.

Carrier, James G. and Achsah H. Carrier 1989. Marine tenure and economic reward on Ponam Island, Manus Province. In *A sea of small boats* (ed.) John Cordell. Cultural Survival Report 26. Cambridge, Mass.: Cultual Survival Inc. Pp.94–121.

Clifford, James 1988. *The predicament of culture: twentieth-century ethnography, literature and art*. Cambridge, Massachusetts and London, England: Harvard University Press.

Cordell, John 1984. Defending customary inshore sea rights. In *Maritime institutions in the western Pacific* (eds) Kenneth Ruddle and Tomoya Akimichi. Osaka: National Museum of Ethnology. Pp.301–326.

1989. A sea of small boats: customary law, tenure and territorial rights in the world of inshore fishing. Cambridge: Cultural Survival.

1991*a*. Lines in the water: sea tenure as 'custom today' in western Oceania. In *Sustainable development for traditional inhabitants of the Torres Strait region* (eds) David Lawrence and Tim Cansfield-Smith. Townsville: Great Barrier Reef Marine Park Authority. Pp.509–517.

1991*b*. Negotiating sea rights. In J. Cordell (ed.) Western Oceania: caring for the ancestral domain. *Cultural Survival Quarterly* :5–10.

1991c. *Managing sea country: tenure and sustainability of Aboriginal and Torres Strait Islander marine resources*. Report on Indigenous Fishing. Canberra: Ecologically Sustainable Development Fisheries Working Group.

1993. Indigenous peoples' coastal-marine domains: some matters of cultural documentation. In *Turning the tide: conference on indigenous peoples and sea rights, 14 July–16 July 1993: selected papers*. Darwin: Northern Territory University. Pp. 159–175.

Crawford, I.M. 1968. *The art of the Wandjina: Aboriginal cave paintings in Kimberley, Western Australia*. Melbourne: Oxford University Press.

Davis, Stephen 1984. Aboriginal claims to coastal waters in north-eastern Arnhem Land, northern Australia. In *Maritime institutions of the western Pacific* (eds) K. Ruddle and T. Akimichi. Senri Ethnological Studies 17. Osaka: National Museum of Ethnology. Pp.231–251.

1988. Aboriginal tenure of the sea in northern Arnhem Land. In *Traditional knowledge of the marine environment in northern Australia* (eds) F. Gray and L. Zann. Workshop Series No.8. Townsville: Great Barrier Reef Marine Park Authority. Pp. 68–99.

Elkin, A.P. 1930*a*. The rainbow serpent myth in north-west Australia. *Oceania* 1(3):349–354.

1930*b*. Rock paintings of north-west Australia. *Oceania* 1(3):257–279.

1932. Social organisation in the Kimberley Division, north-western Australia. *Oceania* 2(3):296–333.

1933. Totemism in north-western Australia (The Kimberley Division). *Oceania* 3(3):257–296; 3(4):435–481.

Fitzgerald, James 1995. Proving native title: a critical guide. *Aboriginal Law Bulletin* : 4–7.

Fong, Gracie 1994. *Case study of a traditional marine management system: Sasa Village, Macuata Province, Fiji.* Rome: Food and Agriculture Organisation of the United Nations.

Frazer, James G. 1937. The totemism of the Karadjeri and other tribes of the Kimberley Division, West Australia. In *Totemica: a supplement to totemism and exogamy.* London: Macmillan and Co.

Graham, Tom 1994. Flexibility and the codification of traditional fisheries management systems. *SPC Traditional Marine Resource Management and Knowledge Information Bulletin* :2–6.

Gribble, E.R. Rev. 1930. *Forty years with the Aborigines.* Sydney: Angus and Robertson.

Haigh, David 1993. Torres Strait and customary marine tenure — a legal baseline. In *Turning the tide: conference on indigenous peoples and sea rights, 14 July–16 July 1993: selected papers.* Darwin: Northern Territory University. Pp.131–159.

Hardin, G. 1968. The tragedy of the commons. *Science* :1243–1250.

Hiatt, L.R. (ed). 1984. *Aboriginal land owners: contemporary issues in the determination of traditional Aboriginal land ownership*. Oceania Monograph 27. Sydney: University of Sydney Press.

Inquirer 1875. Northwest pearl-shell fishery. March.

Jackson, S.E. 1995. The water is not empty: cross-cultural issues in conceptualising sea space. *Australian Geographer* :87–96.

Johannes, R.E. 1981. *Words of the lagoon: fishing and marine lore in the Palau district of Micronesia*. Berkeley, Los Angeles and London: University of California Press.

1988. Research on traditional tropical fisheries: some implications for Torres Strait and Australian Aboriginal fisheries. In *Traditional knowledge of the marine environment in northern Australia* (eds) F. Gray and L. Zann. Workshop Series No.8. Townsville: Great Barrier Reef Marine Park Authority. Pp. 30–42.

Johannes, R.E. and J.W. MacFarlane 1984. Traditional sea rights in the Torres Strait Islands, with emphasis on Murray Island. In *Maritime institutions in the western Pacific* (eds) Kenneth Ruddle and Tomoya Akimichi. Osaka: National Museum of Ethnology. Pp. 253–266.

1991. *Traditional fishing rights in the Torres Strait Islands*. Hobart: Commonwealth Scientific and Industrial Research Organisation, Division of Fisheries.

Kaberry, P. 1939. *Aboriginal woman, sacred and profane*. London: Routledge.

Keen, Ian 1984. Aboriginal tenure and use of the foreshore and seas: an anthropological evaluation of the Northern Territory legislation providing for the closure of seas adjacent to Aboriginal land. *Anthropological Forum* 5 :419–439.

Kilduff, Peter and Neil Lofgren 1996. Native title fishing rights in coastal waters and territorial seas. *Aboriginal Law Bulletin*, 16–17.

Kondos, V. and Gillian Cowlishaw 1995. Introduction: conditions of possibility. In G. Cowlishaw and V. Kondos (eds), Mabo and Australia: on recognising Native title after two Hundred Years. *The Australian Journal of Anthropology* :1–15.

Levi-Strauss, C. 1963. *Totemism*. Harmondsworth: Penguin.

Lommel, A. 1952. *Die Unambal*. Hamburg: Monographen Zur Volkerkunde.

1961. The rock art of Australia. In *The art of the stone age* (ed.) Hans-Georg Bardi. New York: Crown Publishers.

Love, J.R.B. Rev. 1917 Notes on the Wororra tribe of north-western Australia. *Transactions of the Royal Society of South Australia* 4:21–38.

1927–1940. *Notes on the Wororra people*. Unpublished manuscript. Adelaide: State Library of South Australia Archives.

1930. Rock paintings of the Worrora and their mythological interpretation. *Journal of the Royal Society of Western Australia* 16:1–24.

1935a. The Worora tribe of north-west Australia. *Journal of the Royal Anthropological Institute of Great Britain and Ireland*. April, 59–60.

1935b. Mythology, totemism and religion of the Worora tribe of north-west Australia. *Report of the Australian and New Zealand Association for the Advancement of Science* 22:222–231.

1939. The double raft of north-western Australia. *Man* 39:158–160.

Marcus, George. E. and Richard Cushman 1982. Ethnographies as text. *Annual Review of Anthropology* 11:25–69.

McGoodwin, James. R. 1990. *Crisis in the world's fisheries: people, problems and policies*. Stanford: Stanford University Press.

McIntyre, Greg 1993. Mabo and sea rights: public rights, property rights or pragmatism. In *Turning the tide: conference on indigenous peoples and sea rights, 14 July—16 July 1993: selected papers*. Darwin: Northern Territory University. Pp. 107–112.

Memmot, P. 1983. Social structure and use of space amongst the Lardil. In *Aborigines, land and land rights* (eds) Nicolas Peterson and Marcia Langton. Canberra: Australian Institute of Aboriginal Studies. Pp. 33–65.

Mulrennan, Monica E. 1992. *Coastal management: challenges and changes in the Torres Strait Islands. discussion paper.* Darwin: North Australia Research Unit.

Myers, Fred 1986. *Pintupi country, Pintupi self: sentiment, place and politics among western desert Aborigines.* Washington: Smithsonian Institution Press.

Nietschmann, Bernard 1985. Torres Strait Islander sea resource management and sea rights. In *The traditional knowledge and management of coastal systems in Asia and the Pacific* (eds) Kenneth Ruddle and R.E. Johannes. Jakarta: UNESCO-ROSTSEA. Pp. 127–154.

Nor'West Times 1891. Advertisement. 17 October, page 2.

1894. Our pearling industry. 17 February, page 2.

Palmer, Kingsley 1988. Status of documentary information on Aboriginal and Islander fishing and marine hunting in northern Australia. In *Traditional knowledge of the marine environment in northern Australia*, F. Gray and L. Zann. Workshop Series No. 8. Townsville: Great Barrier Reef Marine Park Authority. Pp. 4–19.

Pannell, Sandra 1996. Homo nullius or Where have all the people gone?: refiguring marine management and conservation approaches. *The Australian Journal of Anthropology* 7(1):21–42.

Peterson, Nicolas and Marcia Langton (eds). 1983. *Aborigines, land and land rights.* Canberra: Australian Institute of Aboriginal Studies.

Peterson, Nicolas and Jeremy Long 1986. *Australian territorial organisation: a band perspective.* Oceania Monograph 30. Sydney: University of Sydney.

Petri, Helmut 1954. Sterbende Welt in Nordwest Australien ['The dying world of northwest Australia']. Limoach: Braunschweig.

Piddington, R. 1971. A note on Karadjeri local organisation. *Oceania* 41(4):239–243.

Pink, O. 1936. The landowners in the northern division of the Aranda tribe, central Australia. *Oceania* 6(3):275–305.

Polunin, Nicholas. V.C. 1984. Do traditional marine 'reserves' conserve? A view of Indonesia and New Guinean evidence. In *Maritime institutions in the western Pacific* (eds) Kenneth Ruddle and Tomoya Akimichi. Osaka: National Museum of Ethnology. Pp. 267–283.

Ruddle, Kenneth 1994. *A guide to the literature on traditional community-based fishery management in the Asia-Pacific tropics.* Rome: Food and Agriculture Organisation of the United Nations.

1995. A guide to the literature on traditional community-based fishery management in Fiji. *SPC Traditional Marine Resource Management and Knowledge Information Bulletin* :7–15.

Ruddle, K. and T. Akimichi (eds). 1984. *Maritime institutions of the western Pacific.* Senri Ethnological Studies 17. Osaka: National Museum of Ethnology.

Ruddle, K., E. Hviding and R.E. Johannes 1992. Marine resources management in the context of customary marine tenure. *Marine Resource Economics* :249–273.

Sahlins, M. 1981. *Historical metaphors and mythical realities: structure in the early history of the Sandwich Islands kingdom.* Ann Arbor: University of Michigan Press.

Schama, Simon 1988. *The embarrassment of riches: an interpretation of Dutch culture in the golden age.* Berkeley: University of California Press.

Schug, Donald. M. 1995. The marine realm and the Papua New Guinean inhabitants of the Torres Strait. *SPC Traditional Marine Resource Management and Knowledge Information Bulletin* :16–23.

Schulz, A.S. 1956. North-west Australian rock paintings. *Memoirs of the National Museum of Victoria* :7–57.

Sharp, Noni 1996. *No ordinary judgment: Mabo, the Murray Islanders' land case*. Canberra: Aboriginal Studies Press.

Smyth, Dermot 1993. *A voice in all places: Aboriginal and Torres Strait Islander interests in Australia's coastal zone*. Canberra: Commonwealth of Australia.

1994. *Understanding country: the importance of land and sea in Aboriginal and Torres Strait Islander societies*. Canberra: Australian Government Publishing Service.

Southon, Michael and the Kaurareg Tribal elders 1995. The sea of Waubin: customary marine tenure, traditional knowledge of the marine environment, and contemporary fisheries problems in the waters surrounding the Kaurareg Islands. In *Indigenous management of land and sea and traditional Activities in Cape York Peninsula* (ed.) John Cordel. Brisbane: Cape York Peninsula Land Use Strategy, Office of the Coordinator General of Queensland; Canberra: Department of the Environment, Sport and Territories; Brisbane: The University of Queensland.

Storey, Matthew 1996. The black sea. *Aboriginal Law Bulletin* :4–8.

Sutherland, Johanna 1996. *Fisheries, aquaculture and Aboriginal and Torres Strait Islander peoples: studies, policies and legislation*. Canberra: the Department of the Environment, Sport and Territories.

Taussig, M. 1992. *The nervous system*. New York and London: Routledge.

Teulieres, M.H. 1992. Management of marine resources by Kanak fishermen in New Caledonia: towards what evolution? *SPC Traditional Marine Resource Management and Knowledge Information Bulletin* :14–15.

Tindale, Norman B. 1953. Anthropological field notes on the University of California, Los Angeles—University of Adelaide anthropological expedition, north-west Australia.

1974. *Aboriginal tribes of Australia: their terrain, environmental controls, distribution, limits and proper names*. Berkeley, Los Angeles and London: University of California Press.

White, Duean 1993. The Department of Foreign Affairs and Trade's involvement with indigenous peoples' rights over the sea. In *Turning the tide: conference on indigenous peoples and sea rights, 14 July–16 July 1993: selected papers*. Darwin: Northern Territory University. Pp. 65–77.

Williams, Geoff 1994. *Fisheries and marine research in Torres Strait.* Canberra: Australian Government Publishing Service.

Williams, N.M. 1986. *The Yolngu and their land: a system of land tenure and the fight for its recognition.* Canberra: Australian Institute of Aboriginal Studies.

Zann, Leon. P. 1985. Traditional management and conservation of fisheries in Kiribati and Tuvalu atolls. In *The traditional knowledge and management of coastal systems in Asia and the Pacific* (eds) Kenneth Ruddle and R.E. Johannes. Jakarta: UNESCO-ROSTSEA. Pp. 55–77.

www.ingramcontent.com/pod-product-compliance
Lightning Source LLC
Chambersburg PA
CBHW050642270326
41927CB00012B/2839